READINGS
IN
EDUCATIONAL
AND

Houghton Mifflin Company · *Boston*

Edited by
Clinton I. Chase and
H. Glenn Ludlow
of Indiana University

PSYCHOLOGICAL MEASUREMENT

New York • Atlanta • Geneva, Ill. • Dallas • Palo Alto

HOUGHTON MIFFLIN COMPANY · BOSTON
PRINTED IN THE U.S.A.

Introduction

The burgeoning literature on educational and psychological measurement testifies to its significance as both a method of science and a philosophy of education. No area of either psychology or education has drawn as much criticism as this one — or has had more influence on practice. The variety of instruments is bewildering, the research is voluminous and often superficial. It is too easy to use tests in school administration, teaching, and counseling. The manuals promise much. Sometimes the tests produce also, but only after thousands of subjects have contributed their time and effort to necessary experimentation.

What is seriously lacking is an understanding of the psychological rationale back of all such measurement, the personality assumptions made in the use of tests and inventories, the balance of limitations and of assets to be considered for any given test. The first two-thirds of this book presents basic readings on these points, on what is back of measurement. It is essentially a book on "Basic Principles of Measurement" (a course title that is sometimes used) rather than one on instruments and procedures.

Some of the selections give careful attention to the basic concepts of intelligence, achievement, and aptitude. Many errors are committed under these labels because of superficial understanding. Every teacher and counselor who uses such tests should be deeply concerned about their true meaning — and they will become appropriately concerned if they read the selections in Unit Three, "Assessing Maximum Performance." Perhaps even more errors of understanding exist within the field of personality and interest inventories, which are the subject of the basic readings in Unit Four, "Assessing Typical Performance."

The behavior of teachers in *making* tests, of counselors in *using* tests, and of students in *taking* tests is analyzed in the last third of this book of readings. One of the most serious criticisms of objective tests is that they make possible a depersonalized appraisal of an individual. A boy or girl, man or woman, becomes a score, a point in a distribution. The symbol replaces the person. But teachers and counselors are not computers in their use of tests and students are not robots in responding to them. How to keep selective perception in mind, allow for it, yet maintain a reasonable degree of reliability in appraisal — *that* is the question. Irwin Berg recently commented on "Tantrums over Testing" and quoted from Hawes' *Educational Testing for the*

Millions this statement: "Knowledge about ourselves which testing reveals is vital for each of us to have if we are to operate as self-knowing and, therefore, free agents. We should know the truth about ourselves. . . . And that truth can help make us free." The integrity of the person *can* be protected, even enhanced, with psychological tests, provided they are used within the guidelines of the best psychometric principles and practices. It is the purpose of this book to illuminate those guidelines.

C. GILBERT WRENN

Preface

For several years the editors of this text have taught courses in educational and psychological testing. Through this experience we, as well as many of our students, have noted the very real difficulty in bringing intellectually curious students into contact with the rich variety of supplementary reading materials on hand in the field of measurement. Patently, it is either impossible or impractical to assign large numbers of students the task of seeking out critical journal articles and sections of important works. The answer, therefore, appeared to be in making a collection of these materials available in a single book.

We view this collection of readings as especially useful for the following courses: (a) the commonly offered master's degree course in tests and measurements, for which extension of practical knowledge is important; (b) the second-level course in measurement, offered in schools and departments of education where technical information is emphasized; and (c) undergraduate courses in psychology or education departments where the emphasis is on a sound foundation. Considering the varying amounts of sophistication represented by these audiences, the editors have included articles and materials ranging from introductory, elementary study to fairly complex work. Further, selections have been carefully chosen to provide information on a wide variety of relevant topics. Early in the planning process, the authors questioned approximately twenty leading experts in the measurement field, asking each to recommend one or two articles that he felt would be indispensable to any thoughtful student of measurement. These recommendations provided a basis for the difficult process of deciding which articles to choose and which to omit.

The heart of psychological measurement is test theory, for without a sound theoretical structure, a test is of little practical value. Accordingly, the most extensive unit in the collection is the one on test theory. This unit appears early in the book, since understanding the subsequent topics depends on knowledge of test theory.

Many classifications of tests are extant in the literature; however, we believe that the analysis of various common types of tests is based on essentially the same propositions. We have, therefore, chosen to use the gross classifications of Maximum Performance and Typical Performance. Moreover, we would encourage the reader to generalize the points made in reference to a given test to other tests within the broader classification. In other words, the emphasis in reading should be on arriving at general principles for evaluating a group of tests, not on acquiring detailed information about the specific test used by a given author as an example.

To assist the reader in focusing on crucial problems and questions, all units begin with prefatory comments that point up significant issues, and a brief introduction precedes each selection. We encourage the reader to note these introductory comments before moving on to the articles themselves. A list of Suggested Readings will be found at the end of each unit, offering expansion of concepts and principles presented in the various sections of the book. Beginning students may wish to consult these references first, while more sophisticated readers may wish to use the bibliography on a more selective basis.

Obviously, the compilers of this collection are heavily indebted to the many authors and publishers who so graciously gave permission for the use of their materials. In this period of phenomenal growth of the literature in educational and psychological measurement, we believe that compilations such as this one will greatly aid in bringing students and writers together, thereby giving the student a better opportunity to examine relevant and important ideas in the field; but it is to the authors and publishers whose works appear in this book that the credit for this convenience must go.

We are grateful also to the following persons, who helped us formulate the selection of readings: Herschel T. Manuel, University of Texas; A. S. Barr, Editor, *Journal of Educational Research*; John C. Flanagan, President, American Institute for Research; John M. Duggan, College Entrance Examination Board; Walter W. Cook, University of Minnesota; Frank B. Womer, University of Michigan; Robert D. North, Educational Records Bureau; Max D. Engelhart, Chicago Public Schools; Robert L. Ebel, Michigan State University; Victor H. Noll, Michigan State University; J. Wayne Wrightstone, New York City Board of Education; Robert A. Davis, George Peabody College for Teachers; J. Francis Rummel, University of Oregon; Harold Seashore, The Psychological Corporation; S. A. Courtis, The University of Michigan; Edward C. Roeber, The University of Michigan; Ralph W. Tyler, Stanford University; Robert H. Bauernfeind, Northern Illinois University; and Delmont Byrn, The University of Michigan.

CLINTON I. CHASE
H. GLENN LUDLOW

Contents

ix

Contents   **xi**

READINGS
IN
EDUCATIONAL
AND PSYCHOLOGICAL
MEASUREMENT

Development and Objectives of Measurement and Evaluation

"In darkness dwells the people which knows its annals not," reads an inscription on the Clements Library at the University of Michigan. The history of the standardized testing movement provides an excellent springboard for the more general study of educational goals, content and learning experiences, and organization of content. The process of evaluation, of which standardized testing is an important part, appears to be very closely related to the establishment and evaluation of goals and objectives. Obviously, measurement and evaluation are also closely tied to content and instructional techniques which are used to reach agreed-upon objectives. The improvement of test construction and the better utilization of test results are, although indirect, often the best approach to the improvement of instruction.

Although the history of testing and evaluation is an integral and important part of the entire intellectual history of mankind, the major psychometric developments have occurred in the twentieth century. Beginning with the Binet test of ability in 1905, the standardized testing movement has experienced phenomenal growth. In 1964, about 150 million standardized tests were administered. When the reader considers that standardized tests constitute only approximately 10 per cent of all tests taken, he begins to be impressed with the importance of the concept and process of measurement.

The development of educational measurement can be divided roughly into three stages. First came the age of curiosity, about 1900–1915. In this period educators experimented with standardized tests as novelties. This stage was followed by a period of confidence from approximately 1915 to 1930. Much too often, test results were accepted at face value, being viewed as truly objec-

1

tive and scientific. In addition, too little consideration was given to the limitations of standardized tests. The third stage, beginning about 1930 and including our present era, may be characterized as one of critical caution. Although a large number of new tests are in use in an ever-widening setting, tests today are required to meet increasingly higher standards of validity and reliability. Further, attention is being focused on more creative and intelligent uses of test results. Particularly noteworthy is the expanding role tests are playing in the guidance and counseling field.

A fairly recent development is the marked criticism of multiple-choice tests in college admission batteries. The more vocal critics have attempted to demonstrate the low predictive validity of such instruments. Specifically, these writers believe that truly creative students and divergent thinkers are likely to be penalized on multiple-choice tests. Numerous writers, such as Ebel and Turnbull, have pointed out various fallacies in this argument, but the controversy continues.

Measurement specialists emphasize that test experts must be much more than technicians. Their activities need the direction of a well-defined educational philosophy. Even more, they need to be increasingly concerned with the role of measurement in selecting and clarifying educational goals.

1

Testing Has a History

Henry Chauncey and John E. Dobbin

Tests and measurements have played a far more prominent role in the history of mankind than is generally recognized. Ability, achievement, interest, and personality tests have evolved over a period of many years, but the major portion of their development has occurred in this century.

No student of testing can characterize himself as really informed unless he recognizes the major contributions of such giants as Binet, Goddard, Thorndike, Terman, Otis, Courtis, Thurstone, Strong, Kuder, and others. The following selection presents a broad view of the history of measurement. The reader will find it profitable to note the persistent attempt to relate measurement to the goals and techniques of instructional programs. Another focal point is the current criticism of tests and testing and the reactions of measurement experts.

By the time of the ancient Greeks, the relation of testing to the education of the young was well established and much refined. The Spartans, devoted to physical culture, had an elaborately graduated series of tests through which every boy had to pass in demonstrating his growing mastery of the required skills of manhood. In Athens a more intellectual kind of testing was refined by Socrates to extend and enrich the learning of his pupils — a combination of teaching and testing that is popular in certain fields to this day.

Through the long run of time, those who taught the young also tested them. Teaching was intensely personal. As a rule, the teacher worked with a single pupil, or with a small group of pupils. Under these conditions, testing was a normal part of the give and take of teaching and seldom was regarded as a function separate from teaching.

But times and circumstances changed. Schooling inevitably became more formal as increasing numbers of young people sought an education. The informal class of one to three or four pupils gave way to classes of twenty or thirty pupils per teacher. And this arrangement was generally established practice at the time American education was being organized. The old intimacy was lost. The "teacher" had become the "schoolmaster."

The special problems of teaching created by group instruction were recognized at least as early as the eighteenth century by men concerned about proper education of children. Pestalozzi and Herbart are names as monumental in education as Newton and Darwin in science; for those men saw that even though teachers instructed pupils in groups, they had to understand them as individuals and plan their learning accordingly. What is obvious to us now was an unusual notion two hundred years ago: Students of the same age and approximately the same size do not learn anything at the same rate, in the same sequence, or with the same degree of success, even when they are instructed simultaneously by one teacher. The modern teacher knows that every pupil brings to class his own genes and family background, his own experience, his own interests, his own successes and failures, and his own sense of well-being or lack of it; and that the teacher's instruction is received not by a group but by a collection of quite different individuals.

TESTS OF ABILITY

It is difficult to be at the same time brief and fair to the many gifted people who have contributed to the development of psychological and educational testing techniques. For example, Sir Francis Galton and James McKeen Cattell were major figures in the early attempts at measurement of individual differences and in the development of formal testing methods; yet because their work was less directly concerned with the problems of the schools than Alfred Binet's, it is glossed over with no more than passing mention in this condensed history. So, for the sake of brevity, are the contributions of certain later contributors in the field, illustrious men whose place in the history of psychological measurement is well described in the specialized literature of measurement.

In the late 1800s and early 1900s, certain special problems in education engaged the attention of able men in the emerging science of psychology. One of these problems was that of classifying school pupils so that the dullest of them could be identified and separated from the others for special instruction. Psychologists in the United States as well as in Europe had been looking for some time for connections between a child's physical characteristics and his "intelligence," or ability to do school work. Some of the characteristics they measured were size of skull, strength of grip, speed of tapping, speed of reaction, sensitivity to touch, and keenness of vision and hearing. These tests provided no answers, for pupils who were quick to learn in class and those who were slow did about equally well on all of them.

In 1904 the French psychologist Alfred Binet became a member of a commission asked to recommend to the educational authorities of Paris a method for picking out children who were mentally unable to profit from regular school instruction. Having tried to do this job with many of the earlier methods, Binet concluded that more complex tests were needed, tests that would require a child to use the complex mental processes needed in school study and in everyday life. The problems he posed for youngsters were both complex and sensible: Younger children (ages 3–6) were asked to give their family name, to identify familiar objects, to copy figures, to point to their right and left ear, to obey commands. Ten- and eleven-year-olds were asked to name the months of the year in correct order, to recognize and name various coins, to make up sentences in which various key words were provided, to define abstract words, and to arrange scrambled words into a meaningful sentence.

Binet's logic was straightforward. Most children in a given culture, he assumed, are exposed to similar influences. As they grow they have opportunities to learn about themselves and the world in which they live. They develop skill in dealing with everyday problems as well as in solving problems that involve reasoning. So Binet proposed that the degree of brightness in children could be judged by observing their ability to perform correctly tasks similar in nature to those faced in their daily lives.

It is important here to point out a fact that has escaped most laymen. No test or technique measures mental ability directly. What Binet did, and what all other "intelligence test" builders after him have done, was to set up some tasks for the young intellect to attack and then to observe what happened when that intellect was put to work on them. His method was truly scientific and remarkably like the method used by physicists forty years later to detect and measure the forces released by the atom. The cloud chamber does not permit the physicist to see the atom or its electrically charged components, but it does reveal the tracks of ionizing particles and thus permits the scientist to deduce the nature of the atom from which the particles emanate.

Similarly, psychologists cannot peek through a window to assess the quality or power of the mind. All they can do is set up a job for a person's intellect or "intelligence" and then see how well that job is done. If the job is done better or faster than it usually has been done by others of the same age, the tester deduces that this particular intellect is somehow better or stronger than most. If the job is done more poorly or slowly than the average, the tester deduces that this particular intellect is weaker than most, or not experienced in this kind of work, or not properly focused on the job. Tests of intelligence are *work-samples* of a special kind.

Binet's second contribution to measurement of mental ability was his way of describing the differences he found among the intellectual capacities of children. He did this by establishing rough averages of performance among children at successive age levels. But how to describe the children whose performance is not just at the average for their age? Binet's system was simple and is used to this day. To illustrate: If nine-year-old Pierre solved correctly the tasks appropriate for his own age group plus the tasks appropriate for average ten-year-olds and average eleven-year-olds (but encountered trouble with the tasks for average children of twelve years), he was judged to have an intellectual development roughly comparable to that of an average eleven-year-old. Conversely, if nine-year-old Louis was found to be able to handle the tasks for average seven-year-olds but to have great difficulty with tasks for average eight-year-olds, his intellectual development was judged to be comparable to that of an average youngster of seven years.

The measures that Binet and his co-workers developed for estimating mental ability marked the real beginning of modern psychological testing. These measures demonstrated that complex mental processes, processes generally associated with intelligent behavior, could be called forth and evaluated in a systematic way.

The Binet tests were not long in crossing the Atlantic. In 1910, a translation and adaptation was done by Dr. Henry Goddard, director of the training school for retarded children in Vineland, New Jersey. Goddard's enthusiasm for the tests, and their use in early identification of the retarded, encouraged many teachers and others with little or no background in psychology to become "intelligence testers," with the consequence that the newly imported technique often was badly used and earned an unfairly bad press.

At about the same time, Dr. Lewis Terman, at Stanford University, was working on a further adaptation of the Binet tests. He devised new questions, developed new methods for giving and scoring the tests, prepared new norms based on the performance of American children, and wrote a detailed book of instructions for administering the test and interpreting its results. Terman's 1916 test, known as the *Stanford-Binet*, gained wide acceptance and quickly became the standard American "intelligence test." Like Goddard, Terman recognized the usefulness of a test in discovering children who were mentally deficient, but he also saw the potential of such a test for the identification of superior students. His lifelong work with superior children, and his studies of these same children as adults, constitute a major contribution to our understanding of the "gifted" child.

One less fortunate development got its start with the increasing use of the *Stanford-Binet* test, in spite of Terman's word of caution. Other psychologists had developed a simple procedure for expressing the results of a child's performance on the Binet tests as one number. They divided the child's actual age into the age level earned by the child from the number of test questions he could answer successfully — and multiplied the result by 100 to eliminate the decimal point, as shown belov

Chronological Age	Mental Age	Computation	IQ
8 years 0 months	10 years 0 months	$10 \div 8 = 1.25 \times 100$	125
8 years 0 months	6 years 0 months	$6 \div 8 = 0.75 \times 100$	75

This new single-number index (credited by most historians to the German psychologist Wilhelm Stern) was given a name: "intelligence quotient" — IQ for short. It provided a convenient way of summarizing the comparative performance of a child on a given test; if a child's IQ number was substantially less than 100 he had done less well than the average of his age. Terman used this score device for the interpretation of performance on the *Stanford-Binet*, carefully describing it as a convenient "index of brightness" that had a comparison built into it. With the wide acceptance of the *Stanford-Binet* tests, the term IQ came into popular use among teachers and parents very quickly. In a few years, IQ had become synonymous with "intelligence" in the public mind, and the IQ of a child was erroneously assumed to be a permanent and immutable characteristic, like blue eyes or big ears, rather than a score on a particular test at a particular time.

The shortcomings of the IQ in school test score interpretation were the fault of the users far more often than of the index itself. Probably innumerable children were spiritually handicapped, in the heyday of the IQ, by their teachers' or parents' intimation that their low IQ meant they were just plain stupid. Others, proudly inflated by a high score, mistakenly believed they were generally smarter than most anybody. Since other ways of indicating ability in test scores have been developed, and teachers are becoming aware that the IQ is not necessarily a constant number, the era of overinterpretation may be drawing to a close.

For two decades the 1916 edition of the *Stanford-Binet* held a position of outstanding prestige and usefulness. Its use required a trained examiner if its results were to be trusted, and it could be administered to only one child at a time, but it was a tremendously useful tool for the better understanding of individual children and, hence, for better teaching. Beginning in 1926 and working continuously for a full decade, Terman and his associates completely revised the test, introducing changes which experience and research had shown to be necessary. The *Stanford-Binet* in its current version continues to be the most widely used individual test of the mental ability of children in America. Its only major rival is the *Wechsler Intelligence Scale for Children* (WISC), which appeared in 1949. For the individual testing of adolescents and adults, however, the *Wechsler-Bellevue Intelligence Scales,* first published in 1939, appears to have surpassed the *Stanford-Binet* in frequency of use.

Despite their usefulness in schools and clinics, the individual tests of mental ability were too cumbersome and too time-consuming for efficient use with large numbers of people. The limitations were recognized by Terman as well as by other psychologists. Accordingly, one of Terman's students, Arthur Otis, very early began to experiment with methods by which tests of mental ability could be administered to children in groups. Unlike the majority of Binet's and Terman's tests, which required the individual to think of the answer to a question or problem without any clues from the examiner, the test material with which Otis experimented required the subject to pick out the correct answer from among several alternatives provided.

Example: Which one of these five words means the *opposite* of north?

(1) pole   (2) equator   (3) south   (4) east   (5) west

Questions of this kind are called "multiple-choice" questions, for obvious reasons.

When the United States entered World War I, the Army asked the American Psychological Association to help devise a method for classifying recruits rapidly according to their mental ability. A committee headed by Robert Yerkes drew heavily upon Otis's work in developing the group test soon to be known to millions of doughboys — the _Army Alpha Test_. They also devised a group test for illiterates, using drawings and other nonverbal materials, called the _Army Beta Test_. Nearly two million soldiers took the _Army Alpha_ in the training camps. This test turned out to be a remarkably good instrument for assigning recruits to jobs with different intellectual demands, for picking out promising officer candidates, and for rejecting those who lacked sufficient mental ability to complete military training successfully.

The period of the twenties and thirties was one of active and painstaking research directed toward improvement in measuring mental ability. If a test that worked well under some circumstances, such as the _Army Alpha_, could not be adapted for other uses and did not perform equally well, then new tests were devised for new situations. Sophisticated techniques — description of score reliability and methods for empirical validation, to name just two — began to come into use.

One of the new improvements was an attempt to separate mental behaviors according to content and by different methods. The earlier tests demonstrated mental functioning as a single, general trait. Measurement of separate and distinct mental functions came into prominence with the work of L. L. Thurstone, at the University of Chicago. He and other psychologists here and abroad led the development of a mathematical method known as multiple factor analysis. By applying this method, they were able to describe the abilities measured by a variety of tests in terms of a fairly small number of "primary mental abilities." This approach led many psychologists to place less emphasis on general intelligence and to think in terms of a number of abilities in describing an individual's strengths and weaknesses.

While the search continues to refine the instruments now used to identify known factors and to isolate new ones, testing of children and students indicates that two clusters or factors of mental ability appear to have a closer relationship with school performance (in terms of marks assigned by teachers) than others yet known. These two are verbal ability — involving vocabulary, sentence understanding, and reading comprehension — and ability in numerical reasoning and computation. Because intelligence of the kind required to succeed in school learning seems to be measured most accurately by tests of verbal and quantitative ability, these kinds of tests are commonly used in schools.

In World War II, for the second time within a generation, the growing techniques for measuring human capacity were brought to bear on problems of national defense. Twelve million men and women were inducted into the armed services, each one assigned to his duty or training at least partly on the basis of his test performance. Mistakes were made, of course. Every veteran recalls or has heard of instances in which individuals were grossly or hilariously miscast in the military drama. Nevertheless, the conversion of twelve million citizen-soldiers into the complex and highly technical force of a modern army was accomplished in time because there were ways of predicting whether a recruit could learn the mathematics of gunnery or would serve the country better driving a supply truck.

One illustration will explain how new techniques of testing were used in the course of World War II. Early in the war, selection of aviation cadets was limited to men with at least two years of college who also were bright, in the sense that they all scored high on tests involving the use of words and numbers. Yet a number of these failed in pilot training. What were the characteristics that separated successful pilots from poor ones, or, for that matter, navigators from bombardiers? How could selection be made more effective?

Dozens of different test ideas were tried out, from paper-and-pencil tests to those indicating the trainee's speed of reaction, his coordination, dexterity, and ability to maintain a steady hand under stress. Many of the trial tests failed to prove useful, but some seemed to show signs of being related to pilot success, and these were analyzed and refined and tried again.

Eventually a large sample of men beginning pilot training was given a trial battery of the most promising tests. No applicant was rejected because of a low score, nor was a high score alone sufficient to keep him on the roster, and the results of the tests were not made known during the trial period.

After the entire group had completed the first stage of pilot training, the test results were studied to see whether there might be any relationship between the individual's test performance and his later success or failure in pilot training. Figure 1 shows the results. Ninety-six per cent of the men with the highest scores successfully completed primary training, while 77 per cent of the men who scored lowest "washed out."

The story illustrates the principle most important to an understanding of testing: A test is nothing more than a sample of performance related to

Figure 1

CHANCES OF SUCCESS IN PRIMARY PILOT TRAINING BASED
ON APTITUDE TEST SCORES — 185,367 TRAINEES

Test Score*	Number of Men	Per Cent Failing Primary Pilot Training
9	21,474	4%
8	19,440	10%
7	32,129	14%
6	39,398	22%
5	34,975	30%
4	23,699	40%
3	11,209	53%
2	2,139	67%
1	904	77%

* This type of score, the "stanine," was devised by the Air Force during World War II and refers to a weighted scale on which 9 represents the highest score and 1 the lowest.

the characteristic the examiner is trying to predict or estimate. The Air Force psychologists had to try out many different samples of performance and then wait to see which kinds of test performance were most closely related to later performance in pilot training. This trying-and-waiting procedure is called "validation."

A second important principle is suggested by the results of the Air Force testing reported in Figure 1. Almost no test or combination of tests has an inherently stable yes-no, pass-fail, go–no-go score. The person who is using the test scores may decide to set a "cutting score" arbitrarily and thus make an artificial pass-fail interpretation of the test results, but the test itself will at best yield a score with a fairly reliable set of probabilities.

At the end of the war, testing had a new military role. The return of twelve million veterans to civilian life during a short span of time quite properly concerned those who cared about individuals and about the nation. A high proportion of these veterans were men who had no vocational training other than military training. Others had left jobs which had changed or disappeared altogether during the war years. Many had interrupted schooling to enter the service and soon would be seeking to press on with their education. Could the country afford to release these millions willy-nilly, without guidance or help, into an economy already struggling with the mammoth conversion back to peacetime operations?

Using personal histories, service records, and tests of ability, of aptitude, of school achievement, and of vocational preparation, the Veterans Administration gathered information to be used in counseling each individual veteran toward the postwar activity or occupation for which he seemed to be best suited. He had only to ask for it, and he received the help of the most thorough, and certainly by far the largest, counseling agency the world had known. With VA support and guidance, millions of veterans left the services to continue education in high schools, colleges, technical schools, and vocational training courses. It has been said that the federal investment in education of veterans after World War II contributed as much to the growth and security of the nation as the military victories earned by these same veterans during the war. In the process of finding and training and using the capacities of people, coming out of military service as well as going into it, tests were used as tools.

TESTS OF ACHIEVEMENT

Achievement examinations have as long a history as tests of ability. The Spartan youth demonstrated his hard-earned fitness by running to the top of a mountain. The young Athenian scholar successfully engaged other scholars in disputation. And in the United States of a generation ago the pigtailed eighth-grader in the little red schoolhouse stood up and correctly spelled dis-es-tablish-men-tarian-ism at the Friday afternoon "visitation."

The point of the achievement test is to find out whether the student (or soldier or hunter or worker) has learned what the teacher has been trying to teach him. Sometimes the achievement test is aimed at demonstration of a small piece of learning — recall of a single chapter in a book or demonstration of one new stroke in swimming. Other times the achievement test covers a great deal of learning or a complex set of learnings, as in the examinations for admission of a lawyer to the bar. In every case the achievement test calls for a demonstration of learning in some form that can be observed and assessed. Just as in the case of the ability test, the achievement test is a work sample.

From the first schools of early colonial times down to the present, the most frequently used achievement tests have been those prepared by the teacher. And since the major part of school learning for generations has come out of books, it follows that demonstration of learning should be accomplished by speaking and writing.

A step toward standardized testing was introduced by Horace Mann in 1845, when he substituted a uniform written examination for oral interrogation of students by school committeemen in the Boston public schools. Mann's comments about the superiority of the uniform written examination have a curiously modern sound:

1. These examinations are impartial, and there is no possibility of favoritism or "officious interference" by the examiner.
2. Uniform questions eliminate the chance element inherent in oral examinations, where questions vary so widely that the good pupil may miss a hard question while the dullard answers an easy one correctly.
3. Such examinations conserve the time of examiners and permit many questions to be asked of all pupils — the greater the number of questions, the nearer does the examination approach completeness.
4. Uniform examinations place all students under the same conditions — they all run the same race over the same course.

Horace Mann's uniform examinations had one characteristic that was to be of significance in later standardized tests: They required all students to answer the same questions, and a lot of them. Use of the uniform examination is still growing, as school districts, city school systems, and even states, such as New York State with its Regents examinations, have borrowed and adapted the idea.

Probably the first application of a standardized test to an educational problem was accomplished by a physician, J. M. Rice, in 1897. At that time schools were under considerable pressure to add new subjects to the narrowly academic curriculum, and school people generally were countering with a claim that they had too little time to teach the subjects already required. Rice prepared a list of fifty spelling words and administered his test to pupils as he went from town to town. He found little relationship between scores on his "test" and the amount of time a school spent on formal spelling instruction. This simple experiment pointed the way to an objective method for resolving educational differences of opinion.

A giant of the early years of testing was Professor E. L. Thorndike, of Teachers College, Columbia University. Thorndike in 1904 published the first textbook on educational measurement, *An Introduction to the Theory* of *Mental and Social Measurement,* which is taken by many to mark the beginning of modern times in testing. Thorndike's work was soon followed by other pioneering attempts to measure systematically the outcomes of instruction in various school subjects: In 1908, Stone's arithmetic reasoning test; in 1909, Courtis's arithmetic computation test; in 1910, Thorndike's scale for the handwriting of children; in 1911, the Ayres Handwriting Scale; in 1912, the Hillegas composition scale. The start had been made.

The new aspect of standardized achievement tests was their systematic use of the principles of scientific measurement of human abilities developed in the psychological laboratories. The early workers in the measurement of school achievement carried over from the psychological laboratory a concern for careful control of the conditions of testing and for absolutely objective scoring. Spurring them on in this effort was a series of experiments that showed how unreliable, and often unfair, was the grading of the traditional essay examination.

The educational ferment of the 1920s was basically scientific, in that education generally was shifting from a wholly philosophical base to a position that included scientific self-study. Old ideas were challenged and new ones introduced according to evidence that had been gathered systematically. By 1915 specialists with responsibility for educational research were numerous enough to form a professional organization. Early in the twenties more than one hundred bureaus of educational research were established in large city school systems, in state departments of education, and in state universities.

Many professional articles on testing and applications of testing in educational research began to appear. New educational and psychological journals were established in response to growing activity in these fields. Books on statistical methods for use in educational research were published. Publishers previously engaged in the preparation of textbooks added technicians to their staffs and began the commercial publication of standardized tests. And since the major focus of all this effort was on measuring what and why and how young people learn in school, tests were built and printed or mimeographed by practically everyone who had an interest in the problem — teachers, researchers, psychologists, professors of education, book publishers, graduate students.

The wholesale building of tests in the 1920s had several results. On the good side was the encouragement that testing gave to teachers to re-examine their teaching goals and to think over again the content of their instruction. Also on the good side was the general acceptance of testing, created by the widespread public interest and the multitude of amateur test-builders, which made it possible for the little group of trained professionals in the field to carry on the large tryouts necessary for the building of real standardized tests. A landmark in the history of educational measurement was the publication, in 1923, of the first *Stanford Achievement Test,* a "battery" of standardized achievement tests in elementary school subjects — developed by L. M. Terman (builder of the *Stanford-Binet*), T. L. Kelley, and G. M. Ruch. This test, and the methods used to produce it, foreshadowed many characteristics of modern testing.

On the debit side of the early enthusiasm for testing, the list of effects is longer. Most of the tests put together by eager amateurs and hawked among their colleagues were not very good, and they soured a lot of teachers on the whole idea of testing. Almost without exception, the amateur-made tests measured only recall of specific subject matter content, asking only for regurgitation of the text; so teachers and parents came to feel that all tests covered only a small part of what schools were attempting to teach. Many people grew to think that all objective tests were true-false tests (as many of the slapped-together instruments of the period were).

The most detrimental effect of the early enthusiasm for tests was the disenchantment produced by exaggerating the benefits of tests and overinterpreting their results. Educators and public alike had been oversold on educational testing. When it began to appear that tests did not measure as much or as accurately as their enthusiasts claimed, there was a reaction against school testing — a reaction that persists in some form to this day.

The leaders among the professionals continued with their work — trying new approaches, refining ideas, and running experimental tryouts; and the number of such professionals grew. Teachers College at Columbia University led all others in the number of scholars and researchers devoted to psychological and educational measurement. Other centers of educational thought, too, began in this period to develop leadership in measurement — Stanford, Chicago, Peabody, and Iowa among them. Researchers in the older field of experimental psychology crossed over now and then to the applied problems of education; and still other centers of leadership grew in the emerging "science" of measuring and predicting how people learn: the universities of Harvard, Michigan, Ohio State, Yale, Minnesota, and Princeton, to name just a few.

The first *Stanford Achievement Test* foreshadowed several things to come in the preparation of standardized tests for school use. This elementary school test battery of 1923 stood out over the welter of unsubstantial tests of its time for these reasons: (1) It was built by a group of highly trained professionals working as a team; (2) its content was drawn from a survey of many different courses of study, so that its questions were representative of what was being taught in all parts of the country; (3) its questions were tried out experimentally, to see how well they worked, before they were used in a final test form; and (4) the final test forms were given to thousands of school children in many different school systems to obtain comparative samples of performance (norms). This long, difficult, and expensive process requires the effort of many people and the investment of considerable sums for years before the investment can be recovered through sale of the finished tests.

Publication of this battery of tests brought together in a joint risk venture, for the first time, the combination of resources necessary for development of good standardized tests: a team of professionals in measurement, the help of educators all over the country, an established publisher, and capital to support the venture until the tests could be sold. The *Stanford Achievement Test* proved to be extremely useful to elementary school people in assessing the academic learning of their students; millions of copies were sold, and the original investment was returned. Test publication had passed from an amateur to a professional basis, and the general characteristics of the publication process had been established.

Tests of school achievement are as varied as they are numerous. Most of the earlier ones, and many of the tests now used, measure little more than recall of factual information. There are two reasons for this: (1) Learning and retention of factual information is an important purpose of school instruction, and (2) measurement of other kinds of learning (insights, understandings, attitudes, points of view) is much more difficult to accomplish. But even in the measurement of factual recall, tests are different, one from another, because any school achievement test is just a sample of the things a student is taught. Every test-maker draws on a different sample of learning when he frames his questions.

The limitation of early achievement tests to measurement of recall was recognized from the outset by the professionals in the field. To go beyond the recall or recognition of facts and measure other learnings — the ability to gather information and draw conclusions, for example, or the habit of suspending judgment until information has been obtained — is more difficult. But it was attempted, again and again, by those who wanted to encourage good teaching by providing tests of the harder-to-measure outcomes of good teaching.

A number of promising leads were developed in the direction of testing the broader outcomes of teaching, but three particular efforts, each supported by large resources, will be mentioned here: the Pennsylvania Study, begun in the late 1920s, supported by the Carnegie Foundation for the Advancement of Teaching; the Eight-Year Study of the 1930s, sponsored by the Progressive Education Association; and the Study of General Education (college level) of the 1940s, supported by the American Council on Education. Each of these efforts was partly based upon previous research and each added something important to the techniques of measuring school learning. One enormous contribution of the men who led these researches was development of a rationale and a vocabulary with which they could explain what they were trying to do. The general conclusions might be paraphrased as follows:

The purpose of schools is to educate each young person in such a way that he will be able, to the limits of his natural ability, to contribute to the welfare and strength of American society and to realize a full development of his own potential as a human being. In order to do this, the school teaches each child certain subject matter content, such as English and history and mathematics, so that he may have the knowledge with which to solve his problems; the learning of this content is the immediate goal of instruction. When he has learned some subject matter and mastered some skills, the school teaches the student to apply them in a variety of new situations, so that he will be able to use them when they are needed in nontextbook circumstances; learning to use school-learned knowledge in a variety of ways is the intermediate goal of instruction. When he knows the subject matter and how to apply it, the ultimate goal of the school is that he will apply his learning, bettering his own life and the lives of his fellows.

This is a set of ideas that makes education easier to study and assess. Successful achievement of the ultimate goals of schooling depends on successful achievement of the intermediate goals, which, in turn, depends on the learnings that make up the immediate goals. With this definition, it became clear that achievement tests in subject matter had now reached the point of evaluating how well students attain the immediate goals of instruction. With continued refinement, the direction of the next step in testing was clear — toward measurement of abilities to apply knowledge, the intermediate goals.

A useful application of the new concept was developed by the United States Armed Forces Institute during World War II. With millions of young people in service who wanted somehow to continue their interrupted educations, the Armed Forces Institute set into motion a gigantic program of correspondence courses, in which servicemen enrolled all over the world. The Institute developed tests by which veterans could gain credit for courses taken in service in obtaining high school diplomas or getting into college. How could they equate the physics learned after hours in a supply depot with the physics learned by demonstration and lecture in a classroom? Or ancient history read by flashlight in a dugout with ancient history studied in a hushed library?

USAFI sought the answers by measurement of the intermediate goals of instruction in these subjects; they built tests which attempted to measure the student's understanding of the principles of the subject and his ability to use these principles in the solution of new problems, regardless of the source or nature of his instruction. The product of this USAFI effort was the series of tests called Tests of General Educational Development. By arrangement with thousands of high schools and hundreds of colleges, these tests were used to bring veterans back into formal schooling with full credit for their wartime learning. The work of USAFI and its acceptance by civilian educators constitute one of the most satisfying episodes, in terms of the conservation of human talent, in the history of education. The tests built by USAFI have been models for test improvement ever since.

Measuring the achievement of the ultimate goals of education is something else again. One can test students on their knowledge of the facts of local government (immediate goal) and their ability to apply this knowledge to different kinds of problems (intermediate goal), but it has not yet been possible to test them ten years after they are out of school to find out whether any sizable unit of education — say, a college major in political science — has contributed more to the personal fulfillment or social effectiveness of young people than an equivalent amount of time and effort spent in travel or apprenticeship.

Measuring Student Interests

It is axiomatic that good teaching often depends on the ability of the teacher to ascertain the interests of the learner, as well as his capacities, and to capitalize upon them. Good teachers and counselors often use an individual's special interests as means for reinforcing learning or awakening motivation to learn. For this reason, tests and inventories for discovery of students' interests have been used in schools for many years.

The oldest and best known of the standardized interest inventories used in schools is the *Strong Vocational Interest Blank,* one form for men and the other for women, which had its origins in early research done at Carnegie Institute of Technology. Work on the inventory was continued by its author, E. K. Strong, Jr., while he was at Stanford University. The inventory has been in school use since 1927. Through many revisions and countless research applications, the *Strong Vocational Interest Blank* has built up a body of background information that permits a good counselor in high school or college to help a student in recognizing and interpreting his interests. With the proper administration and interpretation of this inventory, it is possible for a student to discover whether his interests are similar to those of sales managers, of physicists, or of musicians. Such a discovery of shared interest means a great deal to young people who are at that lonely point in the maturation process at which one must decide on directions in which life must turn.

Another inventory of interests related to occupational fields is the *Kuder Preference Record,* which appeared in its original form in 1934. This instrument, too, can be used to help students understand their own interests in the light of how those interests may relate to various occupations.

There are several other inventories of interests used in schools, but the *Strong* and the *Kuder* are both the ancestors and the prototypes of all others concerned with interest and vocation. Both have long histories of research. Both have survived a period in which users with more enthusiasm than information overinterpreted their results.

No standardized inventory or combination of inventories — of interests or of any other attributes — will tell an individual student that he should become a doctor, or an artist, or anything else. Properly used, such an inventory can add one more bit of evidence that may be helpful to him in making up his mind about vocational goals to pursue, but it cannot tell him what he should do. This much has been learned by school people and most parents since the advent of interest inventories; its recognition is an event of some note in the history of measurement.

MEASURING PERSONAL CHARACTERISTICS

Teachers and parents have been interested in the testing of "personality" for as long as they have been interested in the testing of academic achievement. Many human beings are rather more interested in hanging a personality label on other people than in achieving a deeper understanding of themselves. What is lacking is a method for observing and describing personality that is as objective and accurate as description of physical or intellectual characteristics. Psychologists have long been striving to develop such a method. Progress has been painfully slow. The nature of the individual personality is even more difficult to perceive than the nature of intellect. Although there are several different major theories about formation of the individual personality structure, all theories rely on observation of individual reaction to certain factors of environment, natural or artificial, to provide evidence about the nature of a personality. A great deal of research has been undertaken in the field, but there is not yet available for general use in schools any test that will describe or categorize the personality of normal people with the accuracy of academic ability and achievement tests.

PROGRAMS OF TESTING FOR SELECTION

All of the major selection testing programs operate to make the competition for college admissions more equitable, to help students get into the right college, and to assist them in locating scholarship aid. The oldest and best known of these programs is run by the College Entrance Examination Board, an association of over five hundred colleges with additional representatives from secondary schools. The College Board examination program was started at the turn of the century as the result of a proposal that colleges requiring examinations for admission would do both the high schools and the applicants a service by setting a common examination on which an applicant could earn admission to any of a number of colleges. Until the College Board was formed, a student who wanted to enter his application at three colleges had to take three different examinations at three different times and places. The principal of any high school that had many college-going graduates had an exasperating time trying to arrange for and comply with the multitude of examinations his seniors needed to take in order to their various college choices, not to mention preparing the students for the examinations.

A major change occurred in the American educational culture in the fifteen years following World War II. This change was first seen as a mushrooming of the college population and was the result of several forces acting together. The GI Bill brought college education within reach of thousands of veterans who would not have considered going to college without its assistance, and thereby set a "college-going" example in families where it had not existed. The average individual income rose to new highs and stayed there, making a college education possible for youngsters whose parents could not have afforded it a generation earlier, while the technology of business and industry grew at such a furious rate and to such heights of complexity that "Help Wanted" pages were filled with attractive positions for young people requiring at least some college training. The college-educated person had become the object of greater respect in the popular eye, and college education had become more desirable to more people for personal reasons. All together, these forces swamped many colleges with applicants.

In addition to the rapidly growing program of the College Board, several more testing programs, national or regional in scope and focused also on young people in transition between high school to college, were developed in the 1950's. The Westinghouse Talent Search, launched earlier, reached across the country. The Selective Service Examinations provided for draft deferment of able students. Then came other tests for selection of students for scholarship awards — the General Motors Scholarships, the hundreds

of private, industrial, and philanthropic scholarships, and, largest of all, the
National Merit Scholarships. In 1959, the American College Testing Program was established to screen applicants to colleges which did not use the
College Board program.

Thus in a period of sixty years educational testing has developed from
a part-time chore of psychologists to a set of techniques that affects every
student in school and college. The history of testing has been one of
dedicated effort by a great many people to shape and sharpen and wield a
tool that can be of great help to educators everywhere.

2

General Statement on Evaluation

Ralph W. Tyler

*Although this statement on evaluation is only gradually nearing
the quarter-of-a-century mark, it is already a classic in the field; yet it
is still quite relevant to the current problems of testing and evaluation. The author summarizes six significant purposes of evaluation
and six assumptions underlying programs for evaluation. The statements relating to evaluation procedures are just as significant today
as when they were written.*

*A critical reading of this selection should do much to place measurement in its proper perspective in the total educational enterprise. A constructive activity for the reader would be to select some
learning unit in mathematics, social studies, or English and outline
it briefly following the steps presented in Tyler's conceptualization.*

. . . .

PURPOSES OF EVALUATION

In perceiving the appropriate place of evaluation in modern education,
consideration must be given to the purposes which a program of evaluation
may serve. At present the purposes most commonly emphasized in schools
and colleges are the grading of students, their grouping and promotion,

From Ralph W. Tyler, "General Statement on Evaluation," *The Journal of Educational Research*, XXXV (March, 1942), pp. 492–501. Reprinted with the
permission of publisher and author.

reports to parents, and financial reports to the board of education or to the board of trustees. A comprehensive program of evaluation should serve a broader range of purposes than these.

One important purpose of evaluation is to make a periodic check on the effectiveness of the educational institution, and thus to indicate the points at which improvements in the program are necessary.

Another important purpose of evaluation which is frequently not recognized is to validate the hypotheses upon which the educational institution operates. A school or college organizes its curriculum on the basis of a plan which seems to the staff to be satisfactory, but in reality we do not yet know enough about curriculum construction to be sure that a given plan will work satisfactorily in a particular community. On that account, the curriculum of each school or college is based upon hypotheses, that is, the best judgments the staff can make on the basis of information it has. In some cases these hypotheses are not valid, and the educational institution may continue for years utilizing a poorly organized curriculum because no careful evaluation has been made to check the validity of the hypotheses on which the curriculum is operating. Similarly, a program of guidance in any school system is largely based on hypotheses which have not been adequately validated, and again the effectiveness of the program may be greatly reduced because some of these hypotheses are not valid. Furthermore, many of our administrative policies and practices are based upon judgments which in a particular case may not be sound. Every educational institution has the responsibility of testing the major hypotheses upon which it operates and of adding to the fund of tested principles upon which schools may better operate in the future.

A third important purpose of evaluation is to provide information basic to effective guidance of individual students. Only as we appraise the student's achievement and as we get a comprehensive description of his growth and development are we in a position to give him sound guidance. This implies evaluation sufficiently comprehensive to appraise all the significant aspects of the student's accomplishments. Merely the judgment that he is doing average work in a particular course is not enough. We need to find out more accurately where he is progressing and where he is having difficulties.

A fourth purpose of evaluation is to provide a certain psychological security to the school or college staff, to the students, and to the parents. The responsibilities of an educational institution are broad and involve aspects which seem quite intangible to the casual observer. Frequently the staff becomes a bit worried and is in doubt as to whether it is really accomplishing its major objectives. This uncertainty may be a good thing if it leads to a careful appraisal and constructive measures for improvement of the program; but without systematic evaluation the tendency is for the staff to become less secure and sometimes to retreat to activities which give tangible results although they may be less important. Often we seek security through emphasizing procedures which are extraneous and sometimes harmful to the best educational work of the school. Thus, high-school teachers may devote an undue amount of energy to coaching for scholarship tests or college entrance examinations because the success of students on these examinations serves as a tangible evidence to the teacher that something has been accomplished. However, since these examinations may be appropriate for only a portion of the high-school student body, concentration of attention upon them may actually hinder the total educational program of the high school. For such teachers a comprehensive evaluation which gives a careful check on all aspects of the program would provide the kind of security that is necessary for their continued growth and self-confidence. Students and parents are also subject to this feeling of insecurity and in many cases desire some kind of tangible evidence that the educational program is effective. If this is not provided by a comprehensive plan of evaluation, then students and parents are likely to turn to tangible but extraneous factors for their security.

A fifth purpose of evaluation which should be emphasized is to provide a sound basis for public relations. No factor is as important in establishing constructive and co-operative relations with the community as an understanding on the part of the community of the effectiveness of its educational institutions. A careful and comprehensive evaluation should provide evidence that can be widely publicized and used to inform the community about the value of the school or college program. Many of the criticisms expressed by patrons and parents can be met and turned to constructive co-operation if concrete evidence is available regarding the accomplishments of the school or college.

A sixth purpose of evaluation is to help both teachers and pupils to clarify their purposes and to see more concretely the directions in which they are moving. Appraisal demands a clear conception of the results hoped for; hence, both teachers and pupils are stimulated by an evaluation program to define these anticipated results. This definition of results sought serves to guide the efforts of both teacher and learner. For this reason the participation of both teachers and pupils in planning and conducting evaluation processes is of vital importance.

Evaluation can contribute to these six purposes. It can provide a periodic check which gives direction to the continued improvement of the program of the school or college; it can help to validate some of the important hypotheses upon which the program operates; it can furnish data about individual students essential to wise guidance; it can give a more satisfactory foundation for the psychological security of the staff, of parents, and of students; it can supply a sound basis for public relations; and it can help both teachers and pupils to clarify their goals. For these purposes to be achieved, however, they must be kept continually in mind in planning and in developing the program of evaluation. The decision as to what is to be evaluated, the techniques for appraisal, and the summary and interpretation of results should all be worked out in terms of these important purposes.

UNDERLYING ASSUMPTIONS

In the development of a program for evaluating the outcomes of general education, certain basic assumptions are helpful. Six of them are of particular importance. In the first place, it is assumed that education is a process which seeks to change the behavior pattern of human beings. It is obvious that we expect students to change in some respects as they go through an educational program. An educated man is different from one who has no education and presumably this difference is due to the educational experience. It is also generally recognized that these changes brought about by education are modifications in the ways in which the educated man reacts, that is, changes in his ways of behaving. Generally, as a result of education we expect students to recall and to use ideas which they did not have before, to have developed various skills, as in reading and in writing, which they did not previously possess, to have improved their ways of thinking, to have modified their reactions to aesthetic experiences, as in the arts, and so on. It seems safe to say on the basis of our present conception of learning, that education, when it is effective, changes the behavior patterns of human beings.

A second basic assumption involved in evaluation is that the kinds of changes in behavior patterns in human beings which the school or college seeks to bring about are its educational objectives. The aims of any educational program cannot well be stated in terms of the content of the program, or in terms of the methods and procedures followed by the teachers, for these are only means to other ends. Fundamentally, the purposes of education represent these changes in human beings which we hope to bring about through education. The kinds of ideas which we expect students to get and to use, the kinds of skills which we hope they will develop, the techniques of thinking which we hope they will acquire, the ways in which we hope they will learn to react to aesthetic experiences — these are illustrations of educational objectives.

A third basic assumption is that an educational program is appraised by finding out how far the objectives of the program are actually being realized. Since the program seeks to bring about certain changes in the behavior of students, and since these are the fundamental educational objectives, then it follows that an evaluation of the educational program is a process for finding out to what degree these changes in the students are actually taking place.

The fourth basic assumption is that the way in which the student organizes his behavior patterns is an important aspect to be appraised. There is always the danger that the identification of these various types of objectives will result in their treatment as isolated bits of behavior. Thus, the recognition that an educational program seeks to change the student's information, skills, ways of thinking, attitudes, and interests, may result in an evaluation program which appraises the development of each of these aspects of behavior separately, and makes no effort to relate them. We must not forget that the human being reacts in a fairly unified fashion; hence, in any given situation information is not usually separated from skills, or from ways of thinking, or from attitudes, interests, and appreciations. For example, a student who encounters an important social-civic problem is expected to draw upon his information to use such skill as he has in locating additional facts, to think through the problem critically, to make choices of courses of action in terms of fundamental values and attitudes, and to be continually interested in better solutions to such problems. This clearly involves the relationship of various behavior patterns and their better integration. So that this interrelation will not be neglected, it seems necessary to emphasize as a basic assumption that the way in which the student relates his various reactions is an important aspect of his development and an important part of any evaluation of his educational achievement.

A fifth basic assumption is that the methods of evaluation are not limited to the giving of paper-and-pencil tests; any device which provides valid evidence regarding the progress of students toward educational objectives is appropriate. As a matter of practice, most programs of appraisal have been limited to written examinations or paper-and-pencil tests of some type. Perhaps this has been due to the long tradition associated with written examinations or perhaps to the greater ease with which written examinations may be given and the results summarized. However, a consideration of the kinds of objectives formulated for general education makes clear that written examinations are not likely to provide an adequate appraisal for all of these objectives. A written test may be a valid measure of information recalled and ideas remembered. In many cases too, the student's skill in writing and in mathematics may be shown by written tests, and it is also true that various techniques of thinking may be evidenced through more novel types of written test materials. On the other hand, evidence regarding the improvement of health practices, regarding better personal-social adjustment of students, regarding interests and attitudes, may require a much wider repertoire of appraisal techniques. This assumption emphasizes the wider range of techniques which may be used in evaluation, such as observational records, anecdotal records, questionnaires, interviews, check lists, records of activities, products made, and the like. The selection of evaluation techniques should be made in terms of the appropriateness of that technique for the kind of behavior to be appraised.

A sixth basic assumption is that the participation of teachers, pupils, and parents in the processes of evaluation is essential to derive the maximum values from a program of evaluation. They all have a stake in the educational program of school or college. They can all contribute to the formation and clarification of objectives; they are all in a position to obtain evidence about the progress pupils are making; they can all benefit from efforts to interpret the results of appraisal. The processes of evaluation help to guide both teachers and pupils and may help parents in understanding the work of the school. Finally, the development of an increasing degree of self-evaluation is in itself a major goal of democratic education.

A comprehensive program of evaluation utilizes other assumptions, but these six are of particular importance because they suggest the general procedure by which an evaluation program can be developed. They show the necessity of basing an evaluation program upon educational objectives, and they indicate that educational objectives for purposes of evaluation must be stated in terms of changes in behavior of students; they emphasize the importance of the relation of various aspects of behavior rather than the treatment of them in isolation, they make clear the possibility of a wide range of evaluation techniques, and they suggest the co-operative responsibilities of teachers, pupils, and parents.

EVALUATION PROCEDURE

The general procedure followed in evaluation involves several major steps. It is first necessary for the school to formulate a statement of its educational objectives, then these statements of objectives are classified into major types. Without effort at classification, the objectives are likely to be of various levels of generality and specificity, and too numerous for practicable treatment. Furthermore, the classification into types of objectives indicates the kinds of evaluation procedures essential to an adequate appraisal.

The next step is to define each of these types of objectives in terms of behavior. This step is necessary because in any list, some objectives are likely to be stated in terms so vague and nebulous that the kind of behavior they imply is not clear. Thus, a type of objective such as the development of effective methods of thinking may mean different things to different people. Only as "effective methods of thinking" is defined in terms of the range of reactions expected of students can we be sure what is to be evaluated under this classification.

After a clear definition of the kinds of behavior we are trying to appraise has been obtained, the next problem is to identify situations in which students can be expected to display these types of behavior so that we may know where to go to obtain evidence regarding this objective. If each objective has been clearly defined, this step is not difficult. For example, if our definition of objectives has identified as one educational goal, the ability to locate dependable information relating to specified types of problems, then it seems obvious that a situation which would give students a chance to show this ability would be one in which they were asked to find information relating to these specified problems.

One value of this step is to suggest a much wider range of situations which might be used in evaluation than have commonly been utilized. By the time this step has been completed, there will usually be listed a considerable number of types of situations which give students a chance to indicate the sort of behavior patterns they have developed. These can be considered potential "test situations."

The next step in this general evaluation procedure involves the selection and trial of promising methods for obtaining evidence regarding each type of objective. Before attempting to construct any new evaluation instruments, it is generally a good plan to examine tests and other instruments already developed to see whether they will serve as satisfactory means for appraising the objective. Any group working on an evaluation program will find useful bibliographies of evaluation instruments such as the Buros *Mental Measurements Yearbooks*. This bibliography not only lists tests and other appraisal instruments which are commercially available, but also includes several critical reviews of each test written by teachers, curriculum constructers, and test makers. These reviews help in selecting from available instruments those which might be worth a trial.

Usually at this point it is found that no tests are available to measure certain of the objectives emphasized. In such cases it becomes necessary to construct additional new instruments in order to make a really comprehensive appraisal. In constructing these instruments it is helpful to set up some of the potential test situations suggested in the preceding step and actually to try them out with students to see how far they can be used effectively.

The next step is to select on the basis of this preliminary trial the more promising appraisal methods for further development and improvement. The basis of selection will include the degree to which the appraisal method is found to give results consistent with other evidences regarding the student's attainment of this objective and the extent to which the appraisal method can be practicably used under the conditions prevailing in the school or college.

An important problem in the refinement and improvement of an evaluation instrument is the determination of the aspects of student behavior to be summarized and the decision regarding the units or terms in which each aspect will be summarized. The reaction of a human being in any test situation is sufficiently complex so that several aspects could be measured and several possible units of measurement could be used. The choice should be made in terms of the significance of the several aspects and the appropriateness of the results. Another task in refining and improving an evaluation instrument is to make revisions which give more clear-cut measures, which provide a more representative and adequate sample of the student's reaction, and which improve the ease with which the instrument can be used.

A final step in the procedure of evaluation is to devise means for interpreting and using the results of the various instruments of evaluation. The previous steps have resulted in the selection of, or the development of a range of procedures which can be used periodically in appraising the degree to which students are acquiring the several important educational objectives. These instruments will give a series of scores and descriptions which will serve to describe and to measure various aspects of the behavior patterns of the students. Presumably each of these scores or verbal summaries can be compared with scores or verbal summaries previously obtained so that some evidence of change or growth of students is available. However, the meaning of these scores, that is, their significance in interpretation, becomes fuller through various sorts of studies. One such study is the development of norms, that is, the identification of scores typically made by students in similar classes, in similar institutions, or with other similar characteristics. Another helpful study is one involving the typical growth or changes made in these scores from year to year. A third study involves the interrelationship of several scores to identify patterns. It is important in this step to examine the progress students are making toward each of the several objectives in order to get more clearly the pattern of development of each student and of the group as a whole and also to obtain hypotheses which help to explain the types of development taking place. An important purpose of evaluation is to provide evidence which suggests hypotheses for modification and improvement of the curriculum. Each school and college needs to develop methods for interpreting and using the results of appraisal so as to improve the educational program and to guide individual students more wisely.

CONTINUAL EVALUATION

This brief description of the steps followed in evaluation should have indicated that the process of evaluation is an integral part of the educational process. It does not mean simply the giving of a few ready-made tests and the tabulations of resulting scores. It is a recurring process involving the formulation of objectives, their clearer definition, plans to study students' reactions in the light of these objectives, continued efforts to interpret the results of such appraisals in terms which throw helpful light on the educational program and on the individual student. This sort of procedure goes on as a continuing cycle. Studying the results of evaluation often leads to a reformulation and some improvement in the conception of the objectives to be obtained. The results of evaluation and any reformulation of objectives will suggest desirable modifications in the teaching and in the educational program itself. Modifications in the objectives and in the educational program will result in corresponding modifications in the plan and program of evaluation. So the cycle goes on.

This program of evaluation is also a potent method of continued teacher education. The recurring demand for the formulation and clarification of objectives, the continuing study of the reactions of students in terms of these objectives, and the persistent attempt to relate the results obtained from various sorts of measurement are all means for focusing the interests and efforts of teachers upon the most vital parts of the educational process. Evaluation provides a means for the continued improvement of the program of education, for an ever deepening understanding of students, with a consequent increase in the effectiveness of our educational institutions.

3

The Social Consequences
of Educational Testing

Robert L. Ebel

*In this brief article we find a distillation of many current issues
and problems in the area of educational and psychological measurement. The rapid increase in the use of tests in decision making has
brought forth a horde of critics, some of whom see the ultimate solution as the complete abandonment of standardized testing. Dr. Ebel
carefully analyzes four major criticisms and tells why properly interpreted test results are quite compatible with our goals in a free
society.*

*One noteworthy suggestion is that tests should be used as little
as possible to* impose *decisions. Rather, they should be used as
much as possible to provide a sounder basis for* choice *in individual
decision making. An interesting aspect of this selection is the
enumeration of the social consequences of* not *testing. The reader
would find it instructive to explicate further these latter four consequences.*

Tests have been used increasingly in recent years to make educational
assessments. The reasons for this are not hard to discover. Educational
tests of aptitude and achievement greatly improve the precision, objectivity
and efficiency of the observations on which educational assessments rest.
Tests are not alternatives to observations. At best they represent no more
than refined and systematized processes of observation.

But the increasing use of tests has been accompanied by an increasing
flow of critical comment. Again the reasons are easy to see. Tests vary in
quality. None is perfect and some may be quite imperfect. Test scores
are sometimes misused. And even if they were flawless and used with the
greatest skill, they would probably still be unpopular among those who
have reason to fear an impartial assessment of some of their competencies.

From Robert L. Ebel, "The Social Consequences of Educational Testing," *School
and Society*, November 14, 1964, pp. 331–334; excerpted from "Proceedings of the
1963 Invitational Conference on Testing Problems," copyright 1964, Educational
Testing Service, Princeton, N.J. Reprinted with the permission of publishers and
author.

Many of the popular articles critical of educational testing that have appeared in recent years do not reflect a very adequate understanding of educational testing, or a very thoughtful, unbiased consideration of its social consequences. What appears in print often seems to be only an elaboration and documentation of prejudices and preconceptions, supported by atypical anecdotes and purposefully selected quotations. Educational testing has not fared very well in these articles.

Among the charges of malfeasance and misfeasance that critics have leveled against the test makers there is one of nonfeasance. Specifically, they are charged with having shown lack of proper concern for the social consequences of educational testing. These harmful consequences, the critics have suggested, may be numerous and serious. The more radical among them imply that, because of what they suspect about the serious social consequences of educational testing, the whole testing movement ought to be suppressed. The more moderate critics claim that they do not know much about these social consequences. But they also suggest that the test makers don't either, and that it is the test makers who ought to be doing substantial research to find out.

Perhaps so, but it is worth noting that the scarcity of formal research on the social consequences of educational testing does not mean that there is no reliable knowledge about those consequences, or that those engaged in educational testing have been callously indifferent to its social consequences. Further, scientific research on human behavior may require commitment to values that are in basic conflict with our democratic concerns for individual welfare. If boys and girls are used as carefully controlled experimental subjects in tough-minded research on social issues that really matter, not all of them will benefit, and some may be disadvantaged seriously. Our society is not yet ready, and perhaps should never become ready to acquiesce in that kind of scientific research. Finally, and unfortunately, research seldom if ever reveals clearly what society *ought* to do about a particular problem.

Before proceeding further, let us mention specifically a few of the harmful things that critics have suggested educational testing may do:

1. It may place an indelible stamp of intellectual status — superior, mediocre or inferior — on a child, and thus predetermine his social status as an adult, and possibly also do irreparable harm to his self-esteem and his educational motivation.

2. It may lead to a narrow conception of ability, encourage pursuit of this single goal, and thus tend to reduce the diversity of talent available to society.

3. It may place the testers in a position to control education and determine the destinies of individual human beings, while, incidentally, making the testers themselves rich in the process.

4. It may encourage impersonal, inflexible, mechanistic processes of evaluation and determination, so that essential human freedoms are limited or lost altogether.

Consider first the danger that educational testing may place an indelible stamp of inferiority on a child, ruin his self-esteem and educational motivation, and determine his social status as an adult. The kind of educational testing most likely to have these consequences would involve tests purporting to measure a person's permanent general capacity for learning. These are the intelligence tests, and the presumed measures of general capacity for learning they provide are popularly known as IQ's.

Most of us . . . are well aware of the fact that there are no direct, unequivocal means for measuring permanent general capacity for learning. We know that all intelligence tests now available are direct measures only of achievement in learning, including learning how to learn, and that inferences from scores on those tests to some native capacity for learning are fraught with many hazards and uncertainties.

But many people who are interested in education do not know this. Many of them believe that native intelligence has been clearly identified and is well understood by expert psychologists. They believe that a person's IQ is one of his basic, permanent attributes, and that any good intelligence test will measure it with a high degree of precision. They do not regard an IQ simply as another test score, a score that may vary considerably depending on the particular test used and the particular time when the person was tested.

One of the important things test specialists can do to improve the social consequences of educational testing is to discredit the popular conception of the IQ. Wilhelm Stern, the German psychologist who suggested the concept originally, saw how it was being overgeneralized and charged one of his students coming to America to "kill the IQ." Perhaps we would be well advised, even at this late date, to renew our efforts to carry out his wishes.

If human experience, or that specialized branch of human experience we call scientific research, should ever make it quite clear that differences among men in achievement are largely due to genetically determined differences in talent, then we ought to accept the finding and restructure our society and social customs in accord with it. For the present, it will be more consistent with the facts as we know them, and more constructive for the society in which we live, to think of talent, not as a natural resource like gold or uranium to be discovered, extracted and refined, but as a synthetic product like fiberglass or D.D.T. — something that, with skill, effort and luck, can be created and produced out of generally available raw materials to suit our particular needs or fancies.

This means, among other things, that we should judge the value of the tests we use not in terms of how accurately they enable us to *predict* later achievement, but rather in terms of how much help they give us to *increase* achievement by motivating and directing the efforts of students and teachers. From this point of view, those concerned with professional education who have resisted schemes for very long-range predictions of aptitude for, or success in, their professions have acted wisely. Not only is there likely to be much more of dangerous error than of useful truth in such long-range predictions, but also there is implicit in the whole enterprise a deterministic conception of achievement that is not wholly consistent with the educational facts as we know them, and with the basic assumptions of a democratic, free society.

Consider next the danger that a single widely used test or test battery for selective admission or scholarship awards may foster an undesirably narrow conception of ability and thus tend to reduce diversity in the talents available to a school or to society.

Here again, it seems, the danger is not wholly imaginary. Basic as verbal and quantitative skills are to many kinds of educational achievement, they do not encompass all aspects of achievement. Overemphasis on a common test could lead educators to neglect those students whose special talents are neither linguistic nor mathematical.

Those who manage programs for the testing of scholastic aptitude always insist, and properly so, that scores on these tests should not be the sole consideration when decisions are made on admission or the award of scholarships. But the question of whether the testing itself should not be varied from person to person remains. The use of optional tests of achievement permits some variation. Perhaps the range of available options should be made much wider than it is at present to accommodate greater diversity of talents.

The problem of encouraging the development of various kinds of ability is, of course, much broader than the problem of testing. Widespread commitment to general education, with the requirement that all students study identical courses for a substantial part of their programs, may be a much greater deterrent of specialized diversity in the educational product. Perhaps these requirements should be restudied too.

What of the concern that the growth of educational testing may increase the influence of the test makers until they are in a position to control educational curricula and determine the destinies of students?

Those who know well how tests are made and used in American education know that the tests more often lag than lead curricular change, and that while tests may affect particular episodes in a student's experience, they can hardly ever be said to determine a student's destiny. American education is, after all, a manifold, decentralized, loosely organized enterprise. Whether it restricts student freedom too much or too little is a subject for lively debate. But it does not even come close to determining any student's destiny, not nearly as close as the examination systems in some other countries, ancient and modern.

But test makers have, I fear, sometimes given the general public reason to fear that we may be up to no good. I refer to our sometime reluctance to take the layman fully into our confidence, to share fully with him all our information about his test scores, the tests from which they were derived, and our interpretations of what they mean.

Secrecy concerning educational tests and test scores has been justified on several grounds. One is that the information is simply too complex for untrained minds to grasp. However, essential information revealed by the scores on most educational tests is not particularly complex. If we understand it ourselves, we can communicate it clearly to most laymen without serious difficulty. To be quite candid, we are not all that much brighter than they are, much as we may sometimes need the reassurance of thinking so.

Another justification for secrecy is that laymen will not use test scores properly. It is true that the test scores can be misused. They have been in the past and they will be in the future. But does this justify secrecy? Can we minimize abuses due to ignorance by withholding knowledge? We do not flatter our fellow citizens when we tell them, in effect, that they are too ignorant, or too lacking in character to be trusted with the knowledge of their children, or of themselves, that we possess.

Seldom acknowledged, but very persuasive as a practical reason for secrecy regarding test scores, is that it spares those who use the scores from having to explain and justify the decisions they make. Preference is not, and should not, always be given to the person whose test score is the higher. But if score information is withheld, the disappointed applicant will assume that it was because of his low score, not because of some other factor. He will not trouble officials with demands for justification of a decision that, in some cases, might be hard to justify. But all things considered, more is likely to be gained in the long run by revealing the objective evidence used in reaching a decision.

If specialists in educational measurement want to be properly understood and trusted by the public they serve, they will do well to shun secrecy and to share with the public as much as it is interested in knowing about the methods they use, the knowledge they gain, and the interpretations they make. This is clearly the trend of opinion in examining boards and public education authorities. Let us do what we can to reinforce the trend. Whatever mental measurements are so esoteric or so dangerous socially that they must be shrouded in secrecy probably should not be made in the first place.

Finally, let us consider briefly the possibility that testing may encourage mechanical decision making, at the expense of essential human freedoms of choice and action.

Those who work with mental tests often say that the purpose of all measurement is prediction. They use regression equations to predict grade point averages, or expectancy tables to predict the chances of various degrees of success. Their procedures may seem to imply not only that human behavior is part of a deterministic system in which the number of relevant variables is manageably small, but also that the proper goals of human behavior are clearly known and universally accepted.

In these circumstances, there is some danger that we may forget our own inadequacies and attempt to play God with the lives of other human beings. We may find it convenient to overlook the gross inaccuracies that plague our measurements, and the great uncertainties that bedevil our predictions. Overestimating our own wisdom and virtue, we may project our particular value systems into a pattern of ideal goals and behavior for all men.

If we do this, if we ignore our own limitations and those of our tests, if we undertake to manage the lives of others so that they will qualify as worthy citizens in our own particular vision of utopia, we do justify the concern that one harmful social consequence of educational testing may be mechanistic decision making and the loss of essential human freedoms.

A large proportion of the decisions affecting the welfare and destiny of a person must be made in the midst of overwhelming uncertainties concerning the outcomes to be desired and the best means of achieving those outcomes. That many mistakes will be made seems inevitable. One of the cornerstones of a free society is the belief that in most cases it is better for the person most concerned to make a major decision affecting him, and to take the responsibility for its consequences.

The implications of this for educational testing are clear. Tests should be used as little as possible to *impose* decisions and courses of action on others. They should be used as much as possible to provide a sounder basis of *choice* in individual decision making. Tests can be used and ought to be used to support rather than to limit human freedom and responsibility.

Let us now have a brief look at the other side of the coin — the social consequence of *not* testing. If the use of educational tests were abandoned, the encouragement and reward of individual efforts to learn would be made more difficult. Excellence in programs of education would become less tangible as a goal and less demonstrable as an attainment. Educational opportunities would be extended less on the basis of aptitude and merit and more on the basis of ancestry and influence; social class barriers would become less permeable. Decisions on important issues of curriculum and method would be made less on the basis of solid evidence and more on the basis of prejudice or caprice. These, it seems to us, are likely to be the more harmful consequences, by far. Let us not forego the wise use of good tests.

4

Of Testing and Its Tyranny

Stanley E. Ballinger

The following selection is one of the more interesting and informative articles critical of the current role of standardized tests in our educational programs. Dr. Ballinger presents the thesis that our present system of testing will preclude the discovery of a large share of talented youngsters from our twenty million Negro Americans and another twenty million youngsters existing under culturally disadvantaged conditions. He proposes the establishment of a national commission to examine the nature and use of standardized testing instruments. It should be instructive to compare this reading with Professor Ebel's "The Social Consequences of Educational Testing" (Selection 3), and with Dyer's "Is Testing a Menace to Education?" (Selection 5).

Imagine yourself, taking a college entrance examination, encountering Item 23 as in the box at right. Just as you probably thought, the key calls for "e." to be chosen. But is it really correct, at least sufficiently correct to justify the judgment "that it best fits the meaning of the sentence as a whole"? An unsettling question may occur to you, "Does the question refer to the time of the American Revolution or to the pre-Revolutionary period?" You may also waste valuable time if you stop to ask yourself if the colonies of the time are to be taken as Spanish, British, French, or Dutch colonies. Just when you guessed that probably the person who made the test was thinking of British colonies and that "e." is the wanted answer, your eye lights on the word "entirely." Somehow the force of that word in the sentence had escaped you the first time around. The British colonies were certainly not *entirely* independent of the Crown, and that gives "e." a serious blemish. But, looking it over, it gives all the other answers a serious blemish too! Which blemished foil is the "best answer"? No, the rules will not permit one to cross off "entirely" and substitute "somewhat." Even if they did permit such substitution, could you then choose between "b.," "c.," "d.," or "e."? At this point, you may be getting a little frazzled and ask what in the world the point is, anyway?

From Stanley E. Ballinger, "Of Testing and Its Tyranny," *Phi Delta Kappan*, XLIV, (January, 1963), pp. 176–180. Reprinted with the permission of publisher and author.

23. Pick the pair of words below which best fits the meaning of the sentence as a whole, when the first word of the pair is inserted into the first blank and the second word into the second blank:

The American colonies were separate and . . . . entities, each having its own government and being entirely . . . .

a. incomplete	— revolutionary
b. independent	— interrelated
c. unified	— competitive
d. growing	— organized
e. distinct	— independent

It may or may not come as a surprise to you to learn that this item, in substantially this form, appeared in a booklet entitled A *Description of The College Board Scholastic Aptitude Test*, 1956 edition, published by the College Entrance Examination Board, with test items supplied by that most respectable giant of test-makers, Educational Testing Service, known to the trade as ETS. The "colonies item" was printed as a sample, presumably representative of a class of items in the College Entrance Examination for 1956. Everyone is entitled to an occasional slip, isn't he? But ETS does not seem to have gotten around to admitting that the item is in any way defective, even though given quite a sufficient chance to confess to error. This could be passed over, of course, but there are other questionable items and there is a man who has done a lot of worrying about multiple-choice tests. He has some very nagging questions to raise about the whole business.

The man in question is Banesh Hoffmann and the latest product of his worrying about multiple-choice tests is his book, *The Tyranny of Testing* (1). Hoffmann is a professor of mathematics at Queens College in New York City. The chances are pretty good that the reader has run into his writing on the subject of testing at one point or another, for Hoffmann has written a number of articles on the subject, two sharp attacks appearing in *The American Scholar*, Spring, 1959, and *Harper's*, March, 1961. The book is made up essentially of Hoffmann's earlier articles, considerably expanded and reworked. Because of its careful documentation and forceful argument, as well as the gravity of the charges it makes, the book deserves very careful attention by all who have a serious interest in education. For the record, Dr. Hoffmann graduated from Oxford University and was a member of the Institute for Advanced Study at Princeton, collaborating at one point with Einstein on a paper on relativity.

The central theme of *The Tyranny of Testing* is that multiple-choice tests "favor the superficially brilliant and penalize the student who has depth, subtlety, and critical acumen." Hoffmann likes to illustrate this by actual items, such as one from a National Merit Scholarship Test which he learned about from a scholarship winner and then checked out with the test publisher. This was a spelling item in which there were five choices: four separate words, each spelled correctly, and a "none wrong" as the fifth choice. The fourth word, "intensionally," a perfectly good word in this spelling in common use by logicians, was the wanted answer, thus designated as misspelled by the test-maker. Ordinary students would have no problem with the item, not having heard of "intension" and its derivative forms. The more widely read and informed student would be more likely to have encountered the term and learned its meaning and spelling. He would puzzle over the item and perhaps answer it "wrong" according to the key.

Hoffmann places great emphasis upon the student's ability to respond with individuality and creativity to situations, and this is precisely what multiple-choice items by their very nature prevent, since the student must choose among several "pre-determined intellectual snippets." His reason for choosing an answer may be of the most original sort, but on a multiple-choice item such a reason counts for no more than a response chosen for commonplace or even quite invalid reasons. Hoffmann furthermore takes the position that a student's quality is linked to his skill in the disciplined expression of ideas, organized with an eye to persuasiveness, logical coherence, or sheer delight. Multiple-choice items cannot test this skill, says Hoffmann, nor can they get substantially at "the crucial ability to conceive, design, and actually carry out a complex undertaking in an individual way." In the long run the merit they identify turns out to be meretricious, and the effect on education is "pernicious."

Professor Hoffmann has favorite whipping-boys among the various testers and kinds of tests, which is not to say that some of the boys are not in need of a good whipping. He concentrates most of his attack upon "scholastic aptitude" tests of the kind used in the College Entrance Examinations and in the screening phase of the National Merit Scholarship program. It is to be wondered why he left out of consideration the most notorious American scholastic test — the Regents' Examination of the State of New York, unless it is because the Regents' includes a generous sprinkling of essay questions.

ATTENTION FOR OTHER TYPES

In addition to those mentioned above, other types of tests come in for a lesser share of Hoffmann's attention. Reading-readiness tests are criticized for being not "readiness" tests but "unreadiness" tests. "Intelligence tests" are taken to task for creating the impression of testing "intelligence." Hoffmann suggests a term of his own invention, "iquination," as a substitute for "intelligence" in referring to what these tests measure. "There recently has been much discussion of the advisability of letting parents know their children's IQ's. One begins to wonder whether the discussion ought not instead to have been directed at the advisability of letting this information fall into the hands of school psychologists and school principals." He also devotes a few pages to personality tests, severely criticizing their use in business and the schools.

The general criticisms which Hoffmann directs at multiple-choice tests are not new. A substantial group of educators and psychologists have voiced their disturbance before, and Hoffmann seems to be quite aware of this. But, as he points out, this criticism has had little effect. It has confirmed the test-makers in their ways, and they have taken increasingly to beating off their critics with charges of ignorance of statistics and of the science of testing. The two most common lines of defense would appear to be (1) that such a competent team of test-makers (as, for instance, at ETS) surely must know more than any ill-informed critic, or (2) that the critic obviously is ignorant of the meaning of these tests' having been "empirically validated." This smoke-screen of "empirical validity" is by no means a totally invalid notion in the field of testing, but in the context of the defense of the test-makers against the charges of Hoffmann, it is basically a circular notion that avoids issues which should be confronted and also obscures the social premises upon which current scholastic aptitude testing rests. A reasonably adequate explanation of the crucial role which the notion of empirical validation plays in the situation would require a separate article.

HOFFMANN'S STRATEGY FOR REFORM

In view of the test-makers' imperviousness to basic criticism and their general unwillingness to respond in what Hoffmann would regard as a helpful manner, he has decided that what is needed in the situation is a new strategy. This strategy is relatively simple, one in which "the critic merely exhibits defective multiple-choice questions, declares that they are defective, and challenges the test-makers publicly to defend these, their own questions, specifically." It is mainly this strategic task to which *The Tyranny of Testing* devotes itself. From among the sample items (the actual tests are closely guarded, of course) published in the descriptive literature of college entrance examinations prepared by Educational Testing Service, Hoffmann found twelve which he regarded as defective from the point of view of objective scorability. These twelve items represent 5 per cent of the total number of sample items scrutinized by Hoffmann. Except for two of the items in natural science which clearly go beyond his understanding, this writer agrees with Hoffmann that these items are objectively unscorable. The "colonies item" in the box at the head of this article [see page 33] is one of the "defective twelve." The significance of the figure of 5 per cent can be understood as one considers what it would mean in such a test as the first qualifying round of the annual National Merit Scholarships. This first round summarily eliminates from further consideration some 98 per cent of the aspirants, making it a matter of crucial importance, in order to stay in the running, to guess what is in the test-maker's mind for perhaps as many as five defective items out of every hundred on the test.

It is Hoffmann's intention to use the publication of defective items to smoke out the test-makers into public discussion. By the time of the publication of Hoffmann's article in *Harper's* in March, 1961, five of the twelve sample items had been publicly branded as defective. ETS then accepted the challenge to the extent of publishing a booklet, dated April, 1961, called

Explanation of Multiple-Choice Testing. It has the interesting sub-title, "With particular reference to items which have been criticized in articles by Dr. Banesh Hoffmann." Substantial portions of this booklet are quoted in various places in *The Tyranny of Testing.* On the basis of these quoted sections of the booklet and correspondence from Henry Chauncey (president of ETS), and another "high official" of ETS — all published in Hoffmann's book — the defense of the test items must be judged extremely weak and evasive, certainly a long way from the full candor and scholarly responsibility called for in a matter so much in the public interest. It should be remembered here that Hoffmann agrees that his "nitpicking" approach in spotting weak items is very superficial, and that the challenge on particular items is the first step in a long-run strategy to get more basic problems confronted.

Having made what he calls a *prima facie* case against standardized multiple-choice tests, Hoffmann proposes strategy step number two: the forming of a committee to investigate the whole matter. Such a committee should include outstanding "creative individuals of commanding intellectual stature." Only a minority should be professional test-makers and representatives of test-making organizations. The committee should view its task comprehensively, " . . . with particular reference to the effects of tests upon education, business, and the strength and vitality of the nation — for these are the transcendent issues."

This reviewer agrees that there are some very sorry aspects to educational testing today. There is little consolation in observing that the situation is not a new one. Seventy years ago Joseph M. Rice, editor of *The Forum,* went on his crusade for quantitative, "objective" research in education, to be followed shortly by such giants of the educational measurement movement as Edward Lee ("Everything exists in some amount") Thorndike. The dangers of equating quantitative treatment with objectivity were pointed out by a variety of critics of the educational measurement movement in the early twentieth century, but it would appear that this is a hard lesson for the education profession to learn.

The Tyranny of Testing, determined as it is to make a *prima facie* case against the test-makers, has some understandable blind spots and some weaknesses of emphasis. Hoffmann does not always distinguish between the tests and the misuse of tests, or between the reputable professionals in psychological testing in the academic world and those who are apologists for the test-selling corporations. Objectively scorable tests of the multiple-choice variety have much more to offer, in actuality now and potentially, than Hoffmann appears willing to concede. At many places in the book, in spite of covering statements elsewhere, he gives the impression that multiple-choice items, in not testing creativity, can test only for routine information. This overlooks many components of critical thinking in given disciplinary contexts which can be fairly well tested through multiple-choice items when they are directed at carefully prepared textual material included in the test. It is not particularly to his credit that Hoffmann attacks a particular item — the only item considered at all — in the Watson-Glaser Critical Thinking Appraisal, without even a kind word for a test which has tried to get at something more than routine recall of information. Furthermore, the item which is criticized (somewhat justly) calls for the identification of assumptions, an aim which Professor Hoffmann ought to find laudable. The item is of a type which is sound in principle, not necessarily doomed to have the kind of defect noted in the book.

A MORE PROMISING SCHOLASTIC TEST

One wonders why Hoffmann did not mention one of the more promising scholastic tests, one prepared by ETS itself: the Sequential Test of Educational Development. This is a series of tests covering stages of educational development from the lower grades through the first two years of college. The segment that Professor Hoffmann would be interested in covers the first two years of college. It includes a substantial "essay" item and a "listening test," which would appear to call for the ability to listen with care and thought to material of substantial intellectual content.

It would also appear that Hoffmann places too large a share of the blame upon the test-makers. Their defense that they employ the services of a great many subject-matter specialists is not to be dismissed as altogether meaningless. There is merit in the view that if the standardized tests too often test primarily for routine information-recall, this is basically because a great deal of teaching and testing in college courses is information-oriented. It would be instructive to know how many college teachers still make heavy use of true-false tests or even crude short answer "essay" tests, both of which are apt to be far worse than reasonably good multiple-choice tests. If critical thinking, creativity, and profundity were at the heart of most college and high-school teaching today, how much place would there be for tests composed of simple recognition-type multiple-choice items? This line of reasoning does not free the test-makers from responsibility but it does indicate that the responsibility should be spread a little more widely.

It does not seem that Banesh Hoffmann did the kind of homework he should have done with respect to the notion of "creativity," as it has been variously conceived and tested in psychological circles. There is a considerable history of failure, confusion, and, certainly, lack of consensus in the psychological study of creativity. Hoffmann's book gives no indication of any real awareness of this history. He appears to be satisfied with a vague notion which shifts from place to place in its wording: creativity, profundity, subtlety. There is even a literature on "creativity" in Hoffmann's own field of mathematics, but if he has found any way to test creativity in his own teaching, this writer can not recall any reference to it in his book. Hoffmann perhaps does not fully appreciate the difficulty of predicting what seems inevitably to have an element of the unpredictable, or of testing the undefined, if not the undefinable. On the other hand, some support for Hoffmann's position may be found in the following excerpt from a review of an American test, written by the British educator, Stephen Wiseman, for the *Fifth Mental Measurement Yearbook:*

The tendency in England to move away from "recognition" items to "creative" items finds no echo across the Atlantic. Is this mainly because of the prestige, as well as the convenience, of machine scoring? Some of us over here have discovered that the open-ended question, to be answered by a word, a phrase, or a sentence, can be almost as reliable and sometimes more valid and discriminating.

SOCIAL DIMENSIONS OF TESTING

The Tyranny of Testing gives scant attention to some of the important social dimensions of standardized testing. This is not necessarily a defect of the book as such, but these social dimensions are often neglected, and a brief indication of what is involved is important to the discussion here.

The search for "talent" or "merit" is an endeavor in which certain conceptions of the national interest, of social benefit, or of individual satisfaction and fulfillment are heavily implicated. According to one's interpretation of these, singly or in combination, the choice of means will undoubtedly differ. Tests are increasingly important in this world as a means of identifying talent. As in every other case of means-end relationships, the tests should be evaluated as to their adequacy *as means* for achieving desirable *end-conditions*, which include the absence of undesirable, as well as the presence of desirable, consequences. One important consequence of the wide use of standardized tests is the tendency for aspects of the prevailing social structure to be thereby preserved and strengthened. Standardized tests seem by their very nature to be a conservative force. Since even "ability" tests sample some area of achievement already made, how does one identify individuals whose achievement in a given area is all *potentiality* with as yet no *actuality*? How do you find a basis for determining the presence of talent which has not yet found the circumstances under which it can form even the buds for later flowering? Minority groups such as American Negroes, almost twenty million strong, surely must contain many individuals with "talent" for scholastic achievement, yet not a single Negro showed up among the 5,000 or so winners or runners-up of the National Merit Scholarship competition in 1956 (the only year for which such data is at hand for this writer). Of course there was no direct bias operating to keep high-scoring Negroes from receiving scholarships. It was another case of "to those who have shall be given." In this connection, note the words of Horace Mann Bond, Dean of the School of Education, Atlanta University, in a passage from the Inglis Lecture for 1957 at Harvard University:

> We do not know whether the "talented" are also the "gifted," but we use the phrase interchangeably; and we do not know, or seek to discover, whether their "gifts" came from God, from their genes, or from the social order from which these individuals are derived. . . . Search as we may, the present instruments we have will not discover talent masked by verbal insufficiencies grown from social and economic class and regional deprivation. The pressing task is to strip off that mask for the millions of laborers, farm dwellers, and submerged racial castes in this country.

If Americans want the talent that lies buried in the twenty million Negro Americans and in perhaps twenty million other Americans living under "culturally deprived" conditions, not much of it is going to be "discovered" by any pencil and paper test. Before talent can be discovered, it has to be able to develop at least in a small way; it has to be given the social conditions for development so that it can be sampled, on the spot or under contrived test conditions. We seem to be in a situation where, unless we are able and willing to reconstruct some segment of our social arrangements and change some ingrained aspects of our culture, we are forced to seek at least the upper grades of talent mainly among the children of those who have already demonstrated talent, which is to say, in general, among the favored social classes. For what it may be worth, let us remind ourselves that the educational measurement movement began as an essentially conservative social force. It may not have changed very much to date in this respect, but there is no cosmic necessity for it continuing along past lines.

HOFFMANN'S QUESTIONING APPROPRIATE TODAY

The serious questioning of current testing practices which *The Tyranny of Testing* represents is certainly appropriate at this point in our national history. As students pour into our colleges in ever larger numbers during the next decade, one can reasonably predict increased reliance upon standardized tests for screening scholarship applicants, for college-admissions purposes, and for what seems to be a growing trend, advanced college placement. It is likely that the federal government will vastly increase its scholarship and loan programs in its search for talent to help win the cold war on earth and the race for outer space. If ever we needed to take a good look at our tests and policies controlling their use, it would appear to be now. Banesh Hoffmann's book is likely to play a very useful role in this public scrutiny, not only because of the cogency of its argument, but also because, in the field of tests and "mental measurement," where graduate students often are hard put to get the necessary technical sophistication, Professor Hoffmann has managed to write interestingly and informatively.

This reviewer would like to add his second to the proposal that a commission of inquiry into current testing practices be established, along the lines suggested in the book. Foundations looking for a large-scale project to underwrite would do well to give this possibility serious consideration. Even a thorough-going effort with a dozen full-time staff members giving four or five years to such an endeavor would be incredibly cheap in view of the probable benefits. And, likely enough, the work of such a committee of inquiry could be well financed for something less than the cost of an ICBM.

REFERENCE

1. Hoffmann, Banesh. *The Tyranny of Testing.* New York: The Crowell-Collier Publishing Co., 1962. Pp. 233.

5

Is Testing a
Menace to Education?

Henry S. Dyer

It is quite apparent that some opponents of today's widespread testing programs believe that the individual is likely to be lost in a welter of group norms. Further, test results may be used to label youngsters and ultimately create unnecessary anxiety among boys and girls and their parents. Dr. Dyer presents nine misconceptions about tests and points out that the real culprit is ignorance on the part of test users and interpreters. This statement of the problem should be read and reread at least three times annually by guidance counselors, teachers, and all other professional personnel using standardized measurements.

The title of this talk is a question: "Is Testing a Menace to Education?" Knowing who I am and what I do for a living, you would have every reason to believe that I am going to answer the question with a resounding, "No!" But you would be dead wrong, for I am going to answer the question with a tentative, "Yes, but — " Yes, testing *is* a menace to education, *but* probably not for the reasons you think. It is a menace to education primarily because tests are misunderstood and test results are misused by too many educators. In his recent book called *The Schools*, Martin Mayer speaks of testing as a "necessary evil." I disagree. It is not *necessarily* evil. Tests *could* be a blessing to education if only teachers and counselors and educational administrators would divest themselves of a number of misconceptions about what tests can and cannot do and would learn to use test results more cautiously and creatively in the educational process.

There are nine principal misconceptions that seem to stand in the way of the appropriate use of tests.

The *first* misconception is the notion that aptitude or intelligence tests measure something called "native ability," something fixed and immutable within the person that determines his level of expectation for all time. I am

From Henry S. Dyer, "Is Testing a Menace to Education?" *New York State Education*, XLIX (October, 1961), pp. 16–19. Reprinted with the permission of the New York State Teachers Association and the author.

not prepared to say such an inherent entity does not exist. The chances are it does. Studies in genetics certainly support the idea, and so do many psychological studies. But intelligence or aptitude tests do not *measure* such an entity — at least not directly; and certainly not in any interpretable manner.

What intelligence tests do measure is the individual's performance on certain types of mental tasks . . . a long time after the child has first entered the world. The kinds of mental tasks that appear in any intelligence or aptitude test are clearly the kinds that a student *learns* to perform from his experiences in the world around him. The amount of learning based on such experiences may depend on many things that can vary enormously from one child to another — the number and quality of books available in his home, the kind of talk he hears, the richness and variety of his surroundings, the vividness and emotional quality of the thousands of happenings in his life from day to day. It is absurd to suppose that a child's score on an intelligence test bypasses all these factors, to suppose that such a score gets directly at the brains he was born with.

I prefer to think of an intelligence test as essentially indistinguishable from an achievement test — that is, as a measure of how well, at a given point of time, a student can perform certain well-defined tasks. The main difference between the tasks in a so-called achievement test and those in a so-called intelligence test is, generally speaking, that the tasks in an achievement test are usually learned over a relatively short time and those in an intelligence test are learned over a relatively long time.

The consequences of thinking of an aptitude test as measuring some immutable determiner of student performance can be pretty serious. First, such thinking encourages the dangerous idea that one can, from an aptitude score, decide once and for all at a fairly early age what kind and level of educational or vocational activity a student is fitted for. It nurtures that hardy perennial, for instance, that if a student has an IQ of 115 or better he ought to prepare for college, and if his IQ is below 115 he ought to make other plans — this, despite all the studies which have shown that an IQ may be highly variable for a given student, that colleges vary enormously in the quality of students they enroll, and that some low scorers succeed in college while some high scorers fail. I have often wondered how many educational crimes are annually committed on the strength of the theory that intelligence tests measure something they cannot possibly measure.

A second consequence, almost as serious, is the conception that a student with a high aptitude score and low achievement scores (or low grades in school) is an "under-achiever" — another hardy perennial. It was exploded 30 years ago, but it is back and can lead to some rather distressing treatment of individual pupils. The diagnosis goes that a student with a high aptitude score and low achievement scores is "unmotivated" or "lazy" or suffering from some sort of emotional disturbance. Granted there may be some grounds for such diagnoses, nevertheless they are scarcely inferable from the discrepancy in scores alone. And some new and possibly more useful insights about such students might be forthcoming if one frankly regarded the discrepancies simply as differences in performance on one kind of achievement test as compared to another.

Finally, the idea that aptitude tests are supposed to measure native ability leads to the persistent and embarrassing demand that they should be "culture free"; that if they are, as they must be, affected by the student's background of experience in school and at home, then *ipso facto*, they are "unfair" to the underprivileged. I wish we could get it *out* of people's heads that tests are unfair to the underprivileged and get it *into* their heads that it is the hard facts of social circumstance and inadequate education that are unfair to them. If educational opportunities are unequal, the test results will also be unequal.

A *second* misconception about tests is the notion that a prediction made from a test score, or from a series of test scores, or from test scores plus other quantifiable data, are, or should be, perfectly accurate, and that if they are not, the tests must be regarded as no good. This fallacy arises from a confused conception of what constitutes prediction. There are some people — maybe most people — who think of prediction as simply an all-or-none, right-or-wrong business. If a test score predicts that Johnny will get B in American History, the score is right if he actually gets a B; it is wrong if he gets a B— or a C. I suppose this is a legitimate way of thinking about prediction in certain circumstances, but it is scarcely fair to the test and it may well be unfair to Johnny. A more meaningful and useful way of thinking about a prediction is to regard it as a statement of the odds: A given test score might predict that Johnny has 8 chances in 10 of getting a grade of B or better in American History, and 3 chances in a hundred of flunking. This approach recognizes that in forecasting future events, especially human events, we never have sufficient information to be sure of being right every time, but we do have information, in the form of test scores and other data, which, if appropriately organized, can help us make better decisions than would be possible without them.

The *third* misconception is that standardized test scores are infallible or perfectly reliable. Reliability, I remind you, has to do with the degree to which the score of an individual stands still on successive testings. It rarely occurs to the uninitiated that a test can never be more than a *sample* of a student's performance and that, in consequence, the score on any test is afflicted with sampling error. To the man-in-the-street, to many teachers, school administrators and parents, who have never reflected on the problem, a score is a score is a score, and they are shocked to find that when a student takes one test today and an alternate form of the same test tomorrow, his score can change. Anyone who deals with a test score must always be conscious that such a score, like any sort of measurement whatever, is clouded with uncertainty, that it is never more than an estimate of the truth.

A *fourth* misconception is the assumption that an achievement test measures all there is to measure in any given subject matter area — that an achievement test in history, for example, measures everything a high school student should know about the facts of history and how to deal with them. It never seems to occur to some people that the content of a standardized achievement test in any particular subject matter area may be only partially related to what a specific course of study in that area may call for.

If people will only take the trouble to look critically at the insides of achievement tests and not just at their covers, they will almost certainly find that even the test best suited to their purposes still fails to sample *all* the types of learning that are sought in a given subject, or even all the most important types of learning. And it may also often include matters that the student is not expected to know. The consequence is, of course, that on a particular standardized achievement test a student may look considerably better or considerably worse than he really is, and decisions based on his score may miss the boat by a considerable margin.

A *fifth* misconception is that an achievement test can measure only a pupil's memory for facts. This used to be true. But a good modern achievement test gets at far more than a command of facts alone; it usually measures in addition the pupil's skill in reasoning with the facts he remembers and also his skill in reasoning with facts newly presented to him. It is this introduction into achievement tests of the requirement to reason, to cope with problems, to think clearly, critically and even creatively that helps to blur the distinction between aptitude and achievement tests. The modern achievement test recognizes that as students come up through the grades they are, or ought to be, learning to think as well as to know. It recognizes also that there may be many different kinds of thinking to measure, depending upon the subject matter in which the thinking is required. The result is that a well-conceived battery of achievement tests gives the same sort of information one would get from a general intelligence test plus a good deal more.

A *sixth* misconception has to do with profiles of achievement or aptitude scores; that a profile of scores summarizes clearly and efficiently a considerable amount of reliable information about the relative strengths and weaknesses of an individual. Test technicians have inveighed repeatedly against the use of profile charts on the grounds that they are often grossly misleading, that the differences they depict — even when they appear large — may be, and usually are, unreliable differences, that the score scales used for the several tests in the profile may not be comparable, that the several measures which show on the profile may have the appearance of being highly independent measures when, in fact, many of them may be highly correlated — in short, that the apparent clarity and efficiency of a test score profile is really an illusion covering up all sorts of traps and pitfalls in score interpretation which even the most wary can scarcely avoid. Yet the profile chart is still in much demand and in wide use, primarily, I suppose, because it is extraordinarily convenient. Mere administrative convenience is hardly sufficient justification for hiding confusion under a false coat of simplicity. Good test interpretation takes mental effort, a bit of imagination and some willingness to cope with complexity.

A *seventh* misconception is that interest inventories measure some kind of basic orientation of a student irrespective of the kinds of experiences to which he has been or will be exposed. Let me cite just one example. A presumably well-trained guidance counselor in a high school where the large majority of students go on to college was confronted by a girl with top-notch scholastic standing in all of the college preparatory subjects. Her parents were college-trained people, had always expected their daughter would go to a liberal arts college; the daughter had always enthusiastically entertained the same idea. The counselor, however, was apparently bewitched by one of the girl's scores on an interest inventory which indicated her major interest was in clerical work. Disregarding all the other evidence, the counselor insisted that the girl was unfitted for the work of a liberal arts college and would be happy only in a secretarial school. Tears on the part of the child, anger on the part of the parents and hell-to-pay all around. Certainly interest test scores are useful in promoting thought and self-analysis, but certainly also the tests are scarcely capable of probing deeply enough into an individual's past and future to warrant anything approaching the dogmatism which characterized this counselor.

The *eighth* misconception is that on a personality test an individual reveals deep and permanent temperamental characteristics of which he himself may be unaware. I suppose there is nothing about the whole testing business that frightens me more than this. Anyone close to the research in personality testing who has any critical sense at all knows that we have still barely scratched the surface of a field whose dimensions are still far from defined. To put it perhaps a little too strongly, personality tests — the inventories, the projective tests, all of them — are scarcely beyond the tea-leaf-reading stage. To be sure, there is some interesting — even exciting — research going on in the area, but none of it yet adds up to tests that can be trusted as evidence leading to important decisions about children.

There are four major weaknesses in personality tests. First, they purport to measure traits such as introversion-extroversion, neurotic tendency, gregariousness, tolerance for ambiguity, and the like — all of which are highly fuzzy concepts, to say the least, and for none of which there are any agreed-upon definitions. There is not even any general agreement on what we mean by the word "personality" itself. How can you describe or classify a person meaningfully with a test whose scores do not themselves have any clear or rigorous meaning?

Secondly, it is characteristic of current personality tests that the behavior they sample is essentially superficial nonsignificant behavior. By this I mean when a subject answers such a question as "Do you often daydream?" his response of "Yes" or "No" may well be nothing more than a purely random phenomenon quite unconnected with any of his habitual behavior tendencies. The whole essence of the measurement problem is to secure reliable samples of human behavior under standardized conditions which will have strong correlates with the universe of behavior an individual habitually exhibits in his waking life. The personality tests currently available have yet to demonstrate that they can provide such samples.

Thirdly, even if we were able to establish some meaningful personality traits, we still know little or nothing about their stability. We still don't know whether an introvert at age 15 may not turn into an extrovert by the time he is 22.

Finally, of course, practically all personality tests can be faked. I proved to my own satisfaction how fakable such tests are when I gave one to a class I was once teaching. I asked the students to take a personality inventory twice — once to prove that they were thoroughly well adjusted people and once to prove that they were ready for a mental institution. The first set of scores showed that the whole class was a bunch of apple-cheeked extroverts; the second set showed that they were all nuts.

Please do not misunderstand me. I take a very dim view of current personality tests, and I think the general public is being much too frequently taken in by the mumbo-jumbo that goes with them. On the other hand, I am very much in favor of as much solid research as we can possibly get into the fundamental dynamics of human behavior, for we shall never be in full command of the educational process until we have far more understanding than we now have of what makes children tick. There are glimmerings of hope, but we are not out of the woods yet, and who can tell when we will be? In the meantime, let's not kid ourselves by putting our trust in gimmicks.

The *ninth* and final misconception is this: that a battery of tests can tell all one needs to know in making a judgment about a student's competence, present and potential, and about his effectiveness as a human being. The fact is that no test or series of tests now available is capable of giving the total picture of any child. Tests can illuminate many areas of his development, suggest something about his strengths and weaknesses, show in certain respects how he stands among his peers. But there are still many important aspects of learning and human development where we must still rely upon the observation and judgment of teachers if we are to get something that approaches a complete description of the child as a functioning individual. There are subtle but supremely important human elements in the teaching-learning situation that no combination of tests yet devised is able to capture. Such elements are elusive, but if ever we lose sight of them, the educational process in all its ramifications will become something less than the exciting human enterprise it should always be.

These are the nine misconceptions which I think most frequently lead to wide misuse of tests and test results. Some of our brasher critics have argued that, since tests are so widely misused, they do constitute a menace to sound education and therefore should be abolished. This argument is specious. It is the same as saying that automobiles should be abolished because they are a menace to human life when reckless drivers are at the wheel. Or it is the same as saying that teachers should be abolished because too many of them make psychometric hash out of marks and test scores.

In any case, I think it is highly unlikely that tests will be abolished any more than that textbooks will be abolished. Too many schools have discovered that, menace or not, they cannot operate effectively without them. The problem is not one of doing away with tests and testing but of getting people to use tests intelligently. When this happens testing will cease to be a mere administrative convenience or, worse still, a burden on the souls of teachers and pupils; it will become an effective instrument for vitalizing the total educational process and for helping to insure that in these days of sky-rocketing enrollments the individual pupil will not be lost in the shuffle.

SUGGESTED READINGS

American Educational Research Association. "Educational and Psychological Testing," *Review of Educational Research*. Washington, D.C.: The Association, Vol. XXXV, No. 1 (February, 1965).

Research literature on testing is ordinarily summarized in three-year cycles in this review which has been published since 1931. This particular issue contains a very worthwhile treatment of trends in testing.

Dressel, Paul L., and others. *Evaluation in Higher Education*. Boston: Houghton Mifflin Company, 1961.

The comprehensive discussions of evaluation are especially pertinent to the burgeoning problems of higher education. Chapters 1 and 2 provide excellent background material for the student on the nature of evaluation and the objectives of instruction. Chapters 4 through 7 discuss quite specifically evaluation in the fields of social science, the natural sciences, the humanities, and communication skills.

Findley, Warren G. (ed.). *The Impact and Improvement of School Testing Programs*, Part II, Sixty-Second Yearbook of the National Society for the Study of Education. Chicago: The Society (distributed by The University of Chicago Press), 1963.

This yearbook is a valuable resource on issues and problems in testing. The twelve chapters, written by well-known measurement and guidance experts, present the materials in the form of a series of recommendations with supporting arguments based upon a vigorous evaluation of research and practice.

Hoffmann, Banesh. *The Tyranny of Testing*. New York: The Crowell-Collier Press, 1962.

As the title implies, this book presents a strong indictment of objective tests. The author-mathematician warns that these "new-type" tests are blocking our search for superior talent in the schools, community, and nation. The profound student of measurement will enjoy refuting many of the arguments set forth by Professor Hoffmann.

Noll, Victor H. *Introduction to Educational Measurement* (2nd ed.). Boston: Houghton Mifflin Company, 1965.

Chapter 2 gives a brief but interesting treatment of the development of educational measurement. Some good footnotes will lead the reader to source material, and the annotated bibliography at the conclusion of the chapter provides ten references for further reading in this area.

Stanley, Julian C. *Measurement in Today's Schools* (4th ed.). Englewood Cliffs, New Jersey: Prentice-Hall, Inc., 1964.

Chapter Two, "Historical Development of Measurement," is a very readable and carefully documented account. Readers will find several figures and tables which dramatize important developments in the annals of testing.

Wesman, Alexander G. (Chairman). *Proceedings of the 1963 Invitational Conference on Testing Problems*. Princeton, New Jersey: Educational Testing Service, 1964.

This report is illustrative of several valuable contributions to measurement literature emanating from these annual conferences. The papers of Findley, Messick, and Ebel provide some significant thinking on the implications and consequences of measurement.

Test Theory

There are basic principles in test development that apply to all devices used as psychological measurements. Tests are successful indicators of given characteristics to the extent that these basic principles have been recognized in their construction. This unit points up certain salient aspects of test theory in an attempt to promote among test builders and users wider recognition of the relevance of theoretical issues to determining the adequacy of tests.

The unit is divided into three parts by its emphasis on certain issues. The first group of selections deals with the topic of validity, the second with reliability and the third with scores and their interpretation. Each of these points is a limiting condition on the adequacy of any test, and therefore deserves careful consideration by those persons who are diligent in test construction, as well as those who would be intelligent consumers of test data.

In the practical setting — whether it be a school, clinic or industrial plant — test users wish to employ the tools which do the best job possible to assess those human traits important for functioning in that setting. When the test user begins to inventory all the tools publishers claim are relevant to his interest, he must wonder if so many tests can all be excellent measures of the characteristic he has in mind. Therefore, the user must be equipped to question intelligently the adequacy of the tools presented to him.

An initial point of consideration in such an evaluation must deal with reliability. To what extent would several applications of a measuring device report scores that are consistent one with the other? This is the question involved in reliability procedures. However, there are several approaches to answering this question, and which of them is the most appropriate depends on the purpose of the test. In Selections 12 and 13, Wesman and Bloom attempt to elaborate this point, emphasizing conditions which influence reliability and its interpretation.

Validity is the primary quality of a test. A test can be useful only to the extent that we know what characteristic is being measured by it, and to what extent the test is reflecting that characteristic. Several methods of arriving at validity have emerged. Each has its particular ground rules for effective use. Anastasi presents an overview of the topic in Selection 7, while Cronbach, Ebel, and Mosier (Selections 8–11) deal with special topics in relation to test validity. The reader will no doubt note that validity is not a unitary quality, but a many-faceted characteristic; that a test which is valid under one condition may not be so under other conditions. Test validity, then, can only be stated in terms of some objective of measurement. Tests are not merely valid or invalid, but are so in reference to a given measurement problem. The authors presented in the articles ahead not only point out procedures to be followed in determining validity, but equally important, they also illustrate various types of measurement problems in reference to the validation procedures which are appropriate.

Test theory extends beyond reliability and validity. Another important topic deals with the handling of scores. No matter how adequate the content of a test may be, if the scores cannot be dealt with in a meaningful manner, the test's utility will likely be naught. Davis, Gardner, and Angoff, in Selections 14–16, present interesting points in regard to handling scores in a meaningful way.

Since tests are devices for comparing a person to other people in reference to a given trait, a necessary part of test interpretation is the distribution of scores for a defined group of people who may form a basis for the comparison. However, time changes the traits of people, and accordingly may erode the adequacy of the defined group as a reference base. Angoff and Gardner present two sides of a dilemma that rests in this procedure. The resolution of the divergent views is left to the reader.

Regardless of the publicity a test may receive, its ultimate value is tied to the success with which the test maker has dealt with the basic problems of theory. This unit points to these significant issues both in an effort to raise some questions and to provide some solutions.

6

Selecting an Achievement Test:
Principles and Procedures

Martin Katz

Certain concepts are basic to the proper application of any test or other measuring device. The student's first job is to become well acquainted with these basic ideas before attempting to utilize tests themselves. The following selection presents a brief description of the most fundamental concepts in measurement, and should be used as an introduction to these topics. Since later selections will explore some of these concepts in considerable detail, a careful reading of the topics by Katz is strongly advised.

The Question

School people who are responsible for selecting standardized achievement tests often ask: What is the best test to use for such-and-such a subject or grade? or, What is the best achievement testing program for a school system or college? Good answers to these questions are essential to the effectiveness of a testing program. Many problems in test use and test interpretation have their origin in test selection.

However, good answers cannot be drawn from stock. Schools differ so that no one test or one program is equally suitable for all. Certainly, the measurement expert who does not know the individual school should not, in good conscience, try to "fit it in the dark." Fortunately, a large quantity and great variety of standardized achievement tests are available, permitting each school to tailor a program to its own needs and characteristics. But how can educators who are not measurement experts be helped to choose from the vast array of materials?

Major Considerations. Shifting the emphasis from "what" to "how" offers a solution. While no tests can be prescribed as "best" for all schools,

From Martin Katz, *Selecting an Achievement Test: Principles and Procedures.* Evaluation and Advisory Service Series, No.3 (Princeton, N.J.: Educational Testing Service, 1958 [1st ed.], 1961 [2nd ed.]), pp. 3–10. Reprinted with the permission of publisher and author.

there are fundamental principles and procedures for test selection that can be recommended to all. The particular program of tests chosen may be different for each school, applicable to no other; but the process of choosing wisely seems to contain universal elements, applicable by many schools.

These elements include careful inquiry into the following topics: I, the nature of the pupil population; II, the content and objectives of the curriculum; III, the purposes in testing; IV, the ways in which test scores may be used to accomplish those purposes; V, the readiness, willingness, and ability of the school staff to administer tests and interpret scores; VI, the amount of time and money available for testing.

Questions and answers about school staff and time and money (items V and VI) will not be elaborated here. Such circumstances can be quite readily described, and their bearing on test selection quickly understood. It is the other four points — pupil population, curricular objectives and content, testing purposes, and prospective uses of scores — that usually need more specific explanation. Merely to admonish that they "should be taken into account" does not seem sufficiently helpful. Therefore, this pamphlet will try to explain *how* they "should be taken into account." It will discuss in some depth and detail how to analyze these four major considerations as they relate to sound measurement principles in the selection of standardized achievement tests.

Naïve Assumptions. For to many school people "testing achievement" seems in itself like an adequate statement of purpose and use, and the designation of grade level and subject area seems like an adequate description of population and content. They assume that if a test measures achievement it measures achievement, and any application or use can be made of the results with equal relevance. And of course by this naïve reasoning the test which "best" measures achievement is the best one to choose.

Those who have had some exposure to measurement lingo may specify this "best" achievement test they are seeking as the one with the "best" validity, the "best" reliability, the "best" norms. However, their search on these grounds is likely to be confusing and futile because the question — What is *the best* achievement test? — is probably the wrong question. It is more profitable to ask, What test can be most effectively used in a certain way for a designated purpose in a specific school setting? This kind of inquiry shapes more distinctly the questions that should be directed to validity, reliability, and norms. Since these statistical properties of tests must figure in our later discussion of pupil population, curriculum content and objectives, purposes in testing, and uses of test scores, let us review briefly here a few fundamental definitions and concepts that can serve as guide lines and warnings.

DEFINITIONS AND CONCEPTS:
STATISTICAL PROPERTIES OF ACHIEVEMENT TESTS

Validity is often defined as the extent to which a test measures what it is supposed to measure or does the job it is given to do; *reliability* as the extent to which a test is consistent in measuring what it measures; *norms* as the statistics describing the test performance of a specific group which can be used for comparison.

These test characteristics are frequently reported in quantitative terms. For example, a per cent agreement or correlation coefficient (indicating degree of relationship) may figure prominently in validity studies; a correlation coefficient almost always appears as an index of reliability; and a description of norms generally stresses the number of people tested to establish a comparison group.

Common Misconceptions. Sometimes prospective test users, upon being advised to "take into account" the validity, reliability, and norms of tests, are tempted to make a direct comparison of these indices and numbers from one test to another. Some will assume, for example, that if in a certain study or series of studies, Test A had a higher correlation with teachers' marks than Test B, Test A is generally more valid than Test B; that a test which is reported to have a "reliability coefficient" of .93 is more reliable than a test which is reported to have a "reliability coefficient" of .88; that norms based on test performance of 100,000 pupils are "better" — more likely to be a "national sample" — than norms based on test performance of 25,000 pupils. Then, if the test they have selected by these erroneous assumptions as the "best" fails to work out effectively for them, they are likely to view with suspicion the publisher's claims about validity, reliability, and norms. They wonder whether he has been guilty of misrepresentation or statistical skulduggery.

A Standard for Disclosure. Test publishers who try to follow the *Technical Recommendations for Achievement Tests* (1) in their manuals and other publications do much to dispel such suspicions. The *Technical Recommendations*, speaking for the educational research and measurement professions, furnishes standards of approved practice for the guidance of both users and producers of tests. These standards specify what essential information on validity, reliability, and norms (as well as interpretation, administration, and scales) should usually accompany a test to enable users to evaluate it.

Validity

The *Recommendations* will alert the test user to the type of validity and to the kinds of substantiating data he should look for. Four types of validity are defined.

1. Content Validity. "*Content validity* is concerned with the sampling of a specified universe of content."

Sometimes, content validity is completely self-evident. For example, suppose we want to measure pupils' recall of the alphabet, or the names of the 50 states, or Latin verbs that take the dative, or the "multiplication table," or the correct spelling of a certain list of words. We can present the complete task itself to the pupils. In such cases, the entire test is identical with — not merely representative of — the knowledge or skill to be measured.

More often, the knowledge or skill that we are interested in measuring cannot be presented *in toto*. We want to know more about the pupils' reading, social studies, Latin, arithmetic, or spelling achievement than is usually encompassed in such limited tasks. If, for a spelling test, we were to use all the words in an unabridged dictionary (which, for illustrative purposes, we can take to comprehend the entire universe of English words), we should have an uncomfortably long list. Furthermore, this long list is probably not the universe that we are interested in. For example, if we want to test the spelling of 8th-graders, we are not likely to be concerned with words like "syzygy" or "xyster," rarely encountered or used by 8th-graders. Nor are we likely to be concerned with words like "cat" or "boy," which we may prefer to assume all of our 8th-graders can spell. Perhaps we should rather focus on a universe (or solar system) consisting of all words misspelled in the written compositions of a certain large number of 8th-graders, or the words used by them with a certain degree of frequency, or words contained in a certain array of reading materials, or some combination of these. Such a procedure still gives us a long list. But at least it is a list which we can define in specific terms. Then, we can take a *sample* of that list, selected so as to truly represent it. In other words, pupils should spell correctly the same proportion of words from the sample as they would from the complete list. If so, the sample list, or test, has high *content* validity.

2. *Concurrent Validity*. But we cannot expect use of the sample list to tell us any *more* about a pupil's spelling ability than use of the original list would have told us. Therefore we shall probably have questions concerning its *concurrent validity*, which "is concerned with the relation of test scores to an accepted contemporary criterion of performance on the variable which the test is intended to measure." For example, how similar is the 8th-graders' performance on the test-task (say, writing words from dictation, or judging whether a printed word is correctly or incorrectly spelled, etc.) to the kind of spelling skill they show in their own writing? Of course, in writing a composition, some pupils will look up spellings they are not sure of; others will take a guess; others will limit their written vocabulary to words they feel sure they can spell. Or pupils may even have different spelling habits in different types of composition. Nevertheless we shall probably expect to find some relationship between spelling test scores and pupils' spelling in their own compositions. Data demonstrating such relationships will be evidence of concurrent validity.

3. *Predictive Validity*. Research studies showing a relationship between performance on the spelling test and performance in some future activity will be evidence of its *predictive validity* — which "is concerned with the relation of test scores to measures on a criterion based on performance at some later time." Thus, as an example of predictive validity, there may be evidence that scores on this spelling test can help us to differentiate between pupils who will succeed and pupils who will fail in a stenography course. Time — relating test performance to a present or to a future criterion — is the chief difference between concurrent and predictive validity.

4. Construct Validity. When direct criteria are not available for evidence of concurrent or predictive validity, and the universe of content can not be adequately specified, it is necessary to rely more heavily on *construct validity* — logical inferences which can be drawn from indirect evidence that the test measures what it is claimed to measure. We may ask, what hypotheses about the nature of spelling ability does this test reflect? Do test performances of pupils tend to confirm these hypotheses? In what ways do high scorers differ from low scorers? How, for example, are scores related to methods of instruction in reading? What is the factorial composition of this test? Thus, evidence of construct validity is likely to be both more varied and more theoretical than evidence of the other types of validity.

Evidence of each type of validity answers a somewhat different question about the test: **content** — what does the test represent and how truly representative is it? **concurrent** — with what other present observations of pupils' knowledge, understanding, or skill do scores on this test agree and how closely do they agree? **predictive** — what kinds of future performance can be predicted by scores on this test and how accurately can they be predicted? **construct** — what else do we know about the content, relationships, and rationale of this test?

Judging Validity. The sophisticated test-user realizes, then, that validity is not some general, pervasive characteristic that a test "has." Rather, the validity of any test is likely to be specific to the job he wants that test to do. Whether he requires evidence of content validity, concurrent validity, predictive validity, or construct validity depends on his purpose. Whether the evidence is convincing depends on its relevance to the setting in which he expects to use the test. An approach to judging the validity of a test, then, will be implicit in our discussion of pupil population, curriculum content, purpose in testing, and use of scores.

RELIABILITY

Reliability Coefficients. The test-user may expect to find himself concerned with one or more of three kinds of reliability coefficients:

1. *Coefficient of internal consistency* shows consistency of performance on different parts or items of the test taken at a single sitting. This coefficient is usually computed by "split-half" correlation (e.g., Spearman-Brown formula), or by item analysis (e.g., a Kuder-Richardson formula).

2. *Coefficient of equivalence* shows consistency of performance on different forms of a test. It is based on the correlation between performances on the different forms administered at nearly the same time.

3. *Coefficient of stability* shows consistency of performance on a test (or on equivalent forms) over a period of time. It is based on the correlation between performances on initial test and retest after a distinct interval.

Judging Reliability. It is clear that each of these coefficients gives a somewhat different view of reliability, including some different sources of measurement error. Whether we should look to one or another of these coefficients in forming judgments about the reliability of a test depends on how we expect to use the test.

What else must we know about these coefficients to judge whether a test is "sufficiently reliable" for our needs? Let us plant a few seeds of statistical lore concerning reliability now and harvest them later in our discussion of pupil population, curriculum content, purpose in testing, or prospective use of test scores:

1. For speeded tests a coefficient of internal consistency can be quite misleading. In considering any reliability coefficient for a speeded test, we must be sure that speed is one of the important elements we want to measure. Otherwise, the index of reliability will be spuriously high. [content]

2. Other things — such as item quality — being equal, the size of a reliability coefficient can be expected to vary with the number of items in a test. But there is a law of diminishing returns — beyond a certain point, increases in the length of a test may produce relatively small increments in a reliability coefficient. Thus, although "high" reliability is desirable, we must ask ourselves how much additional testing time is a given increase in reliability worth? [purpose]

3. Reliability coefficients can be expected to increase with the performance range or "spread" of the sample of people tested. Conversely, the more homogeneous the group in respect to test scores — i.e., the more restricted their range or spread of achievement — the more likely the rank order of their scores is to change from one part of a test, one form of a test, or one taking of a test to another, and the lower the reliability coefficient will be. [population]

Thus, a publisher may report a high reliability coefficient based on a sample that represents a wide range of ability. But in our use of the test we may be concerned with the scores of individual pupils in a single class representing a much narrower range of ability. Clearly, we cannot expect the test to be so reliable for this group as for the publisher's sample. Therefore, some publishers have adopted the practice of reporting "within class within school" reliability coefficients. These may not seem so impressive in absolute magnitude but are much more realistic for such test usage. [purpose]

4. Test performance and consequent reliability of test scores are also likely to vary with other characteristics of the group tested. For example, a test that is very difficult for a group will result in much guessing, many chance scores, and a low reliability coefficient; whereas a much higher reliability coefficient might be derived from the same test taken by a group which did not find it so difficult. (Thus — taking items 3 and 4 together — when we want to compare the reliability of different tests, we should not simply stack the reliability coefficient reported for one test against the reliability coefficient reported for another. In order to evaluate a reliability cofficient, we should know something about the "reliability sample" on which it is based. Then we should ask, How does the group we want to test compare with the reliability sample for each achievement test we are considering?) [population]

5. An index of reliability which is not governed by the nature of the re-

liability sample is the Standard Error of Measurement. We must bear in mind, however, that the Standard Error of Measurement is expressed in the score units of each test. Therefore, we can best use the Standard Error of Measurement not in direct comparisons between different tests but in judgments about reliability of various scores and score differences on any test. For this purpose, we may do well to note whether the recommended system of reporting scores for a test utilizes the Standard Error of Measurement. Does it thereby help us to avoid making over-fine differentiations between scores of individuals or groups? Also, if the test is a "wide-range" one, we may note whether score reporting allows for variation in size of the Standard Error of Measurement at different score levels. [use]

6. For any test, average scores of groups are more reliable than scores of individuals. Therefore, a test which may not seem sufficiently reliable for evaluating a score difference of a certain size between two pupils may have satisfactory reliability for evaluating an average score difference of the same size between two schools. Or, to put it another way, a test permits finer distinctions to be made among mean achievement scores of groups than among achievement scores of individual pupils. [purpose and use]

7. The nature of the decision to be based on test scores — the degree to which it is tentative or irreversible, coarse or precise — may influence the order of reliability (or validity) required. For example, a final placement or selection test should be more reliable than a preliminary screening test. [purpose]

NORMS

If we want to use the publisher's norms provided for any test, our first question should be: What is this norms group supposed to represent? For instance, is it supposed to be a sample of all 4th-graders in the nation? all the public high school students of a given state who have completed a course in American history? all entering female freshmen in New England teachers' colleges? all male independent secondary school students who have completed two years of algebra?

Suitability of Norms. Norms provide a specific *comparison group*, in relation to which test performance may be meaningfully described. Therefore, whatever the norms group is intended to represent, its characteristics should be clearly defined so that we can judge whether the norms given in the manual will be useful in interpreting scores for the population we want to test. (Incidentally, one of these characteristics should be the time of testing. The distribution of scores for 4th-graders tested in the spring may not look like the distribution of scores for 4th-graders tested in the fall.)

As for the adequacy of the sample, we should probably be concerned more with the basis for sampling than with the total number sampled. For instance, although there is probably no such thing as a truly "national" sample, national norms can be more closely approximated by testing a few pupils at each of a large number of schools (classified according to geographic region, community size, and other specified variables) than by testing a much larger total number of pupils from relatively few schools. Of course, for many purposes local or other specified norms will be much more useful than "national" norms. Local norms will generally have to be developed by the test user himself. (Some test manuals offer specific directions for compiling local norms.)

Using Statistical Information. Armed with these concepts concerning validity, reliability, and norms, we can avoid making unwarranted comparisons among tests. And, thanks to the influence of the *Technical Recommendations,* more and more test publishers are furnishing the essential information about a test to enable the "qualified user to make sound judgments regarding the usefulness of tests and the interpretation of test data." However, it is still up to the test users to relate the published information to: I, the characteristics of their own school population; II, the content and objectives of their own curriculum; III, the purposes of their own staff in testing; IV, the use of test scores in their own school setting.

Let us suppose that we are members of a test selection committee. What should we know about these major considerations, and how should we apply them to selecting achievement tests?

Although these four topics will serve as separate headings, it is clear that they overlap and intermingle to such an extent that no one of them can be treated without reference to the others.

REFERENCE

1. *Technical Recommendations for Achievement Tests.* Committee on Test Standards, American Educational Research Association and Committee on Test Standards, National Council on Measurements Used in Education, January 1955.

7

The Concept of Validity
in the Interpretation of Test Scores

Anne Anastasi

The following article presents a general interpretation of validity in its several principal aspects. The reader should note the various types of validation procedures and compare among them the information that each provides for the test user.

If asked to define "validity," most psychologists would probably agree that validity is the closeness of agreement of a test with some independently observed criterion of the behavior under consideration. It is only as a measure of a specifically defined criterion that a test can be objectively validated at all. For example, unless we define "intelligence" as that combination of aptitudes required for successful school achievement, or for survival on a certain type of job, or in terms of some other observable criterion, we can never either prove or disprove that a particular test is a valid measure of "intelligence." The criterion may be expressed in very broad and general terms, such as "those behavior characteristics in which older children in our culture differ from younger children reared in the same culture," but, however expressed, it defines the functions measured by the particular test. To claim that a test measures anything over and above its criterion is pure speculation of the type that is not amenable to verification and hence falls outside the realm of experimental science.

To the question, "What does this test measure?", the only defensible answer can thus be that it measures a sample of behavior which in turn may be diagnostic of the criterion or criteria against which the particular test was validated. Nor is there any circularity implicit in such a definition of validity, since a psychological test is a device for determining within a relatively short period of time what could otherwise be discovered only by means of a prolonged follow-up. For example, with a psychological test we may be able to predict within a certain margin of error which applicants will succeed on a given job or which students will be able to complete a

From Anne Anastasi, "The Concept of Validity in the Interpretation of Test Scores," *Educational and Psychological Measurement*, X (Spring, 1950), pp. 67–78. Reprinted with the permission of publisher and author.

medical course satisfactorily. Logically, the same information could have been obtained, even more precisely, by hiring all job applicants or admitting to medical school all students wishing to enroll, and observing the subsequent performance of each subject. The latter procedure is obviously so time-consuming and wasteful, however, as to be completely impracticable. Hence the tests make a real contribution in permitting predictions in advance of lengthy observations. Another advantage of standardized psychological tests is that they make possible a comparison of the individual's performance with that of other persons who have been observed in the same sample situation represented by each test. In other words, the tests provide norms for evaluating individual performance.

Prediction and comparison with norms represent valuable contributions which psychological tests can render to our knowledge of individual behavior, the practical benefits of these contributions having been widely demonstrated. It is of fundamental importance, however, to bear in mind that psychological tests do not provide a different *kind* of information from that obtained by any other observation of behavior. The use of such labels as "intelligence," "aptitude," "capacity," and "potentiality" has probably done much to make test users lose sight of the empirical validation of tests. A number of current disagreements regarding the interpretation of test results and the susceptibility of tested abilities to training may be traceable to a failure to take due cognizance of validation procedures. Many test users apparently give only preliminary and possibly perfunctory attention to validation data, in order to reassure themselves at the outset that the test is "satisfactory." Their interpretation of the scores obtained with such a test, however, often takes no account of the validation data and is expressed in terms which bear little or no relation to the criterion.

Perhaps one of the most common examples of such an inconsistent treatment of test validity is provided by what we may call the argument of "extenuating circumstances." Let us suppose that a child obtains an IQ of 58 on a verbal intelligence test, and that the examiner subsequently finds evidence of a fairly severe language handicap in this child owing to foreign parentage. It is a common practice to conclude in such a case that the obtained IQ is not "valid," on the grounds that the verbal content of the test rendered it unsuitable for testing such an individual. At this point we may inquire, however, "On the basis of *what criterion* is this IQ invalid?" Certainly the obtained IQ may be a valid measure of the behavior defined by the criterion against which the particular test was validated. It is very likely that the same language handicap which interfered with performance on this test will interfere with the child's behavior in other linguistic situations of which this test is an adequate index. The correspondence with the criterion may thus be just as close for this child as for children without a language handicap. In school, for example, the language handicap would probably interfere with the child's acquisition of important skills and information. The resulting academic backwardness, together with the original language handicap itself, would, in turn, affect certain aspects of job performance and other areas of adult activities. Conversely, any remedial efforts designed to eliminate the language handicap would produce an improvement, not only in the tested IQ, but also in the broader area of behavior of which this test is a predictor.

It should be added parenthetically that language handicap has been chosen as an example only for purposes of discussion. A number of other "extenuating circumstances," such as visual or auditory defects, emotional and motivational factors, inadequate schooling, and the like, could have served equally well to illustrate the point. Similarly, the discussion has been limited to intelligence tests, since it is chiefly in connection with these tests that many confusions regarding validity have arisen. The entire discussion applies equally well, however, to all types of psychological tests.

Specifically, how does the case cited in our illustration, as well as others of its type, differ from those in which no question is raised regarding the "validity" of the test or its applicability to the particular individual? First, in the present case the examiner has direct and certain knowledge regarding at least one of the factors which *determine* the subject's subnormal performance, viz., language handicap. In other cases, the principal determining factor might be inferior schooling facilities, parental illiteracy, cerebral birth injuries, a defective thyroid, or any of a large number of psychological or biological conditions. Yet it is doubtful whether the IQ would be considered "invalid" in all of these cases simply because it proved possible to point to a specific condition as the determining factor in the poor test performance. To be sure, in many cases of low IQ, the examiner has little or no knowledge about the circumstances or conditions which lead to the intellectual backwardness. But such ignorance is obviously no more conducive to "valid" testing. Quite apart from the question of validity, the examiner should, of course, make every effort to understand why the individual performs as he does on a test. The fullest possible knowledge of the individual's pre- and post-natal environment, structural deficiencies, and any other relevant conditions in his reactional biography is desirable for the most effective use of the test data. But to explain *why* an individual scores poorly on a test does not "explain away" the score. There are always reasons to account for an individual's performance on a test. Language handicap is just as real as any other reason.

A second distinguishing feature of our example is that such a language handicap is usually *remediable*. The individual need not be permanently backward in intellectual performance, but with special training he may in large measure compensate for past losses in intellectual progress. Susceptibility to treatment is, however, a matter of degree. Many of the conditions determining intellectual performance, whether structural or functional, are amenable to change under special treatment. Moreover, conditions for which no effective therapy is now known may yield to newly developed treatments in the future. The distinction in terms of remediability is thus rather tenuous. Nor does such a distinction have any direct bearing upon the validity of a measuring instrument. A thermometer may be a valid index of fever, despite the fact that the administration of medicine will cure the fever.

Thirdly, some may point out that language handicap is not *hereditary* and may maintain that for this reason its influence upon test performance ought to be "ruled out." Such an objection contains a tacit assumption that psychological tests are primarily concerned with those individual differences in behavior which can be attributed to heredity. Since the number of hereditary conditions which have been clearly related to behavior differences are extremely few, such a policy, if followed consistently, would mean the virtual cessation of psychological testing. Moreover, the connection between hereditary mechanisms and behavior is so remote and indirect as to render the distinction between hereditary and environmental factors in behavior largely an academic one (cf., e.g., 2). Above all, it should be noted that no *criterion* against which any psychological test has been validated is itself traceable to purely hereditary factors. Hence no such test has been proved to be a valid measure of individual differences in hereditary characteristics.

A fourth point to be considered is that of *comparability*. It may be objected that the individual who is handicapped by language difficulties, sensory deficiencies, or similar "extenuating circumstances" is not comparable to the validation group on which the test norms were established. The requirement of comparability in the application of psychological tests needs further clarification. If individuals are entirely similar in all of the conditions (psychological, physiological, etc.) which influence the behavior measured by a particular test, individual differences will disappear, all subjects receiving the same score. Obviously no test is designed to measure behavior independently of the conditions which determine such behavior — that would be a logical absurdity as well as an empirical impossibility. When the conditions in which the individual differs from the standardization group affect the test and the criterion in an approximately equal manner and degree, the validity of the test for that individual will not be appreciably influenced by the lack of comparability of the individual to the standardization group.

This question of "comparability" pertains not so much to the measurement of behavior as to the analysis of the etiology of behavior differences. It is only when attributing the observed individual differences in test scores to a particular factor or class of factors that the investigator must make certain that other contributing factors have been reasonably constant. For example, if a few individuals in a group have a language handicap while the rest do not, we could not ascribe individual differences in performance within this group to structural differences in the nervous system, or to any other factor whose contribution to behavior we may be investigating. The same limitation would apply, however, if educational opportunities, family traditions, incentives for intellectual activities, or any other factor were not held constant. The fact that the influence of language handicap, sensory deficiencies, and a few other conditions is more readily apparent does not place such conditions in a different category. The question of comparability applies equally to all conditions other than the one under investigation.

A fifth consideration pertains to the use of test scores in *prediction*. Could an IQ obtained by a child with a language handicap serve as a basis for predicting the subsequent behavior of the individual? As long as the language handicap remains, the test score can provide an accurate prognosis of the child's behavior in situations demanding the type of verbal responses sampled by the test. It is only in this sense that *any* psychological test makes predictions possible. Within a certain margin of error, behavior can be predicted *under existing conditions*. But if, for example, any detrimental conditions such as poor schooling, sensory deficiencies, or the like are corrected, then performance on *both* test and criterion will show improvement. In discussions of test *reliability*, various writers during the past twenty-five years have pointed out that a psychological test should be expected to reflect changes in behavior at different times and under different conditions.[1] For test scores to remain constant when conditions affecting the subject's behavior have altered would indicate a crude and relatively insensitive measuring instrument, rather than a highly "reliable" one. The same logic applies to validity. If the subjects' test scores remain unchanged despite the modification of conditions which affect criterion performance, the test cannot have high validity.

Closely related to the problem of prediction is the *scope or breadth of influence* of any given condition upon the individual's behavior. For example, the presence of a loud, irregular noise during the testing would probably affect the score on that test, without influencing the individual's behavior in other situations. A toothache or a severe cold on the day of the testing would be further illustrations of narrowly limited conditions. In the case of these conditions, the prognostic value of the test for the individual would indeed be reduced, in much the same manner that holding an ice cube in the mouth would invalidate an oral thermometer reading of bodily temperature. Conditions such as language handicap, however, affect the individual's behavior in a much broader area than that of the immediate test situation. They may thus influence both criterion and test score in a similar manner.

The import of the above analysis is that validity should be consistently interpreted with reference to the *specific criteria* against which the given test was validated. It also follows that validity is not a function of the test but of the use to which the test is put. A test may have high validity for one criterion and low or negligible validity for another. The attitude that a good test has "high validity" and a poor test has "low validity" is still too prevalent among test users. Tests cannot be validated in the abstract, nor is the usual concept of validity itself universally applicable to psychological testing. It is only when tests are employed for predictive or diagnostic purposes that the correlation with an external criterion is relevant at all. In many investigations concerned with fundamental behavior research, tests are employed merely as behavior samples obtained under standardized (i.e., uniform) conditions, without reference to the correlations of these samples with other, "everyday-life" behavior samples (i.e., practical criterion measures). When the maze-learning behavior of white rats is tested, for example, the maze is not first "validated" against the rats' success in finding food in a grocery basement, or their ability to avoid contact with prowling cats, or any other criteria of

[1] Cf., e.g., 1, 4, 5, 6, 9, 10, 11, 12, 15, 18, 19.

achievement in the rats' extra-laboratory or workaday world. The investigator may quite reasonably argue that for the study of the particular principles of behavior which he is investigating, maze-learning is as "good" a sample of behavior as cat-avoiding, and that he has no more reason for validating the former against the latter than vice versa.

Fundamentally, any validation procedure provides a measure of the relationship between two behavior samples. As Guilford has recently expressed it, "In a very general sense, a test is valid for anything with which it correlates" (7, p. 429). The process can be regarded as irreversible only when one of the behavior samples has greater importance than the other for a specific purpose.[2] In such a case, the more important behavior sample is designated the "criterion." No basic difference exists between "criteria" on the one hand and "tests" on the other. They are merely different samples of behavior whose interrelationships permit predictions from one to the other. We *could* predict intelligence test scores from school achievement, although the process would be needlessly time-consuming. In such a case, the intelligence test scores would constitute the criterion.

The criterion is not *intrinsically* superior in any sense. It is well known, for example, that many commonly used criteria, such as school grades or job advancement, may be influenced by many factors "extraneous" to the quality of the individual's performance. Yet, if it is our object to predict such criteria, with all their irrelevancies and shortcomings, then the correlation of a given test with such criteria *is* the validity of the test in that situation. To be sure, the immediate criterion against which a test is validated may itself have been chosen as a convenient index or predictor of a broader and less readily observable area of behavior. For example, a pilot aptitude test may be validated against performance in basic flight training, the latter being in turn regarded as an approximate index of achievement in more advanced training and even possibly of ultimate combat performance. Such "successive validation" would be quite consistent with the relativity of predictors and criteria. It might be noted parenthetically that it is only when criterion measures are themselves used as predictors of further behavior that one may legitimately speak of the reliability and validity of the criterion itself (cf. e.g., 8).

Validation against a "practical" criterion is essential for many uses to which tests are put. It should not be assumed, however, that only tests which have been validated against some criterion considered important within a particular cultural setting can be used in behavior research. In order to be able to generalize from any obtained test score, we need only to know the relationships between the tested behavior in question and other behavior samples, none of these behavior samples necessarily occupying the preeminent position of a criterion. Thus, if the investigator is interested in the possible use of maze-learning performance as a basis for predicting the rats' behavior

[2] To be sure, when the relationship between the two variables is curvilinear, prediction will not be equally accurate in both directions, since $\eta_{xy} \neq \eta_{yx}$. In such cases, however, there is no a priori reason to expect that the correlation will be any higher when predicting the "criterion" from the "test" than when predicting the "test" from the "criterion."

in other learning situations, he will have to correlate the subjects' maze-learning scores with their scores in a variety of other learning tasks. If a common factor is identified through these different learning scores, the "factorial validity" (7) of any one of the tests in predicting that which is common to all of them can be determined. On the other hand, if no single learning factor is demonstrated, then the area within which predictions can be made must be accordingly narrowed to fit the confines of whatever common factor does become evident. Investigations conducted to date on human subjects, for example, have failed to indicate the presence of a common "learning factor" (20, 21), and animal studies have revealed even greater specificity (cf., e.g., 14, 16, 17). But such specificity, if further corroborated, is an empirically observed fact whose discovery is useful in its own right in advancing our knowledge of behavior; it should not be construed as a weakness of the tests.

Whether we are dealing with common factors and "factorial validity" or with "practical validity" in the prediction of everyday-life criteria, the question of validity concerns essentially the interrelationships of behavior samples. In the latter case, one sample is represented by the test and another, probably much more extensive sample, by the criterion. In the former case, the different tests which are correlated constitute the behavior samples. Nor should the terminology of factor analysis mislead us into the belief that anything external to the tested behavior has been identified. The discovery of a "factor" means simply that certain relationships exist between tested behavior samples.

The common misconception that the criterion is in some mysterious fashion more basic than the test probably results, in part, from the belief that tests measure hypothetical "underlying capacities" which are distinguishable from observed behavior. Discussions of psychological tests often become hopelessly entangled because of the implicit supposition that tests can be validated against such underlying capacities as criteria. Any operational analysis of actual validation procedures reveals the futility and absurdity of such an expectation.

In this connection we may consider a monograph by Thomas (13), which sounds a note of acute pessimism regarding the use of mental tests as "instruments of science." Through a careful and systematic logical analysis, the author demonstrates the fallacies inherent in any attempts to interpret psychological tests as measures of "innate abilities," hypostatized "fundamental human capacities," and the like. He clearly recognizes that "the methodology of mental testing provides no way of operationally defining an ability and a performance as distinct . . . entities" (13, p. 75). But, in his final conclusions, the author seems to exhibit the same confusions which he had previously sought to eliminate.[3] For example, in the attempt to

---

[3] These confusions in the fundamental argument do not detract from the value of certain more specific points discussed in this monograph, such as the limitations of ordinal scales, and the concepts of difficulty value and homogeneity in test construction. But these problems have also been analyzed by other writers, in a somewhat more constructive manner (cf., e.g., 3, 10).

evaluate the scientific usefulness of psychological tests, he raises such questions as the following: "Do two identical scores mean that the same kind and amount of psychological processes were employed? Do they mean similar sociological backgrounds of experience? Do they mean a qualitatively similar adaptation to the immediate test environment? Do they mean that comparable amounts of psychic tension were built up or that similar amounts of nervous energy were expended?" (13, p. 77). By way of reply he adds: "The achievement of such scientific meanings as these from the current methodology of mental testing is probably too much to expect, for test results at present are notoriously ambiguous in what they signify about the socio-psychological ingredients of the recorded performances" (13, p. 77).

Two weaknesses are apparent in such an argument. First, the testing of behavior is being confused with an analysis of the factors which determine behavior. Secondly, despite his earlier advocacy of an operational definition of "ability," the author now appears to be chasing the will-o'-the-wisp of "psychological processes" which are distinct from performance. He seems thus to be demanding that in order to be proper instruments of science, psychological tests should measure functions which by definition fall outside the domain of scientific inquiry!

In summary, it is urged that test scores be operationally defined in terms of empirically demonstrated behavior relationships. If a test has been validated against a practical criterion such as school performance, the scores on such a test should be consistently defined and treated as predictors of school performance rather than as measures of hypostatized and unverifiable "abilities." It is further pointed out that conditions which affect test scores may also affect the criterion, since both test scores and criteria are essentially behavior samples. The extent or breadth of such influences is a matter for empirical determination, rather than for a priori assumption. Moreover, the validity of a psychological test should not be confused with an analysis of the factors which determine the behavior under consideration. Finally, it should be noted that the distinction between test and criterion is itself merely one of practical convenience. The scientific use of tests is not predicated upon the assumption that criteria are a separate class of phenomena against which all tests must first be validated. Essentially, generalization and prediction in psychology require knowledge of the interrelationships of behavior, regardless of the situation in which such behavior was observed.

REFERENCES

1. Anastasi, A. "The Influence of Practice upon Test Reliability," *Journal of Educational Psychology*, XXV (1934), 321–335.
2. Anastasi, A., and Foley, J. P., Jr. "A Proposed Reorientation in the Heredity-Environment Controversy," *Psychological Review*, LV (1948), 239–249.
3. Coombs, C. H. "Some Hypotheses for the Analysis of Qualitative Variables," *Psychological Review*, LV (1948), 167–174.
4. Cronbach, L. J. "Test 'Reliability': Its Meaning and Determination," *Psychometrika*, XII (1947), 1–16.
5. Dunlap, J. W. "Comparable Tests and Reliability," *Journal of Educational Psychology*, XXIV (1933), 442–453.

6. Goodenough, F. L. "A Critical Note on the Use of the Term 'Reliability' in Mental Measurement," *Journal of Educational Psychology*, XXVII (1936), 173–178.

7. Guilford, J. P. "New Standards for Test Evaluation," *Educational and Psychological Measurement*, VI (1946), 427–438.

8. Jenkins, J. G. "Validity for What?" *Journal of Consulting Psychology*, X (1946), 93–98.

9. Kuhlmann, F. *Tests of Mental Development*. Minneapolis: Educational Test Bureau, 1939.

10. Loevinger, J. "A Systematic Approach to the Construction and Evaluation of Tests of Ability," *Psychological Monographs*, LXI (1947), No. 4.

11. Paulsen, C. B. "A Coefficient of Trait Variability," *Psychological Bulletin*, XXVIII (1931), 218–219.

12. Skaggs, E. B. "Some Critical Comments on Certain Prevailing Concepts Used in Mental Testing," *Journal of Applied Psychology*, XI (1927), 503–508.

13. Thomas, L. G. "Mental Tests as Instruments of Science," *Psychological Monographs*, LIV (1942), No. 3.

14. Thorndike, R. L. "Organization of Behavior in the Albino Rat," *Genetic Psychology Monograph*, XVII (1935), No. 1.

15. Thouless, R. H. "Test Unreliability and Functional Fluctuation," *British Journal of Psychology*, XXVI (1935–1936), 325–343.

16. Van Steenberg, N. J. F. "Factors in the Learning Behavior of the Albino Rat," *Psychometrika*, IV (1939), 179–200.

17. Vaughn, C. L. "Factors in Rat Learning: An Analysis of the Intercorrelations Between 34 Variables," *Psychological Monographs*, XIV (1937), No. 69.

18. Wherry, R. J., and Gaylord, R. H. "The Concept of Test and Item Reliability in Relation to Factor Pattern," *Psychometrika*, VIII (1943), 247–264.

19. Woodrow, H. "Quotidian Variability," *Psychological Review*, XXXIX (1932), 245–256.

20. ———. "The Relation Between Abilities and Improvement with Practice," *Journal of Educational Psychology*, XXIX (1938), 215–230.

21. ———. "Factors in Improvement with Practice," *Journal of Psychology*, VII (1939), 55–70.

8

Construct Validity in Psychological Tests

Lee J. Cronbach and Paul E. Meehl[1]

*The writers of the following article have presented a compre-
hensive discussion of the basic theory of, and indications of evidence
for, construct validity. Since so many psychological measuring devices are based upon construct validity, the reader may well profit
from a careful investigation of the points brought out. A contrasting
viewpoint is presented by Bechtoldt, in the* American Psychologist,
1959, 14:619–629.

Validation of psychological tests has not yet been adequately conceptualized, as the APA Committee on Psychological Tests learned when it undertook (1950–54) to specify what qualities should be investigated before a test
is published. In order to make coherent recommendations the Committee
found it necessary to distinguish four types of validity, established by different
types of research and requiring different interpretation. The chief innovation
in the Committee's report was the term *construct validity*.[2] This idea was
first formulated by a subcommittee (Meehl and R. C. Challman) studying
how proposed recommendations would apply to projective techniques, and
later modified and clarified by the entire Committee (Bordin, Challman,
Conrad, Humphreys, Super, and the present writers). The statements agreed
upon by the Committee (and by committees of two other associations) were
published in the *Technical Recommendations* (59). The present interpretation of construct validity is not "official" and deals with some areas where
the Committee would probably not be unanimous. The present writers are
solely responsible for this attempt to explain the concept and elaborate its
implications.

From Lee J. Cronbach and Paul E. Meehl, "Construct Validity in Psychological
Tests," *Psychological Bulletin*, LII (May, 1955), pp. 281–302. Reprinted with the
permission of the American Psychological Association and the authors.

[1] The second author worked on this problem in connection with his appointment to the
Minnesota Center for Philosophy of Science. We are indebted to the other members of
the Center (Herbert Feigl, Michael Scriven, Wilfred Sellars), and to D. L. Thistlethwaite
of the University of Illinois, for their major contributions to our thinking and their suggestions for improving this paper.

[2] Referred to in a preliminary report (58) as *congruent validity*.

Identification of construct validity was not an isolated development. Writers on validity during the preceding decade had shown a great deal of dissatisfaction with conventional notions of validity, and introduced new terms and ideas, but the resulting aggregation of types of validity seems only to have stirred the muddy waters. Portions of the distinctions we shall discuss are implicit in Jenkins' paper, "Validity for what?" (33), Gulliksen's "Intrinsic validity" (27), Goodenough's distinction between tests as "signs" and "samples" (22), Cronbach's separation of "logical" and "empirical" validity (11), Guilford's "factorial validity" (25), and Mosier's papers on "face validity" and "validity generalization" (49, 50). Helen Peak (52) comes close to an explicit statement of construct validity as we shall present it.

Four Types of Validation

The categories into which the *Recommendations* divide validity studies are: predictive validity, concurrent validity, content validity, and construct validity. The first two of these may be considered together as *criterion-oriented* validation procedures.

The pattern of a criterion-oriented study is familiar. The investigator is primarily interested in some criterion which he wishes to predict. He administers the test, obtains an independent criterion measure on the same subjects, and computes a correlation. If the criterion is obtained some time after the test is given, he is studying *predictive validity*. If the test score and criterion score are determined at essentially the same time, he is studying *concurrent validity*. Concurrent validity is studied when one test is proposed as a substitute for another (for example, when a multiple-choice form of spelling test is substituted for taking dictation), or a test is shown to correlate with some contemporary criterion (e.g., psychiatric diagnosis).

Content validity is established by showing that the test items are a sample of a universe in which the investigator is interested. Content validity is ordinarily to be established deductively, by defining a universe of items and sampling systematically within this universe to establish the test.

Construct validation is involved whenever a test is to be interpreted as a measure of some attribute or quality which is not "operationally defined." The problem faced by the investigator is, "What constructs account for variance in test performance?" Construct validity calls for no new scientific approach. Much current research on tests of personality (9) is construct validation, usually without the benefit of a clear formulation of this process.

Construct validity is not to be identified solely by particular investigative procedures, but by the orientation of the investigator. Criterion-oriented validity, as Bechtoldt emphasizes (3, p. 1245), "involves the *acceptance* of a set of operations as an adequate definition of whatever is to be measured." When an investigator believes that no criterion available to him is fully valid, he perforce becomes interested in construct validity because this is the only way to avoid the "infinite frustration" of relating every criterion to some more ultimate standard (21). In content validation, *acceptance* of the universe of content as defining the variable to be measured is essential. Construct validity must be investigated whenever no criterion or universe of content is accepted as entirely adequate to define the quality to be measured. Determining what psychological constructs account for test performance is desirable for almost any test. Thus, although the MMPI was originally established on the basis of empirical discrimination between patient groups and so-called normals (concurrent validity), continuing research has tried to provide a basis for describing the personality associated with each score pattern. Such interpretations permit the clinician to predict performance with respect to criteria which have not yet been employed in empirical validation studies (cf. 46, pp. 49–50, 110–111).

> We can distinguish among the four types of validity by noting that each involves a different emphasis on the criterion. In predictive or concurrent validity, the criterion behavior is of concern to the tester, and he may have no concern whatsoever with the type of behavior exhibited in the test. (An employer does not care if a worker can manipulate blocks, but the score on the block tests may predict something he cares about.) Content validity is studied when the tester *is* concerned with the type of behavior represented in the test performance. Indeed, if the test is a work sample, the behavior represented in the test may be an end in itself. Construct validity is ordinarily studied when the tester has no definite criterion measure of the quality with which he is concerned, and must use indirect measures. Here the trait or quality underlying the test is of central importance, rather than either the test behavior or the scores on the criteria (59, p. 14).

Construct validation is important at times for every sort of psychological test: aptitude, achievement, interests, and so on. Thurstone's statement is interesting in this connection:

> In the field of intelligence tests, it used to be common to define validity as the correlation between a test score and some outside criterion. We have reached a stage of sophistication where the test-criterion correlation is too coarse. It is obsolete. If we attempted to ascertain the validity of a test for the second space-factor, for example, we would have to get judges [to] make reliable judgments about people as to this factor. Ordinarily their [the available judges'] ratings would be of no value as a criterion. Consequently, validity studies in the cognitive functions now depend on criteria of internal consistency . . . (60, p. 3).

Construct validity would be involved in answering such questions as: To what extent is this test of intelligence culture-free? Does this test of "interpretation of data" measure reading ability, quantitative reasoning, or response sets? How does a person with A in Strong Accountant, and B in Strong CPA, differ from a person who has these scores reversed?

Example of Construct Validation Procedure

Suppose measure X correlates .50 with Y, the amount of palmar sweating induced when we tell a student that he has failed a Psychology I exam. Predictive validity of X for Y is adequately described by the coefficient, and a statement of the experimental and sampling conditions. If someone were to ask, "Isn't there perhaps another way to interpret this correlation?" or "What other kinds of evidence can you bring to support your interpretation?", we would hardly understand what he was asking because no interpretation has been made. These questions become relevant when the correlation is advanced as evidence that "test X measures anxiety proneness." Alternative interpretations are possible; e.g., perhaps the test measures "academic aspiration," in which case we will expect different results if we induce palmar sweating by economic threat. It is then reasonable to inquire about other *kinds* of evidence.

Add these facts from further studies: Test X correlates .45 with fraternity brothers' ratings on "tenseness." Test X correlates .55 with amount of intellectual inefficiency induced by painful electric shock, and .68 with the Taylor Anxiety Scale. Mean X score decreases among four diagnosed groups in this order: anxiety state, reactive depression, "normal," and psychopathic personality. And palmar sweat under threat of failure in Psychology I correlates .60 with threat of failure in mathematics. Negative results eliminate competing explanations of the X score; thus, findings of negligible correlations between X and social class, vocational aim, and value-orientation make it fairly safe to reject the suggestion that X measures "academic aspiration." We can have substantial confidence that X does measure anxiety proneness if the current theory of anxiety can embrace the variates which yield positive correlations, and does not predict correlations where we found none.

KINDS OF CONSTRUCTS

At this point we should indicate summarily what we mean by a construct, recognizing that much of the remainder of the paper deals with this question. [A construct is some postulated attribute of people, assumed to be reflected in test performance.] In test validation the attribute about which we make statements in interpreting a test is a construct. We expect a person at any time to possess or not possess a qualitative attribute (amnesia) or structure, or to possess some degree of a quantitative attribute (cheerfulness). A construct has certain associated meanings carried in statements of this general character: Persons who possess this attribute will, in situation X, act in manner Y (with a stated probability). The logic of construct validation is invoked whether the construct is highly systematized or loose, used in ramified theory or a few simple propositions, used in absolute propositions or probability statements. We seek to specify how one is to defend a proposed interpretation of a test; *we are not recommending any one type of interpretation.*

The constructs in which tests are to be interpreted are certainly not likely to be physiological. Most often they will be traits such as "latent hostility" or "variable in mood," or descriptions in terms of an educational objective, as "ability to plan experiments." For the benefit of readers who may have been influenced by certain eisegeses of MacCorquodale and Meehl (40), let us here emphasize: Whether or not an interpretation of a test's properties or relations involves questions of construct validity is to be decided by examining the entire body of evidence offered, together with what is asserted about the test in the context of this evidence. Proposed identifications of constructs allegedly measured by the test with constructs of other sciences (e.g., genetics, neuroanatomy, biochemistry) make up only *one* class of construct-validity claims, and a rather minor one at present. Space does not permit full analysis of the relation of the present paper to the MacCorquodale-Meehl distinction between hypothetical constructs and intervening variables. The philosophy of science pertinent to the present paper is set forth later in the section entitled, "The nomological network."

THE RELATION OF CONSTRUCTS TO "CRITERIA"

Critical View of the Criterion Implied

An unquestionable criterion may be found in a practical operation, or may be established as a consequence of an operational definition. Typically, however, the psychologist is unwilling to use the directly operational approach because he is interested in building theory about a generalized construct. A theorist trying to relate behavior to "hunger" almost certainly invests that term with meanings other than the operation "elapsed-time-since-feeding." If he is concerned with hunger as a tissue need, he will not accept time lapse as *equivalent* to his construct because it fails to consider, among other things, energy expenditure of the animal.

In some situations the criterion is no more valid than the test. Suppose, for example, that we want to know if counting the dots on Bender-Gestalt figure five indicates "compulsive rigidity," and take psychiatric ratings on this trait as a criterion. Even a conventional report on the resulting correlation will say something about the extent and intensity of the psychiatrist's contacts and should describe his qualifications (e.g., diplomate status? analyzed?).

Why report these facts? Because data are needed to indicate whether the criterion is any good. "Compulsive rigidity" is not really intended to mean "social stimulus value to psychiatrists." The implied trait involves a range of behavior-dispositions which may be very imperfectly sampled by the psychiatrist. Suppose dot-counting does not occur in a particular patient and yet we find that the psychiatrist has rated him as "rigid." When questioned the psychiatrist tells us that the patient was a rather easy, free-wheeling sort; however, the patient *did* lean over to straighten out a skewed desk blotter, and this, viewed against certain other facts, tipped the scale in favor of a "rigid" rating. On the face of it, counting Bender dots may be just as good (or poor) a sample of the compulsive-rigidity domain as straightening desk blotters is.

Suppose, to extend our example, we have four tests on the "predictor" side, over against the psychiatrist's "criterion," and find generally positive correlations among the five variables. Surely it is artificial and arbitrary to impose the "test-should-predict-criterion" pattern on such data. The psychiatrist samples verbal content, expressive pattern, voice, posture, etc. The psychologist samples verbal content, perception, expressive pattern, etc. Our proper conclusion is that, from this evidence, the four tests and the psychiatrist all assess some common factor.

The asymmetry between the "test" and the so-designated "criterion" arises only because the terminology of predictive validity has become a commonplace in test analysis. In this study where a construct is the central concern, any distinction between the merit of the test and criterion variables would be justified only if it had already been shown that the psychiatrist's theory and operations were excellent measures of the attribute.

INADEQUACY OF VALIDATION IN TERMS OF SPECIFIC CRITERIA

The proposal to validate constructual interpretations of tests runs counter to suggestions of some others. Spiker and McCandless (57) favor an operational approach. Validation is replaced by compiling statements as to how strongly the test predicts other observed variables of interest. To avoid requiring that each new variable be investigated completely by itself, they allow two variables to collapse into one whenever the properties of the operationally defined measures are the same: "If a new test is demonstrated to predict the scores on an older, well-established test, then an evaluation of the predictive power of the older test may be used for the new one." But accurate inferences are possible only if the two tests correlate so highly that there is negligible reliable variance in either test, independent of the other. Where the correspondence is less close, one must either retain all the separate variables operationally defined or embark on construct validation.

The practical user of tests must rely on constructs of some generality to make predictions about new situations. Test X could be used to predict palmar sweating in the face of failure without invoking any construct, but a counselor is more likely to be asked to forecast behavior in diverse or even unique situations for which the correlation of test X is unknown. Significant predictions rely on knowledge accumulated around the generalized construct of anxiety. The *Technical Recommendations* state:

> It is ordinarily necessary to evaluate construct validity by integrating evidence from many different sources. The problem of construct validation becomes especially acute in the clinical field since for many of the constructs dealt with it is not a question of finding an imperfect criterion but of finding any criterion at all. The psychologist interested in construct validity for clinical devices is concerned with making an estimate of a hypothetical internal process, factor, system, structure, or state and cannot expect to find a clear unitary behavioral criterion. An attempt to identify any one criterion measure or any composite as *the* criterion aimed at is, however, usually unwarranted (59, pp. 14–15).

This appears to conflict with arguments for specific criteria prominent at places in the testing literature. Thus Anastasi (2) makes many statements of the latter character: "It is only as a measure of a specifically defined criterion that a test can be objectively validated at all . . . To claim that a test measures anything over and above its criterion is pure speculation" (p. 67). Yet elsewhere this article supports construct validation. Tests can be profit-

ably interpreted if we "know the relationships between the tested behavior . . .
and other behavior samples, none of these behavior samples necessarily occupying the preeminent position of a criterion" (p. 75). Factor analysis with
several partial criteria might be used to study whether a test measures a postulated "general learning ability." If the data demonstrate specificity of ability
instead, such specificity is "useful in its own right in advancing our knowledge of behavior; it should not be construed as a weakness of the tests"
(p. 75).

We depart from Anastasi at two points. She writes, "The validity of a
psychological test should not be confused with an analysis of the factors
which determine the behavior under consideration." We, however, regard
such analysis as a most important type of validation. Second, she refers to
"the will-o'-the-wisp of psychological processes which are distinct from performance" (2, p. 77). While we agree that psychological processes are
elusive, we are sympathetic to attempts to formulate and clarify constructs
which are evidenced by performance but distinct from it. Surely an inductive
inference based on a pattern of correlations cannot be dismissed as "pure
speculation."

Specific Criteria Used Temporarily: The "Bootstraps" Effect

Even when a test is constructed on the basis of a specific criterion, it may
ultimately be judged to have greater construct validity than the criterion. We
start with a vague concept which we associate with certain observations. We
then discover empirically that these observations covary with some other observation which possesses greater reliability or is more intimately correlated
with relevant experimental changes than is the original measure, or both. For
example, the notion of temperature arises because some objects feel hotter to
the touch than others. The expansion of a mercury column does not have face
validity as an index of hotness. But it turns out that (*a*) there is a statistical
relation between expansion and sensed temperature; (*b*) observers employ the
mercury method with good interobserver agreement; (*c*) the regularity of
observed relations is increased by using the thermometer (e.g., melting points
of samples of the same material vary little on the thermometer; we obtain
nearly linear relations between mercury measures and pressure of a gas).
Finally, (*d*) a theoretical structure involving unobservable microevents — the
kinetic theory — is worked out which explains the relation of mercury expansion to heat. This whole process of conceptual enrichment begins with what
in retrospect we see as an extremely fallible "criterion" — the human temperature sense. That original criterion has now been relegated to a peripheral
position. We have lifted ourselves by our bootstraps, but in a legitimate and
fruitful way.

Similarly, the Binet scale was first valued because children's scores tended
to agree with judgments by schoolteachers. If it had not shown this agreement, it would have been discarded along with reaction time and the other
measures of ability previously tried. Teacher judgments once constituted the
criterion against which the individual intelligence test was validated. But if

today a child's IQ is 135 and three of his teachers complain about how stupid he is, we do not conclude that the test has failed. Quite to the contrary, if no error in test procedure can be argued, we treat the test score as a valid statement about an important quality, and define our task as that of finding out what other variables — personality, study skills, etc. — modify achievement or distort teacher judgment.

EXPERIMENTATION TO INVESTIGATE CONSTRUCT VALIDITY

Validation Procedures

We can use many methods in construct validation. Attention should particularly be drawn to Macfarlane's survey of these methods as they apply to projective devices (41).

Group Differences. If our understanding of a construct leads us to expect two groups to differ on the test, this expectation may be tested directly. Thus Thurstone and Chave validated the Scale for Measuring Attitude Toward the Church by showing score differences between church members and non-churchgoers. Churchgoing is not *the* criterion of attitude, for the purpose of the test is to measure something other than the crude sociological fact of church attendance; on the other hand, failure to find a difference would have seriously challenged the test.

Only coarse correspondence between test and group designation is expected. Too great a correspondence between the two would indicate that the test is to some degree invalid, because members of the groups are expected to overlap on the test. Intelligence test items are selected initially on the basis of a correspondence to age, but an item that correlates .95 with age in an elementary school sample would surely be suspect.

Correlation Matrices and Factor Analysis. If two tests are presumed to measure the same construct, a correlation between them is predicted. (An exception is noted where some second attribute has positive loading in the first test and negative loading in the second test; then a low correlation is expected. This is a testable interpretation provided an external measure of either the first or the second variable exists.) If the obtained correlation departs from the expectation, however, there is no way to know whether the fault lies in test A, test B, or the formulation of the construct. A matrix of intercorrelations often points out profitable ways of dividing the construct into more meaningful parts, factor analysis being a useful computational method in such studies.

Guilford (26) has discussed the place of factor analysis in construct validation. His statements may be extracted as follows:

"The personnel psychologist wishes to know 'why his tests are valid.' He can place tests and practical criteria in a matrix and factor it to identify 'real dimensions of human personality.' A factorial description is exact and stable; it is economical in explanation; it leads to the creation of pure tests which can be combined to predict complex behaviors." It is clear that factors here function as constructs. Eysenck, in his "criterion analysis" (18), goes farther than Guilford, and shows that factoring can be used explicitly to test hypotheses about constructs.

Factors may or may not be weighted with surplus meaning. Certainly when they are regarded as "real dimensions," a great deal of surplus meaning is implied, and the interpreter must shoulder a substantial burden of proof. The alternative view is to regard factors as defining a working reference frame, located in a convenient manner in the "space" defined by all behaviors of a given type. Which set of factors from a given matrix is "most useful" will depend partly on predilections, but in essence the best construct is the one around which we can build the greatest number of inferences, in the most direct fashion.

Studies of Internal Structure. For many constructs, evidence of homogeneity within the test is relevant in judging validity. If a trait such as *dominance* is hypothesized, and the items inquire about behaviors subsumed under this label, then the hypothesis appears to require that these items be generally intercorrelated. Even low correlations, if consistent, would support the argument that people may be fruitfully described in terms of a generalized tendency to dominate or not dominate. The general quality would have power to predict behavior in a variety of situations represented by the specific items. Item-test correlations and certain reliability formulas describe internal consistency.

It is unwise to list uninterpreted data of this sort under the heading "validity" in test manuals, as some authors have done. High internal consistency may *lower* validity. Only if the underlying theory of the trait being measured calls for high item intercorrelations do the correlations support construct validity. Negative item-test correlations may support construct validity, provided that the items with negative correlations are believed irrelevant to the postulated construct and serve as suppressor variables (31, pp. 431–436; 44).

Study of distinctive subgroups of items within a test may set an upper limit to construct validity by showing that irrelevant elements influence scores. Thus a study of the PMA space tests shows that variance can be partially accounted for by a response set, tendency to mark many figures as similar (12). An internal factor analysis of the PEA Interpretation of Data Test shows that in addition to measuring reasoning skills, the test score is strongly influenced by a tendency to say "probably true" rather than "certainly true," regardless of item content (17). On the other hand, a study of item groupings in the DAT Mechanical Comprehension Test permitted rejection of the hypothesis that knowledge about specific topics such as gears made a substantial contribution to scores (13).

Studies of Change Over Occasions. The stability of test scores ("retest reliability," Cattell's "N-technique") may be relevant to construct validation. Whether a high degree of stability is encouraging or discouraging for the proposed interpretation depends upon the theory defining the construct.

More powerful than the retest after uncontrolled intervening experiences is the retest with experimental intervention. If a transient influence swings test scores over a wide range, there are definite limits on the extent to which a test result can be interpreted as reflecting the typical behavior of the individual. These are examples of experiments which have indicated upper limits to test validity: studies of differences associated with the examiner in projective testing, of change of score under alternative directions ("tell the truth" vs. "make yourself look good to an employer"), and of coachability of mental tests. We may recall Gulliksen's distinction (27): When the coaching is of a sort that improves the pupil's intellectual functioning in school, the test which is affected by the coaching has validity as a measure of intellectual functioning; if the coaching improves test taking but not school performance, the test which responds to the coaching has poor validity as a measure of this construct.

Sometimes, where differences between individuals are difficult to assess by any means other than the test, the experimenter validates by determining whether the test can detect induced intra-individual differences. One might hypothesize that the Zeigarnik effect is a measure of ego involvement, i.e., that with ego involvement there is more recall of incomplete tasks. To support such an interpretation, the investigator will try to induce ego involvement on some task by appropriate directions and compare subjects' recall with their recall for tasks where there was a contrary induction. Sometimes the intervention is drastic. Porteus finds (53) that brain-operated patients show disruption of performance on his maze, but do not show impaired performance on conventional verbal tests and argues therefrom that his test is a better measure of planfulness.

Studies of Process. One of the best ways of determining informally what accounts for variability on a test is the observation of the person's process of performance. If it is supposed, for example, that a test measures mathematical competence, and yet observation of students' errors shows that erroneous reading of the question is common, the implications of a low score are altered. Lucas in this way showed that the Navy Relative Movement Test, an aptitude test, actually involved two different abilities: spatial visualization and mathematical reasoning (39).

Mathematical analysis of scoring procedures may provide important negative evidence on construct validity. A recent analysis of "empathy" tests is perhaps worth citing (14). "Empathy" has been operationally defined in many studies by the ability of a judge to predict what responses will be given on some questionnaire by a subject he has observed briefly. A mathematical argument has shown, however, that the scores depend on several attributes of the judge which enter into his perception of *any* individual, and that they therefore cannot be interpreted as evidence of his ability to interpret cues offered by particular others, or his intuition.

The Numerical Estimate of Construct Validity

There is an understandable tendency to seek a "construct validity coefficient." A numerical statement of the degree of construct validity would be a statement of the proportion of the test score variance that is attributable to the construct variable. This numerical estimate can sometimes be arrived at by a factor analysis, but since present methods of factor analysis are based on linear relations, more general methods will ultimately be needed to deal with many quantitative problems of construct validation.

Rarely will it be possible to estimate definite "construct saturations," because no factor corresponding closely to the construct will be available. One can only hope to set upper and lower bounds to the "loading." If "creativity" is defined as something independent of knowledge, then a correlation of .40 between a presumed test of creativity and a test of arithmetic knowledge would indicate that at least 16 per cent of the reliable test variance is irrelevant to creativity as defined. Laboratory performance on problems such as Maier's "hatrack" would scarcely be an ideal measure of creativity, but it would be somewhat relevant. If its correlation with the test is .60, this permits a tentative estimate of 36 per cent as a lower bound. (The estimate is tentative because the test might overlap with the irrelevant portion of the laboratory measure.) The saturation seems to lie between 36 and 84 per cent; a cumulation of studies would provide better limits.

It should be particularly noted that rejecting the null hypothesis does not finish the job of construct validation (35, p. 284). The problem is not to conclude that the test "is valid" for measuring the construct variable. The task is to state as definitely as possible the degree of validity the test is presumed to have.

The Logic of Construct Validation

Construct validation takes place when an investigator believes that his instrument reflects a particular construct, to which are attached certain meanings. The proposed interpretation generates specific testable hypotheses, which are a means of confirming or disconfirming the claim. The philosophy of science which we believe does most justice to actual scientific practice will now be briefly and dogmatically set forth. Readers interested in further study of the philosophical underpinning are referred to the works by Braithwaite (6, especially Chapter III), Carnap (7; 8, pp. 56–69), Pap (51), Sellars (55, 56), Feigl (19, 20), Beck (4), Kneale (37, pp. 92–110), Hempel (29; 30, Sec. 7).

The Nomological Net

The fundamental principles are these:

1. Scientifically speaking, to "make clear what something *is*" means to set forth the laws in which it occurs. We shall refer to the interlocking system of laws which constitute a theory as a *nomological network*.

2. The laws in a nomological network may relate (*a*) observable properties or quantities to each other; or (*b*) theoretical constructs to observables; or (*c*) different theoretical constructs to one another. These "laws" may be statistical or deterministic.

3. A necessary condition for a construct to be scientifically admissible is that it occur in a nomological net, at least *some* of whose laws involve observables. Admissible constructs may be remote from observation, i.e., a long derivation may intervene between the nomologicals which implicitly define the construct, and the (derived) nomologicals of type *a*. These latter propositions permit predictions about events. The construct is not "reduced" to the observations, but only combined with other constructs in the net to make predictions about observables.

4. "Learning more about" a theoretical construct is a matter of elaborating the nomological network in which it occurs, or of increasing the definiteness of the components. At least in the early history of a construct the network will be limited, and the construct will as yet have few connections.

5. An enrichment of the net such as adding a construct or a relation to theory is justified if it generates nomologicals that are confirmed by observation or if it reduces the number of nomologicals required to predict the same observations. When observations will not fit into the network as it stands, the scientist has a certain freedom in selecting where to modify the network. That is, there may be alternative constructs or ways of organizing the net which for the time being are equally defensible.

6. We can say that "operations" which are qualitatively very different "overlap" or "measure the same thing" if their positions in the nomological net tie them to the same construct variable. Our confidence in this identification depends upon the amount of inductive support we have for the regions of the net involved. It is not necessary that a direct observational comparison of the two operations be made — we may be content with an intranetwork proof indicating that the two operations yield estimates of the same network-defined quantity. Thus, physicists are content to speak of the "temperature" of the sun and the "temperature" of a gas at room temperature even though the test operations are nonoverlapping because this identification makes theoretical sense.

With these statements of scientific methodology in mind, we return to the specific problem of construct validity as applied to psychological tests. The preceding guide rules should reassure the "toughminded," who fear that allowing construct validation opens the door to nonconfirmable test claims. *The answer is that unless the network makes contact with observations, and exhibits explicit, public steps of inference, construct validation cannot be claimed.* An admissible psychological construct must be behavior-relevant (59, p. 15). For most tests intended to measure constructs, adequate criteria do not exist. This being the case, many such tests have been left unvalidated, or a finespun network of rationalizations has been offered as if it were validation. Rationalization is not construct validation. One who claims that his test reflects a construct cannot maintain his claim in the face of recurrent negative results because these results show that his construct is too loosely defined to yield verifiable inferences.

A rigorous (though perhaps probabilistic) chain of inference is required to establish a test as a measure of a construct. To validate a claim that a test measures a construct, a nomological net surrounding the concept must exist.

When a construct is fairly new, there may be few specifiable associations by which to pin down the concept. As research proceeds, the construct sends out roots in many directions, which attach it to more and more facts or other constructs. Thus the electron has more accepted properties than the neutrino; *numerical ability* has more than *the second space factor*.

"Acceptance," which was critical in criterion-oriented and content validities, has now appeared in construct validity. Unless substantially the same nomological net is accepted by the several users of the construct, public validation is impossible. If A uses *aggressiveness* to mean overt assault on others, and B's usage includes repressed hostile reactions, evidence which convinces B that a test measures *aggressiveness* convinces A that the test does not. Hence, the investigator who proposes to establish a test as a measure of a construct must specify his network or theory sufficiently clearly that others can accept or reject it (cf. 41, p. 406). A consumer of the test who rejects the author's theory cannot accept the author's validation. He must validate the test for himself, if he wishes to show that it represents the construct as *he* defines it.

Two general qualifications are in order with reference to the methodological principles 1–6 set forth at the beginning of this section. Both of them concern the amount of "theory," in any high-level sense of that word, which enters into a construct-defining network of laws or lawlike statements. We do not wish to convey the impression that one always has a very elaborate theoretical network, rich in hypothetical processes or entities.

Constructs As Inductive Summaries. In the early stages of development of a construct or even at more advanced stages when our orientation is thoroughly practical, little or no theory in the usual sense of the word need be involved. In the extreme case the hypothesized laws are formulated entirely in terms of descriptive (observational) dimensions although not all of the relevant observations have actually been made.

The hypothesized network "goes beyond the data" only in the limited sense that it purports to *characterize* the behavior facets which belong to an observable but as yet only partially sampled cluster; hence, it generates predictions about hitherto unsampled regions of the phenotypic space. Even though no unobservables or high-order theoretical constructs are introduced, an element of inductive extrapolation appears in the claim that a cluster including some elements not-yet-observed has been identified. Since, as in any sorting or abstracting task involving a finite set of complex elements, several nonequivalent bases of categorization are available, the investigator may choose a hypothesis which generates erroneous predictions. The failure of a supposed, hitherto untried, member of the cluster to behave in the manner said to be characteristic of the group, or the finding that a nonmember of the postulated cluster does behave in this manner, may modify greatly our tentative construct.

For example, one might build an intelligence test on the basis of his background notions of "intellect," including vocabulary, arithmetic calculation, general information, similarities, two-point threshold, reaction time, and line bisection as subtests. The first four of these correlate, and he extracts a huge first factor. This becomes a second approximation of the intelligence construct, described by its pattern of loadings on the four tests. The other three tests have negligible loading on any common factor. On this evidence the investigator reinterprets intelligence as "manipulation of words." Subsequently it is discovered that test-stupid people are rated as unable to express their ideas, are easily taken in by fallacious arguments, and misread complex directions. These data support the "linguistic" definition of intelligence and the test's claim of validity *for* that construct. But then a block design test with pantomime instructions is found to be strongly saturated with the first factor. Immediately the purely "linguistic" interpretation of Factor I becomes suspect. This finding, taken together with our initial acceptance of the others as relevant to the background concept of intelligence, forces us to reinterpret the concept once again.

If we simply *list* the tests or traits which have been shown to be saturated with the "factor" or which belong to the cluster, no construct is employed. As soon as we even *summarize the properties* of this group of indicators — we are already making some guesses. Intensional characterization of a domain is hazardous since it selects (abstracts) properties and implies that new tests sharing those properties will behave as do the known tests in the cluster, and that tests not sharing them will not.

The difficulties in merely "characterizing the surface cluster" are strikingly exhibited by the use of certain special and extreme groups for purposes of construct validation. The P_d scale of MMPI was originally derived and cross-validated upon hospitalized patients diagnosed "Psychopathic personality, asocial and amoral type" (42). Further research shows the scale to have a limited degree of predictive and concurrent validity for "delinquency" more broadly defined (5, 28). Several studies show associations between P_d and very special "criterion" groups which it would be ludicrous to identify as "*the* criterion" in the traditional sense. If one lists these heterogeneous groups and tries to characterize them intensionally, he faces enormous conceptual difficulties. For example, a recent survey of hunting accidents in Minnesota showed that hunters who had "carelessly" shot someone were significantly elevated on P_d when compared with other hunters (48). This is in line with one's theoretical expectations; when you ask MMPI "experts" to predict for such a group they invariably predict P_d or M_a or both. The finding seems therefore to lend some slight support to the construct validity of the P_d scale. But of course it would be nonsense to *define* the P_d component "operationally" in terms of, say, accident proneness. We might try to subsume the original phenotype and the hunting-accident proneness under some broader category, such as "Disposition to violate society's rules, whether legal, moral, or just *sensible*." But now we have ceased to have a neat operational criterion, and are using instead a rather vague and wide-range class. Besides, there is worse to come. We want the class specification to cover a group trend that (nondelinquent) high school students judged by their peer group as least "responsible" score over a full sigma higher on P_d than those judged most "responsible" (23, p. 75). Most of the behaviors contributing to such sociometric choices fall well within the range of socially permissible action; the proffered criterion specification is still too restrictive. Again, any clinician familiar with MMPI lore would predict an elevated P_d on a sample of (non-delinquent) professional actors. Chyatte's confirmation of this prediction (10) tends to support *both:* (*a*) the theory sketch of "what the P_d factor is, psychologically"; and (*b*) the claim of the P_d scale to construct validity for this hypothetical factor. Let the reader try his hand at writing a brief phenotypic criterion specification that will cover both trigger-happy hunters and Broadway actors! And if he should be ingenious enough to achieve this, does his definition also encompass Hovey's report that high P_d predicts the judgments "not shy" and "unafraid of mental patients" made upon nurses by their supervisors (32, p. 143)? And then we have Gough's report that *low P_d* is associated with ratings as "good-natured" (24, p. 40), and Roessell's data showing that high P_d is predictive of "dropping out of high school" (54). The point is that all seven of these "criterion" dispositions would be readily guessed by any clinician having even superficial familiarity with MMPI interpretation; but to mediate these inferences explicitly requires quite a few hypotheses about dynamics, constituting an admittedly sketchy (but far from vacuous) network defining the genotype *psychopathic deviate.*

Vagueness of Present Psychological Laws. This line of thought leads directly to our second important qualification upon the network schema. The idealized picture is one of a tidy set of postulates which jointly entail the desired theorems; since some of the theorems are coordinated to the observation base, the system constitutes an implicit definition of the theoretical primitives and gives them an indirect empirical meaning. In practice, of course, even the most advanced physical sciences only approximate this ideal. Questions of "categoricalness" and the like, such as logicians raise about pure calculi, are hardly even statable for empirical networks. (What, for example, would be the desiderata of a "well-formed formula" in molar behavior theory?) Psychology works with crude, half-explicit formulations. We do not worry about such advanced formal questions as "whether all molar-behavior statements are decidable by appeal to the postulates" because we know that no existing theoretical network suffices to predict even the *known* descriptive laws. Nevertheless, the sketch of a network is there; if it were not, we would not be saying *anything* intelligible about our constructs. We do not have the rigorous implicit definitions of formal calculi (which still, be it noted, usually permit of a multiplicity of interpretations). Yet the vague, avowedly incomplete network still gives the constructs whatever meaning they do have. When the network is very incomplete, having many strands missing entirely and some constructs tied in only by tenuous threads, then the "implicit definition" of these constructs is disturbingly loose; one might say that the meaning of the constructs is undetermined. *Since the meaning of theoretical constructs is set forth by stating the laws in which they occur, our incomplete knowledge of the laws of nature produces a vagueness in our constructs* (see Hempel, 30, Kaplan, 34; Pap, 51). We will be able to say "what anxiety is" when we know all of the laws involving it; meanwhile, since we are in the process of discovering these laws, we do not yet know precisely what anxiety is.

Conclusions Regarding the Network After Experimentation

The proposition that x per cent of test variance is accounted for by the construct is inserted into the accepted network. The network then generates a testable prediction about the relation of the test scores to certain other variables, and the investigator gathers data. If prediction and result are in harmony, he can retain his belief that the test measures the construct. The construct is at best adopted, never demonstrated to be "correct."

We do not first "prove" the theory, and then validate the test, nor conversely. In any probable inductive type of inference from a pattern of observations, we examine the relation between the total network of theory and observations. The system involves propositions relating test to construct, construct to other constructs, and finally relating some of these constructs to observables. In ongoing research the chain of inference is very complicated. Kelly and Fiske (36, p. 124) give a complex diagram showing the numerous inferences required in validating a prediction from assessment techniques, where theories about the criterion situation are as integral a part of the prediction as are the test data. A predicted empirical relationship permits us to test all the propositions leading to that prediction. Traditionally the proposition claiming to interpret the test has been set apart as the hypothesis being tested, but actually the evidence is significant for all parts of the chain. If the prediction is not confirmed, any link in the chain may be wrong.

A theoretical network can be divided into subtheories used in making particular predictions. All the events successfully predicted through a subtheory are of course evidence in favor of that theory. Such a subtheory may be so well confirmed by voluminous and diverse evidence that we can reasonably view a particular experiment as relevant only to the test's validity. If the theory, combined with a proposed test interpretation, mispredicts in this case, it is the latter which must be abandoned. On the other hand, the accumulated evidence for a test's construct validity may be so strong that an instance of misprediction will force us to modify the subtheory employing the construct rather than deny the claim that the test measures the construct.

Most cases in psychology today lie somewhere between these extremes. Thus, suppose we fail to find a greater incidence of "homosexual signs" in the Rorschach records of paranoid patients. Which is more strongly disconfirmed — the Rorschach signs or the orthodox theory of paranoia? The negative finding shows the bridge between the two to be undependable, but this is all we can say. The bridge cannot be used unless one end is placed on solider ground. The investigator must decide which end it is best to relocate.

Numerous successful predictions dealing with phenotypically diverse "criteria" give greater weight to the claim of construct validity than do fewer predictions, or predictions involving very similar behaviors. In arriving at diverse predictions, the hypothesis of test validity is connected each time to a subnetwork largely independent of the portion previously used. Success of these derivations testifies to the inductive power of the test-validity statement, and renders it unlikely that an equally effective alternative can be offered.

Implications of Negative Evidence

The investigator whose prediction and data are discordant must make strategic decisions. His result can be interpreted in three ways:
1. The test does not measure the construct variable.
2. The theoretical network which generated the hypothesis is incorrect.
3. The experimental design failed to test the hypothesis properly. (Strictly speaking this may be analyzed as a special case of 2, but in practice the distinction is worth making.)

For Further Research. If a specific fault of procedure makes the third a reasonable possibility, his proper response is to perform an adequate study, meanwhile making no report. When faced with the other two alternatives, he may decide that his test does not measure the construct adequately. Following that decision, he will perhaps prepare and validate a new test. Any rescoring or new interpretative procedure for the original instrument, like a new test, requires validation by *means of a fresh body of data*.

The investigator may regard interpretation 2 as more likely to lead to eventual advances. It is legitimate for the investigator to call the network defining the construct into question, if he has confidence in the test. Should the investigator decide that some step in the network is unsound, he may be able to invent an alternative network. Perhaps he modifies the network by splitting a concept into two or more portions, e.g., by designating types of *anxiety*, or perhaps he specifies added conditions under which a generalization holds. When an investigator modifies the theory in such a manner, he is now required to *gather a fresh body of data* to test the altered hypotheses. This step should normally precede publication of the modified theory. If the new data are consistent with the modified network, he is free from the fear that his nomologicals were gerrymandered to fit the peculiarities of his first sample of observations. He can now trust his test to some extent, because his test results behave as predicted.

The choice among alternatives, like any strategic decision, is a gamble as to which course of action is the best investment of effort. Is it wise to modify the theory? That depends on how well the system is confirmed by prior data, and how well the modifications fit available observations. Is it worth while to modify the test in the hope that it will fit the construct? That depends on how much evidence there is — apart from this abortive experiment — to support the hope, and also on how much it is worth to the investigator's ego to salvage the test. The choice among alternatives is a matter of research planning.

For Practical Use of the Test. The consumer can accept a test as a measure of a construct only when there is a strong positive fit between predictions and subsequent data. When the evidence from a proper investigation of a published test is essentially negative, it should be reported as a stop sign to discourage use of the test pending a reconciliation of test and construct, or final abandonment of the test. If the test has not been published, it should be restricted to research use until some degree of validity is established (1). The consumer can await the results of the investigator's gamble with confidence that proper application of the scientific method will ultimately tell whether the test has value. Until the evidence is in, he has no justification for employing the test as a basis for terminal decisions. The test may serve, at best, only as a source of suggestions about individuals to be confirmed by other evidence (15, 47).

There are two perspectives in test validation. From the viewpoint of the psychological practitioner, the burden of proof is on the test. A test should not be used to measure a trait until its proponent establishes that predictions made from such measures are consistent with the best available theory of the trait. In the view of the test developer, however, both the test and the theory are under scrutiny. He is free to say *to himself privately*, "If my test disagrees with the theory, so much the worse for the theory." This way lies delusion, unless he continues his research using a better theory.

Reporting of Positive Results

The test developer who finds positive correspondence between his proposed interpretation and data is expected to report the basis for his validity claim. Defending a claim of construct validity is a major task, not to be satisfied by a discourse without data. The *Technical Recommendations* have little to say on reporting of construct validity. Indeed, the only detailed suggestions under that heading refer to correlations of the test with other measures, together with a cross reference to some other sections of the report. The two key principles, however, call for the most comprehensive type of reporting. The manual for any test "should report all available information which will assist the user in determining what psychological attributes account for variance in test scores" (59, p. 27). And, "The manual for a test which is used primarily to assess postulated attributes of the individual should outline the theory on which the test is based and organize whatever partial validity data there are to show in what way they support the theory" (59, p. 28). It is recognized, by a classification as "very desirable" rather than "essential," that the latter recommendation goes beyond present practice of test authors.

The proper goals in reporting construct validation are to make clear (*a*) what interpretation is proposed, (*b*) how adequately the writer believes this interpretation is substantiated, and (*c*) what evidence and reasoning lead him to this belief. Without *a* the construct validity of the test is of no use to the consumer. Without *b* the consumer must carry the entire burden of evaluating the test research. Without *c* the consumer or reviewer is being asked to take *a* and *b* on faith. The test manual cannot always present an exhaustive statement on these points, but it should summarize and indicate where complete statements may be found.

To specify the interpretation, the writer must state what construct he has in mind, and what meaning he gives to that construct. For a construct which has a short history and has built up few connotations, it will be fairly easy to indicate the presumed properties of the construct, i.e., the nomologicals in which it appears. For a construct with a longer history, a summary of properties and references to previous theoretical discussions may be appropriate. It is especially critical to distinguish proposed interpretations from other meanings previously given the same construct. The validator faces no small task; he must somehow communicate a theory to his reader.

To evaluate his evidence calls for a statement like the conclusions from a program of research, noting what is well substantiated and what alternative interpretations have been considered and rejected. The writer must note what portions of his proposed interpretation are speculations, extrapolations, or conclusions from insufficient data. The author has an ethical responsibility to prevent unsubstantiated interpretations from appearing as truths. A claim is unsubstantiated unless the evidence for the claim is public, so that other scientists may review the evidence, criticize the conclusions, and offer alternative interpretations.

The report of evidence in a test manual must be as complete as any research report, except where adequate public reports can be cited. Reference to something "observed by the writer in many clinical cases" is worthless as evidence. Full case reports, on the other hand, may be a valuable source of evidence so long as these cases are representative and negative instances receive due attention. The report of evidence must be interpreted with reference to the theoretical network in such a manner that the reader sees why the author regards a particular correlation or experiment as confirming (or throwing doubt upon) the proposed interpretation. Evidence collected by others must be taken fairly into account.

Validation of a Complex Test "As a Whole"

Special questions must be considered when we are investigating the validity of a test which is aimed to provide information about several constructs. In one sense, it is naive to inquire "Is this test valid?" One does not validate a test, but only a principle for making inferences. If a test yields many different types of inferences, some of them can be valid and others invalid (cf. Technical Recommendation C2: "The manual should report the validity of each type of inference for which a test is recommended"). From this point of view, every topic sentence in the typical book on Rorschach interpretation presents a hypothesis requiring validation, and one should validate inferences about each aspect of the personality separately and in turn, just as he would want information on the validity (concurrent or predictive) for each scale of MMPI.

There is, however, another defensible point of view. If a test is purely empirical, based strictly on observed connections between response to an item and some criterion, then of course the validity of one scoring key for the test does not make validation for its other scoring keys any less necessary. But a test may be developed on the basis of a theory which in itself provides a linkage between the various keys and the various criteria. Thus, while Strong's Vocational Interest Blank is developed empirically, it also rests on a "theory" that a youth can be expected to be satisfied in an occupation if he has interests common to men now happy in the occupation. When Strong finds that those with high Engineering interest scores in college are preponderantly in engineering careers 19 years later, he has partly validated the proposed use of the Engineer score (predictive validity). Since the evidence is consistent with the theory on which all the test keys were built, this evidence alone increases the presumption that the *other* keys have predictive validity. How strong is this presumption? Not very, from the viewpoint of the traditional skepticism of science. Engineering interests may stabilize early, while interests in art or management or social work are still unstable. A claim cannot be made that the whole Strong approach is valid just because one score shows predictive validity. But if thirty interest scores were investigated longitudinally and all of them showed the type of validity predicted by Strong's theory, we would indeed be caviling to say that this evidence gives no confidence in the long-range validity of the thirty-first score.

Confidence in a theory is increased as more relevant evidence confirms it, but it is always possible that tomorrow's investigation will render the theory obsolete. The Technical Recommendations suggest a rule of reason, and ask for evidence for each *type* of inference for which a test is recommended. It is stated that no test developer can present predictive validities for all possible criteria; similarly, no developer can run all possible experimental tests of his proposed interpretation. But the recommendation is more subtle than advice that a lot of validation is better than a little.

Consider the Rorschach test. It is used for many inferences, made by means of nomological networks at several levels. At a low level are the simple unrationalized correspondences presumed to exist between certain signs and psychiatric diagnoses. Validating such a sign does nothing to substantiate Rorschach theory. For other Rorschach formulas an explicit a priori rationale exists (for instance, high $F\%$ interpreted as implying rigid control of impulses). Each time such a sign shows correspondence with criteria, its rationale is supported just a little. At a still higher level of abstraction, a considerable body of theory surrounds the general area of *outer control*, interlacing many different constructs. As evidence cumulates, one should be able to decide what specific inference-making chains within this system can be depended upon. One should also be able to conclude — or deny — that so much of the system has stood up under test that one has some confidence in even the untested lines in the network.

In addition to relatively delimited nomological networks surrounding *control* or *aspiration*, the Rorschach interpreter usually has an overriding theory of the test as a whole. This may be a psychoanalytic theory, a theory of perception and set, or a theory stated in terms of learned habit patterns. Whatever the theory of the interpreter, whenever he validates an inference from the system, he obtains some reason for added confidence in his overriding system. His total theory is not tested, however, by experiments dealing with only one limited set of constructs. The test developer must investigate far-separated, independent sections of the network. The more diversified the predictions the system is required to make, the greater confidence we can have that only minor parts of the system will later prove faulty. Here we begin to glimpse a logic to defend the judgment that the test and its whole interpretative system is valid at some level of confidence.

There are enthusiasts who would conclude from the foregoing paragraphs that since there is some evidence of correct, diverse predictions made from the Rorschach, the test as a whole can now be accepted as validated. This conclusion overlooks the negative evidence. Just one finding contrary to expectation, based on sound research, is sufficient to wash a whole theoretical structure away. Perhaps the remains can be salvaged to form a new structure. But this structure now must be exposed to fresh risks, and sound negative evidence will destroy it in turn. There is sufficient negative evidence to prevent acceptance of the Rorschach and its accompanying interpretative structures as a whole. So long as any aspects of the overriding theory stated for the test have been disconfirmed, this structure must be rebuilt.

Talk of areas and structures may seem not to recognize those who would interpret the personality "globally." They may argue that a test is best validated in matching studies. Without going into detailed questions of matching methodology, we can ask whether such a study validates the nomological network "as a whole." The judge does employ some network in arriving at his conception of his subject, integrating specific inferences from specific data. Matching studies, if successful, demonstrate only that each judge's interpretative theory has some validity, that it is not completely a fantasy. Very high consistency between judges is required to show that they are using the same network, and very high success in matching is required to show that the network is dependable.

If inference is less than perfectly dependable, we must know which aspects of the interpretative network are least dependable and which are most dependable. Thus, even if one has considerable confidence in a test "as a whole" because of frequent successful inferences, one still returns as an ultimate aim to the request of the Technical Recommendation for separate evidence on the validity of each type of inference to be made.

RECAPITULATION

Construct validation was introduced in order to specify types of research required in developing tests for which the conventional views on validation are inappropriate. Personality tests, and some tests of ability, are interpreted in terms of attributes for which there is no adequate criterion. This paper indicates what sorts of evidence can substantiate such an interpretation, and how such evidence is to be interpreted. The following points made in the discussion are particularly significant.

1. A construct is defined implicitly by a network of associations or propositions in which it occurs. Constructs employed at different stages of research vary in definiteness.

2. Construct validation is possible only when some of the statements in the network lead to predicted relations among observables. While some observables may be regarded as "criteria," the construct validity of the criteria themselves is regarded as under investigation.

3. The network defining the construct, and the derivation leading to the predicted observation, must be reasonably explicit so that validating evidence may be properly interpreted.

4. Many types of evidence are relevant to construct validity, including content validity, interitem correlations, intertest correlations, test-"criterion" correlations, studies of stability over time, and stability under experimental intervention. High correlations and high stability may constitute either favorable or unfavorable evidence for the proposed interpretation, depending on the theory surrounding the construct.

5. When a predicted relation fails to occur, the fault may lie in the proposed interpretation of the test or in the network. Altering the network so that it can cope with the new observations is, in effect, redefining the construct. Any such new interpretation of the test must be validated by a fresh body of data before being advanced publicly. Great care is required to avoid substituting *a posteriori* rationalizations for proper validation.

6. Construct validity cannot generally be expressed in the form of a single simple coefficient. The data often permit one to establish upper and lower bounds for the proportion of test variance which can be attributed to the construct. The integration of diverse data into a proper interpretation cannot be an entirely quantitative process.

7. Constructs may vary in nature from those very close to "pure description" (involving little more than extrapolation of relations among observation-variables) to highly theoretical constructs involving hypothesized entities and processes, or making identifications with constructs of other sciences.

8. The investigation of a test's construct validity is not essentially different from the general scientific procedures for developing and confirming theories.

Without in the least *advocating* construct validity as preferable to the other three kinds (concurrent, predictive, content), we do believe it imperative that psychologists make a place for it in their methodological thinking, so that its rationale, its scientific legitimacy, and its dangers may become explicit and familiar. This would be preferable to the widespread current tendency to engage in what actually amounts to construct validation research and use of constructs in practical testing, while talking an "operational" methodology which, if adopted, would force research into a mold it does not fit.

References

1. American Psychological Association. *Ethical Standards of Psychologists*. Washington, D.C.: American Psychological Association, Inc., 1953.
2. Anastasi, Anne. "The Concept of Validity in the Interpretation of Test Scores," *Educational and Psychological Measurement*, 1950, 10, 67–78.

3. Bechtoldt, H. P. "Selection," in S. S. Stevens (ed.), *Handbook of Experimental Psychology*. New York: John Wiley & Sons, Inc., 1951, 1237–1267.

4. Beck, L. W. "Constructions and Inferred Entities," *Philosophy of Science*, 1950, 17. Reprinted in H. Feigl and M. Brodbeck (eds.), *Readings in the Philosophy of Science*. New York: Appleton-Century-Crofts, Inc., 1953, 368–381.

5. Blair, W. R. N. "A Comparative Study of Disciplinary Offenders and Non-offenders in the Canadian Army," *Canadian Journal of Psychology*, 1950, 4, 49–62.

6. Braithwaite, R. B. *Scientific Explanation*. Cambridge: Cambridge University Press, 1953.

7. Carnap, R. "Empiricism, Semantics, and Ontology," *Revue Internationale de Philosophie*, 1950, II, 20–40. Reprinted in P. P. Weiner (ed.), *Readings in the Philosophy of Science*, New York: Charles Scribner's Sons, 1953, 509–521.

8. ———. *Foundations of Logic and Mathematics*. International Encyclopedia of Unified Science, I, No. 3. Pages 56–69 reprinted as "The Interpretation of Physics," in H. Feigl and M. Brodbeck (eds.), *Readings in the Philosophy of Science*. New York: Appleton-Century-Crofts, Inc., 1953, 309–318.

9. Child, I. L. "Personality," *Annual Review of Psychology*, 1954, 5, 149–171.

10. Chyatte, C. "Psychological Characteristics of a Group of Professional Actors," *Occupations*, 1949, 27, 245–250.

11. Cronbach, L. J. *Essentials of Psychological Testing*. New York: Harper & Brothers, 1949.

12. ———. "Further Evidence on Response Sets and Test Design," *Educational and Psychological Measurement*, 1950, 10, 3–31.

13. ———. "Coefficient Alpha and the Internal Structure of Tests," *Psychometrika*, 1951, 16, 297–335.

14. ———. "Processes Affecting Scores on 'Understanding of Others' and 'Assumed Similarity,'" *Psychological Bulletin*, 1955, 52, 177–193.

15. ———. "The Counselor's Problems from the Perspective of Communication Theory," in Vivian H. Hewer (ed.), *New Perspectives in Counseling*. Minneapolis: University of Minnesota Press, 1955.

16. Cureton, E. E. "Validity," in E. F. Lindquist (ed.), *Educational Measurement*. Washington, D.C.: American Council on Education, 1950, 621–695.

17. Damrin, Dora E. "A Comparative Study of Information Derived from a Diagnostic Problem-Solving Test by Logical and Factorial Methods of Scoring." Unpublished Doctor's dissertation, University of Illinois, 1952.

18. Eysenck, H. J. "Criterion Analysis — An Application of the Hypothetico-Deductive Method in Factor Analysis," *Psychological Review*, 1950, 57, 38–53.

19. Feigl, H. "Existential Hypotheses," *Philosophy of Science*, 1950, 17, 35–62.

20. ———. "Confirmability and Confirmation," *Revue Internationale de Philosophie*, 1951, 5, 1–12. Reprinted in P. P. Weiner (ed.), *Readings in the Philosophy of Science*. New York: Charles Scribner's Sons, 1953, 522–530.

21. Gaylord, R. H. "Conceptual Consistency and Criterion Equivalence: A Dual Approach to Criterion Analysis." Unpublished manuscript (PRB Research Note No. 17). Copies obtainable from ASTIA-DSC, AD-21 440.

22. Goodenough, Florence L. *Mental Testing*. New York: Rinehart & Company, Inc., 1950.

23. Gough, H. G., McClosky, H., & Meehl, P. E. "A Personality Scale for Social Responsibility," *Journal of Abnormal and Social Psychology*, 1952, 47, 73–80.

24. Gough, H. G., McKee, M. G., and Yandell, R. J. "Adjective Check List Analyses of a Number of Selected Psychometric and Assessment Variables." Unpublished manuscript. Berkeley: IPAR, 1953.

25. Guilford, J. P. "New Standards for Test Evaluation," *Educational and Psychological Measurement*, 1946, 6, 427–439.

26. ———. "Factor Analysis in a Test-Development Program," *Psychological Review*, 1948, 55, 79–94.

27. Gulliksen, H. "Intrinsic Validity," *American Psychologist,* 1950, 5, 511–517.
28. Hathaway, S. R., and Monachesi, E. D. *Analyzing and Predicting Juvenile Delinquency With the MMPI.* Minneapolis: University of Minnesota Press, 1953.
29. Hempel, C. G. "Problems and Changes in the Empiricist Criterion of Meaning," *Revue Internationale de Philosophie,* 1950, 4, 41–63. Reprinted in L. Linsky, *Semantics and the Philosophy of Language.* Urbana: University of Illinois Press, 1952, 163–185.
30. ———. *Fundamentals of Concept Formation in Empirical Science.* Chicago: University of Chicago Press, 1952.
31. Horst, P. "The Prediction of Personal Adjustment," *Social Science Research Council Bulletin,* 1941, No. 48.
32. Hovey, H. B. "MMPI Profiles and Personality Characteristics," *Journal of Consulting Psychology,* 1953, 17, 142–146.
33. Jenkins, J. G. "Validity for What?" *Journal of Consulting Psychology,* 1946, 10, 93–98.
34. Kaplan, A. "Definition and Specification of Meaning," *Journal of Philosophy,* 1946, 43, 281–288.
35. Kelly, E. L. "Theory and Techniques of Assessment," *Annual Review of Psychology,* 1954, 5, 281–311.
36. Kelly, E. L., and Fiske, D. W. *The Prediction of Performance in Clinical Psychology.* Ann Arbor: University of Michigan Press, 1951.
37. Kneale, W. *Probability and Induction.* Oxford: Clarendon Press, 1949. Pages 92–110 reprinted as "Induction, Explanation, and Transcendent Hypotheses," in H. Feigl and M. Brodbeck (eds.), *Readings in the Philosophy of Science.* New York: Appleton-Century-Crofts, Inc., 1953, 353–367.
38. Lindquist, E. F. *Educational Measurement.* Washington, D.C.: American Council on Education, 1950.
39. Lucas, C. M. "Analysis of the Relative Movement Test by a Method of Individual Interviews," *Bureau of Naval Personnel Research Report,* Contract Nonr-694 (00), NR 151–13, Educational Testing Service, March 1953.
40. MacCorquodale, K., and Meehl, P. E. "On a Distinction Between Hypothetical Constructs and Intervening Variables," *Psychological Review,* 1948, 55, 95–107.
41. Macfarlane, Jean W. "Problems of Validation Inherent in Projective Methods," *American Journal of Orthopsychiatry,* 1942, 12, 405–410.
42. McKinley, J. C., and Hathaway, S. R. "The MMPI: V. Hysteria Hypomania, and Psychopathic Deviate," *Journal of Applied Psychology,* 1944, 28, 153–174.
43. McKinley, J. C., Hathaway, S. R., and Meehl, P. E. "The MMPI: VI. The K Scale," *Journal of Consulting Psychology,* 1948, 12, 20–31.
44. Meehl, P. E. "A Simple Algebraic Development of Horst's Suppressor Variables," *American Journal of Psychology,* 1945, 58, 550–554.
45. ———. "An Investigation of a General Normality or Control Factor in Personality Testing," *Psychological Monographs,* 1945, 59, No. 4 (Whole No. 274).
46. ———. *Clinical vs. Statistical Prediction.* Minneapolis: University of Minnesota Press, 1954.
47. Meehl, P. E., and Rosen, A. "Antecedent Probability and the Efficiency of Psychometric Signs, Patterns or Cutting Scores," *Psychological Bulletin,* 1955, 52, 194–216.
48. *Minnesota Hunter Casualty Study.* St. Paul: Jacob Schmidt Brewing Company, 1954.
49. Mosier, C. I. "A Critical Examination of the Concepts of Face Validity," *Educational and Psychological Measurement,* 1947, 7, 191–205.
50. ———. "Problems and Designs of Cross-Validation," *ibid.,* 1951, 11, 5–12.
51. Pap, A. "Reduction-Sentences and Open Concepts," *Methodos,* 1953, 5, 3–30.
52. Peak, Helen. "Problems of Objective Observation," in L. Festinger and D. Katz (eds.), *Research Methods in the Behavioral Sciences.* New York: Dryden Press, 1953, 243–300.
53. Porteus, S. D. *The Porteus Maze Test and Intelligence.* Palo Alto: Pacific Books, 1950.

54. Roessel, F. P. "MMPI Results for High School Drop-outs and Graduates." Unpublished Doctor's dissertation, University of Minnesota, 1954.
55. Sellars, W. S. "Concepts as Involving Laws and Inconceivable Without Them," *Philosophy of Science*, 1948, 15, 287–315.
56. ———. "Some Reflections on Language Games," *ibid.*, 1954, 21, 204–228.
57. Spiker, C. C., and McCandless, B. R. "The Concept of Intelligence and the Philosophy of Science," *Psychological Review*, 1954, 61, 265–267.
58. "Technical Recommendations for Psychological Tests and Diagnostic Techniques: Preliminary Proposal," *American Psychologist*, 1952, 7, 461–476.
59. "Technical Recommendations for Psychological Tests and Diagnostic Techniques," *Psychological Bulletin Supplement*, 1954, 51, 2, Part 2, 1–38.
60. Thurstone, L. L. "The Criterion Problem in Personality Research," *Psychometric Laboratory Report*, No. 78. Chicago: University of Chicago, 1952.

9

Obtaining and Reporting
Evidence on Content Validity[1]

Robert L. Ebel

A principal measuring tool of the educator is the achievement test, a type of test that rests on content validity for its adequacy. As the reader explores the ideas presented by Ebel, he may well profit from a perusal of several achievement test manuals to see to what extent Ebel's procedures have been acknowledged by test publishers.

THE CONCEPT OF CONTENT VALIDITY

In dealing with the complex problems of validity, test specialists (4) have found it convenient to designate four different types: content validity, concurrent validity, predictive validity, and construct validity. The main concern of this paper is with content validity. The other types will be discussed only as they relate to content validity.

From Robert L. Ebel, "Obtaining and Reporting Evidence on Content Validity," *Educational and Psychological Measurement*, XVI (Summer, 1956), pp. 269–282. Reprinted with the permission of publisher and author.

[1] Contribution to a symposium on "Content Validity of Non-factual Tests," American Psychological Association, San Francisco, September, 1955.

It is often said that an educational achievement test possesses content validity to the degree that it samples adequately some clearly specified universe of educational content. This statement lends itself to a common and rather serious misinterpretation. It suggests that the validity of a test is to be judged in terms of its relevance to the *materials* of instruction, rather than the *ultimate objectives* of instruction. But the validity of an educational achievement test cannot be judged solely, or even principally, in terms of its sampling of the subject matter of a course. Only when the "content" of education is conceived as a set of goals to be attained, rather than as a set of lessons to be studied, or as a set of class activities to be carried out, is it educationally useful to seek content validity in a test.

An educational achievement test is one designed to measure the extent of attainment of the ultimate goals of instruction in a particular area by the individuals in a particular group. In passing judgment on the content validity of an educational achievement test one asks, "To what extent does this test require demonstration by the student of the achievements which constitute the objectives of instruction in this area?" The more directly, completely, and reliably a test measures the attainment of these goals the greater is its content validity.

There is a common and widespread tendency on the part of both teachers and pupils to place primary emphasis on "covering" the subject matter and remembering the materials of instruction, rather than on achieving the objectives of that instruction, i.e., developing abilities for more effective behavior. No subject has ever been introduced into the curriculum that was not, in the first instance, designed to enable those who studied it to behave more effectively. But teaching procedures are habit forming. The transmission of learning from teachers to scholars, who in their turn become the teachers of other scholars, tends to shift attention away from the ends of instruction, and to focus it on the means.

OPERATIONAL DEFINITIONS OF GOALS

When tests are derived directly from desired behavioral goals the tests constitute operational definitions of those goals. Such tests are sometimes called "self-defining" tests. This term seems unfortunate, since it suggests that the contents of the test are immune from criticism. A test does not define itself. It defines an educational achievement, and some definitions of that achievement are likely to be more soundly based, or more rational, than others.

Three objections have been raised to the statement that achievement tests constitute operational definitions of the goals of achievement. The first is that not all of the ultimate goals of education can be measured effectively in a test situation. This is true, and ought to be recognized frankly. An achievement test provides an operational definition of only those goals whose achievement can be observed in test situations. Operational definitions of other goals of achievement must be sought in non-test procedures appropriate for revealing the extent of their achievement.

A second objection is that, since any achievement test constitutes a sample of items from a much larger potential population of items, it provides a very incomplete definition of the goals of achievement. This also is true, but how serious a limitation it is depends on the complexity of the field to be covered by the test and the adequacy of sampling of items in the test. For measurement purposes the particular sample used does constitute the operational definition of achievement. For instructional purposes it is better to regard the hypothetical population of items, from which this particular sample is presumed to have been selected, as constituting a better operational definition of the goals of achievement.

A third objection is that each test constitutes a different operational definition of achievement. The existence of such a multiplicity of definitions, it is argued, is likely to contribute more to confusion than to clarity in thinking. Again there is some truth in this argument. However it discounts the very considerable areas of agreement in the definitions of the same achievement provided by different tests. Further, it implies that agreement on the goals of instruction can be purchased at the price of clarity in the definitions of those goals. This is certainly true, as many vague statements of educational goals attest, but it is a poor bargain. The use of achievement tests as operational definitions of the goals of achievement does not cause disagreements. It simply brings them to light. There is no better way to define many educational goals concretely than to construct tests of the achievement of them.

With these considerations in mind a more precise description of the concept of educational achievement tests as operational definitions of the goals of achievement may be stated. Any educational achievement test may be regarded as a sample of items from a hypothetical population of items which constitutes one operational definition of the testable goals of instruction in the area.

GOALS, CURRICULA AND TESTS

It is possible to conceive of a neat division of educational labor in which the educational philosopher defines the goals of education, the curriculum maker devises methods for attaining those goals, and the test constructor devises instruments to measure the extent to which they have been attained. But the problems of education are too complex, and our abilities to construct and communicate ideas too limited, to make this neat system workable. Each of the specialists needs not only to have his eye on what the other fellow is doing, but needs also to help him do it. This does not mean that education can do without specialists who are philosophers, curriculum builders or test constructors. What is does mean is that no one of these specialists can stake a claim to one field of operation and insist that all other specialists keep off.

Emphatic, even angry, words have been spoken from time to time concerning the harmful influences of tests on education and the evil influences of test makers on the curriculum. Certainly bad tests, or the improper use of good tests, can affect education adversely. Certainly any intended or accidental enforcement of uniformity in educational procedures through a wide scale testing program cannot be defended. But it is foolish to disregard, and it would be more foolish to abandon, the powerful forces for educational improvement that are available through proper use of good educational achievement tests.

Consider these alternative sequences in the development of an educational program.

First Sequence —
Step 1. Areas of agreement in desired behavior are identified.
Step 2. Curricula calculated to develop these desired behaviors are designed.
Step 3. Tests are constructed on the basis of the curricula to determine each student's degree of mastery of it.

Second Sequence —
Step 1. Areas of agreement in desired behavior are identified.
Step 2. These behaviors are translated, as directly and completely as possible, into an extended series of test problems.
Step 3. Curricula are designed to equip students to do as well as possible on problems like those presented in the test.

The first alternative is the one which is commonly followed. The second is equally sound from a logical point of view, and might well, in practice, prove to be more effective. It is easier to define desirable behavior in terms of test exercises than in terms of curricular procedures. The best of our current educational achievement tests have been derived, not indirectly from curricula, but directly from the ultimately desirable goals of behavior.

QUALITATIVE VS. QUANTITATIVE EVALUATION OF CONTENT VALIDITY

Validity is concerned with the relation between the information the user expects from a test, and the information actually supplied by it. There are two bases on which this relationship can be examined, qualitative and quantitative. In using the qualitative basis one asks how closely the behavior *apparently called for by the test* represents or indicates the desired behavior which constitutes the goal of instruction. At one extreme, a test of competence in shorthand may require behavior identical with the desired behavior. Such a test would be judged highly valid on a qualitative basis. At the other extreme is a test of honesty based on an analysis of handwriting. Since there appears [to be] no rational relationship between the behavior called for by the test and the desired behavior, such a test would be judged qualitatively to be low in validity.

Most users of educational achievement tests place considerable faith in the qualitative comparison of the behavior called for by a test with the behavioral goals of instruction. But this process is regarded with considerable mistrust by some specialists in psychological testing. Qualitative examination, they feel, involves personal and highly subjective judgments. Appearances may be deceiving, so that false relationships are accepted as true, and true relationships overlooked. Incidental relationships may be weighted heavily and more fundamental relationships neglected. These specialists discount the importance of content validity, arguing for a more objective, systematic, quantitative approach.

In using the quantitative approach, the behavior on the test is quantified in the form of a single score. The behavior which the test ought to measure is also quantified, preferably by observing the desired behavior directly and assigning precisely defined scores to various aspects of it. These scores are referred to as criterion scores. A correlation coefficient is then calculated to express the degree of relationship between the test scores and the criterion scores.

On the surface, but on the surface only, this quantitative approach appears to avoid some of the subjective difficulties involved in the qualitative approach. For even in the quantitative approach, the selection of acts of behavior to become part of the criterion measure, and the assignment of different score values to various manifestations of this behavior, involves the exercise of personal, subjective judgment. There are, in fact, added opportunities for error in the quantitative approach for it involves three steps instead of one. Test behavior must be quantified, desired behavior must be quantified, and the relation between the two must be examined. In the qualitative evaluation of a test, a single, direct comparison is made between test behavior and desired behavior.

The fundamental fact is that one cannot escape from the problem of content validity. If we dodge it in constructing the test, it raises its troublesome head when we seek a criterion. For when one attempts to evaluate the validity of a test indirectly, via some quantified criterion measure, he must use the very process he is trying to avoid in order to obtain the criterion measures.

RELATION OF CONTENT VALIDITY TO OTHER TYPES

The nature and importance of content validity may be made clearer by relating it to other types of validity. The degree of *content validity* of a test is a function of the directness, completeness, and reliability with which it measures attainment of the ultimate goals of instruction in a given area. The degree of *concurrent validity* of a test is a function of the correlation between scores on it and scores obtained from an alternative, presumably more valid but less convenient, measurement procedure, *and of the degree of content validity of the alternative procedure.* The degree of *predictive validity* of a test for a given group is a function of the correlation between scores on the test and future measures of the status to be predicted, *and of the content validity of future measures of status.* The degree of *construct validity* of a test is the extent to which a system of hypothetical relationships can be verified on the basis of measures of the construct derived from the test (1). But this system of relationships always involves measures of observed behavior *which must be defended on the basis of their content validity.* In every case quantitative validation builds on qualitative validation. Statistical validation is not an alternative to subjective validation, but an extension of it. All statistical procedures for validating tests are based ultimately upon common sense agreement concerning what is being measured by a particular measurement process.

OBTAINING EVIDENCE OF CONTENT VALIDITY

The simplest and most direct evidence of content validity is obtained from examination of the test itself by a competent judge. A cursory inspection, skimming the test, is better than no inspection at all. But if the judge is seriously interested in determining the relationship between what the test asks an examinee to do and what the typical user expects of a test of that sort, he should take the test himself, just as a student would do. Only by this means can he give sufficiently close, careful attention to the individual items of the test.

It is true that the judge may not always respond to the items on exactly the same basis as a typical examinee would, and thus may misjudge what a particular item measures. But this does not mean that his judgments of what the test as a whole is measuring are completely untrustworthy. It simply means that he must be competent and work carefully, and that he should, if possible, check his interpretations against those of other competent judges or typical examinees.

To obtain a summary view of test content it is often helpful to classify the items in broad areas of subject matter and student ability. Areas of content will vary from test to test, of course. In straight subject examinations these areas will ordinarily follow the customary divisions of the subject, as shown in representative text books. Even in skills examinations such as reading comprehension the items may be regarded as belonging to different areas of content. Some of the reading passages may be historical, others scientific, others literary prose, and still others poetry.

TYPES OF ABILITY MEASURED

Equally important in judging the content validity of a test is the distribution of items with respect to the types of ability or achievement they require. Many of the items found in educational achievement tests can be classified in one or more of the following broad categories: content detail, vocabulary, fact, generalization, understanding, and application. A *content detail* item is one of no significance outside the classroom. Its function is to indicate that the examinee has or has not done some particular learning exercise. A *vocabulary* item is one which requires essentially knowledge of the meaning of a particular term for successful response. A *factual* item is one dealing with an isolated bit of information, frequently a *Who? What? When?* or *Where?* type of item. A *generalization* item is one dealing with a law, principle, general summary or basic method of procedure. An *understanding* item is one beginning with the word "Why?", or calling for completions beginning with the word "because." An *application* item is one which presents a problem to be solved, a decision to be given, or a recommendation to be made, in terms of some specifically described situation. Items are classified in these categories, not on the basis of assumed psychological functions involved, but in terms of overt characteristics of the items. While it is seldom possible to classify all of the items in the test with complete confidence that they have been properly classified, the over-all process usually gives a good indication of the emphasis found in the test.

It is sometimes argued that differences in the type of ability called for by a test item are relatively unimportant. A test of factual knowledge was shown in one study to rank pupils in nearly the same order as a test of their problem solving ability. Other studies have given a contrary indication. Much appears to depend on the character of the previous teaching. If applications *are not* stressed, pupils may do much better in a test over factual details than on a test involving applications. If applications *are* stressed, pupils may do equally well on both, since factual knowledge is prerequisite to effective application. Failure to find significant differences in the ranking of a particular group of pupils on different types of test items cannot be accepted as conclusive evidence that the items are measuring identical achievements. In the long run tests which emphasize primarily factual information will tend to direct teaching and learning to the acquisition of factual knowledge. Unless it can be shown, which it has not been and is not likely to be, that pupils who possess factual knowledge can, without further emphasis or training, achieve desired understanding and make desired applications, emphasis on understanding and applications will be essential in both teaching and testing.

Within both subject matter and pupil ability classifications either important or unimportant questions can be asked. The content validity of a test depends on the significance or importance of the questions asked, and on the appropriateness of the balance among various subject matter and pupil ability categories. It depends also on the quality of the items themselves. Are they clearly expressed? Is the intended correct answer an adequate answer? Are the distractors plausible, yet not sufficiently defensible to attract many good students? Is the item as a whole of appropriate difficulty?

The User as a Judge of Content Validity

The content validity of a test depends not only on the characteristics of the test itself, but also on the purposes and needs of the user. A test of achievement in first year high school algebra can be regarded as a generally valid test only to the extent that it measures what good algebra teachers try to teach. It is inevitable that the aims and values of different teachers will differ. It is also obvious that greater weight should be attached to the judgments of certain individuals than to those of others. But it is beyond question that a competent teacher or administrator, clearly aware of appropriate educational goals and familiar with the functions and limitations of various test procedures, can obtain direct evidence concerning the content validity of a test by careful examination of the test itself. Other types of evidence may be useful in judging content validity, but none is more fundamental.

Evidence from the Test Manual

Evidence of content validity may sometimes be obtained by examining the test manual. If the manual presents the test outline, defines the universe of content sampled, summarizes the unique characteristics of the test, and calls attention to the principles guiding the authors and editors of the test in their selection of items, the manual can be extremely helpful in judging the content validity of the test. Since concrete information is more meaningful than abstract, actual items from the test should be used to illustrate the major classifications in the test outline.

In the development of a test, experts are sometimes asked to judge the relationship between the tasks required by the test and the desired behavioral goals. The number of judges used, their competence, and the process they use in evaluating the test help to determine the value of their contributions, and should be reported in the manual. Another factor of great importance, but one which is difficult to assess and report accurately, is the conscientiousness with which they undertook the task of evaluation. In the long run there probably would be greater incentives for the judges to assume responsibility for a careful job if their names were listed on the test booklet or in the manual.

The presentation in test manuals of detailed analysis of the content of a test has sometimes been criticized on the ground that this information tends to encourage teachers to "teach for the test." It cannot be denied that efforts to coach pupils to respond to specific test items is educationally harmful. But it is open to question that a test manual which outlines the contents of the test, or even which indicates the items that fall under each general heading, encourages this practice. Any misguided teacher who regards the final achievement test for her pupils as appropriate lesson material would not be likely to waste time on the manual. As a matter of fact, the manual, in calling attention to the broad categories of items from which the particular items have been drawn, should have the effect of generalizing instruction rather than making it more specific.

Validity and Reliability

Validity has two aspects, relevance and reliability (2). What has been said thus far about determining the content validity of a test has been concerned with determining its content relevance. To be valid a test must not only be closely related to the function it is used to measure, but it also must measure that something with reasonable precision. Internal analysis of the data obtained from a single administration of the test under typical conditions to a representative group of examinees can provide adequate evidence concerning the reliability of the test. If item analysis data has been obtained, one of the Kuder-Richardson formulas for reliability is usually most convenient to use. If not, the odds-even coefficient may be more convenient. Either will ordinarily provide quite adequate information on the reliability of the test.

When items are selected empirically on the basis of item analysis data from a particular sample, reliability coefficients should not be computed by rescoring the selected items on the same sample of papers. Nor should the originally obtained indices of discrimination and difficulty be reported as un-biased estimates of these parameters for the selected items. In all cases the reliability coefficient and final item characteristic data should be obtained from a cross-validation sample.

Item analysis data are ordinarily obtained by contrasting the performance of students who scored high on the test with those who scored low. It is pos-sible, and sometimes profitable, to use other sources for the contrasting groups. Two such independently defined groups were used in a recent study which required a test of the grasp of certain concepts in geography. Materials presenting and explaining these concepts were prepared and given to a small group of scholars whose ability to comprehend them was beyond question. Then the test was administered to these scholars. The test was also given to a group of students typical of those to be used later in the main experiment. These students had not had an opportunity to study the explanatory materials. Any item which was not answered correctly by all of the informed experts and which was not missed by all except a chance proportion of the unin-formed students was rejected.

In the construction of reading interpretation tests it should be more com-mon practice than it is to administer the test questions independent of the background material. Any item which can be answered correctly by a large proportion of students without reference to the background material can hardly be regarded as a valid test of comprehension of that material.

Reporting Evidence on Content Validity

What has been said thus far about obtaining evidence on the content validity of educational achievement tests carries with it in most cases obvious implications for reporting that evidence. Such evidence ought to be reported more fully than is the usual practice. The purpose for reporting this evidence is not to convince the test user that the test is valid. It is rather to help him judge whether or not the test is valid *for his purposes*. The validity of a test is relative to the user and his purposes, as well as to the nature of the group on which it is used.

Test developers can aid test users to judge the content validity of their tests by stating the criteria and principles which guided them in choosing item topics and in writing items, by presenting an outline of the achievements covered by the test, and by indicating which items are intended to measure each of the achievements outlined. They can also aid test users by presenting detailed data on the internal analysis of the test, recognizing that these analyses are likely to be somewhat specific to the population tested.

A form for reporting results of the analysis of classroom tests has been developed in the Examination Service at the State University of Iowa. This form provides for reporting a partial analysis of relevance, and a rather com-plete internal statistical analysis of the test. Arbitrary but not irrational standards have been worked out for each category in the analysis. These pro-vide useful bench marks for judging the validity of the test. A copy of the

Figure 1

TEST ANALYSIS REPORT

University Examinations Service   *State University of Iowa*

Test Title_____k = _____Job Number_____
Group Tested_____N = _____Date of Test_____
Time Limit_____Calculator_____Checker_____

Characteristic	Ideals		Observed	Rating
I. Relevance				
A. Content details		0%	_____	_____
B. Vocabulary	less than	20%	_____	_____
C. Facts	less than	20%	_____	_____
D. Generalizations	more than	10%	_____	_____
E. Understanding	more than	10%	_____	_____
F. Applications	more than	10%	_____	_____
II. Discrimination				
A. Item				
1. High (.41 and up)	more than	25%	_____	_____
2. Moderate (.21 to .40)	more than	25%	_____	_____
3. Low (.01 to .20)	less than	15%	_____	_____
4. Zero or Negative	less than	5%	_____	_____
B. Score				
1. Mean	(a)____		_____	_____
2. Standard Deviation	(b)____		_____	_____
3. Reliability	more than	.70	_____	_____
4. Probable Error			_____	
III. Speededness				
A. Percent of Complete Papers	more than 90%		_____	_____

(a) Midpoint of range between highest possible and expected chance score.
(b) One-sixth of range between highest possible and expected chance score.

analysis report form is presented as Figure 1. The use of this form was described in a previous article (3).

SUMMARY

This article has dealt mainly with eleven points of view.

1. That the content validity of a test is determined by its relevance to the objectives of instruction rather than by its coverage of the materials of instruction.

2. That good tests of educational achievement provide good operational definitions of the goals of instruction.

3. That tests based on educational goals directly can influence teaching procedures constructively.

4. That there is no essential difference between the rational judgments involved in determining the content relevance of a test and those involved in determining the adequacy of criterion scores.

5. That all types of validity are based ultimately on the content validity of some measurement procedures.

6. That the best evidence of content validity is obtained by detailed, systematic, critical inspection of the test itself.

7. That it is possible to analyze the types of achievement required by the items as well as the content covered by the items in judging content validity.

8. That the test user is more competent than anyone else to judge the relevance of the test to his purposes.

9. That presentation of detailed test specifications and outlines in the test manual helps the user judge its relevance to his purposes.

10. That data from internal analysis of test reliability and item discriminating power are helpful in judging content validity.

11. That evidence of content validity should be reported more fully than is usually true.

REFERENCES

1. Cronbach, Lee J., and Meehl, Paul E. "Construct Validity in Psychological Tests," *Psychological Bulletin*, LII (1955), 281–302.
2. Cureton, Edward E. "Validity," Chapter 16 in *Educational Measurement*. E. F. Lindquist (ed.). Washington, D.C.: American Council on Education, 1951.
3. Ebel, Robert L. "Procedures for the Analysis of Classroom Tests," *Educational and Psychological Measurement*, XIV (1954), 352–364.
4. *Technical Recommendations for Achievement Tests*. AERA and NCMUE Committee on Test Standards, American Educational Research Association, January 1955.

10

A Critical Examination
of the Concepts of Face Validity

Charles I. Mosier

No one selects a test for use sight-unseen. Yet one cannot help being influenced by the appearance of the content of a test, and at times this appearance may carry considerable weight in determining whether the test is chosen for use. Is face validity desirable or not? What are its limitations? Mosier's presentation should allow the student to put face validity in its proper place among the various procedures for validating tests.

Face validity is a term that is bandied about in the field of test construction until it seems about to become a part of accepted terminology. The frequency of its use and the emotional reaction which it arouses — ranging almost from contempt to highest approbation — make it desirable to examine its meaning more closely. When a single term variously conveys high praise or strong condemnation, one suspects either ambiguity of meaning or contradictory postulates among those using the term. The tendency has been, I believe, to assume unaccepted premises rather than ambiguity, and beautiful friendships have been jeopardized when a chance remark about face validity has classed the speaker among the infidels.

An examination of the ways in which the term "face validity" has been used indicates three frequent meanings. These are sufficiently similar as to be confused, yet so different in their implications that to understand one meaning where another was intended leads to a wholly erroneous interpretation. This paper will analyze the various meanings which have been attributed to the term and it will then recommend that the term (and one of its meanings as well) be banished to outer darkness.

The three meanings which have been attributed to the term may be characterized as: (1) validity by *assumption*, (2) validity by *definition*, and (3) the *appearance* as well as the reality of validity. A fourth concept, validity

From Charles I. Mosier, "A Critical Examination of the Concepts of Face Validity," *Educational and Psychological Measurement*, VII (Summer, 1947), pp. 191–205. Reprinted with the permission of the publisher.

by hypothesis, is closely related to the first two and deserves consideration in connection with them, although this concept has not generally been termed "face validity."

Validity by assumption: As used in this way, the term "face validity" carries the clear meaning that a test is assumed to be valid for the prediction of an external criterion if the items which compose it "appear on their face" to bear a common-sense relationship to the objective of the test. The assumption of validity in this case is asserted to be so strong that statistical evidence of validity is unnecessary; indeed, statistical evidence showing a lack of validity may be set aside by the strength of the assumption.

Validity by definition: For some tests, the objective is defined solely in terms of the population of questions from which the sample comprising the test was drawn, e.g., when the ability to handle the one hundred number facts of addition is tested by a sampling of those number facts. In these cases, the test is considered to be valid if the sample of items appears to the subject-matter expert to represent adequately the total universe of appropriate questions. The objective of the test is so defined that the index of reliability (the square root of the reliability coefficient) is, by definition, the measure of validity. This is so, because of a definition of validity, but because of the way the objective of the test is defined. This situation is the one for which the term "face validity" was apparently coined.

Appearance of validity: In this usage, the term "face validity" implies that a test which is to be used in a practical situation should, in addition to having pragmatic or statistical validity, appear practical, pertinent and related to the purpose of the test as well; i.e., it should not only *be* valid but it should *also appear* valid. This usage of the term assumes that "face validity" is not validity in any usual sense of the word but merely an additional attribute of the test which is highly desirable in certain situations.

Validity by hypothesis: This concept, not generally associated with the term "face validity," is nevertheless sufficiently related to validity by assumption and validity by definition as to call for analysis at this point. The term "validity by hypothesis" is used to characterize the following situation. Often, before the validity of a test can be empirically verified for a particular group by demonstration of its relationship to a satisfactory criterion, the test must be used to meet an immediate practical need. In such instances, the use of the test involves the hypothesis that it has a useful degree of validity. This hypothesis is based upon the designed similarity of the particular test to other tests already demonstrated to have known validity for the purpose in question. The validity of the test is not assumed in the sense that no further proof is required; neither is the objective of the test defined in such a way that the reliability of the test is evidence of its validity for the defined purpose. Rather the hypothesis is stated that, because of the sum total of previous knowledge relating to methods of predicting this particular criterion it is reasonable to suppose that a test of this sort will prove to be valid by the conventional statistical tests. This reasonable presumption, however, is subject to empirical verification by fact. Pending the opportunity for such verification, the presumption may be sufficiently strong as to justify the use of the test. Similarly, the physician studies the symptoms and the general condition of the patient and then, on the basis of his knowledge of the past effects of remedies upon similar symptoms in similar patients, prescribes treatment. He does this even though this combination of remedies has not occurred before in his experience and certainly not with this patient(who may have an unsuspected allergy which will defeat the purpose of the remedy).

With these four possible meanings of the term before us, it becomes profitable to examine each one in more detail.

VALIDITY BY ASSUMPTION

This conception of "face validity" is illustrated by the following quotations from a widely circulated testing handbook:

> Generally speaking, the validity of the test is best determined by using common sense in discovering that the test measures component abilities which exist both in the test situation and on the job. This common-sense approach to the problem of validity can be strengthened greatly by basing the estimate of the component of the job on a systematic observation of job analysis.

The term "face validity" is thus used to imply that the appearance of a relationship between the test and the external criterion is sufficient evidence of pragmatic validity. This use is a pernicious fallacy. This illegitimate usage has cast sufficient opprobrium on the term as to justify completely the recommendation that it be purged from the test technicians' vocabulary, even for its legitimate usage. The concept is the more dangerous because it is glib and comforting to those whose lack of time, resources, or competence prevent them from demonstrating validity (or invalidity) by any other method. Moreover, it is readily acceptable to the ordinary users of tests and its acceptance in these quarters lends the concept strength. This notion is also gratifying to the ego of the unwary test constructor. It implies that his knowledge and skill in the area of test construction are so great that he can unerringly design a test with the desired degree of effectiveness in predicting job success or in evaluating defined personality characteristics, and that he can do this so accurately that any further empirical verification is unnecessary. So strong is this ego complex that if statistical verification is sought and found lacking, the data represent something to be explained away by appeal to sampling errors or other convenient rationalization, rather than by scientific evidence which must be admitted into full consideration.

The concept of validity by assumption gains strength from the legitimate use of the term "face validity" to mean validity by definition. The superficial similarity, however, between the two concepts should not deceive us into accepting either the truth of the one or the necessary falsity of the other.

Any experienced test constructor can cite numerous instances of tests which appear so closely related to the external criterion that a high validity coefficient seems inevitable. The following example is to be considered merely one illustration which most readers can reproduce almost without limit from their own experience.

Two test construction agencies, each having a fairly large and competent staff, began work about the same time on an objective test to measure the clerical skills involved in alphabetical filing. Up to a certain point the two agencies worked independently, each devising its own test. Agency A, after an analysis of the job, constructed a test of which the following item is representative:

> Below are five names, in random order. If the names were placed in strict alphabetical order, which name would be *third:* (1) John Meeder; (2) James Medway; (3) Thomas Madow; (4) Catherine Meagan; (5) Eleanor Meehan.

The second agency designed a test of skill in alphabetical filing in which the task was as follows:

> In the following items you have one name which is underlined and four other names in alphabetical order. If you were to put the underlined name into the alphabetical series, indicate by the appropriate letter where it would go:
>
>   Robert Carstens
>
>   A._____
>   Richard Carreton
>   B._____
>   Roland Casstar
>   C._____
>   Jack Corson
>   D._____
>   Edward Cranston
>   E._____

There was a general agreement that each of these tests was face-valid and that each consisted of work-samples representative of the filing of alphabetical material. It was also agreed that if one were going to use two different tests to measure filing ability, it would be difficult to get two tests more closely similar than these and still have different tests. Had the concept of validity by assumption prevailed, there is little question that each test would have been considered highly valid.

An actual tryout, however, revealed quite different results from those expected. The correlation of the two tests in a sample of 43 clerical workers was .01, although the Kuder-Richardson reliabilities of the two tests were .81 and .98, respectively. We have here two tests which, on the basis of face validity by assumption, would be equally valid but which correlate substantially zero with one another. If one is valid, the other is not likely to be. What happens when the two tests are studied, not for their correlation with each other, but for their correlation with what seems to be a reasonable criterion, namely supervisors' ratings of speed and accuracy in filing? For 72 employed workers where accuracy of filing materials was an important part of the job, the correlation between the first of the two tests described and the supervisors' rating was .09.[1] For the second test the correlation with the supervisors' ratings of accuracy in alphabetizing was .00. (That these results cannot be attributed to the unreliability of the supervisors' ratings is indicated by correlation coefficients of .40 and above between the same ratings and scores on other tests.) These two examples, therefore, as well as those which the reader's experience will readily bring to bear, are sufficient to demonstrate the fallacy involved in the statement that a test can be assumed to be valid without further verification if only it "measures component abilities which are judged by common sense to exist both in it and in the job."

VALIDITY BY DEFINITION

The foregoing discussion has assumed an outside criterion measurable apart from the test itself. The discussion which follows is applicable rather to the situation, very frequent in educational measurement, in which the only available measure of the criterion (that which the test is intended to measure) is, because of the nature of the criterion, directly and intimately related to the test questions themselves. If the objective is the measurement of the pupils' skill in forming the elementary number combinations of addition, a test consisting of the one hundred possible combinations is presumably valid by definition. In this case the index of reliability can be taken as the validity coefficient. Even in this simple situation, the actual validity is limited by the reliability of the particular test, by the form in which the problems are presented, e.g., in words, in columns or in equations (e.g., four

plus two equals ———; $+\ 2$; $4 + 2 =$ ———), the arrangement of the items and by the conditions of administration. As soon, however, as the test is reduced from the totality of all situations which constitute the objective of measurement to a sample of those situations, the question recurs as to the extent to which the universe can be predicted from the sample. Moreover, it must be remembered that the relationship between test items and criterion behavior requires careful scrutiny. It is quite possible to design a test which apparently depends on the ability to perform the indicated additions, but is at the same time so dependent on verbal facility in understanding the directions, on speed of reaction, and on coding skills needed to record the answers, that the similarity between test situation and criterion situation is more apparent than real.

A further point which must be remembered in interpreting validity by definition is that it is frequently possible to establish several definitions of the criterion behavior, each obviously valid and yet each bearing far less than perfect relationship to the other. In the investigation of spelling ability, one obviously valid criterion of ability to spell might be the number of words correctly spelled from dictation. Should the words be dictated singly or in sentences, in a Brooklyn, Mobile, or Chicago accent? Another criterion

---

[1] The test did, however, show substantial correlation with other clerical skills and hence was useful in a general clerical battery, though not for its "face-valid" objective.

which might be used, however, is a count of the number of words misspelled in compositions written by the pupils. Either of these criteria is, upon its face, a valid reflection of spelling ability. Nevertheless, empirical investigation is unlikely to show a perfect correlation between dictation and correct spelling in compositions, even after correction for attenuation. Which universe should be sampled to provide a face-valid test of spelling?

Finally, in the validation of a test by definition, it must be remembered that *the direction of the argument flows from the test to the definition of the criterion* rather than from the conceptually defined criterion to the test as a valid measure. The only proper statement which can be made about a test in terms of face validity by definition is that this test is a valid measure of that and only that universe of individual behavior patterns for which these items constitute a representative sample. If one is prepared to infer such a universe and consider *that* universe rather than one defined in any other way, such a concept of validity may be useful. The necessity for inferring the conceptual nature of the universe from an examination of the sample still exists as a judgmental process and as one which is peculiarly subject to error.

If we return to the example of the two alphabetizing tests given in the section above we see how readily one may be misled into generalizing beyond the nature of the facts given. It is not difficult to draw the conclusion, from an inspection of the items, that these two tests were representative of the same universe and that therefore either test is a valid measure of the same set of skills. The fallacy of the conclusion, however, is attested by the absence of correlation between the two tests as cited above.

In educational achievement tests it is possible to outline the concepts to be covered in a particular course of study. These concepts may be sampled so systematically and so comprehensively that we are prepared to say the test questions constitute an adequate representation of all of the questions which might be asked on this course, in the light of its content and stated objectives. Even so, the questions may be so formulated that the crucial skills for achieving a high score on the examination are quite different from a knowledge of course content and the achievement of the stated objectives. We are correct in saying that the test is a valid measure of "whatever it measures reliably." We may be far from correct in inferring that the hypostatized "whatever" is what it appears to be on the face of the test. Nevertheless if we rely on validity by definition, we face the obligation of defining that "whatever" in some meaningful terms without running into the pitfall of *assuming* that the "whatever" is synonymous with the test constructor's objective in preparing the test.

As we examine critically the distinction between validity by assumption and validity by definition, we are led to see how tenuous is the dividing line between the scientifically defensible use, "validity by definition," and the totally unscientific and indefensible use, "validity by assumption."

Moreover, we do not escape the dilemma by refusing to recognize anything except external criteria. The validity of the external criterion is just as much open to question as is the validity of the test which is being checked against it. Consider the situation in which a test purporting to measure clerical aptitude is "validated" by correlating test scores with salary (where salary is presumed to reflect the level of duties and responsibilities assigned). A high correlation between test score and salary level might well be taken, however, not as validation of the test but as validation of the agency's promotional system and an indication of the effectiveness with which the placement office had sought out and recommended for promotion the employees with the highest level of knowledge and skill. As Toops has pointed out, the criterion is a complex and elusive concept (1). This paper is not the place for a systematic analysis of the nature of the criterion. It suffices to point out here that it is frequently possible to define in verbal, as distinct from operational, terms a criterion which is a socially significant independent measure of the behavior to be predicted by the test; such a definition is not in itself a sufficient guarantee that the criterion used to validate the test is itself valid.

THE APPEARANCE OF VALIDITY

In many situations it is highly desirable that the testing instrument should have a high degree of "consumer acceptance." These situations are most commonly found in, but by no means limited to, the field of employment testing. If a test is to be used effectively in achieving its objectives, it is essential that it actually be selected for use and that the results of the test be acceptable to those responsible for action on the basis of these results. In the area of public employment testing, e.g., civil service examining, the test must be acceptable not only to those using the test but to those taking the test as well. To a large extent this is also true in educational situations, particularly in the field of counseling. Up to a certain point the acceptability of the test can be carried by weight of authority. The board of examiners, the test technicians, or the counseling experts assert on the basis of their technical knowledge that the test is good, and their assertion is accepted without question. In other situations, however, this assertion of authority is not sufficient to carry conviction. Moreover, the technical evidence on which such authoritative statements should be based is often neither comprehensible nor completely convincing to those who must be convinced.

In Civil Service situations, the candidate whose score is less than he expected is inclined to attribute his low score, not to his own deficiencies, but to the impractical nature of the test in relation to the job for which he is being examined. His dissatisfaction with the test results and his feeling of injustice may, of course, have real merit. We have not yet reached the era of public personnel examining where all tests are technically sound. Whether or not there is merit in his claim, the legislature, the courts, and public opinion, the court of last appeal, are more readily impressed by superficial appearances than by correlation coefficients. It becomes highly important, therefore, that a test to be used in such a situation not only *be* valid in the pragmatic sense of affording reasonably accurate predictions of job competence, but *have the appearance of validity* as well.

This appearance of validity as an added attribute is important in terms of the acceptance of the test, not only by the persons being examined, but also by those operating officials who are charged with the responsibility for taking action based upon the test results. If sound tests are given and accurately reported, but the supervisor, interviewer, or counselor has no confidence in them, the results will not be used effectively.

In passing it should be noted that the concern of the Civil Service or merit system agency with the consumer acceptance of the test should not be merely a negative one of avoiding appeals or legislative pressures. In a democratic society the quality of public service is dependent to a large extent upon the public's opinion of the quality of public servants. If the examination by which public servants are selected (whether it be an objective test or an examination of the candidates' voting records) is such that competent persons in a particular occupation are convinced that they have no opportunity to demonstrate their competence, they will not file for the examination or apply for the position. Since even the best Civil Service system can do no more than to select the best qualified persons of those who apply for positions, it is essential that every possible step be taken to insure that the most competent ones make application. They certainly will not do so if they believe that their examination will be impractical, theoretical, and deny them an opportunity to demonstrate their real ability. Moreover, in the face of such an attitude, statistical evidence on the validity of the test is likely to prove convincing only after an educational campaign extending to several generations of test-takers.

The foregoing discussion does not imply that predictive value is to be sacrificed to superficial appearances. Neither does it imply that a statistically valid test may be used only if it also has the appearance of practicality. It does imply, however, that the appearance of practicality is an objective sufficiently desirable in its own right that it may often be sought as an additional end consistent with the principal objective — predictive value.

The use of the term "face validity" to denote the appearance of a relationship to job performance as an attribute in addition to rather than instead of a statistical relationship, is frequently and unjustifiably confused with the notion of "face validity" by assumption. There is, however, a much clearer distinction between these two usages than between validity by assumption and validity by definition.

VALIDITY BY HYPOTHESIS

This fourth view of validity has not, to the writer's knowledge, been explicitly termed face validity, although it contains certain elements of confusion with validity by assumption. In the construction of any test it is necessary to formulate certain hypotheses as to the most valid type and content to achieve a particular purpose. These hypotheses are held with a greater or less degree of confidence depending upon (a) the amount and the convincingness of available data showing that test items X have proved valid in situation Y, (b) the similarity of test item X to the proposed test items X', and (c) the degree of similarity between situation Y and situation Y' in which the test is to be used. If the new test is very similar to one previously shown to be valid and if the new situation is very similar to that in which the test was valid, then we may proceed with a high degree of confidence that the proposed test will be valid in the situation in which it is to be used. This confidence, of course, never approaches certainty, and a verification of the hypothesis is always necessary.

Even though the questions and the methods of administration are identical for the two tests (if we may speak of two sets of identical questions as two tests), the measuring instrument will not be identical in its effect if its application has shifted from one group of subjects to another or from one testing situation to another. When a test has been adequately standardized on one population and found to be highly valid for the prediction of a particular skill in that population, the use of the same test for another population involves merely a hypothesis, rather than the certainty, of its validity as a measure of the same skill in the new situation. Even though we may have a high degree of confidence that the hypothesis will be confirmed, it is nevertheless a hypothesis. As we construct alternate forms of a test and apply them to new situations to predict the same set of skills, our degree of confidence becomes substantially less. The confidence level is also reduced when we use the same test to predict a somewhat different set of skills. For example, a test may be used to predict competence in clerical office work of a certain type in one agency when the test has been validated against proficiency in office work of a similar type but in another agency. In all these cases we are dealing with varying amounts of confidence in the validity of a test in a particular situation. The degree of confidence which justifies the use of an examining instrument in advance of its validation in the specific situation is a question of administrative judgment which is not wholly answerable by statistical techniques.

The foregoing discussion makes it clear that a validation study does not completely validate the test for use with another group of subjects but that it merely increases our confidence that the test when applied to a group of "similar" subjects will prove similarly valid. Any selection of an existing test to serve a particular purpose (or construction of a new test to serve that purpose) therefore involves validity by hypothesis to a certain extent. The only situation in which we can escape the conclusion that our knowledge of the validity of a test is a hypothesis is the extremely limited one in which the test is validated on the identical subjects for which it is to be used administratively. Since validation of the test involves obtaining criterion measures (which are presumably superior to the test itself and would be used if it were not for the greater time and cost of securing them), the absurdity of using a test which has been prevalidated in this sense becomes immediately apparent. This does not lead, of course, to the absurd conclusion that a test may never be used; rather, it makes clear that when a test is used, its use is based upon a hypothesis in which we have more or less confidence depending upon the amount of research which has preceded its formulation. Our confidence in the test also depends upon the similarity between the research situation and the service-testing situation. Needless to say, this conclusion applies with equal force to all personnel evaluation and prediction devices.

It will be noted that validity by hypothesis departs from the concept of "face validity" in the preceding usages of the term. The first three usages discussed involve a superficial, common-sense similarity between test content and test objective. For example, in validity by assumption the similarity between test and job, without regard to statistical evidence of validity, is taken as sufficient. In validity by hypothesis, the similarity to a test for which there is statistical evidence of validity is tentatively accepted, without regard to its resemblance to the criterion. In validity by hypothesis, no such superficial similarity is assumed. On the basis of extensive previous research, one might legitimately propose that the ability to identify pictured hands as right hands or left hands would be a valid test for the prediction of the ability to read blueprints, although the superficial resemblance between the two tasks is slight. Nevertheless, certain controversies which have been raised about face validity and the presumed necessity for prevalidating any test before it is used[2] make the discussion of validity by hypothesis appropriate in connection with the other uses of face validity.

Moreover, in validity by assumption, hypothesis, or definition, we are dealing with varying points on a continuum of degrees of certainty. In "assumption" we have, within the scientific frame of reference, no confidence whatever; in "hypothesis" we have varying degrees of confidence depending on the amount, quality and pertinence of the evidence from previous experience; in "definition," our confidence usually is greatest, but — and this must always be remembered — that confidence applies only to the trait or traits actually represented by the test items in relation to the sample and *not* to traits defined in any other way.

SUMMARY AND CONCLUSIONS

1. This paper has attempted an analysis of the various meanings of the term "face validity." These meanings, although superficially similar, lead to widely different conclusions.

2. The results of the analysis may be summarized as follows. Face validity is variously used to mean that:

   a) The test bears a common-sense relationship to the measurement objective and therefore no statistical verification is necessary (*assumption*).

   b) The test sets such a task that the universe of possible tasks (of which the test is a representative sample) is the only practicable criterion and the test is therefore a valid measure of the universe defined in terms of the sample. This implies merely that the test is a valid measure of whatever trait is measured reliably by the test (*definition*).

   c) In the interests of the acceptability of the test to those most intimately concerned with its use, it is highly desirable that a test possess not only statistical validity, but also, as an added attribute, the appearance of practicality (*appearance*).

   d) In the construction or selection of a particular test to be used for a particular objective with a particular group of subjects, recourse is always had to previous knowledge of the effectiveness of the same or similar tests applied to the same or similar subjects for the prediction

[2] Strangely enough, many of those who insist upon the prevalidation of each written test continue to urge reliance upon other types of selection techniques which numerous research studies have almost unanimously shown to be without predictive value.

of the same or similar attributes. On the basis of this previous research, the hypothesis is proposed that this test will be valid for the particular objective. The hypothesis is one which carries varying degrees of confidence: in some cases enough to justify the use of the test immediately, pending further investigation; in other cases so little confidence that such further investigation seems unprofitable. Even after there has been further investigation, however, we are left with a degree of confidence which is somewhat less than certainty, unless we are dealing with the same test, the same population and the same objectives (*hypothesis*).

3. Since the term "face validity" has become overlaid with a high degree of emotional content and since its referents are not only highly ambiguous but lead to widely divergent conclusions, it is recommended that the term be abandoned. Anyone intending to use the term should, instead, describe fully the *concept* which he originally intended to denote by "face validity." Even though writers may not always follow this recommendation, it is hoped that the foregoing analysis will prevent readers from drawing the improper conclusions that have frequently resulted from the indiscriminate uses made of the term in recent years.

Reference

1. Toops, H. A. "The Criterion," *Educational and Psychological Measurement,* IV (1944), 271–297.

11

Problems and Designs
of Cross-Validation[1]

Charles I. Mosier

*To a considerable extent the value of a test depends on the ade-
quacy of the methods used in trying out the tool prior to its release
for general use. When a test is tried out on a given group of subjects, sampling errors may result in conclusions about the test and
its content which may not be substantiated by further application
on successive samples of subjects. Mosier prescribes some basic
formats for trying out tests during their validation phase. The reader
may wish to note specific tests that have used the various procedures
described.*

The term "cross-validation" is often loosely applied to any one of several
distinct, though closely related, experimental designs. Before we get lost in a
swamp of semantic confusion, it may be well to identify each of these, to
point out their similarities and differences and to make clear the objectives
which [they] serve. What name we give to each is secondary, although for
convenience I shall attach a different name to each. Having done this, I
shall consider in greater detail more of the problems posed by the basic cross-
validation pattern.

The first, and what I consider the classic, design is the one referred to by
Kurtz in his 1948 *Personnel Psychology* paper on the Rorschach (3), and
by Cureton in his paper, "Validity, Reliability and Boloney" (1). If the
combining weights of a set of predictors have been determined from the
statistics of one sample, the effectiveness of the predictor-composite *must* be
determined on a separate, independent sample. This is the case whether the
combining weights are multiple-regression beta weights or item-analysis
weights of one or zero. Anyone who doubts the necessity of determining
effectiveness on a separate sample from that on which the weights are
determined should go back and read Kurtz and Cureton.

From Charles I. Mosier, "Problems and Designs of Cross-Validation," *Educational
and Psychological Measurement*, XI (Spring, 1951), pp. 5–11. Reprinted with
the permission of the publisher.

[1] This paper by Dr. Mosier [was] given [in] a symposium before the Psychometric
Society as part of the A.P.A. convention program in September, 1950.

This is the design for which I shall reserve the term "cross-validation." Since both combining weights and their effectiveness should be determined on samples representative of the group in which the battery will be applied, it is obvious that the two samples should be randomly selected from the same universe. It is this design to which I shall return later to consider in greater detail.

There is a variant of this design, however, which is superficially similar but quite different in purpose. This I shall term "validity generalization." If a set of weights has been determined and found effective in one situation, how effective will it be for another different situation, i.e., for a differently selected population? Let me cite two examples: In the Personnel Research Section, Dr. Brogden has recently developed a self-description blank for prediction of leadership potential in ROTC cadets by item-analyzing and cross-validating on samples from military schools. Its cross-validated validity was .42. How well will the instrument work in the quite different setting of ROTC units at civilian colleges? To answer this, the validity in a sample from civilian ROTC units was computed and found to be .41. Thus, in this case the validity could be generalized from military to civilian schools. The other example goes back a number of years. Young and Estabrooks developed a scholastic interest key for the *Strong Vocational Interest Blank,* using the liberal arts students at Colgate University (4). They found a correlation of .45 with school grades. I applied the same key to University of Florida students. It did not work. To find out why, I computed validities separately by curriculum with interesting, if not surprising, results. For Florida liberal-arts students the scale was quite as valid as it had been at Colgate. For B.S. candidates its validity was significant, but much lower; for students of engineering, business administration, education and agriculture, its validity was nil. Thus, the validity of the combining weights determined in one situation may or may not hold up if applied to other, differently selected populations. Note the essential difference between this design and that of cross-validation. In cross-validation we have weights based on one sample and we determine their effectiveness on a second sample where both samples are representative of the population to which the weights will be applied for prediction. In validity generalization we have combining weights known to work in one population and we wish to know whether they will also work in another population, which differs systematically from the first in some characteristic. Our problem is not to get an unbiased estimate of validity but to see whether validity will generalize to a different population. In this problem the criterion is substantially the same, though probably not identical in the two populations: ratings of leadership in civilian or military ROTC units; college grades at Colgate or Florida.

In still another possible design, probably of limited usefulness, we may extend validity generalization to different criteria as well as to different populations. This case we may call validity extension and it is, I think, clear enough to need no extended discussion.

Thus far we have explored two basic designs, cross-validation and validity-generalization. Both are alike in basing combining weights on the statistics of one group and determining the effectiveness of those weights applied to an independent group. They differ in objectives and in the consequent relationship between the groups. Two other designs deserve mention here. In these designs, the problem is to determine the combining weights separately on two or more samples and to use these data in establishing the final combining weights. As in cross-validation and validity generalization the two designs differ principally in objective and in the relationship between the two samples. The first of these we will call "simultaneous validation." We desire a single test or battery which will be effective in either of two situations. We recognize that we might do better by building two tests, one for each situation. Nevertheless, from convenience or necessity we are limited to one. That one must work equally well, however, for either situation. As a concrete example we may take an experimental vocabulary test containing both general and, inadvertently, sex-differentiated items. It is to be used for the prediction of school grades of either boys or girls. If item validities are computed on a combined population, items highly valid for one sex and wholly invalid for the other may be retained over items moderately valid for both sexes. To avoid this we item analyze separately and retain only those items which meet the specified validity for each sex, rejecting those which are invalid for either group as well as those invalid for both.

Here we have used two groups, systematically different in characteristics, as the basis for determining the combining weights. The effectiveness of those weights must still be determined by cross-validation.

The final variant of these designs we will call "replication." It is similar to the preceding in that weights are determined on each of a series of samples. It differs, however, in dividing the available cases into a series of random or representative sub-samples and selecting items whose validities exceed a specified value in some specified percentage of sub-samples. There is a question in my mind, which I hope one of the other speakers will resolve, as to whether or not this fractionation of the data, with resulting increase in the sampling error of the validity indices or beta weights, has any advantage over using the total group as a single sample with correspondingly smaller sampling errors (2).

Thus far, then, we have distinguished five distinct designs closely related to cross-validation.

1. Cross-validation — weights determined on one sample and their effectiveness tested on a second, similarly drawn sample.

2. Validity-generalization — weights determined on a sample from one population (and presumably cross-validated) but the effectiveness tested against the same criterion on a second sample drawn from a differently defined population.

3. Validity-extension — as in validity-generalization except that the criteria as well as the populations differ.

4. Simultaneous validation — item selection or battery weighting on each of two, differently drawn samples in order to develop a single battery useful in either population.

5. Replication — determination of weights in a series of samples drawn

from the *same* population with the final weights (or items selected) based on some combination of the values in the several samples.

With these types of designs distinguished, I should like to consider some of the problems of cross-validation, the first of these designs, and ways of meeting them.

In prediction problems, exemplified by cross-validation, we are faced with two distinct (and, as we shall see later, incompatible) goals. The first of these is the determination of those weights which will best predict the criterion from the predictor information; the second is the most accurate determination of how effective our prediction will be — usually in terms of a simple or multiple-correlation coefficient. As we analyze these objectives further, we shall see that they are incompatible — if we use all of our data to make the best determination of weights, we cannot arrive at an unbiased estimate of the effectiveness of prediction. If, on the other hand, we use some of our data to get a more stable and unbiased estimate of multiple R, we necessarily settle for less than the most stable weights which could be obtained from the data at hand.

Though we cannot resolve the dilemma, we should be aware of it. We can then make the appropriate adjustments in our experimental design as the emphasis shifts from one to another of the two objectives. I should like to explore the problem and to suggest several experimental and analytic designs.

In cross-validation the usual pattern is as follows: (a) the collection of both prediction and criterion data on Sample One, (b) the determination by the method of least squares of the multiple regression weights and the multiple correlation coefficient (or the "shrunken multiple") for Sample One, and (c), then the cross-validation of the findings on Sample Two.

The first, and obvious, point in our analysis is that we are not interested in either the optimal weights or the effectiveness of prediction in the samples at hand. Why should we predict the criterion scores for the sample cases? We have criterion measurements for them! Our sole interest in the samples is to determine β weights and multiple R *as the values which will most likely apply in those other samples for which criterion measures are not or will not be available.* But multiple R obtained on Sample 1 is a biased estimate of predictive effectiveness, since it capitalizes on the idiosyncrasies of the sample. To get an unbiased estimate of R, we must resort to Sample 2. There we compute, in effect, not multiple R but the zero-order coefficient between the criterion and the weighted sum of the predictors. The difference in the two coefficients lies in that, in cross-validation, we use the combining weights from Sample 1. (In computing a true multiple, we would use, not the combining weights from Sample 1, but those recomputed from Sample 2, and our measure would again be biased.) Thus, in order to get an unbiased estimate of predictive effectiveness, we must resort to the cross-validation sample, S_2, on which we have both predictor and criterion measurements. But it now becomes immediately apparent that the best available β weights are not those based on Sample 1 alone but those based upon the larger sample, Sample One plus Two. The nature of our dilemma now becomes clear. To obtain an unbiased measure of predictive effectiveness, we must have a second cross-validation sample, S_2; as soon as we have such a sample we could improve our weights by basing them on the combined sample $S_1 + 2$. But if we do this, we lose the possibility of an unbiased estimate of R. If we seek to escape by getting a new cross-validation sample, S_3, the argument merely repeats itself *ad nauseam*.

Faced with this confusion, let us see what can be done. One possibility is that of double cross-validation (the location of the hyphen is important). If we use a prescript to identify the sample on which a statistic is based, our analysis will be simpler. Thus, $_1\beta_{01.23} \ldots$ n would represent the partial regression of variable 1 on the criterion (variable 0) computed in Sample 1 whereas $_2\beta_{01.23} \ldots$ n would represent the same statistic computed on Sample 2. The design of double cross-validation is seen in Figure 1. We determine weights separately for Sample 1 and Sample 2. We apply each set of weights back on the *other* sample to compute the predictive effectiveness. Hence, the name — double cross-validation.

Figure 1

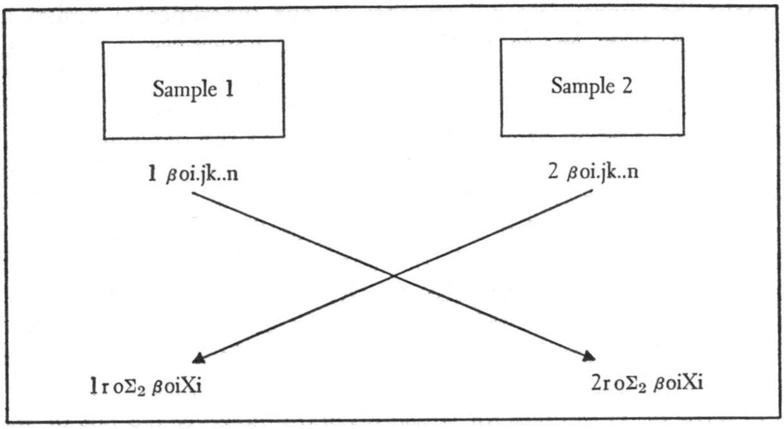

Compared with this design, simple cross-validation while simple, wastes half of the data and, in particular, determines the β's on only half of the available cases.

For most purposes, the principal goal is the maximum accuracy of prediction, with an estimate of that accuracy an important but secondary objective. We may, therefore, be willing to accept a less than optimally accurate estimate of R in return for the best set of weights and a substantial reduction in computing time. If so, another variation in the basic design presents itself. This design proceeds as in a simple cross-validation to the determination of β weights in each sample. Rather than use the values of β thus determined as the final values, however, these are employed merely for the purpose of obtaining an unbiased estimate of R. If that estimate is high enough to warrant prediction of the values, the weights based on the half samples are ignored and a new final set obtained, based upon the combined samples, S_{1+2}. We will have no accurate estimate of R for these β's but we may use the average of the ones obtained for the half sample β's as an approximation. This value, though I cannot assert it is the minimum value, is more likely to be below the universe value than above it. Possibly one of the other speakers knows of a proof that the R based on half sample β's is always lower than that based on the full sample β's.

References

1. Cureton, E. E. "Validity, Reliability and Boloney," *Educational and Psychological Measurement*, X (1950), 94–96.
2. Katzell, Ray. "Cross Validation and Item Analysis," *Educational and Psychological Measurement*, XI (1951), 16–22.
3. Kurtz, A. K. "A Research Test of the Rorschach Test," *Personnel Psychology*, I (1948), 41–53.
4. Young, C. W., and Estabrooks, G. H. "Report on the Young-Estabrooks Studiousness Scale," *Journal of Educational Psychology*, XXVIII (1937), 188–196.

12

An Experimental Comparison of Test-Retest and Internal Consistency Estimates of Reliability with Speeded Tests[1]

Alexander G. Wesman and John P. Kernan

All reliability coefficients do not provide the same kind of information, nor are all reliability techniques equally appropriate for a given kind of measurement. Wesman and Kernan show how imposing a time limit on a test influences two kinds of reliability data. Do the findings reported here provide information for evaluating standardized test construction methods?

It has been pointed out by a number of writers, including Cronbach (2), McNemar (5), Thorndike (6), and others that the use of internal consistency methods in the estimation of the reliability of speeded tests results in spuriously high coefficients. Nevertheless, test builders persist in utilizing internal consistency formulae with such tests and, indeed, frequently compound the error by claiming that the estimates are unduly low.[2] There are relatively few demonstrations in the literature comparing the coefficients resulting from internal consistency methods with those obtained by test-retest techniques. Bennett, Seashore, and Wesman present the results of one such experiment in the Differential Aptitude Tests Manual (1) which reports split-half and test-retest coefficients for a simple clerical test; the split-half coefficients are shown to be consistently (and sometimes dramatically) higher.

From Alexander G. Wesman and John P. Kernan, "An Experimental Comparison of Test-Retest and Internal Consistency Estimates of Reliability with Speeded Tests," *The Journal of Educational Psychology*, XLIII (May, 1952), pp. 292–298. Reprinted with the permission of Abrahams Magazine Service, Incorporated, and the authors.

[1] This paper utilizes some of the findings from Kernan, J. P., *An Empirical Determination of Test Reliability by Different Experimental Designs,* Fordham University, New York, 1950, an M.A. dissertation done under the mentorship of Wm. J. E. Crissy.

[2] Such claims apparently stem from a statement made by Kuder and Richardson that violation of any assumptions underlying their Method of Rational Equivalence would yield underestimates of reliability (4).

The spurious character of internal consistency coefficients is obviously in part a function of the degree to which the tests are speeded — that is, the extent to which subjects who could have correctly answered later items in the tests failed to reach those items. If the items are all so easy that everyone could correctly answer them if given unlimited time, the internal consistency coefficient under speed conditions should approach 1.00 regardless of the size of the test-retest reliability. If, on the other hand, the items are heterogeneous in difficulty for the group and are arranged in order of increasing difficulty, the spuriousness of the internal consistency coefficient will not be so great — depending in part on the extent to which speed and power are intercorrelated.

The correlation between speed and power probably varies from one content area (or one skill) to another. It is the writers' belief that a steeply graded test in mathematics, for example, will show very high correlation between speed and power, whereas in English literature or social studies, the correlation between speed and power is not likely to be so high. Mathematics as a discipline has a vertical hierarchy of knowledge; the student who can solve problems in trigonometry can almost certainly solve those in elementary algebra and is likely to arrive at the answers to the lower level problems quickly. There is no such assurance that a student who knows Eighteenth Century literature is equally conversant with modern drama or oriental literature; the student may puzzle for a long time over a question which has little difficulty for the group as a whole. These hypotheses are the product of the senior writer's experience in building tests, rather than being based on clearcut experimental evidence.

It seems evident, then, that a number of empirical comparisons of test-retest and internal consistency coefficients are needed. We need to know more about the extent of artificial inflation of the reliability coefficient under varying conditions. How great is the overestimate if 90 per cent finish the test — or 80 per cent, or 70 per cent? What assumptions can we make with tests in Biology — in Reading Comprehension — in Logical Reasoning or Productive Thinking? How do split-half coefficients compare with methods of rational equivalence in each of these circumstances? The present study is intended to contribute data which, when coördinated with the results of many similar experiments, will shed some light on these topics.

The test used was The Psychological Corporation's *General Clerical Test* (3). It consists of nine parts which yield three subtotal scores and a total score. The parts are: Checking and Alphabetizing (Clerical subscore); Arithmetic Computation, Error Location, and Arithmetic Reasoning (Numerical subscore); and Spelling, Reading Comprehension, Vocabulary and Grammar (Verbal subscore). These parts are all more or less speeded; they vary also in the homogeneity of the difficulty levels of the items. The test was administered to 197 twelfth-grade commercial high school students, a month intervening between testings.[3] Thirty-nine of the students were boys, 158 girls; they ranged in age from sixteen to nineteen years.

[3] We are grateful to Dr. Robert E. Carey, Director of Guidance, Yonkers, New York, for his coöperation in making these students available to us.

Table 1

TEST-RETEST RELIABILITY COEFFICIENTS ON THE GCT
SCORES AND THE MEANS AND SD'S OF SCORES ON THE
FIRST AND SECOND TESTINGS

Test Parts	Max. Poss. Score	r	1st Testing		2nd Testing	
			Mean	SD	Mean	SD
Part I	19	.59	7.70	2.63	9.69	3.28
Part II	61	.87	29.05	9.07	35.18	9.43
Clerical Subscore	80	.87	36.75	10.57	44.87	11.38
Part III	20	.67	11.55	2.66	12.88	2.82
Part IV	20	.67	11.17	4.91	14.64	4.44
Part V	16	.76	5.64	2.56	6.40	2.93
Numerical Subscore	56	.82	28.35	8.16	33.92	8.36
Part VI	29	.88	19.72	5.42	20.44	5.28
Part VII	14	.65	7.44	2.85	9.23	2.59
Part VIII	40	.86	19.15	6.04	20.96	5.73
Part IX	24	.68	9.99	3.32	11.20	3.25
Verbal Subscore	107	.91	56.30	13.08	61.83	13.08
Total Score	243	.94	121.41	25.42	140.62	26.33

Table 1 presents the test-retest coefficients for each of the nine parts, the three subscores, and the total score, together with the respective means and standard deviations. The consistent increase in score on the second testing is to be expected; since the same form of the test was used, practice effect may be present, and learning also might well have occurred during the period between testings. Table 2 presents these same coefficients together with three sets of internal consistency estimates: split-half and Kuder-Richardson formulas 20 and 21.[4]

A number of interesting observations may be made with regard to the data in Table 2. One generalization is that Kuder-Richardson formulas do not always underestimate. In all but one instance the reliability estimates obtained by formula 20 are larger than the test-retest coefficient (though not always significantly so). K-R No. 21, on the other hand, exceeds the test-retest

[4] The Formulas used were:

Split-half:
$$r = \frac{2r}{1+r}$$

KR 20:
$$r_{tt} = \frac{n}{n-1} \cdot \frac{\sigma_t^2 - n\overline{pq}}{\sigma_t^2}$$

KR 21:
$$r_{tt} = \frac{n}{n-1} \cdot \frac{\sigma_t^2 - n(\overline{p}\,\overline{q})}{\sigma_t^2}$$

Table 2

TEST-RETEST, SPLIT-HALF, K-R No. 20 AND K-R No. 21
RELIABILITY COEFFICIENTS

Test Parts	Test-retest	Split-half	K-R No. 20	K-R No. 21
Part I	.59	.71	.71	.36
Part II	.87	.99	.96	.83
C. Subscore	.87	.97	.95	.83
Part III	.67	.69	.69	.33
Part IV	.67	.91	.92	.84
Part V	.76	.68	.71	.47
N. Subscore	.82	.89	.90	.81
Part VI	.88	.86	.89	.81
Part VII	.65	.83	.81	.62
Part VIII	.86	.87	.88	.75
Part IX	.68	.57	.69	.47
V. Subscore	.91	.91	.92	.85
Total Score	.94	.96	.96	.91

coefficient in only one instance (Part IV-Error Location). We may note also that in four instances (Parts I, III, V, and IX) K-R No. 21 is too conservative; it underestimates reliability to an extent which would cause important differences in judgment about the test part.

The split-half estimate also exceeds the test-retest coefficient for most of the subtests, sometimes by more than K-R No. 20, sometimes by less. Just as with K-R No. 20, the split-half estimates are sometimes quite close approximations to the test-retest coefficients, but sometimes they are gross exaggerations. The fact that in all but one comparison (for Part IX) the difference is no greater than .03, demonstrates the closeness of the split-half and K-R No. 20 estimates.

Several points seem to be suggested by the data:

1) K-R No. 20 and split-half estimates resemble each other very closely, at least with these test parts.

2) It has once again been demonstrated that the K-R formulas do not always underestimate the 'true' reliability. They may, in fact, yield gross overestimates.

3) K-R No. 21 generally provides an underestimate of reliability, which is usually assumed good since the error is on the side of conservatism. Practically, however, the use of this formula may be quite dangerous, since the underestimate may be so great as to deceive the test constructor with regard to appropriate action. For example, the test constructor might consider the

development of Part III to a point at which its reliability was .80. If he had before him only the estimate provided by K-R No. 21, he would be led to believe that a test part eight times the length of the present Part III was needed, and he might well abandon the project.[5] Yet the evidence from the test-retest coefficient is that the part would need to be only twice its present length to attain a reliability of .80. Similarly, for Part V, the K-R No. 21 estimates indicate that a part ten times as long would be required to reach .90; the test-retest coefficient suggests that to reach .90, the part would have to be only three times as long as at present. The practical decisions based on these methods may well be quite opposite to each other.

4) Inspection of the test content in this study yields no clear insight with regard to the effect of the materials on the spurious results of internal consistency techniques. Part I appears to be most homogeneous in content and range of difficulty; it is probably the 'purest' of the nine parts as a speed test. K-R and split-half methods overestimate the test-retest coefficient by about .12; K-R No. 21 underestimates by .23. Part II, which is almost as simple a task (Part I requires comparing names and numbers; Part II requires a knowledge of the alphabet) and seemingly equally homogeneous in content and range of difficulty is overestimated by split-half and K-R No. 20 by about .10; with this part, however, K-R No. 21 underestimates by only .04. Part III, an arithmetic computation test, shows essentially the same coefficient for K-R No. 20, split-half and test-retest, while K-R No. 21 underestimates appreciably; Part IV, an arithmetic error location test, is overestimated by split-half, K-R No. 20 and K-R No. 21 estimates.

It will have been obvious to the reader that our treatment has considered the test-retest estimate of reliability as the criterion against which the spuriousness of internal consistency coefficients has been judged. This procedure is in general accord with present measurement theory; it should nonetheless be recognized that our criterion itself is not perfect, even with these tests and this population. Since the same form of the test was used twice, there may have been enough memory of previous response to add a touch of spuriousness to the test-retest coefficient. On the other hand, an interval of a month might quite possibly be long enough for differential growth to have taken place in some of the abilities measured, which would depress the coefficient.

It is the writers' belief that neither of these factors was seriously operative in the experimental situation. But the possibilities are at least real enough to lead to the question as to how much time ought to elapse in order to yield the best estimate of reliability for each kind of test. This question leads naturally to a consideration of what aspect of reliability concerns us. If we are concerned with what Cronbach (2) has called the 'coefficient of equivalence,' i.e., how precisely the test measures the person's performance at the particular moment, our best estimate for speeded tests would be

[5] The familiar Spearman-Brown formula for estimating the increased length of test required to achieve a desired coefficient is:

$$r_{AA} = \frac{Ar_{11}}{1 + (A-1)r_{11}}$$

obtained only by having two forms administered in a single day. When only one form is available this is impossible; and administration of the same form twice in the same day would, except in the rarest of instances, result in an ambiguous reliability coefficient. How much time, then, should elapse? Only a general answer is possible: enough time to eliminate the influence of memory and immediate practice effect, and too little for changes in the measured traits to occur. A series of studies investigating this principle with specific tasks and specific groups could contribute valuably to our understanding of reliability. Until enough such investigations have been conducted, we shall have to continue to rely on our experience and our intuitions.

Spurious coefficients also deserve empirical study. There has been considerable progress recently in the theoretical development of estimates of spuriousness present in internal consistency coefficients derived from speeded tests. Unfortunately, all too often the assumptions which are required for the theoretical developments are hard to accept. Until such time as there is general agreement as to the acceptability of measures of spuriousness, empirical findings such as those reported in this paper can provide useful clues for the everyday practitioner.

REFERENCES

1. Bennett, George K., Seashore, Harold G., and Wesman, Alexander G. *The Differential Aptitude Tests.* New York: The Psychological Corporation, 1947.
2. Cronbach, L. J. *Essentials of Psychological Testing.* New York: Harper and Brothers, 1949.
3. *General Clerical Test Manual* (rev. ed.). New York: The Psychological Corporation, 1950.
4. Kuder, G. F., and Richardson, M. W. "The Theory of the Estimation of Test Reliability," *Psychometrika,* 2 (1937), 151–160.
5. McNemar, Quinn. *Psychological Statistics.* New York: John Wiley and Sons, Inc., 1949.
6. Thorndike, Robert L. *Personnel Selection: Test and Measurement Techniques.* New York: John Wiley and Sons, Inc., 1949.

13

Test Reliability for What?

Benjamin S. Bloom

A common problem in the interpretation of reliability data is determining what constitutes adequate reliability for a test. Bloom points out that objectives of measurement are related to solving this problem. This article should help the student evaluate reliability reports such as those found in test manuals and technical reports.

Reliability has been defined as the consistency with which a test measures what it measures. A reliability coefficient does not tell us what the test measures. Without further analysis one cannot decide what specific degree of consistency is desirable or necessary for the purpose to which the test results are to be put.

Kelley (1) has pointed out that when a test is to be used for group measurement purposes a reliability coefficient of .50 or higher is needed. When the test is to be used for individual measurement purposes a reliability coefficient of .94 or higher is needed. No one would question the desirability of high reliability coefficients at all times for educational measurements, but often we are confronted with the problem of what to do with evidence about students based on tests with reliability coefficients which do not satisfy the standards indicated above. This paper is an attempt to point out some methods whereby tests with low reliability coefficients can be utilized for making generalizations about student behavior.

It must be pointed out that tests may be utilized for such varied purposes as: The prediction of scholastic achievement, diagnosis of individual strengths and weaknesses, assignment of grades to students, selection of individuals for certain educational and vocational opportunities, and the surveying of individual and group status. The precision required of the test should in general correspond to the extent to which the test results will be used to reach decisions vitally affecting the student. Also, the number of categories into which students are to be distinguished on a distribution of test scores should serve to indicate the lowest reliability coefficient which will be acceptable.

Preoccupation with precision in educational measurements has resulted in

From Benjamin S. Bloom, "Test Reliability for What?" *The Journal of Educational Psychology*, XXXIII (October, 1942), pp. 517–526. Reprinted with the permission of Abrahams Magazine Service, Incorporated, and the author.

an emphasis on long and reliable tests for all purposes. When the length of a test is increased its reliability is improved. Each item in the test which is positively intercorrelated with the other items will improve the reliability of the test. Since positive correlations in educational tests and measurements are the rule rather than the exception, the summing of a large number of not uncorrelated items or subtests having low intercorrelations yields high reliability coefficients.

Emphasis is placed on the total test score rather than on the many sub-test scores which are contained within the total test. We tend to ignore the way in which the student approaches the problem, the types of questions which he answers correctly, and the types of questions which he answers incorrectly. Adding together many relatively unrelated sub-abilities yields reliable total scores but may obscure much valuable information about the configuration of abilities and skills which an individual possesses. These abilities may not be additive, but perhaps should be combined in some unique fashion if we are to secure meaningful insights into the student's behavior.

To use a physical analogy, the volume of a box expressed in cubic inches or feet gives an adequate concept of the size of the box, but tells nothing about its shape. A specified volume might be secured by an infinite number of differently shaped boxes. We must know the length, width, and depth of the box before its shape is known. Also, the volume represents a unique combination of these dimensions of the box. Another combination of these same dimensions would yield the surface area of the box. However, a knowledge of these dimensions tells nothing about the color of the box, its weight, strength, cost, age, length of time required to make the box, whether it is air tight, etc.

This analogy can be applied to the field of testing. A total reading score is frequently a mixture of many different elements of reading. Such a total score is not a direct index of the individual's reading rate, his ability to comprehend material taken from various subject fields, his ability to comprehend groups of words in various organizations, physiological handicaps, eye movements, etc. Nor can we add scores for each of the above characteristics in any meaningful way. We must keep them separate and make our judgment about the appropriate remedial procedures by considering all the scores in some unique combination. For certain purposes an index composed of many different scores may be useful, but it must be remembered that this statistically useful index is a non-meaningful combination.

Before we construct or use a test, we must first determine why we want evidence about the students' aptitudes and achievements, and what evidence should be gathered. Then, having gathered the desired evidence, one should combine the various bits of evidence in some meaningful fashion. Simply to add various subscores to secure a total score may be not only meaningless but actually misleading. To secure a reliable test merely by adding different tests together may be a very vicious practice which gives a false sense of precision and scientific accuracy in tests and measurements. Users of tests sometimes confuse high reliability coefficients with scientific accuracy in measurement, and too often neglect a consideration of the extent to which a single score is an index of the specific ability or skill in which they are interested.

However, as the total test is broken into smaller and smaller useful units, the reliability of each subtest score decreases. Thus we are faced with the dilemma of increasing the diagnostic value of a test by decreasing the reliability of the test units under consideration, or increasing the reliability of the test by decreasing its diagnostic value.

Diagnostic testing is an important adjunct to teaching and educational guidance. The teacher in order to do an effective job must first determine the particular aptitudes and achievements of students which are desired, measure progress in these aptitudes and achievements, and then, before the students leave the class, measure their final status in these aptitudes and achievements. Through such practices the instructor will best be able: Firstly, to help each student; secondly, to present his subject-matter in the most economical and efficient manner; and, finally, to revise the presentation of a particular course in the light of changes shown by students from the initial to the final test.

To do this it will be necessary to use many tests, some of which will not be as long or as reliable as might be desired. In lieu of other evidence about the students and because the testing time is limited, the teacher must content himself with this material. The following will attempt to point out various ways in which these "unreliable" tests may be used with various degrees of confidence.

I. Use of Test Results Without Modification

(A) *For Developing Likely Hypotheses About the Student.* A short unreliable test dealing with some aspect of reading or, perhaps, with the types of errors students make in handling certain laboratory instruments may reveal an aspect of student behavior which the instructor has not taken into consideration. If no other evidence is available on these phases of student behavior, the instructor is confronted with the problem as to whether he should make use of this evidence or should dismiss it because of low reliability.

In a situation of this type, great confidence cannot be placed in this evidence, and we cannot make any decision on this basis which would vitally affect the student. But, in the absence of contradictory evidence, we may use these test results as the basis for likely hypotheses about the student, taking care to recognize the error of measurement associated with the score. These hypotheses should be explored and checked in the light of subsequent evidence about the student.

Although, on subsequent repetitions of comparable tests of this specific ability, it may be expected that the student's score will fluctuate considerably, in the absence of further evidence it may be expected that the student's scores will fluctuate around his present score. That is, in the absence of other evidence, the present score may be assumed to be the most likely score for the student on this ability.

(B) *For Making Decisions About the Student.* If the ability under consideration is one for which some definite decision must be made which will to a considerable extent affect the student, the instructor should seek out further evidence. Thus, if two or more partially independent scores are available, the instructor can make a judgment based on each score, and a decision made on the basis of these two judgments will be more reliable than a decision made on only one of the scores.

The test user can place increased confidence in his decisions if they are based on judgments made on a large number of partially independent tests and if the judgments made on one of the tests are substantiated by the judgments made on the other tests.

Instead of the reliability resulting from the collection of relatively unrelated items to make a single test score, the test user can substitute the consistency of judgments from a number of test scores.

II. STANDARD ERROR OF MEASUREMENT

The reported reliability of a test is very misleading. Symonds (3) has pointed out the many ways in which the reliability coefficient of a test may be affected. In particular, it is possible to secure high reliability coefficients by constructing tests with large numbers of items or by administering short tests to a large and extremely varied group of subjects. Thus, a short test intended for sixth-grade students may be administered to students in all grades from the first to twelfth grade, and, because of the heterogeneity of the students represented, a high reliability coefficient may be secured. Then again, a test intended for one school may be administered to a large number of extremely varied schools and the reliability coefficient for the total group of schools will be much higher than for a single school.

As the heterogeneity of the group tested increases, both the standard deviation and the reliability coefficient of the test increase. However, the standard error of measurement which is a function of the standard deviation of the test scores and of the reliability coefficient of the test remains quite stable. A fictitious numerical example of this stability is:

For one school
  Standard deviation 10   Reliability coefficient .... .64
  Standard error of measurement $\sigma \sqrt{1 - r_{11}} = 10 \sqrt{1 - .64} = 6$
For several schools
  Standard deviation 15   Reliability coefficient .... .84
  Standard error of measurement $\sigma \sqrt{1 - r_{11}} = 15 \sqrt{1 - .84} = 6$

In the above example, in spite of large differences in the standard deviations and the reliability coefficients, the standard error of measurement is constant. The standard error of measurement is an index of the scatter of the observed scores around the estimated true score.

Before it is possible to determine whether a specified reliability coefficient is high enough to give satisfactory precision, something must be known about the heterogeneity of the group on which this coefficient was determined.

The writer would recommend that the number of statistically significant classes into which the test scores may be divided be determined by the ratio:

$$\frac{\text{Range of scores}}{3\sigma \sqrt{1 - r_{11}}}$$

This ratio indicates the number of categories which may be obtained from this range of test scores so that the chances of a point in one category overlapping with the corresponding point in the next category is only about one in one thousand. The test user can then determine whether this yields a sufficient number of statistically distinct categories for the purpose to which he intends to put the results from this test.

If a normal distribution is assumed in which the range of scores on a test is six times the standard deviation, it is possible to determine the number of distinct categories available for different reliability coefficients by the proper substitutions in the above formula. The following represents some possible substitutions:

Reliability Coefficients	*Number of Categories*
40	2.58
60	3.16
80	4.47
90	6.33
95	8.97

III. Use of Extreme Scores

A profile of test scores is usually analyzed by pointing out the tests on which the student is extreme. Thus the scores on an interest test are analyzed by pointing out those interests in which the individual deviates markedly from the average.

If a normal distribution is assumed and the raw test scores are transmuted to percentile ranks, certain characteristics of the distribution are altered. Equal raw score units are being exchanged for rank units in which the number of people rather than the size of the score is the unit. As the extreme percentile ranks are approached, the distance in raw score units from the mean becomes increasingly large. Thus the difference between percentile ranks of 50 and 55 in terms of raw scores is much less than the raw score difference between percentile ranks of 90 and 95.

If the standard error of measurement of percentile ranks is computed, it will be found that the precision with which we can speak about a score is a function of the distance of that score from the mean and of the reliability of the test. Table 1 shows the fiducial limits associated with specified percentile ranks and specified reliability coefficients. If these limits are adopted, such estimates of the true score will be right 95 per cent of the time.

If the reliability of a test is .90 and a student's percentile rank is 50, the true percentile rank may be found (ninety-five out of one hundred times) within the limits 27 and 73 or a range of forty-six percentile points. For the

Table 1

GIVEN A SPECIFIED RELIABILITY COEFFICIENT AND SPECIFIED PERCENTILE
SCORE BASED ON A NORMAL DISTRIBUTION, THE FIDUCIAL LIMITS WHICH
MAY BE EXPECTED NINETY-FIVE OUT OF ONE HUNDRED TIMES

Percentile Score	Reliability Coefficients							
	40	50	60	70	80	85	90	95
99	999+ 791	999+ 827	999+ 861	999+ 895	999 926	999 942	998 956	997 971
98	999+ 704	999+ 748	999+ 792	999 837	998 881	998 902	996 924	994 947
97	999+ 642	999 690	999 739	998 790	997 842	996 867	994 869	990 896
96	999+ 592	999 642	999 695	998 751	996 809	994 839	991 871	986 905
95	999 550	999 602	998 657	997 716	994 779	992 812	988 847	981 886
90	997 407	996 460	994 517	991 582	985 657	979 699	971 746	957 801
85	995 315	992 363	989 420	983 485	972 564	964 609	951 662	930 725
80	991 249	987 293	981 345	972 408	957 486	945 533	928 588	900 657
70	980 160	972 195	961 237	945 291	919 362	900 407	874 462	832 534
60	962 103	949 129	932 162	908 206	871 267	844 307	809 357	755 427
50	936 065	917 083	892 108	859 142	810 190	776 224	732 268	669 331

Note: The complements of the above figures may be used for percentile scores below 50.

same reliability coefficient, a percentile rank of 90 may (ninety-five out of one hundred times) really be somewhere within the limits 75 and 97 or a range of twenty-two points. Contrast this with the limits within which the true rank may be found ninety-five out of one hundred times for other ranks and other reliability coefficients.

As the ranks become more and more extreme we can have greater and greater confidence in a narrower and narrower range of possible true ranks.

Although greatest confidence can be placed in the most extreme rank on a test with the highest reliability, much confidence can be placed in extreme ranks even when the reliability of the test is low. Thus we can speak with as much confidence about a percentile rank of 98 when the reliability coefficient is .60, as we can speak about a percentile rank of 85 when the reliability coefficient is .95. This holds true for ranks at the lower extremity as well as for those at the higher extremity.

Thus, short and unreliable tests can be utilized for quite precise generalizations about individuals with extreme ranks, but only for the formulation of venturesome hypotheses about individuals who receive non-extreme ranks.

IV. USE OF A COMBINATION OF PROBABILITIES

If an individual student has taken a number of tests and a profile is drawn to represent his scores, we might want to know whether it is possible that he might really have received the mean score on these tests. That is, we would like to know the probability that this particular profile of abilities and disabilities is due to the errors associated with the tests, rather than to the presence of true abilities or disabilities.

The standard error of measurement can be used to determine the probability that one score is different from another in the same distribution. The difference between two scores may be divided by the standard error of measurement and the ratio referred to the x/σ column of a normal probability integral. Thus, if Individual A's score is 38, the mean in this case is 30, and the standard error of measurement is 3, then $\frac{38 - 30}{3} = 2.67$. The probability of these two scores being different is 9,924 out of 10,000. It is reasonable to suppose that these two scores are statistically different. It is also possible to determine the probability that on the other tests taken by this individual his score is different from the mean by following the above procedure.

Having determined the probability that each of the scores received by this individual is different from the mean, it is now desired to determine the probability that this combination of scores is different from a combination of mean scores on these tests. Lindquist (2) has pointed out a method whereby the probabilities from independent tests of significance can be combined. This is done by converting each probability to a chi-square value and then determining the probability of getting the sum of these chi-squares by chance.

A more direct technique for appraising the significance of a number of critical ratios may be determined. If we have

$$\text{sum} = \frac{x_1}{\sigma_1} + \frac{x_2}{\sigma_2} = Z_1 + Z_2 = CR_1 + CR_2,$$

then, if the tests are unrelated,

$$\sigma^2{}_{\text{sum}} = \sigma_{z_1}{}^2 + \sigma_{z_2}{}^2$$
$$\sigma_{\text{sum}} = \sqrt{\sigma_{z_1}{}^2 + \sigma_{z_2}{}^2}$$

Since $\sigma_{z_1}{}^2 = 1$ and $\sigma_{z_2}{}^2 = 1$

$$\sigma_{\text{sum}} = \sqrt{1+1} = \sqrt{2}$$

then $\dfrac{Z_1 + Z_2}{\sqrt{2}} = $ new critical ratio

Thus, to test the significance of a number of critical ratios it is necessary to determine their sum and divide by the square root of the number of critical ratios in the sum. See the following example:

	$\sigma \sqrt{1 - r_{11}}$	Mean	Individual A's Score	Critical Ratio
Test 1.............	4	15	23	2.00
Test 2.............	3	17	25	2.67
Test 3.............	5	10	21	2.20
				6.87

Since $\dfrac{6.87}{\sqrt{3}} = 3.97$, the probability of getting a critical ratio as great as this by chance is less than one in one thousand times.

It is obvious that the comparisons need not always be made from the mean. If the test user has found that individuals with a certain profile of test scores are ordinarily aided most by certain remedial measures or should be given certain types of guidance, the above procedure should be useful in determining the probability that the scores for a given individual are like or different from the profile of scores in question. When the comparison is with another score, the difference between the two scores should be divided by $\sqrt{2}$ times the standard error of measurement.

This procedure makes possible the testing of a number of hypotheses about the scores for a particular individual. Since it can be applied to a set of scores regardless of the size of the reliability coefficients, it should prove useful in the analysis of any type of profile where the characteristics in question can be expressed in quantitative terms.

The above method will yield lower probabilities of scores being different than is actually the case. Since most achievement tests are positively correlated, high scores on one test will quite likely be associated with high scores on another test. Thus the individual who has a certain score on one test will tend to make certain scores on other related tests. The method described above was based on the assumption that the test scores are unrelated; when related measures are used, a slightly different procedure should be adopted.

If the tests are related, the significance of a number of critical ratios may be derived.

If we have

$$\text{Sum} = \frac{x_1}{\sigma_1} + \frac{x_2}{\sigma_2} = Z_1 + Z_2 = CR_1 + CR_2$$

then

$$\sigma_{sum}^2 = \sigma_{z_1}^2 + \sigma_{z_2}^2 + 2r_{12}\sigma_{z_1}\sigma_{z_2}$$
$$\sigma_{sum} = \sqrt{\sigma_{z_1}^2 + \sigma_{z_2}^2 + 2r_{12}\sigma_{z_1}\sigma_{z_2}}$$

Since $\sigma_{z_1}^2 = 1$ and $\sigma_{z_2}^2 = 1$

$$\sigma_{sum} = \sqrt{1 + 1 + 2r_{12}} = \sqrt{2(1 + r_{12})} = \sqrt{2}\sqrt{1 + r_{12}}$$

If we assume that $r_{12} = r_{13} = r_{23}$, etc., then

$$\sigma_{sum} = \sqrt{N}\sqrt{1 + (N-1)r_{11}}$$

where N = number of critical ratios. The average correlation between the critical ratios can hardly be greater than the average reliability coefficients of the tests involved, so this may be used as a conservative upper bound of the intercorrelations.

Thus we may proceed as before to find the critical ratio on each test for the individual in question, sum these critical ratios and divide by σ_{sum} to secure the critical ratio of the sum.[1] This value may be referred to the normal probability integral to determine the probability that such a set of critical ratios might be obtained by chance.

[1] The writer is indebted to Dr. John H. Smith of the University of Chicago for certain suggestions on the significance of a sum of critical ratios.

REFERENCES

1. Kelley, T. L. *Interpretation of Educational Measurements.* New York: World Book Company, 1927, 210–211.
2. Lindquist, E. F. *Statistical Analysis in Educational Research.* Boston: Houghton Mifflin Company, 1940, 47.
3. Symonds, P. M. "Factors Influencing Test Reliability," *Journal of Educational Psychology,* XIX, 73–87.

14

Use of Correction for Chance
Success in Test Scoring

Frederick B. Davis

Much has been said about the use of scoring formulas to eliminate chance elements from test scores, and arguments have arisen as to the adequacy of such procedures. Davis presents some interesting evidence in the matter that should aid the student in deciding whether the use of scoring formulas is worthwhile.

The September, 1957, issue of the *Journal of Educational Research* contained an interesting article (2) on the use of the conventional scoring formula for true-false tests $(S = R - W)$. The basic data presented in that article are important enough to warrant further analysis. Mead and Smith administered 148 difficult true-false items to 100 volunteers, mostly college students, who indicated for each item they marked whether they did so (1) with confidence that they knew the correct answer, (2) with some doubt that their answers were correct, or (3) with no confidence on the basis of guessing. Examinees were allowed to refrain from marking any item if they had no idea of the correct answer and did not care to venture a guess. That the items were difficult is shown by the fact that the number of items marked correctly by the average examinee was 76.08 (where the most likely chance score was 74). The average number of items omitted was 10.69. After correction for chance by the conventional formula, the average score was 14.85. It is easily shown that this is significantly higher than the most likely chance score. A sample item follows:

T   F   John Cleves Symmes' theory of the nature of the earth at the poles has proved erroneous.

The 14,800 possible responses may be classified as shown in Table 1. Of the 3,594 responses made with confidence on the part of the examinees that their answers were correct, 1,271 (or 35.4 per cent) were actually wrong. According to the examinees, guessing did not enter into their marking of these

From Frederick B. Davis, "Use of Correction for Chance Success in Test Scoring," *The Journal of Educational Research*, LII (March, 1958), pp. 279–280. Reprinted with the permission of publisher and author.

Table 1

CLASSIFICATION OF 14,800 POSSIBLE RESPONSES BY 100 EXAMINEES

Basis for Response	R Correct Response	W Incorrect Response	0 No Response
1. Marked with confidence on the basis of information	2323		
2. Marked with confidence on the basis of mis-information		1271	
3. Marked with some doubt on the basis of partial information	2067		
4. Marked with some doubt on the basis of partial misinformation		1849	
5. Marked as a guess on the basis of chance and some partial information or misinformation	3218	3003	
6. Omitted on the basis of ignorance			1069
Totals	7608	6123	1069

responses. Errors must, therefore, be ascribed to misinformation. It is highly likely that the amount of misinformation displayed reflects the esoteric nature of the points tested. Of the 3,916 responses made with less than assurance on the part of the examinees of their correctness, 1,849 (or 47.2 per cent) were actually wrong. The partial information possessed by examinees permitted them to do significantly better than they could have expected to do by chance alone. Of the 6,221 responses described as made on the basis of guessing, 3,218 (or 51.7 per cent) were correct. It is unlikely that if chance had been the only basis for marking these items so large a number of them would have been marked correctly. We must attribute the outcome to the use of partial information that was unrecognized as such by the examinees. Their "guesses" were sometimes based on hunches. This deduction is consonant with the behavior of the examinees in refusing to respond 1,069 times. In the absence of even vague hunches, the examinees often made no responses.

It has been shown that the conventional formula for correcting multiple-choice items for chance success yields a maximum-likelihood estimate of an individual's true knowledge of the field measured provided that all items to which he responds are marked on the basis of either (1) knowledge sufficient for him to look for and mark the correct answer, or (2) chance. The corrected score of the average of the 100 examinees for whom response data are summarized in Table 1 may be written as follows (where the entries in the table are identified by the letters of the columns and the numbers of the rows, entry R1 being 2323, etc.):

$$S = R + R3 + R5 - W2 - W4 - W5; \text{ or}$$
$$S = 23.23 + 20.67 + 32.18 - 12.71 - 18.49 - 30.03$$
$$= 14.85.$$

In this computation, only term R1 is based on information. Term W2 is based on misinformation. Term R3 is based on partial information and term W4 on partial misinformation. Term R5 is based on partial information and chance while term W5 is based on partial misinformation and chance.

If we accept as accurate the reports of the examinees regarding the bases of their responses and our deductions concerning them, only the responses in terms R1 and 06 satisfy the assumptions underlying the correction formula as a maximum-likelihood estimator of true knowledge. Given the data available, then, our best estimate of the true knowledge of the average examinee is S = R1 = 23.23. As already pointed out, use of the formula yields a corrected score of 14.85. Thus, the formula "overcorrects" by 8.38 points in this specific application of it. The overcorrection is traceable mainly to the presence of misinformation (term W2). Note that the effect of partial misinformation in terms W4 and W5 is more than compensated for by the effect of partial information in R3 and R5. This tendency for the effect of partial information to offset the effects of partial misinformation and misinformation is often overlooked in evaluating the usefulness of the correction formula. Fortunately, these bases for marking items (that use of the formula as a maximum-likelihood estimator of true knowledge assumes are not present) tend to cancel each other out.

The average number of items marked correctly by the 100 examinees has already been given as 76.08. In terms of our analysis of the correction formula, it may be written as: S = R1 + R3 + R5 = 23.23 + 20.67 + 32.18 = 76.08. The resulting score is 52.85 points higher than 23.23, our best estimate of the true knowledge of the average examinee. It is obviously less representative of 23.23 than is the corrected score of 14.85.

It is the writer's belief that, for most tests and groups of subjects for whom the tests are suitable, the relative effects of misinformation and partial information are more nearly in balance than they are in the data presented by Mead and Smith. In fact, there are reasons to believe that the test situation represented by these data is such as to cause correction for chance success to yield almost its minimum of value. Yet, even under these circumstances, it yields scores that are better estimates of the true levels of knowledge of the examinees than does the scoring formula "Number Right," and it eliminates the labor of scanning answer sheets to prevent the giving of unjustified credit for the multiple marking of items. Important additional advantages that accrue from using the correction formula when ordinary tests are given under conditions of administration that teachers and school psychologists know exist during the practical use of tests in schools are explained by the writer in *Educational Measurement* (1).

Additional experiments of the general type reported by Mead and Smith should be conducted, using various kinds of subject matter and items at various levels of difficulty and with various numbers of choices. Tape recordings of the verbalized introspections of a group of examinees might well serve as one medium for obtaining basic data.

REFERENCES

1. Lindquist, E. F. (ed.). *Educational Measurement.* Washington: American Council on Education, 1953. Chapter 9, 268–278.
2. Mead, A. R., and Smith, B. M. "Does the True-False Scoring Formula Work? Some Data on an Old Subject," *Journal of Educational Research*, 51, 1957, 47–53.

15

Normative Standard Scores

Eric F. Gardner

If tests are going to be devices for comparing a given person's performance with that of other people in a defined group, some kind of meaningful procedure must be devised to make such a comparison possible. A rather carefully substantiated plan is proposed by Gardner.

A single isolated test score is of little or no value. For a score to have meaning and be of social or scientific utility, some sort of frame of reference is needed. A number of different frames of reference have been proposed and have been found to have value.

One possible frame of reference is the content of the test itself. Among derived scores one of the earliest was the per cent of a defined sample of tasks which an individual has completed satisfactorily. The deficiencies inherent in these kinds of scores have been discussed so many times in the literature no attempt will be made here to go into detail again. A few of the issues are the lack of comparability of per cent scores on the same test for different people, the lack of comparability from test to test, and the lack of algebraic utility. The following comments illustrate these points. John and Jane might each have scores of 60 per cent on the same test but have answered correctly very different items. A score of 80 per cent on a hard test is obviously not comparable to a score of 80 per cent on an easy test. For algebraic utility, equal units throughout the scale are desirable. It is not reasonable to assume that the difference between scores of 60 per cent and 70 per cent represent the

From Eric F. Gardner, "Normative Standard Scores," *Educational and Psychological Measurement*, XXII (Spring, 1962), pp. 7–14. Reprinted with the permission of publisher and author.

same difference in ability as that between 90 per cent and 100 per cent. Such scores ignore differences between items of the test in representativeness, difficulty and importance. Also it is obvious that the meaning of such scores is entirely dependent upon the particular sample of items included.

The content provided by the items of a test yields scores which may be directly related to standards set by the examiner who prepared the test. He may regard a score as good or poor on the basis of his judgments of the difficulties of the items and the expected performance of those taking the examination. Such judgments are difficult to make and frequently are not related to the realities of the situation. For example, when teachers or examining boards discover that very large proportions of those examined have fallen below the standard they originally built into the examination, they generally revise their judgments about the test and re-evaluate the test results. Thus the content or "absolute" frame of reference is supplemented by a relative frame of reference based upon knowledge of the performance of the group of examinees.

The inadequacy of the content frame of reference led to a consideration of additional approaches. One of the most commonly used frames of reference is the performance of some well-defined group of examinees. The College Board score scale, with a mean of 500 and a standard deviation of 100 for a group of examinees on which it was established some years ago, is one type of normative standard score. The I.Q. and grade scores are different types of basically normative standard scores.

This type of score provides a meaningful report of the examinee's performance in relation to those of members of a defined reference group. For example, it may be more useful to know how an examinee's performance on a particular test compares with those of his peers, than to know how it compares with the standards of the examiners. For many purposes, such as selection, placement and prediction, it is useful to know the location of a given score with respect to a particular frequency distribution of scores. For example, a grade score of 6.5 incorporates in it the information that the subject has obtained a score that is the same as the average of the normative group of sixth-graders who have been half a year in school. An I.Q. of 100 indicates that on the particular intelligence test the subject performed at the same level as the average of the normative group. A standard score of 600 indicates performance which is one standard deviation above the mean of the normative group.

In most cases the test user is concerned with frames of reference based on both content and group performance. He is interested in having knowledge about the specific responses of the individual to the items of the test and also knowledge about the performance of the individual relative to that of other individuals.

SOME DESIRABLE PROPERTIES OF ITEMS

If we ignore practical considerations and concern ourselves with characteristics of items that would aid in scaling and test interpretation, there are a number of desirable properties that can be mentioned. Some of these are difficult or impossible to obtain; while others, if obtained, would almost certainly prevent our achieving more important characteristics. Considering each specific issue in isolation and simultaneously assuming that all other necessary requirements for a good test are met, we could argue the following properties would be desirable:

1. *The test consists of items which constitute a representative sample of the domain tested.* It should be a sample of behaviors that represent the objectives which have previously been defined.

2. *The items in the test form a Guttman Scale.* This property implies that the items selected can be ranked in the same order of difficulty for each individual. Once the items have been so ranked, any examinee will answer correctly all those items of less difficulty and incorrectly all those of greater difficulty. Thus a score of 17 means that the person answered correctly the first seventeen items and incorrectly all others. Such an arrangement of items permits an unambiguous interpretation of the score 17 in that all people who score 17 have answered correctly the same items.

3. *The items in the test can be arranged along a continuum of the variable under consideration in such a way that the raw scores constitute an interval scale.* The items included in such a test would have the property of representing equal differences in ability between adjacent items. For example, the difference in ability represented by scores of 53 and 54 would be the same as that represented by scores of 85 and 86.

4. *The items are of such nature that a zero score on the test represents zero amount of the ability being tested.* If the condition specific in property 3 is now added, the scale becomes a ratio scale which is amenable to all four arithmetic operations.

5. *The items provide a scale unit which is meaningful.* There are advantages in having the size of unit related to the standard error of measurement in such a way that a user has some idea as to the likelihood of a difference being entirely due to error.

A test possessing the properties just enumerated (that is, consisting of items which (1) adequately represent the domain to be tested and (2) can be ranked in order of difficulty, and starting with an absolute zero will provide successively equal increments of knowledge) provides a raw score scale with very desirable characteristics. Unfortunately these properties, although desirable, are difficult to achieve and in many practical situations the achievement of one results in less success in achieving another. For example, I would argue that property 1 is paramount for any achievement test. That is, a good achievement test should itself define the objectives measured. These objectives are set up by those agents of society who are responsible for decisions concerning educational objectives, and the test constructor must attempt to incorporate that definition in the building of the examination. This point of view implies that the method of scaling an educational achievement test should not be permitted to determine the content of the test or to alter the definition of objectives implied in the test. It is most probable that an attempt to select items so that the raw score scale produced has properties 2 and 3 (an interval Guttman Scale) would eliminate from the test sample important concepts and skills.

SAMPLING FROM POPULATIONS OF ITEMS AND EXAMINEES

This discussion so far has suggested that the interpretation of achievement test scores requires one to consider two very different types of frames of reference, each associated with a particular sampling problem.

The first problem is concerned with an acceptable sample of items. For a test score to be meaningful the particular variable under consideration must be defined, and the user must have knowledge about the adequacy of the items to sample this domain. Hence, specific knowledge of the field and of the items included in the test is necessary for the adequate interpretation of a raw score.

The second problem is concerned with a sample of examinees. Information about such things as item or test difficulty functioning of decoys, norms and predictive effectiveness are dependent upon empirical data. To be meaningful these indices must be derived from an acceptable sample of people obtained from a well-defined population. A difficulty index for a reading item obtained from a typical fourth grade obviously does not have the same meaning as one obtained from a typical sixth grade. A person scoring at the eighty-fourth percentile, or obtaining a T-score of 60 in an arithmetic test where the score is calculated from a typical seventh grade sample, is not performing at the same level as one whose standing at the eighty-fourth percentile on the same test is calculated from a below-average seventh grade. Likewise a pupil with a vocabulary grade score of 6.2 obtained from a representative sample of fifth graders, in say, Mississippi, is certainly not comparable to a pupil making a score of 6.2 based on a national representative sample. By the same token, one would hardly expect a set of decoys for an arithmetic multiple-choice item to function in the same fashion in both a fifth and ninth grade. The importance of the particular reference population which is used cannot be overemphasized.

CURRENT PRACTICE

In the construction of an achievement test, the issue of the sampling of the items is considered under the concept of validity — usually content validity. Appropriate objectives are defined, tables of specifications are established, and trial items are constructed to sample the variable described.

Data are then obtained to give information about the statistical characteristics of the items. In the light of this additional information, the test is assembled in such a way that the items will sample both content defined by the objectives and the ability of the examinees for which it is designed.

Attempts are then made by scaling procedures to approximate some of the other desirable properties which the test does not acquire solely through the relationship of the items to each other. Current methods of scaling educational achievement tests are based upon the statistical properties of the test, or of the individual items constituting the test with reference to a particular population of examinees. That is, such scales are derived from normative data.

Raw scores on some educational achievement tests are meaningful in themselves in terms of content of the test. For example, a score of 30 on a test built of 50 basic addition combinations gives some information about the particular student without regard for the performance of any other person. However, groups of such items arranged with reference to such a meaning do not constitute scales. You cannot compare 30 out of these 50 basic addition facts with 30 out of a different set, or 6 out of 15 rules of grammar, or with a possible number of vocabulary items in Russian. Some frame of reference is needed so that performance from person to person and group to group can be compared. The scaling job still remains to be done.

Any added meanings of scaled scores is due entirely to the contribution of the normative data, and that meaning applies, strictly speaking, only to the particular reference population involved in the scaling process. This statement holds whether the scale is based solely upon item statistics or upon some operations on the total score. Normative standard scores are dependent upon the sample of subjects selected (4).

Let us consider the role of the population in several common scaling procedures. A familiar frame of reference is provided by the performance of individuals in a single well-defined group on a particular test at a particular time. Two commonly used scales have been derived within such a frame of reference. The simplest are ordinal scales, such as percentile scores, in which the scale number describes relative position in the group. The second type are interval scales where an effort has been made to obtain algebraic utility by definition. The T-scores of McCall represent an interval scale where equal units have been defined as equal distances along the abscissa of a postulated normal population frequency distribution. A variation is the College Entrance Examination Board scores with a mean of 500 and standard deviation of 100 for the parent, normally distributed population.

A second type of frame of reference is provided by the test performance of individuals belonging to well-defined subgroups where the subgroups have a specific relationship to each other within the composite group.

Within this frame of reference both ordinal and interval scales have been derived. Initially the basic problem is to obtain ordinally related subgroups such as grades 1 to 9 or age groups from a specific population for the scaling operation. Age scores and grade scores provide ordinal scales which have had wide utility in the elementary grades. Attempts have been made to obtain the merits of an algebraically manipulatable scale by utilizing ordinal relationship of subgroups but introducing restrictions in terms of the shape of frequency distributions. Efforts to obtain interval scales within such frames of reference have been made by Flanagan (1) in the development of Scaled Scores of the Cooperative Tests and by Gardner (3) in the development of K-Scores.

Test scores are used by administrators, teachers and research workers to make comparisons in terms of rank, level of development, growth and trait differences among both individuals and groups. Hence many types of scales and norms have been developed depending upon the intended use. Each is consistent within itself but the properties of the scales are not completely consistent from one type of scale to another. For example, a grade scale is not appropriate for measuring growth in a function unless one is willing to accept the assumption that growth is linearly related to grade. The scaling of the Binet items involves the assumption of a linear relationship between Mental Age and Chronological Age. As valuable and useful as the Binet Scale has been for the purpose for which it was designed, it has obvious limitations when we try to infer the "true" nature of intellectual growth.

It should be emphasized that the adoption of any one of the scales available does not exclude the use of any of the others. In fact, most situations require the test user to utilize more than one type of scale or norm for an adequate interpretation of test results.

CONCLUSION

Normative standard scores are measures obtained from scales having certain specific properties, and they incorporate in the numerical values certain information about the normative group used. They are obtained by statistically manipulating the raw score responses of a defined group of people on a defined sample of content. It is desirable to facilitate the interpretation of test scores by giving them as much direct meaning as possible. As Flanagan (2) has said ". . . if much information is built into the score itself, continual use makes its interpretation more and more direct and immediate. It is also of great assistance if such fundamental built-in meanings can be as constant from one test to the next as possible." However, the amount of meaning that can be built into any single reference scale will constitute only a very small part of the total amount of meaning to be desired by all of the test users from those results. It is almost always necessary to supplement the knowledge inherent in the scores with other normative data. Norms based on a variety of different groups have considerable merit. Different types of norms such as grade scores, percentile scores and various types of standard scores all have their place. The case for all normative standard scores stands or falls on their ability to provide additional and more useful information than can be obtained from the raw scores from which they were derived.

REFERENCES

1. Flanagan, John C. "Scaled Scores." The Cooperative Test Service of the American Council on Education, 1939.
2. ———. "Units, Scores and Norms." In *Educational Measurement* (E. F. Lindquist, ed.). Washington, D.C.: American Council on Education, 1950.
3. Gardner, Eric F. "Comments on Selected Scaling Techniques with a Description of a New Type of Scale," *Journal of Clinical Psychology*, VI (1950), 38–42.
4. ———. "The Importance of Reference Groups in Scaling Procedure," *Proceedings of the 1952 Invitational Conference on Testing Problems.* Princeton, N.J.: Educational Testing Service, 1953, 13–21.

16

Scales with Nonmeaningful Origins and Units of Measurement

William H. Angoff

Although there are arguments in favor of normative standard scores, they also have their limitations. It is these limitations that concern Angoff, and his recommendations for dealing with them are very provocative.

The three speakers before me have all made the point that scores should have the characteristic of yielding direct interpretive information; and two of the speakers, Dr. Gardner and Dr. Ebel, have quoted Dr. Flanagan as sharing their general viewpoint. That seems to make it unanimous, and judging from the title of the present paper, leaves me with the only dissenting opinion. However, I would like to make it clear that there is only one point with which I would take issue with the other members of the panel: whether meaning should be incorporated into the scores directly by the test publisher or whether meaning should more properly be brought to the scores directly by the user himself and indirectly by the publisher.

If we were to examine the various reasons that are given for preferring systems of derived score scales for standardized tests rather than the original raw score scales, we might find that the reasons fall into about four categories:

One, for the sake of convenience in handling test score data, it is frequently desirable to convert raw scores to scales with pre-assigned characteristics in round numbers that are easy to recall and easy to use. The stanine scale is a good example of a scale that possesses this characteristic, as is the IQ scale, the 50-10 scale, and others.

Two, it is frequently maintained that the original raw score scale of a test is no more than an ordinal scale and cannot be used, for example, to compare score changes in different regions of the scale. In an effort to make comparisons of this sort possible, raw score scales are converted to derived scales in which the unit separations between scores are in some sense equal. Dr. Flana-

From William H. Angoff, "Scales with Nonmeaningful Origins and Units of Measurement," *Educational and Psychological Measurement,* XXII (Spring, 1962), pp. 27–34. Reprinted with the permission of publisher and author.

gan's Scaled Score System and Dr. Gardner's K-Scores are derived scales of this type.

Three, derived scales are used when more than one form of a test is available and the forms are used interchangeably. In such instances it is considered desirable to equate the forms in order to make the reported scores independent of the form used to obtain them. It is also considered desirable to report scores on a scale which is different from the raw score scale of any form. The derived scale, then, exists as a referent for all test forms, which are interrelated through a process of equating. This process accomplishes the result that, within the limits of random error, the reported score earned by an examinee would be the same, irrespective of the particular test form which actually yielded the score. The College Board Scale is one of a number of scale systems that purport to relate test forms in this way.

Four, it is frequently maintained that the raw score scale yields little or no immediate meaning of its own. For that reason, derived score scales are established in which normative meaning is directly incorporated. The simplest process by which this is accomplished may be described as consisting of the following steps: The test forms are administered to a random or representative sample of a defined population, one whose characteristics are presumably well known. The raw scores for the sample are then collected, pertinent statistics are drawn up, and a conversion applied, either to yield a mean and standard deviation with certain pre-assigned numerical values, or to yield a particular distribution-form with certain pre-assigned numerical values. This scale is then said to have normative meaning because the knowledge of any derived score yields immediate evaluative knowledge of test performance in comparison with the members of a known population. McCall's T-Scores represent a scale of this type, as do many others.

Regarding each of these four characteristics that test constructors consider for their test scales, there appears to be no problem, first of all, in connection with the characteristic of convenience. Unless there were some overriding consideration, it is difficult to imagine why one would choose to assign a number like 81.27 as the mean, for example, of a distribution of derived scores rather than a more convenient one like 50 or 100. Secondly, as far as equality of units is concerned, there is no question about the importance of this problem in measurement. There appears to be no issue here either.

With regard to the question of form-to-form equating, it seems not only reasonable but essential, in a continuing testing program where new test forms are frequently introduced, or in a system of test offerings where more than one form of a test exists, that some means be provided to report scores on a single scale independent of test form. A system of this sort, which can exist only as a result of form-to-form equating, makes it possible to ensure that within the limits of equating error, an examinee's reported score will be unbiased by the form he happened to take. It also ensures that over the course of time, irrespective of the introduction of new forms and the abandonment of old forms, the scale will continue to stand and will continue to yield interpretable data comparable with data collected at earlier times. The characteristic of scale constancy makes it possible to observe, among other things, shifts and changes in the ability of the groups tested over a period of time.

With regard to the normative characteristic of the scale, there *is*, it seems to me, some serious question whether this is always essential or even always desirable. The definition and construction of this type of scale presupposes that there exists a population which is sufficiently unique among all those possible to warrant its choice as the referent population for the system of tests and scores under consideration. This is questionable. There are usually many populations that can be used for this purpose. What frequently happens in scaling the test is that the group chosen to form the normative basis for the scale is a very general one, often too general to use for specific score interpretation. In order, then, to provide data for specific decisions — such as for guidance, placement, or remedial education — additional interpretive aids have to be devised — for example, differentiated norms, local norms, regression equations, and content interpretations — and the group that was originally incorporated into the scale to give it normative meaning often goes unused — or, perhaps, is used when it shouldn't be.

This would lead us to ask: What kind of scale should take the place of the normative scale? The answer to this is particularly difficult to give because it appears to take away and not to give in return. What is suggested here is a non-normative scale — a scale that has no normative meaning at all. The mechanics of defining the scale of numbers can be as simple as one wishes. If the conversion is to be a linear one, one can set the minimum and maximum scores on one of the forms at desired scale values, say 20 and 80, and the scale for the system of equated test forms, when such a system exists, is automatically defined. *Or,* one can choose some convenient group of examinees who are not seriously atypical of those who will be expected to take the tests in the future, and set the mean and standard deviation of this group equal to a pair of convenient numbers in order to transform the raw scores. This group, it should be emphasized, is only a conveniently available group. It need not possess special normative characteristics; indeed, it may be a group that would not ordinarily be used for normative interpretation. If the scale is to be so defined that unit separations are to be made equal in some sense, then this can be done by adjusting the raw score intervals in the desired fashion. This system of adjusted raw score units can then be translated to a new, more convenient system in direct linear fashion in either of the ways described above. The final derived scale would still, of course, retain the relationships among the interpoint distances of the desired interval scale.

The significant point here is simply that it does not matter how the number system is originally defined. The scale can be referred to as a general range of numbers, one that exists without inherent meaning and one that serves only as a referent or vehicle for equating the system of test forms when such a system of test forms is in operation.

One of the difficulties in describing the properties of the non-normative scale is that its advantages are negative ones, negative in the sense that what it contributes is an avoidance of the problems of the alternative, the normative scale. It may therefore be helpful to examine these problems.

There are a number of criteria for the appropriateness of a scale system, but the particular criterion I would like to discuss is the one that is imposed by the passage of time. Let us suppose that the situation for scaling a new test is ideal, one where the unique or the particularly desirable norms population does exist and can be sampled. Having gone to the trouble to establish a sound, acceptable normative basis for the scale, we would want to ask ourselves what assurance we would have that the built-in norms would not be obsolete in ten or twenty years and that the normative scale would exist without normative meaning. At that time the real dilemma would have to be faced: whether to maintain the scale and abandon any pretense of current normative meaning, or to redefine the scale in terms of a currently meaningful group and give up automatic continuity with the past. Personally I see little hope of a satisfactory compromise here.

The point is made here that it is the passage of time and the changes brought on with the passage of time that test the usefulness of a scale. And changes do occur — sometimes dramatic ones. In a 1948 article in the *American Psychologist*, Tuddenham reported that when the Wells Revision of the Army Alpha was administered to a sample of World War II enlisted men it was found that their median score of 104 fell at the 83rd percentile for the soldiers tested in World War I with the original Army Alpha. The World War I median of 62 corresponded to the 22nd percentile of the World War II soldiers. Even allowing for the small differences in difficulty in the two tests, the difference in these norms is still striking. Tuddenham attributes the change to increased familiarity with objective tests and, even more, to superior educational opportunity in the 1940's. Whatever the reasons are, there is no question that populations can and do change with time. Test scales must be built to be adaptive to the change.

For purposes of illustration I would like to consider a testing program like the Scholastic Aptitude Test Program of the College Board. Here is a program in which there are a number of extant forms of, say, the Verbal Test in current use, all interrelated on a single scale which is maintained through a system of equating, going back to the time when the scale was first established. This scale, still in use today, was originally defined as one which yielded a mean of 500 and standard deviation of 100 for the group of candidates who were tested in April, 1941, a group of 10,766 candidates applying to one or more of the 45 colleges who constituted the membership of the College Board at that time. In the academic year 1959–60 the comparable number of College Board candidates had risen to over 566,000 — approximately *thirty* times the number tested in the entire year 1941. The number of member colleges of the College Board has also grown — from 45 in 1941 to 287 in 1960. The point does not have to be made any more emphatically than is already made by these figures that the last twenty years have brought about some considerable changes in the character of the College Board applicant group, changes which, it seems to me, render the original group inappropriate as a normative group today. Indeed, there is some serious question in this instance whether the scale ever had normative meaning, since the group was not defined for its highly meaningful normative value, but simply because, you might say, *it was there*, and there was no other immediately available. In any case, normative or not at the time of its definition, it most certainly does not have any normative meaning today. Yet it is very significant that, in spite of the absence of inherent normative meaning, the scale does have meaning of another kind, meaning that is provided in the normative data published by the College Board, and even more, meaning that is acquired in the minds of the test users in dealing with the scores over the course of time. Obviously, then, while a scale can derive one kind of meaning from its definition, it can also derive meaning from the experience that the user acquires in applying the scale to the measurement of familiar objects. Therefore, these principles can be stated here: One, that the meaning that is invested in a scale at the time of its definition is not lasting; indeed, there is some question whether it is useful. The real meaning in a scale is the meaning given to it by the user over a period of time with experience and familiarity and with normative aids. *Two*, that a scale has a reasonable chance of being meaningful to the user if it does not change. For both of these principles an analogy taken from everyday measurement is helpful, it seems to me. There is hardly a person here who knows the precise original definition of the length of the foot used in the measurement of height or distance, or which king it was whose foot was originally agreed upon as the standard; on the other hand, there is no one here who does not know how to evaluate lengths and distances in terms of this unit. Our ignorance of the precise original meaning or derivation of the foot does not lessen its usefulness to us in any way. Its usefulness derives from the fact that it remains the same over time and allows us to familiarize ourselves with it. Needless to say, precisely the same considerations apply to other units of measurement — the inch, the mile, the degree of Fahrenheit, and so on. In the field of psychological measurement it is similarly reasonable to say that the original definition of the scale is or should be of no consequence. What is of consequence is the maintenance of a constant scale — which, in the case of a multiple-form testing program, is achieved by rigorous form-to-form equating — and the provision of supplementary normative data to aid in interpretation and in the formation of specific decisions, data which would be revised from time to time as conditions warrant.

Let us suppose that a suitable norms population had been chosen for the College Board Program in 1941. How suitable would that population be today, not only because the numbers of candidates are so much greater today than they were then, but also because qualitatively they are different kinds of people? And it is entirely proper to ask this question, even though the mean performance of all candidates tested today is not much different from the mean performance of all candidates tested in 1941.

Suppose further that the candidate population changes, not only in qualitative characteristics but also in level or dispersion of performance. Should the scale be redefined in terms of a normative group relevant to current examinees, or should the scale be retained and simply defined as one which does not yield automatic normative information, in much the same way as the commonly used physical units are defined? Even more significant than the considerations discussed thus far is the fact that if the scale is redefined in terms of an appropriate current normative group, then the act of altering the scale through redefinition would necessarily bring about the loss of that very characteristic of the scale that made it possible to observe the change in the group's relevance in the first place — the characteristic of the constancy or continuity of the scale. It would seem that the appropriate decision here is to retain the existing scale, however one cares to regard its meaning or lack of it, and direct the larger effort toward maintaining and improving a stable and continuing score reporting system.

The definition of the number system for a test scale is a commitment for the future. If a single normative group is available and if it is meaningful above all others for making score interpretations, and if future populations of examinees are not expected to differ in any significant way from the population tested today, then the test scale can be defined in a normative fashion. If this is not the case — and quite often it will not be — then the scale of numbers should be chosen in the most arbitrary way possible and then quickly forgotten. If the test constructor feels that this process of scale definition will deprive it of meaning, he is unduly pessimistic. Meaning will come — but only through his efforts to provide a variety of current and useful norms, and through the experience of the users of his tests.

SUGGESTED READINGS

Ahmann, J. Stanley, and Glock, Marvin D. *Evaluating Pupil Growth* (2nd. ed.). Boston: Allyn and Bacon, Inc., 1963.

Part Three of this text presents a simple description of basic test theory. The concepts are presented at the introductory level and are supplemented with descriptions of practical examples.

Anastasi, Anne. *Psychological Testing* (2nd. ed.). New York: The Macmillan Co., 1961.

In Chapters 4, 5, 6, and 7 of this text the basic concepts of test theory are presented in some detail and precision. Anastasi is clear as to the basic assumptions and requirements associated with each technique, and although she gives considerable attention to test theory, she also devotes time to the interpretation aspects of theory. Some knowledge of simple statistics is helpful in understanding the ideas presented.

Cronbach, Lee J. *Essentials of Psychological Testing* (2nd. ed.). New York: Harper and Brothers, 1960.

Chapters 4, 5, and 6 of this text deal with theoretical issues in testing. Basic concepts are presented along with modes of interpretation and their use in making personnel decisions. Knowledge of basic statistics is assumed in the presentation.

Gulliksen, Harold. *Theory of Mental Tests.* New York: John Wiley and Sons, Inc., 1952.

This book is a rigorous development of basic measurement theory, involving extensive statistical developments of procedures. It is especially recommended for students who wish to progress beyond the introductory level of knowledge in test theory.

Helmstadter, G. C. *Principles of Psychological Measurement.* New York: Appleton-Century-Crofts, Inc., 1964.

The author deals with basic concepts at a somewhat sophisticated level; however, the statistical rigor of Gulliksen is in a large part avoided. A good text for students with an introductory knowledge of statistics who wish to extend their knowledge of test theory.

Thorndike, Robert L., and Hagen, Elizabeth. *Measurement and Evaluation in Psychology and Education* (2nd. ed.). New York: John Wiley and Sons, Inc., 1961.

Chapters 6 and 7 of this text present a simple, nontechnical discussion of test theory topics. These chapters are recommended for students who are at the elementary level of acquaintance with test theory.

Assessing Maximum Performance

The concepts of intelligence, aptitude, and achievement have been the subject of much extended debate, yet controversies persist. The principal issues center around defining and delimiting the basic constructs. What is intelligence? How is it different from achievement or aptitude? Can we think of achievement without also dealing with aptitude?

To a considerable extent tests have influenced the definitions of variables they have been designed to measure. Thorndike's claim that intelligence is what intelligence tests measure is not entirely facetious. The behaviors that are called for by various tests are of course only a sample of a universe of behaviors, but a sample which defines how the universe is to be perceived. For example, an achievement test in arithmetic may have only twenty-five computations on it, but these are chosen so as to be representative of the many computations that could reasonably be included in the curriculum, and as such they define what computation is. Therefore, one needs to investigate intelligence, aptitude, and achievement tests to see how the behaviors called for are samples of the same population of behaviors.

The reader may also wish to consider differences between intelligence, aptitude, and achievement tests in terms of the validation procedure which applies to each. For example, is it possible that an item of knowledge would not reasonably be included in an achievement test based on a content analysis of the curriculum, but could be an item that discriminates on a criterion of intelligence?

Coleman and Cureton (Selection 18) and Levine (Selection 23) deal with the problem of delineating the concepts of intelligence and achievement as different behavior functions. The reader will notice readily that the two articles reflect opinions that may very well lead to different modes of test classification.

Since intelligence testing is so widespread and has probably received more attention than any other single area in mental measurement, Unit Three includes a variety of comments about assessing intelligence. At times test makers become involved with mechanics to the neglect of the basic theory out of which test content must emerge. McNemar (Selection 20) reviews theories and tries to jolt the reader toward bringing some synthesis to the controversies. The remaining articles on intelligence testing deal with how to handle the results produced by these tools.

The reader should find some evidence here to support his views about the stability of the I.Q. Various physical characteristics fluctuate in their rate of development. Is this also true of intelligence? Do all intelligence tests produce the same results for a given child? Can the idea that comes from comparing I.Q.'s taken from several tests for a given child be generalized to comparing grade norms from several achievement tests for that child? And what about the content of intelligence tests? Is some content, non-verbal items, for example, more appropriate for assessing the intelligence of some children, whereas other content, for example, verbal items, more appropriate for others? If so, do the intelligence test results of one child reflect a different class of behaviors than those of another child? If the answer is yes, can a teacher apply the results of intelligence tests in the same manner to all problems? The content of this unit should provide some answers to these problems.

The basic question that the reader should hold before him as he proceeds through the next group of selections should be: What do these different kinds of test results tell me in terms of the behaviors I should expect from children and adults? The articles have been selected not only to point out what tests can be expected to do, but also to illustrate the limitations in the use of these tests' results.

The Stability of Mental Test Performance Between Two and Eighteen Years[1]

Marjorie P. Honzik, Jean W. Macfarlane, and Lucile Allen[2]

A child's I.Q. at one age is very likely not going to be his I.Q. at another age, even though the same test is used at both ages. How much change should be expected during the school age years? At what ages do the greatest changes appear? Are there any clues as to the direction of changes on intelligence test results? Honzik et al. provide some interesting data on these questions.

In an earlier study, the constancy of mental test performance was reported for a group of normal children during their preschool years (8). These children are now young adults, and it is possible to show the relative stability or lability of their mental test scores over the entire period of testing, 21 months to 18 years, inclusive. The contribution of the present study lies in the fact of repeated individual tests given at specified ages over a 16-year period to more than 150 children; and, second, in the fact that this group of children was selected so as to be a representative sample of the children born in an urban community during the late 1920's. Furthermore, since the Guidance Study has as its primary purpose the study of personality development and associated factors, it has been possible to note the relation of fluctuations or stability in rate of mental growth to physical ills, unusual environmental strains or supports, and to evidences of tension or serenity within the individual child.

From Marjorie P. Honzik, Jean W. Macfarlane, and Lucile Allen, "The Stability of Mental Test Performance Between Two and Eighteen Years," *The Journal of Experimental Education*, XVII (December, 1949), pp. 309–324. Reprinted with the permission of publisher and authors.

[1] The data of this investigation are those of the Guidance Study, which is being carried on at the University of California Institute of Child Welfare under the direction of Dr. Jean W. Macfarlane.

[2] Over 2500 individual mental tests were given the 252 children observed; of this number, over 1500, or 60 per cent, were given by Lucile Allen, who also assembled certain of the case material. The case summaries were written by J. W. Macfarlane. M. P. Honzik is largely responsible for the analysis of the data and certain of the conclusions drawn. Acknowledgement is also due to the many statisticians who have helped in the data compilation, J. Delaney, M. Snyder, E. Laws, L. Klein, and H. H. Hoffman.

The Sample

The Guidance Study has been described in detail in previous publications (10, 11, 12). Suffice it to say here that the two groups, which are referred to as the Guidance and Control Groups, constitute representative subsamples of the Berkeley Survey. The names of every third child born in Berkeley between January 1, 1928, and June 30, 1929, were included in the Berkeley Survey (15). A total of 252 children from the Berkeley Survey Group were asked to come to the Institute for their first mental test at the age of 21 months. At this age level, the group of 252 children was divided into two matched subsamples of 126 children on the basis of socio-economic factors (parents' national derivation, income, father's occupation, socio-economic rating, neighborhood, and mother's age and education). One of these subsamples (of the Berkeley Survey) has been called the "Guidance Group" because of the program of intensive interviews had with the parents and children; the second group, which has had physical examinations and mental tests but fewer and less intensive interviews and these at a much later age of the child, has been called the "Control Group." The children in both groups were given mental tests at the age of 21 months. At ages 2 and 2½ years, only the children in the Guidance Group were tested. Thereafter, the testing program was the same for the two groups.

Every effort was made to test the children as nearly as possible on or near their birthdays. Actually, from 72 to 95 per cent of the children were tested within one month of their birthdates at the various ages up to and including 8 years (8).

As was to be expected in a longitudinal study, a number of children were unable to come in for one or more of the mental tests. The most frequent cause of a missed test was the family being "out of town." However, a number of families lost interest or became uncooperative as their children grew older; one child was killed in an automobile accident. Tables 1 and 2 show the number of children tested at each age level. It will be seen that at 18 years 153 of the 252 children were tested on the Wechsler-Bellevue. The reasons that the remaining 99 did not come in for a test are listed in the following table:

	Guidance n	Control n
"Out of town"	24	26
Uncooperative	17	16
Died	—	1
Case closed early, cause unknown	—	6

Missed 18-year test
    (due to changes in
    staff, illness, or
    transportation difficulties)
	5	4

	46	53

The reasons for lack of cooperation on the part of the parents and children are many and varied. Three children were embarrassed by the physical examinations. One father objected to his daughter having a physical examination. Two children objected to taking mental tests (their I.Q.'s were 101 and 110, respectively, at 15 years). One uncooperative family was in legal difficulties and did not want to discuss their affairs. A rough method of evaluating the selectiveness of the sample not tested at 18 years is to compare the education of their parents with that of the children who were tested at 18 years:

Education of Parents	Tested at 18 Years %	Not Tested at 18 Years %
College	40	33
High school	40	46
Grammar school	20	21
	100	100

This comparison shows that more of the parents of children who were tested at 18 years were college trained; fewer had a high school education, and the same proportion had a grammar school education, as was true of the group as a whole. These differences may modify but do not invalidate our conclusions.

The Testing Program

The testing program followed in the Guidance Study is summarized in the following table:

Ages	Test
21 months–5 years	California Preschool Schedule I or II
6 and 7 years	Stanford-Binet, 1916 Revision
8 years	Stanford Revision, Form L
9–15 years	Stanford Revision (either Form L or M)
18 years	Wechsler-Bellevue

During the preschool years, 21 months to 5 years, inclusive, each child was tested at successive age levels on the same test, either the California Preschool Schedule I or California Preschool Schedule II.[3] Beginning at age 9, a program of test alternation was begun which was designed to show the effects of a change in the form of the test on mental test constancy.... All the children in both groups were tested on either Form L or Form M of the Stanford Revision at age 9 years. But at ages 12 and 14 years, only two-thirds of the groups were given mental tests; the remaining third of the groups was

[3] The published California Preschool Scale Form A (9) is composed largely of items from the California Preschool Schedule I, together with a few items from the California Preschool Schedule II. The test items for the California Schedules I and II include selections made by Dr. Adele S. Jaffa from several standardized tests, together with some original items first validated at the Institute. These scales have been normed by the Thurstone method of absolute scaling.

Table 1

Means and Standard Deviations of I.Q.'s for Children in the Guidance Study

Age in Years	Test	Guidance Group			Control Group			Total*		
		n	Mean	S.D.	n	Mean	S.D.	n	Mean	S.D.
6	Stanford-Binet	109	118.8	11.6	102	118.3	13.5	211	118.6	12.6
7	Stanford-Binet	104	119.6	14.3	104	117.0	11.8	208	118.3	13.1
8	Stanford Revision Form L	100	119.4	17.4	99	117.9	17.0	199	118.7	17.2
9	Stanford Revision									
	Form L	36	126.1	20.7	54	119.0	19.7			
	Form M	64	117.5	16.7	40	123.4	13.9			
	Total Form L and M							194	120.7	18.2
10	Stanford Revision									
	Form L	65	118.3	18.0	42	123.7	15.0			
	Form M	33	121.6	17.8	50	121.1	19.5			
	Total Form L and M							190	120.8	17.9
12	Stanford Revision									
	Form L	35	114.9	15.3	57	121.4	15.3			
	Form M	34	125.1	16.9	8	126.9	19.4			
13	Form L	29	⁻⁻121.8	20.1	28	115.4	17.7			
	Form M					- - - -				
12 or 13	Total Form L and M							191	120.3	17.4
14	Stanford Revision									
	Form L	28	128.2	16.8	23	118.8	17.9			
	Form M	32	117.0	17.6	35	127.6	13.5			
15	Form M	30	124.2	15.8	20	121.5	17.3			
14 or 15	Total Form L and M							168	123.2	16.9
18	Wechsler-Bellevue	80	118.4	12.0	73	117.9	11.0	153	118.2	11.6

* These means and standard deviations were used in computing the sigma scores for individual children.

Table 2

CORRELATIONS BETWEEN TEST SCORES GIVEN AT DIFFERENT AGES

Test	Age	n	California Preschool Schedule I or II						Stanford-Binet		Stanford Revision Forms											W-B
			2	2½	3	3½	4	5	6	7	L 8	L 9	M 9	L 10	M 10	L 12	L (12 or 13)	M (12 or 13)	L 14	L (14 or 15)	M (14 or 15)	18
California Preschool Schedule I or II	1¾	234.	.71	.62	.52	.48	.38	.39	.27	.29	.27	.26	.17	.22	.19	.19		.13	.07	.21	.21	.07
	2	113		.71	.69	.60	.46	.32	.47	.46	.43	.45	.29	.37	.37	.49		.26	.21	.34	.34	.31
	2½	114			.73	.64	.57	.46	.37	.38	.37	.53	.32	.36	.55		.36	.42	.26	.31	.31	.24
	3	229				.71	.58	.57	.57	.55	.49	.59	.49	.59	.60		.51	.52	.35	.37	.37	.35
	3½	215					.76	.71	.54	.60	.50	.59	.60	.66	.62		.48	.63	.49	.46	.46	.42
	4	211						.72	.52	.59	.61	.68	.71	.75	.67		.62	.68	.54	.44	.44	.42
	5								.71	.73	.70								.61	.62	.62	.56
Stanford-Binet	6	214								.82	.77	.80	.67	.71	.76	.74	.65		.67	.70	.70	.61
	7	208									.83	.82	.80	.77	.78	.71	.82		.73	.76	.76	.71
Stanford Revision Forms:	L 8	199										.91	.93	.88	.88	.85	.85	.82	.85	.81		.70
	L 9	90												.88		.90			.87			.76
	M 9	104													.90			.79			.91	.66
	L 10	107														.87			.85			.70
	M 10	83																.91			.87	.76
	L 12	92																	.92			.76
	L (12 or 13)	120																		.89		.78
	M (12 or 13)	71																			.88	.84
	L 14	51																				.73
	M (14 or 15)	117																				.79

tested at ages 13 and 15 years. In presenting group results, the scores for ages 12 and 13 years have been considered together, as have scores for ages 14 and 15 years.

The I.Q.'s obtained on the Stanford tests and the Wechsler-Bellevue were converted into sigma or standard scores so that they would be in comparable form to the mental test sigma scores obtained between 21 months and 5 years. The means and standard deviations of the I.Q.'s which were used in computing the sigma scores are given in Table 1. The mean I.Q.'s for the combined Guidance and Control Groups shown in the last columns of the table were the ones used in computing sigma scores for individual children.

Table 1 also shows that, although these children were selected as a representative sample of urban children, their scores are considerably above the test norms. The average I.Q. on the Stanford-Binet at ages 6 and 7 years and on the Stanford Revision, Form L at 8 years varied from 118.3 to 118.7. During the age period 9 to 13 years, the average I.Q. was approximately 120. The highest average I.Q. of 123 was obtained for the test period 14 and 15 years; and the lowest I.Q. average (118.2) was earned on the Wechsler-Bellevue at 18 years.

The distribution of the I.Q.'s may be seen in Figure 1 for age periods 6 through 18 years. These percentage distributions of I.Q.'s are relatively normal at all ages at which the Stanford-Binet or Form L or M of the Stanford Revision were the tests given. But at 18 years, the distribution of I.Q.'s on the Wechsler-Bellevue suggests that this test lacks "top" or at least does not differentiate between the children earning the highest scores at the earlier ages.[4] Bayley (1) has another explanation for the decreased variability at maturity. She suggests that variability is greatest during the age periods when the children are acquiring the functions being tested and that variability becomes restricted with the approach to maturity of the particular processes being measured.

Group Trends in Mental Test Stability

Pearsonian coefficients of correlation between test scores earned at specified ages between 21 months and 18 years are shown in Table 2. These correlation coefficients are based on the scores of the children in the combined Guidance and Control Groups for all but two age levels (2 and 2½ years) when only the children in the Guidance Group were tested.

Correlations for adjacent ages indicate a fair degree of mental test constancy when the interval between tests is at a minimum. The range of correlations for adjacent ages varies from $r = .71$ (between ages 21 months and 2 years; 2 and 2½ years; 3 and 3½ years; and 5 and 6 years) to $r = .92$ for the ages 12 and 14 years on the Stanford Revision, Form L. However, the correlations decrease markedly with the interval between tests but tend to increase with the age of the children when tested.

---

[4] J. H. Ranzoni and R. D. Tuddenham are preparing a more detailed evaluation of the scores earned by these children on the Wechsler-Bellevue in contrast to their scores on earlier tests.

Figure 1
FREQUENCY DISTRIBUTIONS OF I.Q.'S AT DIFFERENT AGES

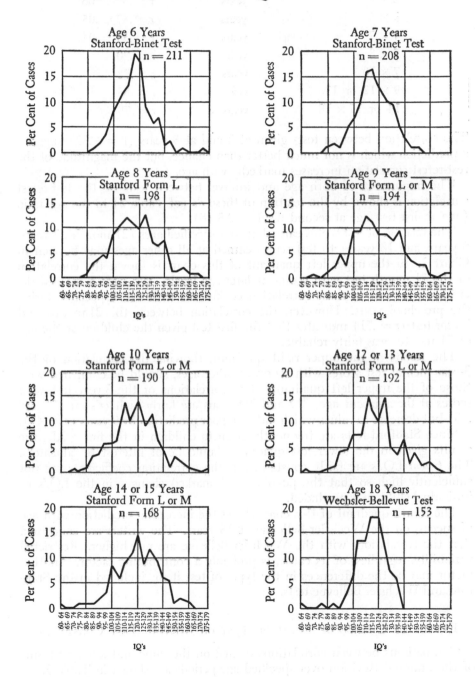

Comparison of the correlation coefficients for three-year intervals shows clearly the increase in mental test constancy with age:

2×5	years	$r = .32 \pm .06$
3×6	years	$r = .57 \pm .05$
4×7	years	$r = .59 \pm .04$
5×8	years	$r = .70$
7×10	years	$r = .78$
9×12 or 13	years	$r = .85$
14 or 15×18	years	$r = .79$

The correlation between tests given at 2 and at 5 years ($r = +.32$) suggests a prediction which is not much better than chance, but the magnitude of the test-retest correlation increases markedly with age.

The importance of both age and interval between tests on the test-retest correlation is shown by the relation of these r's (of Table 2) to the age ratio (age at first test/age at second test), $= .85$ (8).

The relation of test scores earned at four specified ages (21 months, 3 years, 6 years, and 18 years) to test scores earned at all other ages may be seen in Chart 1. In the upper left quadrant of this chart is shown the correlation of the 21 month test with scores at later age levels. We note a marked decrease in the size of these correlation coefficients with age, especially during the preschool years. However, the correlation between the 21-month and 2-year test ($r = .71$) indicates that the first test given the children at the age of 21 months was fairly reliable.

The results of the upper right quadrant, showing the correlation of the 3-year mental test scores with scores at other ages, should be compared with those of the upper left quadrant. The correlations of the 3-year test with scores at the adjacent ages 2½ and 3½ years are fairly high (r's are .71 and .73) but decrease to values which indicate poor prediction by 9 years ($r = .43$).

Since Stanford tests are frequently given to children in the first grade, the results given in the lower left quadrant should be of interest to educators. The 6-year I.Q.'s are fairly constant, but the correlation coefficients are not sufficiently high so that the possibility of marked changes in the I.Q.'s of individual children is precluded.

The fourth quadrant of this chart shows the increasing prediction with age of success on the Wechsler-Bellevue at 18 years. The writers are concerned that the correlations with the Wechsler-Bellevue are not higher. Restricted variability, regardless of its cause, is probably a contributing factor. Another factor may be the differences in the types of test items included in the Stanford and Wechsler-Bellevue tests.

Effect of Change of Form of Test on Mental Test Constancy

Comparisons between correlations earned on the same and different forms of the Stanford Revision over specified age periods are shown in Table 3.

Chart 1

Relation of 21 Month Mental Test Scores to Scores at Other Age Levels

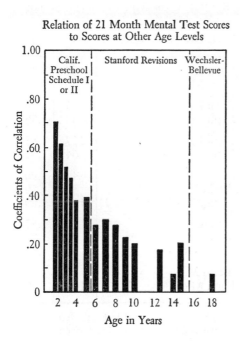

Relation of 3 Year Mental Test Scores to Scores at Other Age Levels

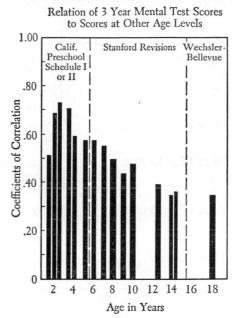

Relation of 6 Year Mental Test Scores to Scores at Other Age Levels

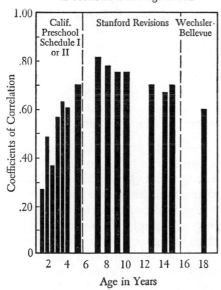

Relation of 18 Year Mental Test Scores to Scores at Other Age Levels

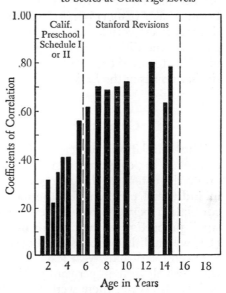

Table 3

EFFECT OF CHANGE OF TEST ON THE STABILITY OF MENTAL TEST SCORES

Age Levels Compared	Tests Given	n	r
8 × 9 years	Form L × Form L	87	.91
	Form L × Form M	100	.93
8 × 10 years	Form L × Form L	105	.88
	Form L × Form M	83	.88
8 × 12 or 13 years	Form L × Form L	117	.85
	Form L × Form M	64	.82
9 × 12 or 13 years	Form L × Form L	49	.90
	Form M × Form M	32	.79
	Form L × Form M or Form M × L	101	.89
10 × 12 or 13 years	Form L × Form L	70	.87
	Form M × Form M	38	.91
	Form L × Form M or Form M × L	48	.89
12 or 13 years × 14 or 15 yrs.	Form M × Form M	33	.88
	Form L × Form M or Form M × L	114	.89

Average r when same form of test repeated   .87
Average r when different form of test given   .88

The correlation between the 8- and 9-year tests for children tested on the same form of the Stanford (Form L) is .91; but the correlation is even higher for the remainder of the group who were tested on Form L at 8 years and Form M at 9 years ($r = .93$). Comparison of the effect of change of form on the test-retest correlations is made for six age periods. In all of these comparisons, the difference between the test-retest coefficients, when the same or different forms of the Stanford test were used, was negligible. Bayley obtained similar results in the Berkeley Growth Study (1).

CHANGES IN SCORES OVER CERTAIN AGE PERIODS

The correlation coefficients in Table 2 indicate the group trends with respect to the constancy of mental test performance. It is also of interest to know the extent of the changes in sigma scores or I.Q. which are occurring in individual children. Furthermore, the question arises as to whether the correlation between mental test scores is largely determined by a relatively small proportion of the cases or by the group as a whole. In a previous study (8), we published the distribution of changes in sigma scores which occurred between the 6- and 7-year tests ($r = .82$) for these children. This distribution was normal, with 80 per cent of the group showing sigma score changes of .5 or less. However, there were six children whose scores differed on these two tests by 1.5 sigma (approximately 20 I.Q. points since the standard deviation for ages 6 and 7 years is approximately 13) or more. The average change in score between 6 and 7 years was .5 of a sigma (6.5 I.Q. points).

If changes in I.Q. of 20 points can occur between the 6- and 7-year tests, it would be reasonable to expect rather marked changes in scores over the entire test period, 21 months to 18 years. We have, therefore, prepared distributions of the range of sigma score changes for the entire 16-year period of testing. We find that the scores of three children have increased between 4 and 4½ sigma (roughly between 70 and 79 I.Q. points, assuming an approximate standard deviation of 17.5 I.Q. points); and the scores of two children have decreased a similar amount. The sigma score curves for four of these five children are depicted in Figure 2D and Figure 2E. The most interesting aspect of these tremendous changes in scores is the fact that the changes are not made abruptly but consistently over a long period of time. However, the greatest changes do occur on the preschool tests. We have, therefore, prepared distributions showing the range of changes in sigma scores and I.Q.'s between 6 and 18 years. No child's sigma score changes as much as 4 sigma during the school years. But the scores of one child (case 764, Figure 2D) changes 3 sigma; and those of four others between 2.5 and 2.9 sigma.

Since educators and clinical workers use I.Q.'s rather than standard scores, we have prepared a distribution of the range of changes in I.Q. during the 12-year period 6 to 18 years for the two groups, Guidance and Control:

I.Q. Changes Between 6 and 18 Years	Guidance n = 114 %	Control n = 108 %	Total n = 222 %
50 or more I.Q. pts.	1	—	.5
30 or more I.Q. pts.	9	10	9
20 or more I.Q. pts.	32	42	35
15 or more I.Q. pts.	58	60	58
10 or more I.Q. pts.	87	83	85
9 or less I.Q. pts.	13	17	15

The mental test curve of the boy in the Guidance Group whose I.Q. varied by more than 50 points of I.Q. is described in Figure 4 (case 967). We are impressed not only by the extent of the changes in I.Q. during the school years but also by the fact that the results are so similar for the two groups, Guidance and Control. This finding suggests the reliability of these figures and that they would probably be duplicated under similar conditions of testing. Changes in I.Q. of 30 or more points of I.Q. are shown by 9 per cent of the children in the Guidance Group and 10 per cent in the Control Group. The I.Q.'s of over half of the children showed a variation of 15 or more points of I.Q. at some time during the school years, and a third of the group varied as much as 20 points of I.Q.

Although it is extremely important to point out the possibility of marked changes in scores in individual cases, it is equally important to emphasize that the scores of many children change only slightly with respect to the group from one age period to the next. And it is only when the changes are consistently in one direction, or the other, over a period of years that the range of variation becomes as great as 3 or 4 sigma (or over 50 I.Q. points).

Figure 2

STABILITY OF MENTAL TEST SCORES IN INDIVIDUAL CHILDREN

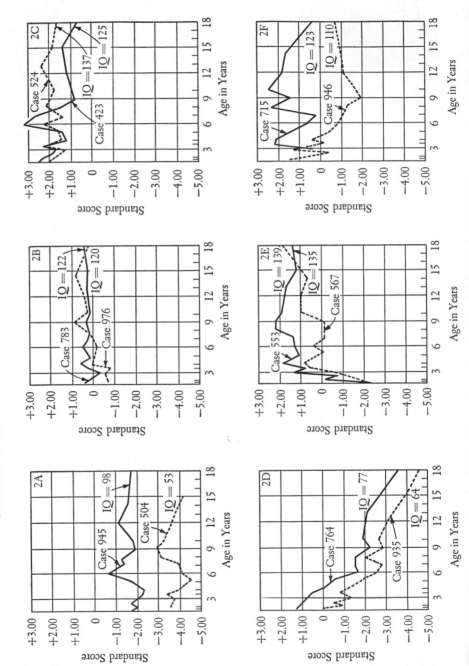

Stability and Instability in the Mental Test Scores of Individual Children

Mental test sigma score curves have been drawn for all of the children in the Guidance Study. In this sample of 252 children, we have found individuals whose mental test scores have remained relatively stable at either a high, average, or low level over the entire period of testing (21 months to 18 years). Other children have shown highly inconsistent scores in their mental test performance. Examples of varying degrees of constancy of mental test performance are shown in Figures 2, 3, and 4.

Consistently Low Scores (Figure 2A)

Case 504, a girl, had a mother who attended college two years and a father who graduated from college. The child was defective at birth, which showed up not only in tests (her I.Q.'s varied from 67 to 53, sigma scores from -3 to $-4\frac{1}{2}$) but in her whole developmental history. Clinical diagnosis was microcephaly, probably secondary to prenatal injury early in M.'s pregnancy.

Case 945, a boy. This child's scores are nearly all between -1 and -2 sigma, but he has one I.Q. as high as 110 and one as low as 87. He comes from a minority group of relatively low economic status. His mother reached the tenth grade; his father finished high school. Additionally, his life has been characterized by the chronic emotional and economic strain and the divorce of his parents, by poor health of both parents and himself, by inadequate supervision, and episodes of acute anxiety which showed themselves in severe psychosomatic disturbances.

Consistently Average Test Scores (Figure 2B)

Case 783, a boy earning consistently average scores, presents the least variability in our group with respect to test scores (I.Q. 120 to 125, after the preschool years). What factors lead to this stability of performance? His health history shows, as an infant, impetigo, severe bronchitis, a critical thymus disturbance, and chickenpox. As a preschool child, he had frequent colds, obstructive adenoids, infected tonsils (removed at 7). During his elementary school years, he had a chronic nasal discharge, a systolic murmur. His adolescent years showed poor dental hygiene, acne. At age 18 he had mumps, measles, and scarlet fever. But in spite of this history, he was energetic when well and interested in athletics.

The family situation was markedly sub-standard. Eight people, sometimes nine or ten, lived in four rooms, the boy sleeping in his parents' room until 11. The father was irregularly employed, insecure, drank too much, and when drinking, got into trouble (fights and women). The mother was mature and steady but had a hernia, chronic endocarditis, and worked away from home and, frequently, worked far beyond her strength. The mother did not finish high school; the father had two years of college. Two sibs of the boy attended the University; one graduated.

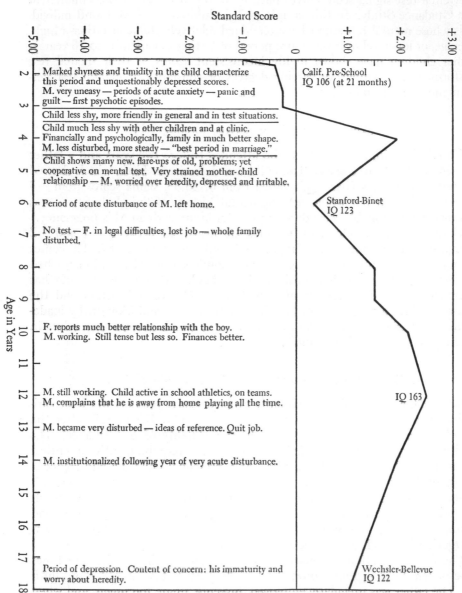

Standard Score

Age in Years

2 — Marked shyness and timidity in the child characterize this period and unquestionably depressed scores. M. very uneasy — periods of acute anxiety — panic and guilt — first psychotic episodes.

3 — Child less shy, more friendly in general and in test situations.

4 — Child much less shy with other children and at clinic. Financially and psychologically, family in much better shape. M. less disturbed, more steady — "best period in marriage."

5 — Child shows many new, flare-ups of old, problems; yet cooperative on mental test. Very strained mother-child relationship — M. worried over heredity, depressed and irritable.

6 — Period of acute disturbance of M. left home.

7 — No test — F. in legal difficulties, lost job — whole family disturbed.

8

9

10 — F. reports much better relationship with the boy. M. working. Still tense but less so. Finances better.

11

12 — M. still working. Child active in school athletics, on teams. M. complains that he is away from home playing all the time.

13 — M. became very disturbed — ideas of reference. Quit job.

14 — M. institutionalized following year of very acute disturbance.

15

16

17

18 — Period of depression. Content of concern: his immaturity and worry about heredity.

Calif. Pre-School
IQ 106 (at 21 months)

Stanford-Binet
IQ 123

IQ 163

Wechsler-Bellevue
IQ 122

MENTAL TEST PERFORMANCE OF CASE 802 (BOY)

Figure 3

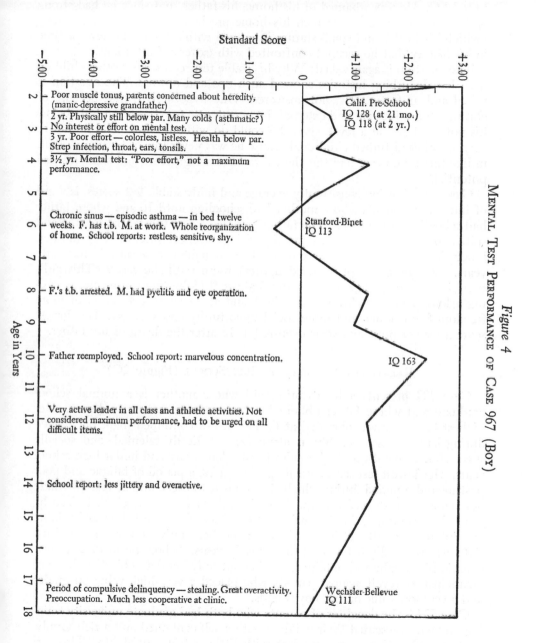

Figure 4

MENTAL TEST PERFORMANCE OF CASE 967 (Boy)

The boy was a bed-wetter until 18, had an acute stammer from 9 to 12, was and is a chronic nailbiter. His school grades were considerably below his tested I.Q. He was ashamed of his home, his father, and since he had strong social affiliative interests (which his home precluded) and athletic interests (which his health and small stature interfered with), there was never a time in his history that he was not confronted with extreme frustrations.

The question is again asked: Why his stable test scores, since other children with less disturbing histories showed such ups and downs? The question is raised and, unfortunately, not answered. One hypothesis is that because of chronic strain, internal and external, he persistently functioned on tests below his potential and at a level which he could do without effort. Did he fail to vary, as other disturbed children, because he was never free of tension so that, unlike them, he never had the chance to have a high score and show his real potential?

Case 976, showing consistently average and fairly stable test scores, is a girl of immigrant parents whose mother had schooling until 16 and whose father had schooling until age 12. The father provided a very substantial income and status to his family with his prestige-giving business success. Her mother, lonely in a new country, over-protected her daughter, especially in her early years. The mother slept in her daughter's room until she was 9. This girl's two highest scores (I.Q. 137) occurred at age 9 (following tonsillectomy ending a long period of chronic infection) and at 14 (during a period of more freedom from home, and more social opportunity and success). Her lowest score after her preschool years occurred at 18 after the death of her father.

Relatively Consistent High Scores (Figure 2C)

Case 423 presents a high-scoring girl whose mother is a normal school graduate and whose father obtained a post-graduate university degree. Her highest test score was obtained at 6. Her scores continued high, but sagged during late adolescence. She is attractive, artistically talented, and socially successful. She got very high grades in the elementary and junior high school years. Her lowest test scores are at ages 9 and 10, a period of fatigue and poor posture and a period during which she strained to excel, and at year 18 where her sigma score showed a drop. Her high school years were characterized by much less interest in intellectual success, which she regarded as unfeminine and interfering with getting good dates; and her motivation in all test situations was markedly below that of her early years. Scholastic mediocrity was consciously sought and obtained, serving not only her date objective, but her emancipatory revolt against parents who placed a very high value on grades and a very low value on her boy friends.

Case 524 is the daughter of parents who both had graduate university training and who presented their children with a self-contained and a rich family-centered recreational program but with little outside social life. This girl showed continuously high scores, although there were frequent shifts of as much as .8 of a sigma over two-year periods and I.Q. variations from a low of 137 to a high of 162. Her most outstanding handicaps were tongue tie, corrected early; strabismus corrected at 11½; and more or less chronic reserve. Sociometric findings appraised her as being the most quiet and reserved in her class. Her main interests were less in persons than in reading and writing. Her highest score was obtained at 13, just after menarche and at a time when she was doing excellent school work (greatly approved by her education-oriented family, including aunts, uncles, and a grandmother who had been active educators). Social participation, which was always a strain for her, was particularly restricted at this time.

STEADILY DECREASING MENTAL TEST SCORES (Figure 2D)

Case 935 is a girl, an only child, who did well on tests at 21 months (I.Q. 120) but lost I.Q. points steadily at the rate of about 5 or 6 points per year, reaching an I.Q. of 64 (Wechsler-Bellevue) at 18 years. This is a decrease of 4½ sigma. School reports after the second or third grade showed consistent failures. Intensive physical tests, including encephalograms, disclosed no discoverable physical factors or disease processes. The estimated I.Q.'s of the parents are around 80 to 85, grammar school education. The mother reports that she, as a girl, was "held over" several times. Chronic emotional and economic strain characterized the home after the early preschool years. Estimates of intelligence on the Rorschach and Thematic Apperception Test indicated average intelligence or only slightly below average. Her fantasy life is apparently richer than her overt test performance or school performance. The question is unsettled as to whether this is a case of mental deficiency or possible hebephrenia.

Case 764 is an example of a gradual lowering of I.Q. from 133 to 77, and sigma scores from +1 to 3. She is an only child, born when the mother was 44, the father, 37. The estimated I.Q. of the mother is 65 to 70. The father is a skilled mechanic. The parents went to school until age 14.

Obesity began in late preschool years and increased steadily until medical advice was finally followed at age 14 (height 5 ft. 2 in., weight 160 lbs. at 13). Weight was normal at 17. There were, however, no I.Q. variations in relation to these physical changes. She was always over-indulged by the mother, who lived to feed her and keep her young, and who was always complaining that her daughter never gave her enough affection.

CASES WITH INCREASING SCORES (Figure 2E)

Case 553 is a boy whose mental test scores increased from a preschool sigma score of −2 to later sigma scores of +2.4 in spite of a bad physical history. He is small-statured, thin, with very poor musculature, and presents a history of early ear infections and chronic bronchitis from infancy — headaches (early glasses), stomach pains (appendectomy); he has had three operations and three serious accidents. He has had only one six-month period in his life free of illness. In spite of a frail frame, which has suffered many serious indignities, an early strained family situation, and relatively low mental test scores in his early preschool years, his tested ability steadily increased until 9, from which time he has maintained high and fairly stable scores. His mother is a normal school graduate; his father completed high school. His greatest security lies in his intellectual interests and achievements, but he has made good social adjustments and an amazingly good adjustment to his handicaps.

Case 567. The early preschool history of this girl (the period of her lowest test scores) was characterized by the critical illnesses of her mother and brother and the emotional and financial strain that these entailed. Further, the girl had very poor muscle tonus, fatigue posture, and was very shy and reserved. At 6½ years she had pneumonia. From 10 on, while still reserved, she had many supports in her life — music, athletic success, summer camps, the honor roll at school. Eighteen years marks her first year in college and away from home and her first really completely satisfying social life, which resulted in great expansiveness. Both parents are college graduates who did advanced work in their fields.

HIGHLY VARIABLE SCORES (Figure 2F)

Case 715, a girl whose I.Q. varies from 121 to 165, presents a history that was characterized by intermittent but severe eczema and asthma throughout the entire testing period. Ages 3 to 7 constituted a particularly bad period; age 9, where there was a drop in I.Q. of 12 points, was a period not only of asthma and poor vision but of acute economic insecurity and family uneasiness. At age 10, during her highest test period, she was taking two cc. of adrenalin daily to keep her asthma under control.

Added to health strain, social strain became more acute for her at 12 when she entered junior high school and continued through high school. It was a period of overweight, disfiguring eczema, and marked mother-daughter strain. Not only did the girl belong to a racial minority group, but she was not at one with them because of her marked intellectual interests, unshared by others in her racial age group, at school or in the neighborhood. Her mother is a high school graduate; her father had three years in college.

At the time of the 18-year test she was very much below par as she was recovering from an acute period of asthma.

Case 946, a girl, has varied in I.Q. between 142 (preschool) and 87. Her sigma scores have varied from +1½ to −2; her preschool years were clearly higher than later years. Her lowest score (I.Q. 87, sigma −2) occurred at 9 years, a period of acute body concern and excessive modesty. Immigrant parents of grammar school education, both unstable and involved in chronic, acute marital tension, were divorced when the girl was 7. This child was acutely uneasy around her young stepfather for the first years of her mother's new marriage. Much internal as well as external turmoil has characterized her life.

In selecting mental test curves to include in this study, the writers were impressed by the fact that the children whose scores showed the greatest fluctuations were children whose life experiences had also fluctuated between disturbing and satisfying periods. Two such cases are 715 and 946 in Figure

2F. Two more cases whose scores show marked instability are presented in Figures 3 and 4.

There is only one further generalization that seems justifiable on the basis of mental test curves of only 14 children, and that is the fact that the records of all eight children showing consistent trends have final mental test scores which are similar to their parents' ability, as judged by their education, and socio-economic rating. Of the four children whose scores either decreased markedly or were consistently below the average for the group, three children were from homes which were low in the socio-economic scale and had parents with less education than the average for this Berkeley sample. One common factor in the decreasing scores of cases 935 and 764 may be the stimulating effect of affectionate parents on their only children in the early years. These parents with less than average ability could not continue to offer intellectually stimulating environments as their children grew older, nor can the hereditary factors with which they were endowed be discounted. The microcephalic youngster with low scores was the child of parents with above average intelligence. This case should probably be considered the result of an intra-uterine disturbance unrelated to hereditary or post-natal environmental factors.

On the other hand, the four children with increasing or consistently high scores had parents with more than average education (seven of the eight parents were college graduates). Superior hereditary and environmental factors were unquestionably contributing to the mental test records of these children.[5]

Summary and Conclusions

A group of 252 children, who comprise a representative sample of the children living in an urban community, were given mental tests at specified ages between 21 months and 18 years. These data have been analyzed to show the extent of the stability of mental test performance for this age period. The results may be summarized as follows:

1. Mental test constancy for the age period 21 months to 18 years is markedly dependent upon the age at testing and the interval between tests. That is, group prediction is good over short age periods, and mental test scores become increasingly predictive after the preschool years.

2. Test-retest correlations are as high for children tested on different forms (L or M) of the 1937 Stanford Revision as for children tested on the same form over the same age periods.

3. Distributions of the extent of the changes in I.Q. for the age period 6 to 18 years show that the I.Q.'s of almost 60 per cent of the group change 15 or more points; the I.Q.'s of a third of the group change 20 or more points; and the I.Q.'s of 9 per cent of the group change 30 or more points. The I.Q.'s of

---

[5] A more intensive and extensive study of factors related to the mental test curves of individual children is planned. The findings given here on only 14 children should be considered suggestive.

15 per cent of the group change *less* than 10 points of I.Q. The group averages, on the other hand, show a maximum shift in I.Q. over this age period of from 118 to 123.

4. Some individuals show consistent upward or downward trends in I.Q. over a long period, resulting in changes of as much as 4½ sigma or 50 I.Q. points.

5. Inspection of the mental test curves of the individual children included in this paper indicates that changes in mental test scores tend to be in the direction of the family level, as judged by the parents' education and socio-economic status. (Group findings showing an increasing relationship of family status to the children's test scores were presented in an earlier study.) (6)

6. Children whose mental test scores showed the most marked fluctuations had life histories which showed unusual variations with respect to disturbing and stabilizing factors. However, there were other children whose scores remained constant despite highly disturbing experiences.

In conclusion, it should be re-emphasized that, whereas the results for the group suggest mental test stability between 6 and 18 years, the observed fluctuations in the scores of individual children indicate the need for the utmost caution in the predictive use of a single test score, or even two such scores. This finding seems of especial importance since many plans for individual children are made by schools, juvenile courts, and mental hygiene clinics on the basis of a single mental test score. Specifically, it could be noted that a prediction based on a 6-year test would be wrong to the extent of 20 I.Q. points for one out of three children by the age of 18 years, and to the extent of 15 I.Q. points for approximately six out of ten children.

References

1. Bayley, Nancy. "Consistency and Variability in the Growth of Intelligence from Birth to Eighteen years," *Journal of Genetic Psychology*, 1948.

2. ———. "Factors Influencing the Growth of Intelligence in Young Children," *Yearbook of the National Society for the Study of Education*, 1940, 49–79.

3. Bradway, Katharine P. "I.Q. Constancy on the Revised Stanford-Binet from the Preschool to the Junior High School Level," *Journal of Genetic Psychology*, LXV (1944), 197–217.

4. Goodenough, F. L. "Studies of the 1937 Revision of the Stanford-Binet Scale, I: Variability of the I.Q. at Successive Age Levels," *Journal of Educational Psychology*, XXXIII (1942), 241–251.

5. ———, and Maurer, K. M. *The Mental Growth of Children from Two to Fourteen Years*. Minneapolis: University of Minnesota Press, 1942, 130.

6. Honzik, M. P. "Age Changes in the Relationship Between Certain Environmental Variables and Children's Intelligence," *Thirty-Ninth Yearbook of the National Society for the Study of Education*, (1940), 185–205.

7. ———. "The Constancy of Mental Test Performance During the Preschool Period," *Journal of Genetic Psychology*, LII (1938), 285–302.

8. ———, and Jones, H. E. "Mental-Physical Relationships During the Preschool Period," *Journal of Experimental Education*, VI (December, 1937), 139–146.

9. Jaffa, A. S. *The California Preschool Mental Scale (Form A)*. Syllabus Series No. 251. Los Angeles: University of California, 1934, 66 pp.

10. Macfarlane, J. W. "Studies in Child Guidance, I. Methodology of Data Collection and Organization," *Monograph Society for Research in Child Development*, III (1938), 1–254.

11. ———. "The Guidance Study," *Sociometry*, II (1939).

12. ———. "Study of Personality Development," Barber, Kounin, and Wright in *Child Behavior and Development*. Chapter XVIII.

13. Terman, L. M., and Merrill, M. A. *Measuring Intelligence*. Boston: Houghton Mifflin Company, 1937, 461.

14. Wechsler, D. *The Measurement of Adult Intelligence*. Baltimore: Williams and Wilkins, 1944, 258.

15. Welch, F. M. *The Berkeley Survey: A Study of the Socio-Economic Status of Four Hundred Berkeley Families in Years 1928–1929*. MS, Berkeley, California: Institute of Child Welfare, University of California.

18

Intelligence and Achievement: The "Jangle Fallacy" Again

William Coleman and Edward E. Cureton

The typical measurement of intelligence involves many test items that could be classified as evidence of achievement. On the other hand, the assessment of achievement cannot be thought of as occurring in the absence of intelligence. The comments by Coleman and Cureton are germane to the interpretation of scores on these two kinds of tests. The reader should go over the points carefully; then decide if he wishes to agree with the authors.

Kelley defines the jangle fallacy (4, p. 64) as . . . "the use of two separate words or expressions covering in fact the same basic situation, but sounding different, as though they were in truth different." Despite his demonstration (4, pp. 193–209) that the traits measured by group intelligence tests and school achievement tests overlap about 90 per cent, many psychologists

From William Coleman and Edward E. Cureton, "Intelligence and Achievement: The 'Jangle Fallacy' Again," *Educational and Psychological Measurement*, XIV (Summer, 1954), pp. 347–351. Reprinted with the permission of publisher and authors.

as well as school people go on interpreting intelligence test scores as measures of native capacity primarily, and achievement test scores as measures of native capacity plus school motivation and effectiveness of instruction. The present study contributes one more item of evidence showing that a group intelligence test and selected subtests from a school achievement battery measure substantially identical functions.

The *Otis Quick-Scoring Test Beta*, Forms CM and DM, and the Word Meaning, Paragraph Meaning, and Arithmetic Computation subtests of the *Stanford Achievement Test*, Forms DM and EM, were administered to the sixth grades of two elementary schools in Knox County, Tennessee, by members of the staff of the Tennessee State Testing and Guidance Program.[1] The testing sessions were arranged as follows:

	First Session	Second Session
Stanford	February 25, 1953 (1)	March 4, 1953 (3)
Otis	March 2, 1953 (2)	March 9, 1953 (4)

At each first session approximately half the pupils took one form and half the other; at the second session each pupil took one form and half the other; at the second session each pupil took the form he had not taken at the first session. At the conclusion of testing there were 117 pupils who had properly completed all four forms. The number in parentheses following each date designates the test and session: odd numbers indicate *Stanford* and even *Otis*; numbers 1 and 2 indicate the first session, and 3 and 4 the second. Since two forms of each test were used in each session, the scores used were the sum of the three Stanford equated scores, and the Otis raw scores (which were pre-equated in the standardization of the test).

The four correlations between tests each of which was given at a different session are:

$$r_{13} = .8416 \quad \text{(Stanford reliability)}$$
$$r_{24} = .9077 \quad \text{(Otis reliability}$$
$$r_{14} = .8416 \quad \text{(intercorrelation)}$$
$$r_{23} = .8254 \quad \text{(intercorrelation)}$$

Since the average time interval for r_{13} and r_{24} is the same as that for r_{14} and r_{23}, any time-generated error correlation should be the same in the two intercorrelations as in the two reliability coefficients. Hence the correlation corrected for attenuation, based on these four correlations, should give an unbiased estimate of the intercorrelation between two perfectly reliable tests of the same types administered simultaneously. The corrected correlation is

$$r_{so} = \sqrt{\frac{r_{14}\,r_{23}}{r_{13}\,r_{24}}} = .9536.$$

[1] We are indebted to Mr. Lloyd E. Fish and Mrs. Annie W. Ward, who did most of the examining (the rest was done by the first-named author), and to the principals and teachers of Inskip School and Fountain City School, for their cooperation in making the subjects available and in scheduling the test sessions.

If we make the reasonable assumption that the relative variability of "real" (non-error) functions measured by *Otis* but not *Stanford* is equal to the relative variability of "real" functions measured by *Stanford* but not *Otis*, the "real" functions measured by the two tests overlap about 95 per cent. Even if we make the most extreme assumption possible, that one test measures *all* "real" functions measured by the other, plus some unique to itself, the per cent overlap is given by the square of the correlation corrected for attenuation — in this case about 91 per cent.

What will happen in this situation if we compare the mental ages and educational ages of individual students, using the scores from these tests, and compute accomplishment quotients? Over a one-grade range, we can assume that the transformations to age-scores will be essentially linear so that the correlations between the age scores will be the same as those between the raw scores. The accomplishment quotient is defined by the formula,

$$AQ = EA/MA.$$

The standard response error of the AQ as given by Huffaker (3) is

$$\sigma_{AQ} = \frac{100\sigma}{M} \sqrt{2 - R_{EE} - R_{MM}},$$

where σ is the standard deviation of the mental ages and the educational ages (assumed equal), and M is the mean of the mental ages and the educational ages (also assumed equal). For the data of this study, $\sigma = 33.9$. Hence before we can be sure whether an AQ from these tests is above or below 100, at the 95 per cent confidence level, the obtained AQ must be 166 or higher, or 34 or lower. If it is between 166 and 34 we cannot with 95 per cent confidence assume that the "true AQ" is above or below 100 in the direction indicated by the actual value.

Eells, *et al.* (2), Cattell (1), and various others have attempted to construct culture-fair or culture-free intelligence tests. The essential assumption for the inference of differences in native capacity corresponding to differences in test scores is that all members of the group tested have had equal opportunities and equal incentives to develop their capacities into the abilities measured by the test. One of the major objectives of the school as a social institution (and in most cases *the* major *de facto* operating objective) is to provide as nearly equal opportunities and incentives as possible to all children to develop their verbal and arithmetical capacities into functioning abilities. Modern education stresses the reasoning aspects of these abilities along with their rote aspects. With school education now almost universal, any valid school achievement test of reading and arithmetic whose items are based on the commonest elements of school curricula in these fields must therefore come about as close as possible to measuring differences in native capacity in verbal-arithmetical intelligence. Uniformity of curricula is lower in all other areas, and there is no other social institution whose major working objective is the development of one or more specific intellectual abilities in every member of the population. So long as we are content to measure merely verbal-arithmetical intelligence, therefore, the best available test is likely to be a valid school achievement test of vocabulary, reading, and arithmetic. The battery used in this study would probably have been improved by adding the Arithmetic Reasoning subtest to the three that were used.

In measuring "general intelligence" with a view to making inferences about differences in native capacity, there is good reason to limit the functions tested to the verbal and arithmetical. Reasoning, which most of us will agree to be the most important aspect of "general intelligence," consists essentially in the mental manipulation of symbols, and it can be measured only by the use of symbolic test materials. Verbal symbolism is by all odds the type most frequently used in thinking about practical problems, and arithmetical symbolism, though not a close second, far exceeds all other systems in the generality of its use in problem solving. Hence a verbal-arithmetical intelligence test, while covering only a fraction of all types of intellectual ability, covers perhaps the only fraction which is developed with any uniformity in the population as a whole, and covers that fraction which is by all odds the most widely used in practical thinking.

SUMMARY

This study indicates that a good school achievement test of reading and arithmetic measures essentially the same combination of functions as a typical group intelligence test, the overlap being on the order of 95 per cent. The proposition is advanced that the school achievement test may well permit better inferences about differences in native capacity than can be made on the basis of the group intelligence test (insofar as there are any differences at all). It is suggested that verbal and arithmetical intelligence are the types most frequently used, and the only types which in our culture can be used as bases for inferences about capacity.

REFERENCES

1. Cattell, R. B. "A Culture Free Intelligence Test: I," *Journal of Educational Psychology,* XXXI (1940), 161–179.
2. Eells, Kenneth, *et al. Intelligence and Cultural Differences.* Chicago: University of Chicago Press, 1951.
3. Huffaker, C. L. "The Probable Error of the Accomplishment Quotient," *Journal of Educational Psychology,* XXI (1930), 550–551.
4. Kelley, T. L. *Interpretation of Educational Measurements.* Yonkers, New York: World Book Company, 1927.

19

Misconceptions About Intelligence Testing

Warren R. Good

There are many misunderstandings about intelligence tests and what their results say. Good reviews the principal misconceptions and points out why these ideas are not valid.

There seems to be a lot of confusion nowadays about intelligence tests and the meaning of intelligence quotients. Most teachers now in service have been taught that 60 per cent of the children have IQ's 90–109, 14 per cent 110–119 and again 80–89, 6 per cent 120–129 and 70–79, 1 per cent above 130, and 1 per cent below 70; and that those with IQ's below 70 are feeble-minded. None of this is true today.

Too, many teachers have been easily converted to an ill-informed confidence in verbal and nonverbal IQ's, primary abilities, and culture-free tests. Whatever the merits of these "newer" developments may be, teachers should choose and interpret on the basis of understanding rather than acceptance of the propaganda devised for commercial exploitation.

Another sign of confusion is the growing tendency of some teachers to consider intelligence tests as a special kind of achievement test. The blunder apparently results from poor knowledge of fundamental intelligence-test theory.

When we try to measure intelligence we seek an indication of *native capacity* for learning and adaptation. This indication must be obtained by inference, because the potentiality for development is constantly in the process of being realized. Hence we must resort to the assumption that mental ability — what the individual knows and can do on intellectual tasks — will vary with native capacity if opportunities for development have been equal. And we infer "native intelligence" from mental ability. But we cannot measure ability directly, either; what we measure is performance. And so, it goes like this: we measure performance, from which we infer ability, from which we infer capacity.

From Warren R. Good, "Misconceptions About Intelligence Testing," *The University of Michigan School of Education Bulletin*, XXV (May, 1954), pp. 117–120; *The Education Digest*, XX (October, 1954), pp. 14–16. Reprinted with the permission of publishers and author.

The basic condition for validity of our inferences — equality of opportunity — demands what might reasonably be called "normal" environment, comparable, so far as test effects are concerned, with that of the children on whom the test was standardized. And opportunities to have learned the kinds of things involved in the specific test items must be equalized.

Our chances of getting such equalization are certainly best at zero (no opportunity at all) and infinity, or to be practical, at *plenty* — far more opportunity than would be needed to learn the thing if the individual were mature enough.

Intelligence tests are often at fault because a good many items relate to special interests or opportunities, but even the best tests will be unsatisfactory for some children in almost any group, because of differences in background. Once this principle of equal opportunity is understood, teachers can judge for themselves whether test items are suitable for measuring intelligence and will soon learn to choose good tests for the purpose.

The pathetic arguments favoring "nonverbal" IQ's for duller children are at best questionable. In general, language is a highly sensitive indicator of intelligence and, barring specific handicap, there is no evidence that those who cannot understand or use their native language with facility are compensated with some special kind of "general mental ability" that cannot be adequately measured by verbal tests.

The issue here, as always in intelligence testing, is equality of opportunity to have learned the kind of thing demanded. But to avoid language in an intelligence test is to reject the most versatile and most important means of communicating thought. In case of specific handicap — defect of speech or hearing, or difference of languages — we resort to nonlanguage tests through necessity, not because they are "just as good." As for verbal and nonverbal IQ's, there has never been any justification for such terminology. What we have is verbal and nonverbal test items or tests, all designed to measure general intelligence; and if IQ's obtained with verbal and nonverbal tests differ greatly there is reason for grave doubt of the validity of either or both.

The search for "primary mental abilities" is concerned with finding the major components of the groups of abilities which may be judged to reflect intelligence. But so far, competent analysts are not agreed on the identification of such abilities or on the validity of tests which purport to measure them as separate abilities.

A common characteristic of intelligence tests is that they yield IQ's. The original Binet tests measured directly in mental-age credits, but nearly all tests nowadays are point scales, the IQ's being determined statistically from the distribution of point scores. If these determinations were valid in relation to the definition of an IQ, the distribution of IQ's obtained from the various tests on the market would be alike — they would have the same standard deviation — and the IQ's would be comparable.

But these standard deviations, rarely published in the test manuals, vary from about 10 to about 26; so a very bright youngster might have, taking extremes, an IQ of 130 on one test and an IQ of 178 on another. Or, a child might have an IQ of 80 on one test and be judged a bit subnormal, and have an IQ of 48 on another and be classified as an imbecile by the scoring.

The standard deviation of IQ's on the first Stanford-Binet scale was about 13. The distribution of IQ's given in the first paragraph of this article was based on that scale, which has been obsolete since 1937, when it was superseded by the present revision. The newer standard deviation is reported as 16.4, and the makers of other intelligence tests now try to get about the same dispersion — with considerably varying degrees of success.

An IQ, then, is likely to be a pretty shifty measure of mental ability unless it is interpreted in terms of how commonly such an IQ occurs in the general population; that is, in terms of the statistical characteristics of the test used. The IQ's yielded by different tests are not likely to be comparable. At least some teachers in each school, therefore, should know enough about elementary statistics to make the necessary analysis.

Many teachers are disturbed by the increasing numbers of "feeble-minded" children in school, as indicated by IQ's below 70. As Tredgold pointed out many years ago, the sound definition of feeblemindedness refers to the lowest x per cent of the population. Without an agreement on x, we formerly had estimates running all the way from one feebleminded person in 2500 to one in 16. The American consensus on what x should be was expressed for the old Stanford-Binet as the portion having IQ's below 70. That was 1 per cent. On the present Stanford-Binet it's nearly 4 per cent. We don't have more feebleminded — an entirely arbitrary classification — we just have a lot of people using the wrong figures.

The term IQ has been so grossly abused and it is so inappropriate to the shifting values yielded by various tests that we probably should abandon it altogether. The test scores would be far easier to interpret if the school made its own conversion of the raw-point scores into standard scores of some sort (Z scores, for example, which have a mean of 50 and a standard deviation of 10), and made comparisons with national norms if requisite data were available.

In any case, I should say that we do too much intelligence testing and then misinterpret — or ignore — the results. Once in three or four years should be often enough to measure a student's mental ability, and the test then used should not attempt the speculative or the impossible. In considering tests for selection, fancy claims and high costs should be automatically suspect, and tests under favorable consideration should be carefully studied (and actually taken, by the teachers who make the selection) to make judgments of local validity, ease of administration and scoring, adequacy of manuals, and so on.

Finally, the results of the intelligence testing should be interpreted in light of the characteristics of the test used, and especially — until we can do better — of the IQ distribution of that test.

20

Lost: Our Intelligence. Why?

Quinn McNemar

The history of intelligence testing is essentially the history of the entire mental measurements movement. McNemar reviews significant events that have led to various practices in intelligence testing, and comes up with some provocative ideas about current practices and their prospects.

The Greeks had a word for it, but the Romans had a word with better survival properties. Regardless of the word, what is now called intelligence has been talked about for at least 2,000 years. And as long as 2,000 years before the advent of attempts to measure intelligence, there seems to have been recognition of the fact that individuals differ in intellectual ability.

The earlier attempts at measuring were based on either of two quite distinct conceptions: the Galton-Cattell idea that intellectual ability manifests itself in simple, discrimination functioning, and the Binet notion that cognitive ability reflects itself in more complex functioning. The Binet concept proved to be more fruitful, and by 1925 there was on the market, in addition to various versions of the Binet scale, a flood of group tests of so-called general intelligence.

A few words about definition may be in order. First, it might be claimed that no definition is required because all intelligent people know what intelligence is — it is the thing that the other guy lacks. Second, the fact that tests of general intelligence based on differing definitions tend to intercorrelate about as highly as their respective reliabilities permit indicates that, despite the diversity of definitions, the same function or process is being measured — definitions can be more confusing than enlightening. Third, that confusion might have been anticipated is evident from a recent reexamination of the problem of definition by Miles (1957) [17]. This British chappie found himself struggling with the awful fact that the word "definition" itself has 12 definitions. Perhaps the resolution of this problem should be assigned to the newly formed Division of Philosophical Psychology, or maybe the prob-

From Quinn McNemar, "Lost: Our Intelligence. Why?" *American Psychologist,* XIX (December, 1964), pp. 871–882. Reprinted with the permission of the American Psychological Association and the author.

lem should be forgotten since psychologists seem to have lost the concept of general intelligence.

Why has the concept been abandoned? Was it replaced by something else? By something better? Must we admit that the millions who have been tested on general intelligence tests were measured for a nonexistent function? If it is possible that the notion of general intelligence is not lost but merely gone astray, in what corners of what psychological fields should we search for it?

Reasons for Discarding the Idea of General Intelligence

Apparently one reason why concepts are either discarded or modified beyond recognition is that too much is claimed for them. Among the supposed strikes against general intelligence are the following: the earlier false claims about IQ constancy; prediction failures in individual cases; unfounded claims that something innate was being measured by the tests; equally unfounded assertions that nothing but cultural effects were involved; the bugaboo that IQ tests reflect middle-class values; the notion that an IQ standing fosters undesirable expectations regarding school achievement; the idea that IQ differences are incompatible with democracy and lead to educational determinism; and, finally, the great stress on general intelligence caused us to ignore other possible abilities.

This last point leads us right into the problem of factor analysis. Spearman died in battle defending his theory of g. Under pressure he reluctantly conceded that factors other than g might exist, and he frequently said, in effect, I told you so as long ago as 1906. Actually, Spearman was on the run before the invention of modern factor analysis, but it was not until Thurstone's (1938) first major application of his centroid factor method that Spearman's g became, seemingly, nonexistent [23]. Thurstone said, "We have not found the general factor of Spearman" and "We cannot report any general common factor in the battery of fifty-six tests [p. vii]." As anticipated by some, Spearman was not prone to admit defeat. He reworked Thurstone's data and a g was found, plus some group factors. He charged that Thurstone's rotational process had submerged the general factor.

American factorists found Thurstone convincing. The description of abilities in terms of seven primaries was an attractive package. The so-called primaries were more amenable to specific definition than the old hodgepodge called general intelligence. Despite the fact that Thurstone was able to replicate his findings on samples from two other populations, thus giving credence to his method and results, there were a couple of events that led to some turbulence in his seven-dimension rarefied atmosphere. The first of these was a minor study, by one of his own students, based on the intercorrelations of 1916 Stanford-Binet items, in which the g refused to be rotated out. But rather than admit that this might be some kind of general intelligence, the author renamed it "maturational level." Incidentally, this illustrates the first cardinal Principle of Psychological Progress: *Give new names to old things.*

The second disturber of the neat little set of primaries, sans a g, resulted when Thurstone took the next logical step, that of constructing tests to measure the primaries. It was found that the primaries were themselves inter-correlated whereas it had, at the time, been expected and hoped that they would be independent. The Thurstones (1941 [24], p. 26) readily admitted that a general factor was needed to explain the interrelatedness of the pri-maries. This eventually led to the idea of oblique axes, which axes were re-garded as representing the primaries as first-order factors, whereas the general factor pervading the primaries was dubbed a second-order factor. It began to look as though Spearman was being revisited, except for the little matter of labeling: anything called second-order could not possibly be regarded as of much importance. Furthermore, it could always be said that, in the ability domain, it is less difficult to attribute psychological meaningfulness to first-order than to second-order factors, so why pay much attention to the latter? Thus it was easy for most American factorists to drop the concept of general intelligence and to advocate that tests thereof, despite their proven usefulness over the years, should be replaced by tests of the primaries. Hence the emergence of differential aptitude batteries, about which more later.

Meanwhile, our British cousins did not tag along with the factor methods preferred on this side of the Atlantic. After all, it is possible to use factor methods that permit a sizable general factor, if such exists, to emerge as the very first factor. Being first, it is, presto, the most important, as indeed it is as a factor explaining, for the starting battery as a whole, more variance for more tests than attributable to any American-style primary factor. The methods preferred by the British also yield group factors, apt to bear the same name as the primaries, but of attenuated importance. Apparently the British are skeptical of the multitude of ability factors being "discovered" in America. The structure of intellect that requires 120 factors may very well lead the British, and some of the rest of us, to regard our fractionization and fragmenta-tion of ability, into more and more factors of less and less importance, as indicative of scatterbrainedness. This statement presumes that intellectual abilities are brain centered.

In practically all areas of psychological research the demonstration of trivially small minutia is doomed to failure because of random errors. Not so if your technique is factor analysis, despite its being based on the correlation coefficient — that slipperiest of all statistical measures. By some magic, hypotheses are tested without significance tests. This happy situation permits me to announce a Principle of Psychological Regress: *Use statistical tech-niques that lack inferential power.* This will not inhibit your power of sub-jective inference and consequently will progress you right back to the good old days when there was no strangling stat or sticky stix to make your in-significant data insignificant.

It may be a long time before we have an ivory tower, strictly scientific reso-lution of the issue as to whether a scheme involving primary abilities plus a deemphasized g is preferable to one involving an emphasized g plus group factors. With bigger and better computers we will have bigger, though not necessarily better, factor-analytic studies, but it seems unlikely that such further studies will, in and of themselves, settle the issue under discussion. Until such time as some genius resolves the broader question, so ably discussed by Lee Cronbach in 1957 [5], of the place, if any, of correlational method in a science that aspires to be experimental, we may have to turn to the criterion of social usefulness as a basis for judging whether it is wise to discard general intelligence. Like it or not, much of our heritage in this area is that earlier workers, from Binet on, had as their motivation the solution of social problems, and currently many in the area have a similar motivation.

THE BEARING OF SOCIAL USEFULNESS

In practice, if you believe that the concept of general intelligence has outlived its usefulness, you may choose from among several differential, or multiple, aptitude batteries, which will provide measures of some of the so-called primary mental abilities. If you happen to believe that there is something to general ability, you can find tests to use. The novice looking for these latter tests may have to alert himself to the first Principle of Psychological Progress — the test labels may have changed from "general intelligence" to "general classification" or "scholastic aptitude." If you enjoy riding the fence, you might become a devotee of the practice of the College Board, and others, and measure just two abilities: Verbal and Quantitative.

This is certainly not the place to review the voluminous literature that amply demonstrates the practical utility of tests of general intelligence. Nor is it the place to catalog the misuses of the Stanford-Binet for purposes which Terman never claimed for it, or the misuses of the Wechsler scales for purposes which Wechsler *has* claimed for his scales. Neither the Binet nor the Wechsler provides a factorially pure, unidimensional measure of a *g*. The current Stanford-Binet was in reality constructed too early to benefit from the implication of factor analysis for test purity, whereas the Wechsler scales were based on the impossible premise that 10 or 11 subtests can simultaneously provide diagnostic subscores and a meaningful total score. Of the many group tests that appeared between 1920 and 1945 it can be said that few, if any, provide unidimensional measures of general intelligence. The chief difficulty is that most of them lead to a total score based on a mixture of verbal and mathematical material. Thus, with two main sources of variance, marked qualitative differences can exist for quantitatively similar total scores. The College Board — Educational Testing Service people have justifiably refrained from giving a total score involving verbal plus math, but there are those who question the usefulness of the Board's math score and there are those who criticize the Educational Testing Service for failing to change over to a differential aptitude battery.

Let us next turn to a somewhat more detailed examination of the various so-called multiple aptitude batteries. What and who influenced whom in the development of these batteries is difficult to disentangle. At the risk of oversimplification, it might be said that two prime influences operated.

First, the early factor studies by the Thurstones, by Holzinger, and by Guilford are the progenitors of the Science Research Associates' Primary Mental Abilities (PMA) Test, the Holzinger-Crowder Unifactor Tests, the

Guilford-Zimmerman Aptitude Survey, and the Segel-Raskin Multiple Aptitude Tests (MAT).

The second influence, which seems to have emerged from testing experience in the Armed Services during World War II, is the job-element approach, an approach which may or may not differ from the old job-analysis method. For whatever jobs you are dealing with, you study the activities involved in order to decide what aptitudes are called for. Whether or not these aptitudes have been previously isolated by factor analysis is totally irrelevant. It is hoped that some jobs will have aptitudes in common so that the needed number of tests will be less than the number of jobs. The one battery that is built on this approach is the Flanagan Aptitude Classification Tests, a battery that just happens to have the catchy abbreviation, FACT. If we cannot muster any facts in psychology, we can at least have FACT scores!

A cross between testing for factorially defined abilities and job-element derived aptitudes is apparently involved in the General Aptitude Test Battery (GATB) of the United States Employment Service and the Differential Aptitudes Tests (DAT) of the Psychological Corporation, since in both batteries some of the tests seem to have sprung from factor-analysis results and some tests seem to have been thrown in as possible predictors of specific performances.

It is not our purpose to rank order the seven above-mentioned multitest batteries, but a few remarks may be relevant as background for the sequel. Apparently the Employment Service's GATB was made available (but not put on the commercial market) with the idea that there would be a continuing program of validities studies — the accumulation is now impressive. For the DAT of the Psychological Corporation there is an overabundance of data on validity, collected and analyzed prior to marketing the test. Both the Science Research Associates' PMA and FACT were made available without backing for the claimed usefulness of the tests. Belatedly, that is, 6 years after its appearance, some evidence on the predictive validity of FACT has been reported. Validity information for the other three batteries is not entirely lacking, though far from ample. Some will have noted that that fuzzy dodge called factor validity is being ignored here.

Now to get back to our main theme, to what extent have the seven batteries contributed to the demise of general intelligence? In attempting to answer this, one encounters a paradox: Some test authors want to eat their cake and have it too — they attempt to measure factors and g with the same instrument. This is understandable in a couple of instances. Three of the 15 tests of the Employment Service GATB were included to provide a measure of general intelligence, apparently because the authors still saw some merit in a g and were not committed to the factor schemata. Holzinger and Crowder suggest a weighted score for a measure of g, perhaps because of Holzinger's long-time alignment with Spearman. The real teaser is why Thurstone ever sanctioned, if he did, the summing of Science Research Associates' PMA scores to obtain an IQ. One has the uncomfortable feeling that his publishers wished to g garnish the factor cake to make it more palatable in the market place.

Although Segel [19] says nothing in his 1957 article about a general score from the Segel-Raskin MAT, the test publishers say that, in addition to yielding scores for four factors, it also provides a "Scholastic Potential" score. Perhaps Flanagan has not completely broken with tradition since he states that four tests of the FACT battery measure "General College Aptitude" — a statement made with the same lack of empirical validity as the claim, which should be anxiety producing for those of you who fly a certain airline, that your highly paid pilot shares four of the aptitudes of a plumber!

Apparently, Guilford and Zimmerman and the test people at the Psychological Corporation are willing to stick to the sound principle that a differential test battery cannot provide factor scores that can be summed to obtain a meaningful IQ, or measure of a g.

Parenthetically, it might be said that the California Test of Mental Maturity (CTMM), which, according to the publisher's 1963 catalog, was originally "designed as a group test of intelligence patterned after the individual Stanford-Binet," serves as an illustration of factor icing a g cake. Some multitest batteries and the CTMM have a Madison Avenue advantage: The advertising claims the measurement of not only factors but also g; not only g but also factors. This measurement absurdity is all too apt to go unrecognized by many test users, and hence a sales advantage for the aptitude battery that produces both factor scores and an IQ.

Just how successful have the multitest batteries been? Since by far the most extensive social use of tests has been, and continues to be, in the schools, let us look at the evidence of validity studies therein. As indicated previously, little is known about the predictive usefulness of some of the seven batteries discussed above. The DAT of the Psychological Corporation is the only battery for which adequate predictive (and concurrent) validity data, derived from school sources, are available. It is also the battery that has fared best in the hands of the test reviewers; therefore if we allow the case for differential batteries to rest thereon, we will be looking at the best. So, what is the story?

Recall that the hoped-for advantage of a multitest battery over the old-fashioned general intelligence test was that it would have greater predictive power, a power which could manifest itself in higher validity coefficients for specific subject matter and, perhaps, for over-all achievement. It was hoped that such a battery would be truly differential in that particular factors (or subtests) would correlate higher with achievement in some areas than in other areas. Presumably each factor (or subtest) should have unique usefulness. If a battery were truly differential, it would be a boon to school guidance personnel.

Now the manual of the DAT of the Psychological Corporation contains a staggering total of 4,096, yes I counted 'em, validity coefficients. With such a large pool to draw from, one could by gracious selection "show" that the DAT is the answer to the prayer of every counselor, male or female, or by malicious selection one could "prove" that the DAT is far worse than any test ever published. The validity coefficients range all the way down to −.37, which is presumably a chance deviation downward from 0, and all the way up to .90, which is likely not a chance deviation downward from unity. But ranges tell us nothing. After a careful perusal of the 4,096 correlations, it seems safe to summarize DAT validities as follows:

1. Verbal Reasoning (analogies to most of you) is the best single predictor; Language Usage, as represented by a sentence test dealing with grammar and word usage, and admittedly more achievement than aptitude, is a close second.

2. Numerical Ability, as measured by a test of simple arithmetic operations, designed to tap arithmetic reasoning without the usual verbal component, is the best predictor of achievement in school mathematics. It does not, however, correlate as well with grades in science as does Verbal Reasoning.

3. Aside from the Numerical Ability test, the only other test that shows differential power as a predictor is the Spelling test — if you cannot spell you may have trouble learning shorthand.

4. The remaining five tests in the battery simply fail to show compelling evidence that they are good in the differential predictive sense. For the Mechanical Reasoning and the Clerical Speed and Accuracy tests this may be understandable in that little of school curricula for Grades 8 through 12 requires such abilities, but one would expect that Abstract Reasoning and Space Relations would fare better than they seem to.

Such data as we have been able to locate for the other six multitest batteries tend to support these findings on the DAT. Aside from tests of numerical ability having differential value for predicting school grades in math, it seems safe to conclude that the worth of the multitest batteries as differential predictors of achievement in school has not been demonstrated. Incidentally, the fact that the Verbal and Numerical tests stand out as the only two useful predictors tends to provide some support for the Educational Testing Service — College Board practice of providing scores for just these two abilities.

And now we come to a very disturbing aspect of the situation. Those who have constructed and marketed multiple aptitude batteries, and advocated that they be used instead of tests of general intelligence, seem never to have bothered to demonstrate whether or not multitest batteries provide better predictions than the old-fashioned scale of general intelligence. Be it noted that we are not discussing experimental editions of tests. Some may say that insofar as a test publisher provides validity data for a new battery it is not necessary to show that the validities are, for the given school condition, better than those of other tests. With this one can agree, but only in case no claims are made, explicity or implicitly, regarding superior merits for the new battery.

It is far from clear that tests of general intelligence have been outmoded by the multitest batteries as the more useful predictors of school achievement. Indeed, one can use the vast accumulation of data on the validity of the Psychological Corporation's DAT to show that better predictions are possible via old-fashioned general intelligence tests. Consider the fact that a combination of the tests Verbal Reasoning (analogies) and Numerical Ability would be, in terms of content, very similar to many group tests of general intelligence. Consider also that an equally weighted combination of these two tests correlates in the mid-.80s with the Otis S-A, Higher Form. Then, when you turn to a careful study of the empirical validities, as reported in the DAT manual, you will not be surprised at the outcome of the application of a little arithmetic, which leads to the definite conclusion that a simple un-weighted combination of the Verbal Reasoning and Numerical Ability tests predicts as well as or, in most instances, better than any subtest taken singly, or in the differential sense.

The manual for the DAT contains the following statement (Bennett, Seashore, and Wesman, 1952):

> Apparently the *Verbal Reasoning* and *Numerical Ability* tests can serve most purposes for which a general mental ability test is usually given in addition to providing differential clues useful to the counselor. Hence, the use of the so-called intelligence test is apparently unnecessary where the *Differential Aptitude Tests* are already being used [2, p. 71].

Anyone who disagrees with this quotation could, with better justification, say that an intelligence test can serve nearly all, if not all, the purposes for which a multiple aptitude battery is given in the schools because the former, in general, is a better predictor and because, as we saw earlier, the differential clues are too fragmentary to be of use to the counselor. And there is a bonus: one classroom period of testing, compared to six periods. A second bonus: much less costly. A third bonus: fewer scores to confuse the already confused minds of most school counselors.

Thus, we come to the conclusion that general intelligence has not been lost in the trend to test more and more abilities; it was merely misplaced by a misplaced emphasis on a hope that a lot of us, including the speaker, once entertained, a hope that in turn was based on a misplaced faith in factor analysis: *the* hope that factors, when and if measured, would find great usefulness in the affairs of society. By the criterion of social usefulness, the multiple aptitude batteries have been found wanting. Now, I have no desire to furnish ammunition for those test critics who would have us stop all testing merely because they find a trivially faulty item in a standardized test. At a time when there is shouting about the tyranny of the testers and the brass of the brain watchers, at a time when school people are showing resentment at the disruption caused by too many national testing programs, at a time when federal and state legislators are all too willing to write legislation that places restrictions on the use of tests, and at a time when both majorities and minorities are being denied the benefits of test-based guidance because certain well-intentioned persons fail to realize that scores for the under-privileged minorities are useful indices of *immediate,* or present, functioning — at a time when all these and other forces are operating to throw out the tests, it is high time for the profession to establish a bureau of standards to test the tests instead of coasting down a road that is tinged with some of the trappings of Madison Avenue. Better to have informed internal control than ignorant, hostile, external control.

INTELLIGENCE ELSEWHERE?

Aside from the near loss of the idea that progress in school may depend on general intelligence, one wonders whether intelligence has come to be regarded as unimportant in other areas.

Any of you who have money invested in stocks and wish some reassurance regarding the intelligence level of business and industry managers should read Edwin Ghiselli's (1963) Bingham Lecture [7]. His summary of his own work indicates that the average intelligence of those in the upper and middle management levels falls at the ninety-sixth percentile of the population. Thomas Harrell (1961) came to a similar conclusion [9]. Furthermore, management level is correlated with intelligence — you can be too dumb to succeed as a manager. Also you can be too bright to be a managerial success! Now it must be admitted that little, if anything, is known about whether management success might be better predicted by measures of factor-analytic defined abilities. On this you are free to guess — most of you will have already guessed my guess.

A one-by-one cataloguing of what we know or do not know about what abilities contribute to success within various occupational and professional groups would merely add to the dullness of this presentation, so let us turn to some of the more esoteric fields of psychology to see whether the concept of general intelligence has or has had any relevance. One such field, and a very broad one, is creativity. Anyone who peeks over the fence into this field is apt to be astonished at the visible chaos. The definition of creativity is confounded by the diversity of subareas within the field, the criterion problems are far from licked, and so little is known about the creative process that measuring instruments are, seemingly, chosen on a trial-and-error basis.

We might presume that the role, if any, of general intelligence in creativity would increase as we pass from art to music, to architecture, to literature and drama, to science. Your presumption about the ordering may be different and more nearly correct. I would like to discuss briefly the extremes of my ordering.

At the risk of being called a heretic and a has-been statistician, I would like first to resort to the single case of a painter, examples of whose works were reproduced in color recently by Desmond Morris (1962) in a journal called *Portfolio and Art News Annual* [18]. To my uncultured eye these paintings have the general appearance of the so-called school of modern art, and the running comment on the paintings involves what I must presume is the jargon of contemporary art critics: talk about self-rewarding activities, compositional control, calligraphic differentiation, thematic variation, optimum heterogeneity, and universal imagery. Since authors may use pen names, I would guess that this painter is using "Congon" as a "brush" name. Supposedly by now some of you will be guessing that this single case is of interest in the context of this paper because of Congon's IQ. Well, because of this painter's underprivileged cultural background, no test scores are available. Congon, despite striking contribution to art, happens to be a chimp. Aside from a rather obvious conclusion, one wonders what would emerge from a blind (as to source) analysis of Congon's paintings by the personality boys. We might even tell them that Congon was breast fed.

Without in any way implying that creativity in the arts is unimportant, we hasten on to scientific creativity, a specific area in which it seems likely, because of the Sputnik-inspired spurt of interest, that we can learn something of the role, if any, of general intelligence. But immediately we encounter skulls that have been cracked on the criterion problem.

One elaborate study (C. Taylor, Smith, Ghiselin, and Ellison, 1961), on a sample of 166 physical scientists working at Air Force research centers, came up with 150, yes, believe it or not, 150 *criteria* of scientific productivity and creativity [21]. By combining some scores and eliminating others, the number of criteria was reduced to 48. A factor analysis of the intercorrelations of the 48 reduced the number to 14 "categories." Apparently the 150 original criterion measures included everything except success at turning on a kitchen faucet, so one need not be surprised at the outcome of the factor analysis. For example, one factor-derived criterion of scientific productivity and creativity is "likeableness," another is "status seeking," another is extent of membership in scientific and professional societies — the joiners, no doubt.

The fact that the intercorrelations among the 14 criterion categories, derived from factor analysis, range from $-.08$ to $+.55$, with a median of only .18, indicates either criterion complexity or else a whale of a lot of vagueness as to what is meant by productivity and creativity in science. Now this criterion mess emerged from a study of interview results of 166 "physical scientists," but nearly half of these so-called scientists were engineers, and the education of the total group indicates only 2 years of graduate work on the average; so when is a scientist a scientist a scientist?

The next step in this study was to collect data on 107 of these so-called scientists for a whopping total of 130 potential predictors, which, when pitted against 17 criterion measures, produced 2,210 "validity coefficients." The distribution of these, excluding 30 values involving un-cross-validated empirical keys, almost restores one's faith in the random-sampling distribution of correlation coefficients around zero! There were 16 predictors based on aptitude tests, hence 16×17, or 272, "validities" for this area. Since only 4% of them reach the 5% level, we can do no more than accept the null hypothesis: Aptitude ain't important in scientific productivity and creativity. The idea that some scientists are more equal in ability than others apparently is not true.

But this criterion-based study did not contribute to my worry about the role of general intelligence — the failure to include a general intelligence measure as a potential predictor may be interpreted as indicating that the authors already had the answer.

Let us turn to another criterion-based study (D. Taylor, 1961) [22]. The criterion measures for creativity and productivity were based on the checking by supervisors of statements that had been scaled by Thurstone's equal-appearing interval method. Creativity and productivity, so gauged, correlated .69 with each other on a sample of 103 researchers (electronic scientists and engineers). For this same group, intelligence, as measured by the Terman Concept Mastery Test (CMT), correlated only .20 or less with the criteria. Two Psychological Corporation tests and an American Institute for Research test did a little better. Creativity is slightly more predictable than productivity. Insofar as these two criteria are themselves valid, the findings indicate that within a group of research workers, precious little of the variance in creativity, and still less in productivity, can be predicted by the tests.

A third study (MacKinnon, 1962) based on criterion (rated) measures of performance was concerned with the creativity of architects [16]. Although the author reports that *within* a creative sample the correlation is essentially zero between intelligence (CMT) and rated creativity, it is not clear from the context what is meant by "within" sample. If this means within the sample of 40 creative architects selected as the "most creative" in the country, then we indeed have such a drastic restriction in range on the *criterion* variable that little, if any, correlation can be expected for any and all predictors. Now the author says, without presenting any evidence, that "Over the whole range of intelligence and creativity there is, of course, a positive relationship between the two variables [16, p. 488]." One wonders just what is meant by creativity in architecture as rated either by fellow architects or by editors of architectural journals. If judged creativity reflects engineering-structural innovation, then intelligence would likely be a correlate; if judged creativity depends on new artistic designs, then the intelligence component would likely be of less importance. It would seem that when the author says we "may have overestimated . . . the role of intelligence in creative achievement [16, p. 493]," he should have included some marked qualifications as to what type of creativity he had in mind.

That such qualification is indeed necessary is supplied by a finding of still another investigator (Barron, 1963) [1]. For a group of highly creative writers it was estimated, by way of the Terman CMT, that their average IQ is about 140, which we interpret as meaning that a high IQ is a necessary, though not sufficient, condition for outstanding success as a writer. On the basis of his own studies and those of other persons, this same investigator suggests that "over the total range of intelligence and creativity a low positive correlation" of .40 probably obtains. This sweeping generalization is for all areas of creativity.

And speaking of sweeping generalizations, consider the suggestion in a 1961 study (Holland, 1961) that "we need to use nonintellectual criteria in the selection of students for scholarships and fellowships [12, p. 146]." The author did not say so, but presumably he meant in addition to intellectual ability; maybe he did not, since he had previously concluded that "intelligence has little or no relationship to creative performance in arts and science . . . [12, p. 143]" at the high school level. His data back up this conclusion, as might have been expected when correlations are based on groups restricted in range to the top 1%!

If the foregoing examples of criterion-based studies of creativity seem to indicate that general intelligence is relatively unimportant for creativity, it should be remembered that drastic but unknown or unspecified curtailment of range exists for both ability and criteria. Why do correlational studies under such adverse circumstances?

Next we turn to a few studies of creativity which cannot be criticized because of restriction of range on the criteria — these studies simply avoid this problem by never having actual criterion information. The approach is to claim that certain tests, which typically are scored for novel responses or novel solutions to problems, *are* measures of creativity, with no evidence whatsoever that the tests have predictive validity for nontest, real-life creative performance. This bit of ignorance does not prove to be a handicap to those who think that creativity can be studied without the nuisance of obtaining criterion measures. We reluctantly accept the test-based criteria solely for the sake of seeing what happens to general intelligence as a part of the picture. Time permits only three examples.

We first note that general intelligence has not manifested itself as a correlate of so-called creativity tests in the factor-analytic studies of creativity. The explanation for this is easily found — no measures of general intelligence are used in these studies. When discussing his plans for studying creativity, a certain author (Guilford, 1950) said that "we must look well beyond the boundaries of the IQ if we are to fathom the domain of creativity [8, p. 448]." He went on to say, the conception "that creative talent is to be accounted for in terms of high intelligence or IQ . . . is not only inadequate but has been largely responsible for lack of progress in the understanding of creative people [8, p. 454]." With a part of this one can agree, but does it follow that one should prejudge the role of general intelligence as a source of variance in creativity tests or factors derived therefrom? Does the failure to include an IQ test help one learn the extent to which one must go beyond the boundaries of the IQ to fathom creativity? Apparently the author, although willing to predict that the correlations between IQ and the many types of creativity tests "are only moderate or low," was unwilling to include an IQ test for the sake of finding out. However, negation by omission is not very convincing.

That at least one test bearing the label "creativity" is correlated more than moderately with IQ is evidenced by the value of .67 (average for boys and girls) for the carefully chosen sample of 15-year-olds in Project Talent (Shaycoft, Dailey, Orr, Neyman, and Sherman, 1963) [20]. This sample-stable r (based on a total N of 7,648) becomes .80 when corrected for attenuation.

In a recent extensive study (Getzels and Jackson, 1962) [6] already extensively criticized, creativity is defined as the sum of scores on five tests (median intercorrelation of only .28). Although the investigators use the sum score for most of their analyses, they do not bother to report the correlation of creativity, so defined, with IQ. From the published report I have ascertained (via the correlation-of-sums formula) that creativity and IQ correlate to the extent of .40 for the total of 533 cases. Now this r of .40 has been greatly attenuated because of three things: first, the usual measurement errors; second, the cases were highly selected on IQ (mean of 132); third, the IQs are a mixture from the Stanford-Binet, Henmon-Nelson, and Wechsler Intelligence Scale for Children (the use of regression-estimated Binet IQs from the other two scales aggravates rather than improves the mixture). We deduce that intelligence and the creativity tests used here have far more common variance than the authors believe.

Much is made of the finding that the creativity tests tended to correlate higher than did IQ with verbal-content school achievements. Again the IQ comes in for an unfair drubbing because of the same mixture of IQ scores and, what is more pertinent, because of explicit selective curtailment on the IQ variable and only incidental selection on the creativity variable.

Of more importance to the present paper is the analysis, by these same authors, based on a high IQ group and a high creative group, these groups being selected as the top 20% for each variable but excluding those who were in the top 20% on both variables. These two selected groups were then contrasted on total school achievement (and a host of other variables that are of no interest here). The mean IQ for the high IQ group was 150 whereas the mean IQ for the high creative group was 127, yet the achievement means of the two groups were "unexpectedly" equally superior to the school population mean despite the 23-point difference in mean IQ. The authors say that it "*is* quite surprising" that the high creativity group achieved so well. From this it is concluded that the "creative instruments account for a significant portion of the variance in school achievement [6, p. 24]," and the subsequent argument implies that creativity is more important for ordinary school achievement than is the IQ. Now anyone who is at all familiar with a three-variate problem will not be "unexpectedly" surprised at the foregoing results — indeed, if the authors had bothered to give the three basic correlations among the three variables (IQ, creativity, and total school achievement) for the entire group, any person versed in simple multivariate analysis could deduce the results. Furthermore, he could deduce a further result (and this one has been overlooked by the critics) which might be unpleasantly surprising to the thesis of these authors: namely, the high IQ and the high creative groups did equally well in school achievement despite an unreported difference in mean creativity that is of the same order as the much stressed difference in IQ.[1] Utilizing the half-blind logic of the authors, one can say that creative ability is not as important as IQ for school achievement — just the opposite of their position.

Now the fact that seven of nine replications of this study confirm the original findings merely indicates that repetition of the same faulty design and false logic will lead to the same false conclusions. The design being used is such that, if two variables are equally correlated with a third, the conclusion will be reached that the two are actually unequally correlated with the third. This is the neatest trick of the decade for supplying educationists with an antidote for the IQ virus. I cannot refrain from saying at this point that, although discouraged, I am still hopeful that people who do statistical studies will first learn a modicum of elementary statistics!

Time does not permit a discussion of other studies in which creativity is defined in terms of test performance instead of being based on actual creativity of the sort prized by society. In summary of this brief on creativity studies, I

---

[1] Since this was written, the replication study of Yamamoto (1964) gives data that corroborate this deduction [27].

would like to offer a few dogmatic-sounding observations. First, one need not be surprised at the fact that so-called creativity tests do not yield high correlations with IQ tests — but the correlations are generally far higher than those found in typical studies with range restrictions. I would anticipate that for normalized scores, the uncurtailed scatters for IQ versus creativity tests will be bivariate normal. Second, if we have honest to goodness criterion measures of literary or architectural or scientific creativity, the scatter diagram between IQ and such creativity (not normalized, since it makes sense to expect a skewed distribution for actual creativity) will be triangular in shape for unselected cases. That is, at the high IQ levels there will be a very wide range of creativity, whereas as we go down to average IQ, and on down to lower levels, the scatter for creativity will be less and less. Having a high IQ is not a guarantee of being creative; having a low IQ means creativity is impossible. Third, it remains to be seen whether or not the so-called creativity tests and/or factors derived therefrom have appreciable value as predictors of actual creative performance. Such tests may or may not yield better predictions than a test of general intelligence. Fourth, as far as I am concerned, to claim factorial validity for creativity tests, along with definitions of creativity in terms of tests, is an unwarranted avoidance of the fundamental problem of validity.

The recently renewed interest in "gifted" children, along with the flurry of creativity studies, has led to a reexamination of methods for identifying the gifted. It has long been recognized that identification in terms of high IQ is too narrow — those gifted in such areas as art and music would be overlooked. The argument against the IQ is now (Torrance, 1962) [25] being reinforced by the claim that the selection of the top 20% on IQ would mean the exclusion of 70% of the top 20% on tested creativity. This startling statistic, which implies a correlation of only .24 between IQ and creativity, is being used to advocate the use of creativity tests for identifying the gifted. Be it noted that these creativity tests will also miss those gifted in art and music.

We are being told that it is important "to identify creative talent early in life," hence you need not be surprised that the search goes down to the kindergarten level, with claims of successful identification. The creativity tests are presumed to be better for this purpose than the IQ tests because of the failure of the IQ to be constant, an argument that completely overlooks the fact that the IQ does have some constancy whereas absolutely nothing is known about the stability of standings on creativity tests. The IQ tests, known to be imperfectly valid as predictors of outstanding achievement in life, are to be replaced by the creativity tests, known to be of unknown validity as predictors. Anyway, progress, defined as change, is in the offing.

The IQ is being linked with *learning* as an outmoded educational objective; the new objective involves an emphasis on *thinking*. Somehow or other creativity, not general intelligence, is being associated with thinking. The horrible idea of underachievers and overachievers, in terms of expectancies based on the IQ, will be abolished. But no thought is given to the fact that the use of creativity tests will simply define a new crop of under- and overachievers.

In an apparent zeal to rid us of general intelligence, it is argued that measured creativity is significantly related to ordinary school achievement. Maybe so, but never, never does one find complete data reported as to the relative sizes of validity coefficients. And, as we have seen, the technique being used will show that equal coefficients are unequal. Why not the full facts, free of fantasy?

An additional difficulty is not being faced by those who would replace IQ tests by creativity tests, or creative-thinking tests. The factor-analytic studies indicate either no, or a trivially small, general creativity factor in these tests, yet these self-characterized "bold, adventurous" reformers (see Torrance, 1963) [26] do not hesitate to advocate a total score which is nearly devoid of meaning. Changing the curriculum to the teaching of creativity and creative thinking will not overcome this measurement difficulty. Again, I express the hope that the IQ is replaced by something better rather than by something worse.

There are other areas, such as reasoning, problem solving, and concept formation, in which one might expect to find some consideration of intelligence as an aspect. One might also expect that investigators of thinking would have something to say about individual differences in thinking being dependent upon intelligence, but for some unintelligent reason these people seem never to mention intelligence. Surely, it cannot be inferred that thinking about thinking does not involve intelligence!

IN CONCLUSION

It has been the thesis of this paper that the concept of general intelligence, despite being maligned by a few, regarded as a second-order function by some, and discarded or ignored by others, still has a rightful place in the science of psychology and in the practical affairs of man. It has not been argued that the nature of general intelligence is well understood. Much, however, has been written about its nature. Over 40 years ago (Intelligence, 1921a, 1921b), an editor secured and published the reasoned views of 13 well-known test psychologists. Later, Spearman set forth his speculations about the nature of g. Prior to these, Binet had, of course, given much thought to the problem.

More recent discussions exist. Hebb (1949) has considered the problem from the viewpoint of neurology and brain functioning [11]. Cyril Burt (1955), always a vociferous defender of the concept of general intelligence, has reviewed the evidence for a g and restated the idea, dreadful to some, that intelligence is innate [3]. Perhaps it was inevitable that Raymond Cattell (1963), who has camped with the general intelligence contingent, should gaze into his crystal n-dimensional factor ball and find evidence for crystallized as opposed to fluid general intelligence [4]. Joseph McVicker Hunt's (1961) book on *Intelligence and Experience* [13] is in large part devoted to questions pertaining to the nature of intelligence.

By far the most provocative recent discussion that I have encountered is the closely reasoned 44-page paper by Keith Hayes (1962) [10]. He puts forth a motivational-experiential theory of intelligence. In essence, he presumes that there are hereditary differences in motivation. "Experience-producing drives" and environmental differences produce differences in experience, which in turn, by way of learning, lead to differences in ability. Therefore, differences called intellectual are nothing more than acquired abilities. I think that Hayes has ignored the possibility of individual differences in learning ability, but if such a formulation leads to experimental manipulation of variables, we may eventually make progress in an area that has too long been dominated by ever increasing fractionization by factor analysis, with little thought as to how the fractured parts get put together into a functioning whole.

Abilities, or capacities, or aptitudes, or intellectual skills, or whatever you choose to call them, are measured in terms of response products to standardized stimulus situations. The *stimulus* is presented to an *organism* which by some *process* comes up with a *response*; thus any attempt to theorize and/or study intellect in terms of a simple stimulus-response (S-R) paradigm seems doomed to failure unless drastically modified and complicated by the insertion of O for organism and P for process.

There have been thousands of researches on the multitudinous variations from organism to organism, and the results fill books on individual differences. These studies can be roughly classified into two types. First, those that ascertain the intercorrelations among scaled response products to various stimulus situations, known as tests, have to do with the structure of intellect; and whether the resulting factors are anything more than dimensions for describing individual differences need not concern us here. The second type of study seeks the nontest correlates of test performance, and whether or not any of the found correlates can be regarded as explaining individual differences is not of interest here. Both types of studies certainly force one to stress the overwhelming diversity exhibited among the organisms.

But these studies of individual differences never come to grips with the *process*, or operation, by which a given organism achieves an intellectual response. Indeed, it is difficult to see how the available individual difference data can be used even as a starting point for generating a theory as to the process nature of general intelligence or of any other specified ability.

As a basis for a little speculation, let us conceive of a highly hypothetical situation in which the two members of a pair of identical twins, with identical experiences, find themselves cast up on an uninhabited tropical island. Let us assume that they are at the supergenius level, far beyond that of your favorite man of genius. Let us also assume that, though highly educated in the sciences, they have been fortunate enough to have had zero exposure to psychology. In addition, we presume that, being highly involved and abstracted in the pursuit of science, they have never noticed what we call individual differences in abilities.

A quick exploration of the island assures them that food is plentiful, that shelter is available, and that clothing is not a necessity. To allay the boredom that they foresee as an eternity in this laborless heaven, they decide to spend their time in the further pursuit of science, but the lack of the wherewithal for constructing gadgets rules out any research in the physical sciences. Having had a college course in Bugs and Bites they proceed to study the life of the island's insects, then the habits of the birds, and the antics of a couple of monkeys. The manner in which the monkeys adjust to the environment leads them to set up some trial situations for more systematic observation. Needless to say, the monkeys show evidence of what we call learning and what we call problem solving.

Eventually they decide that attempting to outwit each other might be more fun than being outwitted by the monkeys, so they begin to cook up and use games and problems for this purpose. This activity leads each to speculate and introspect about how problems are invented and how solved. Then by cleverly designed experiments, preceded of course by theory, they set forth highly developed laws and principles about what we call reasoning and problem solving. Incidentally, they switch back and forth between the roles of experimenter and subject, there being no college sophomores available. They continue for years the study of their own mental operations, constantly on the alert for new phenomena to investigate.

And now with apologies to the ancient Greeks, who did have some ideas along these lines, we leave with you the 64-million drachma question: Will our two identical supergeniuses, being totally unaware of individual differences, ever hit upon and develop a concept of intelligence?

REFERENCES

1. Barron, F. *Creativity and Psychological Health*. Princeton, N.J.: D. Van Nostrand Co., Inc., 1963.
2. Bennett, G. K., Seashore, H. G., and Wesman, A. G. *Differential Aptitude Tests, Manual* (2nd ed.). New York: The Psychological Corporation, 1952.
3. Burt, C. L. "The Evidence for the Concept of Intelligence," *British Journal of Educational Psychology*, 25 (1955), 158–177.
4. Cattell, R. B. "Theory of Fluid and Crystallized Intelligence: A Critical Experiment," *Journal of Educational Psychology*, 54 (1963), 1–22.
5. Cronbach, L. J. "The Two Disciplines of Scientific Psychology," *American Psychologist*, 12 (1957), 671–684.
6. Getzels, J. W., and Jackson, P. W. *Creativity and Intelligence*. New York: John Wiley and Sons, Inc., 1962.
7. Ghiselli, E. E. "Managerial Talent," *American Psychologist*, 18 (1963), 631–642.
8. Guilford, J. P. "Creativity," *American Psychologist*, 5 (1950), 444–454.
9. Harrell, T. H. *Manager's Performance and Personality*. Cincinnati, Ohio: South-Western, 1961.
10. Hayes, K. J. "Genes, Drives, and Intellect," *Psychological Reports*, 10 (1962), 299–342.
11. Hebb, D. O. *The Organization of Behavior*. New York: John Wiley and Sons, Inc., 1949.
12. Holland, J. L. "Creative and Academic Performance Among Talented Adolescents," *Journal of Educational Psychology*, 52 (1961), 136–147.
13. Hunt, J. McV. *Intelligence and Experience*. New York: The Ronald Press Company, 1961.
14. "Intelligence and Its Measurement: A Symposium," *Journal of Educational Psychology*, 12 (1921), 123–147.   (a)
15. "Intelligence and Its Measurement: A Symposium," *Journal of Educational Psychology*, 12 (1921), 195–216.   (b)

16. MacKinnon, D. W. "The Nature and Nurture of Creative Talent," *American Psychologist*, 17 (1962), 484–495.
17. Miles, T. R. "On Defining Intelligence," *British Journal of Educational Psychology*, 27 (1957), 153–165.
18. Morris, D. "The Biology of Art," *Portfolio Art News Annual*, No. 6 (1962), 52–63, 122–124.
19. Segel, D. "The Multiple Aptitude Tests," *Personnel and Guidance Journal*, 35 (1957), 424–432.
20. Shaycoft, M. F., Dailey, J. T., Orr, D. B., Neyman, C. A., Jr., and Sherman, S. E. "Project Talent: Studies of a Complete Age Group — Age 15," Pittsburgh: University of Pittsburgh, 1963. (Mimeo.)
21. Taylor, C. W., Smith, W. R., Ghiselin, B., and Ellison, R. "Explorations in the Measurement and Predictions of Contributions of One Sample of Scientists," *USAF ASD Technical Report*, (1961), No. 61–96.
22. Taylor, D. W. "Variables Related to Creativity and Productivity Among Men in Two Research Laboratories," in C. W. Taylor and F. Barron (eds.), *Scientific Creativity*. New York: John Wiley and Sons, Inc., 1961.
23. Thurstone, L. L. *Primary Mental Abilities*. Chicago: University of Chicago Press, 1938.
24. ————., and Thurstone, T. G. *Factorial Studies of Intelligence*. Chicago: University of Chicago Press, 1941.
25. Torrance, E. P. *Guiding Creative Talent*. Englewood Cliffs, N.J.: Prentice-Hall, Inc., 1962.
26. ————. *Education and the Creative Potential*. Minneapolis: University of Minnesota Press, 1963.
27. Yamamoto, K. "Role of Creative Thinking and Intelligence in High School Achievement," *Psychological Record*, 14 (1964), 783–789.

21

A Comparison of Results of
Three Intelligence Tests

Roger T. Lennon

*It is often assumed by the layman that the results of one intelli-
gence test are essentially the same as those of another. Lennon has
compared data on three separate tests to illustrate the extent to
which these tests are indeed comparable. The results have a definite
implication for interpretation of I.Q., indeed the interpretation of
any two or more tests proposing to measure a common trait. The
persistent student may wish to investigate Millman and Lindlof,
"The Comparability of Fifth-Grade Norms of the California, Iowa,
and Metropolitan Achievement Tests," in the* Journal of Educational Measurement, *1964, 1:135–137, for information regarding
the comparability of achievement test norms.*

Teachers and workers in educational research, child guidance, school and
college admissions work, and related fields are frequently faced with the
problem of reconciling mental ability ratings based on different tests. It is
commonly recognized that results derived from various intelligence measures
cannot be assumed to be directly comparable one with another. This is so for
a number of reasons: different standardization populations, different factorial
compositions of the tests, different methods of computing intelligence quotients, and so forth.

Whatever the reasons, it is generally agreed that there is need for data that
will permit conversion of scores or IQ's derived from one test to comparable
measures derived from other tests. This [article] reports the results of a study
conducted by Harcourt, Brace & World's Test Department for the purpose
of determining the equivalence among scores and IQ's derived from three
widely used mental ability measures for secondary school pupils: *Terman-
McNemar Test of Mental Ability, Otis Quick-Scoring Mental Ability Tests:
Gamma Test,* and *Pintner General Ability Tests: Verbal Series, Advanced
Test.*

From Roger T. Lennon, "A Comparison of Results of Three Intelligence Tests,"
Test Service Notebook, No. 11 (1953), pp. 14–17. Published by Harcourt, Brace &
World, Incorporated, New York. Reproduced by permission.

Methods of Approach

The ideal approach to the determination of equivalent or comparable scores on several different tests is to administer the several tests to the same group of students in such fashion as to allow for practice effect, and within a sufficiently short span of time so that no appreciable growth in the functions measured takes place between testings. The many practical difficulties of this method, particularly with a group sufficiently large to yield dependable results, constitute one of the principal reasons that so few studies of this kind have been made.

A second approach, perhaps less satisfactory on theoretical grounds, involves the administration of each of the tests to groups known, or believed on some reasonable bases, to be equivalent or matched with respect to the abilities measured by the tests. The study here reported is of this second type: distributions of scores and IQ's on the three tests were obtained for matched groups, and tables of equivalent scores and IQ's were derived by the equipercentile method from these distributions.

Source of Data

The data on which the study was based became available as a result of the administration of one or another of the three tests to all students who were tested, during the spring of 1950, in the national standardization of the *Essential High School Content Battery,* a general achievement battery for secondary school students. The schools in the standardization program were required to administer one of the three intelligence tests, but were permitted to use whichever of the three they preferred. Thus it was possible to select, from the total normative population, groups taking each of the three intelligence tests. These groups were then matched in the manner described below.

Bases for Matching Groups

The bases for matching the three groups were (1) grade status, (2) chronological age within grade, and (3) total score on the *Essential High School Content Battery.* Thus three groups (one for each test) were selected, known to be equivalent with respect to grade status, chronological age, age-within-grade, and achievement. Only students of "modal age" within each grade were included — that is, students in the one-year interval most typical for each grade (see Table 1).

The age groups included represent ages at which all three tests are designed to function most effectively; the Terman-McNemar test is designed for use in grades 7 to 12 and the Pintner and Otis tests for grades 9 and above. The students in each group were drawn from a large number of communities widely distributed geographically so that local peculiarities in the relationship between intelligence and achievement test results do not bias the matching.

Table 1

MEANS AND STANDARD DEVIATIONS OF CHRONOLOGICAL AGES, BY GRADE,
OF MATCHED GROUPS TAKING TERMAN-McNEMAR, OTIS, AND PINTNER TESTS

Grade	No. Cases	Age Range	Terman-McNemar		Otis Q-S		Pintner	
			Mean	S.D. (in Mos.)	Mean	S.D. (in Mos.)	Mean	S.D. (in Mos.)
9	243	14–6 to 15–5	14–11	3.2	15–0	3.0	14–11	3.5
10	336	15–5 to 16–4	15–10	2.8	15–11	3.2	15–10	3.5
11	313	16–5 to 17–4	16–10	3.2	16–11	3.0	16–10	3.0
12	295	17–5 to 18–4	17–10	3.0	17–10	3.3	17–10	3.0

The matching of the three groups on the basis of *Essential High School Content Battery* scores was done in such fashion as to yield groups having not only the same means and standard deviations, but identical distributions throughout the entire range.

The use of achievement test scores as a basis for matching groups in terms of mental ability may seem sufficiently novel at first glance to disturb those accustomed to thinking of matching groups only on the basis of intelligence test scores. It should be pointed out, however, that the *Essential High School Content Battery* is a comprehensive achievement measure covering the areas of mathematics, science, social studies, and English. Scores on the battery have a correlation of approximately .75 with any one of the three intelligence tests, which is only slightly less than the correlations among the intelligence tests themselves. It is believed that the use of total scores on this achievement battery, in conjunction with controls on age and grade status, yielded groups closely matched in mental ability.

PROCEDURE

Distributions of intelligence test scores for students in all grades combined were obtained for each of the three groups, and the scores corresponding to given percentile points were determined. The scores corresponding to given percentile points for each pair of tests were then plotted on cross-section paper, and smoothed lines of relation between scores on the tests were drawn (see Figure 1). From these smoothed curves, a table of corresponding scores was read (see Table 2). The same procedure was followed for IQ's from the three tests; the resulting table of equivalent IQ's is shown as Table 3.

Tables of correspondence were derived for both score and IQ because comparability in terms of one or the other of these units from test to test may be desired, depending on the uses to be made of the data. However, Table 3,

Figure 1

LINE OF RELATION BETWEEN SCORES ON OTIS QUICK-SCORING MENTAL
ABILITY TESTS: GAMMA, FORM BM, AND PINTNER GENERAL ABILITY
TESTS: VERBAL SERIES, ADVANCED

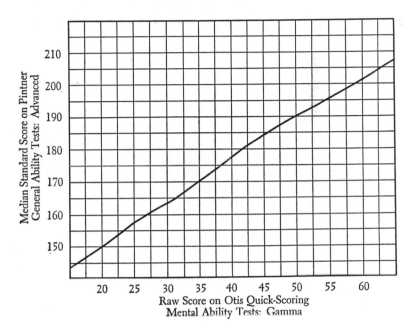

showing the corresponding IQ values for the three tests, is likely to be the more generally useful for the ordinary user of the tests.

RESULTS

Systematic study of Table 3 reveals the following to be true with reference to the comparability of IQ's from the three tests:

1. The Pintner test yields IQ's that are consistently lower than the Terman-McNemar IQ's by amounts varying from 2 to as much as 5 points.

2. The Otis test yields IQ's lower than corresponding Terman IQ's for IQ values of 90 and above.

3. An IQ of 100 on the Pintner test corresponds very closely to an IQ of 100 on the Otis test, but differences in the variability of IQ's on the two tests result in systematic differences between the IQ's, except for values fairly close to 100.

4. Pintner IQ's and Terman IQ's are of about equal variability; the standard deviations for these groups were 12.9 and 12.0 respectively. Otis IQ's are significantly less variable, having a standard deviation of 10.2 for this group. (The standard deviations for these modal-age groups are all lower, of course, than the tests would yield for unselected age groups; Terman and Pintner

Table 2

EQUIVALENT SCORES[1] ON TERMAN-MCNEMAR TEST OF MENTAL ABILITY,
FORM C OR D
OTIS QUICK-SCORING MENTAL ABILITY TESTS: GAMMA TEST,
FORM AM OR BM
PINTNER GENERAL ABILITY TESTS: VERBAL SERIES, ADVANCED TEST,
FORM A OR B

Terman	Otis	Pintner	Terman	Otis	Pintner	Terman	Otis	Pintner
159	74	218	118	48	188	80	32	166
—	—	217	117	48	187	79	31	165
158	73	216	116	47	187	78	31	165
157	72	215	115	47	186	77	31	165
156	71	214	114	46	186	76	30	164
155	70	213	113	46	185	75	30	163
153	69	212	112	45	184	74	29	163
152	68	211	111	45	184	73	29	162
151	—	210				72	29	162
			110	44	183	71	28	161
150	67	209	109	44	183			
149	66	208	108	43	182	70	28	160
147	65	207	107	43	181	69	27	160
146	64	206	106	43	181	68	27	159
145	—	205	105	42	180	67	27	159
144	63	—	104	42	180	66	26	158
143	—	204	103	41	179	65	26	158
142	62	203	102	41	178	64	25	157
			101	40	178	63	25	156
140	61	202				62	25	156
139	60	201	100	40	177	61	25	155
137	59	200	99	39	177			
136	59	199	98	39	176	60	24	155
135	58	198	97	38	176	59	24	154
134	57	197	96	38	175	58	23	154
133	57	197	95	38	175	57	23	153
132	56	—	94	37	174	56	23	153
131	—	196	93	37	174	55	22	152
			92	37	173	54	22	152
130	55	195	91	36	172	53	21	151
129	55	195				52	21	151
128	54	194	90	36	172	51	20	150
127	53	193	89	35	171			
126	53	193	88	35	171	50	20	150
125	52	192	87	35	170	49	19	149
124	52	192	86	34	170	48	19	149
123	51	191	85	34	169	47	18	148
122	50	190	84	33	168	46	18	148
121	50	190	83	33	168	45	17	147
120	49	189	82	33	167	44	17	147
119	49	189	81	32	167	43	16	146

[1] "Score" is raw score (number right) on the Terman and Otis tests, and median standard score on the Pintner test.

Where a value is repeated in the Otis or Pintner column, use of the lower value will yield the more accurate estimate of the equivalent Terman score.

Table 3

EQUIVALENT IQ'S[1] ON TERMAN-MCNEMAR TEST OF MENTAL ABILITY
OTIS QUICK-SCORING MENTAL ABILITY TESTS: GAMMA TEST
PINTNER GENERAL ABILITY TESTS: VERBAL SERIES, ADVANCED TEST

Terman IQ	Otis IQ	Pintner IQ	Terman IQ	Otis IQ	Pintner IQ
142	135–136	139–140	103	—	100
141	134	138	102	100	99
			101	99	98
140	132–133	136–137			
139	131	135	100	98	96–97
138	130	134	99	97	95
137	129	133	98	96	94
136	128	131–132	97	—	93
135	127	130	96	95	92
134	126	129	95	94	91
133	125	128	94	93	89–90
132	124	127	93	92	88
			92	—	87
130	123	126	91	91	86
129	122	125			
128	121	124	90	90	85
127	120	123	89	89	84
126	119	122	88	88	83
124	118	121	87	—	81–82
123	—	120	86	87	80
122	117	—	85	86	79
121	—	119	84	85	78
			83	—	77
120	116	118	82	84	76
119	115	117	81	—	75
118	114	116			
117	—	115	80	83	74
116	113	114	79	82	—
115	112	113	78	—	73
114	111	112	77	81	72
113	110	111	76	—	71
112	109	110	75	80	—
111	108	109	74	—	70
			73	79	69
110	107	108	72	—	68
109	106	107	71	78	—
108	105	106			
107	104	105	70	—	67
106	103	103–104	69	77	66
105	102	102	67–68	—	65
104	101	101	66	76	64

[1] IQ's are not ratio $\frac{(MA)}{(CA)}$ IQ's, but "deviation IQ's" in all cases, computed in accordance with directions in respective manuals.

Table 4

Mental Age Values[1] Corresponding to "Equivalent" Scores on
Terman-McNemar, Otis, and Pintner Tests

Terman-McNemar		Otis Q-S		Pintner	
Score	*MA*	*Equiv. score*	*MA*	*Equiv. score*	*MA*
60	13–0	24	11–10	155	12–8
71	14–0	28	12–9	161	13–6
82	15–0	33	14–0	167	14–6
91	16–0	36	14–10	172	15–3
99	17–0	39	16–0	177	16–1

[1] According to published norms.

IQ's have a standard deviation of about 16½, and Otis IQ's of about 13, for unselected age groups.)

Mental Age Variations

The authors of each of the three tests have provided mental-age norms, which permit conversion of scores to mental ages, although they recommend in all cases that IQ's *not* be computed by the usual ratio of MA to CA method, but by a deviation method. The wisdom of the authors in discouraging the use of mental ages is evident if one compares the mental ages that correspond to "equivalent" scores on the three tests. Table 4 illustrates the discrepancies among mental ages that correspond to presumably equivalent scores at several points along the range covered by these tests. The mental age values above approximately 16 years for these tests, as for most intelligence tests, are derived by extrapolation and are admittedly fictitious. Table 4 clearly reveals the lack of any common meaning of "mental age" in this part of the range.

"Average" Equivalent Scores

It is important to call attention to one characteristic of the table of equivalent values that is not immediately apparent. If these equivalences are computed separately for each grade or age (as was done in checking the original findings of the study) it is found that the "comparability" of scores or IQ's is in part a function of the particular group on which the equivalences are based. Thus the tables of equivalent scores or IQ's presented here represent an average or composite set of relationships that are probably the best single estimates that can be derived. However, more accurate results could be obtained by using, at any given age level, a table of equivalent scores derived for students of that particular age.

The differences here reported in IQ's derived from various tests underscore the necessity for identifying the test from which an IQ was derived whenever the IQ is entered on a student's record. They also make clear how important it is for the psychologist, counselor, or other test user to be aware of any systematic differences between various intelligence tests whose results he is likely to be interpreting. Although, in general, the differences between IQ's yielded by any of the three tests under consideration are not great, in some instances they are so large as to cause quite different decisions to be made about an individual, according as one or the other test was used — e.g. between Otis and Pintner IQ's at the lower end of the scale.

It is to be stressed that the differences among IQ's yielded by the three intelligence tests under study here are not unusually large. If anything, quite the contrary is true; there is evidence that these tests agree more closely with one another than do intelligence tests generally.

The tables of equivalent scores and IQ's presented in this [article] permit more accurate comparison of results from these three tests, and may profitably be used in any study involving results from two or more of the tests. Suggested uses include the following:

a. In any appraisal of student capacity where results from two or three of these tests are available, expressing all results in terms of any one of tests will make for greater precision.

b. More exact measurement of changes in measured intelligence between successive testings involving these tests can be achieved through use of the tables of equivalent values, which permit all results to be converted to comparable terms.

c. Admissions officers, guidance counselors, and others who must make decisions based on results from a variety of intelligence tests, will be able to make these decisions somewhat more accurately, insofar as results from these three tests are concerned, by use of the tables of equivalent values.

d. If it is desired to compare the mental maturity of students who have taken different ones of the three tests, this may be done by means of Table 2, which gives equivalent scores. Where studies involving mental ages are being made, such conversion is absolutely necessary, as the earlier section on variations among mental ages clearly indicates.

22

Some Recent Research
on the Davis-Eells Games

H. Glenn Ludlow

Although the word "recent" in the title may have lost some of its meaning, the generalizations in the report probably have not. The current emphasis on the effect of different cultural backgrounds on school performance and on test results has directed new attention to culture-fair tests. Although the Davis-Eells Games have recently been withdrawn from circulation, they have served as a good example of this type of test. Ludlow's article may help the student place these tests in proper perspective.

Few psychometric questions have been more hotly contested than the measurement of intellectual ability. Readers undoubtedly recall the antithetical claims of the hereditarians and the environmentalists. "Ninety per cent of intelligence is due to hereditary make-up; ten per cent to the environment," cried one extreme group. "Your figures are just reversed," retorted the opposing immoderates. Fortunately, the smoke of this unresolvable conflict has been dissipated. Now, in the same psychological arena, a more scientifically healthy collision has arisen.

Davis and his associates at the University of Chicago (3) have advanced the interesting and testable hypothesis that inferior performance by certain groups on conventional mental ability tests is due largely to the highly verbal and academic nature of the items. Further, if intelligence is defined as problem-solving ability, a "culture-fair" test can be developed to make apparent hidden potentials of youngsters from the wrong side of the tracks. The Davis-Eells Games (2), constructed on the basis of this thinking, have been available just long enough to provoke a few engaging research studies, three of which will be here summarized and evaluated.

Fowler (4) furnishes a rather extensive comparative analysis of pupil performance on conventional and culture-controlled mental tests. The sample was composed of 355 Detroit and Hamtramck, Michigan, 10-year-old pupils

From H. Glenn Ludlow, "Some Recent Research on the Davis-Eells Games," *School and Society*, LXXXIV (October, 1956), pp. 146–148. Reprinted with the permission of publisher and author.

from 14 elementary schools and three race-ethnic groups (201 white American non-cthnics, 70 Negroes, and 84 Polish). Using a modified Warner socio-economic index, he put 99% of the Negro group in the lower class; 62% of the Polish in the lower class and 37% in the lower-middle class; and 49% of the white American non-ethnic pupils in the lower class and 49% in the middle class.

Table 1 presents the test means for the lower-lower socio-economic level, since only in that class were there enough Negro pupils to justify a three-way comparative analysis.

Table 1

Test Means for the Lower-Lower Socio-Economic
Level in I.Q. Points (4, p. 141)

	Race and Ethnic Group		
Item	Polish (N-21)	White American Non-ethnic (N-48)	Negro (N-67)
Conventional Tests			
California Mental Maturity	98.8	100.0	98.0
Detroit Alpha (Boys)[1]	94.3	87.8	79.8
Detroit Alpha (Girls)[1]	89.8	98.9	87.4
Henmon-Nelson (Boys)[1]	101.0	92.4	88.6
Henmon-Nelson (Girls)[1]	97.3	98.2	90.6
Culture-Controlled Tests			
Davis-Eells Games	96.7	101.9	89.8
Cattell, Form A	91.0	95.4	90.8
Cattell, Form B	94.1	97.9	82.0

[1] The Detroit Alpha and Henmon-Nelson results are presented by sex since a preliminary analysis revealed significant sex differences.

Student-Fisher t-tests revealed that the significant (one per cent level) differences disclosed by an analysis of variance existed mainly between the Negro group and each of the other two race and ethnic groups. Although mean test score differences within the three race and ethnic groups were not checked for significance, inspection shows that the Davis-Eells Games results are generally not superior to conventional test means except in the case of the white American group. And in this case, the differences appear to be small except for the Detroit Alpha (Boys) and Henmon-Nelson (Boys).

Fowler also employed the correlational technique to test his hypothesis that a higher positive relation would obtain between conventional mental tests and socio-economic status than between culture-controlled tests and socio-economic status. Table 2 presents these results.

Table 2

CORRELATION BETWEEN SOCIO-ECONOMIC STATUS
AND I.Q. FOR THE TOTAL GROUP OF PUPILS
(N-355) (4, p. 154)

Test	*r*
California Mental Maturity	0.47
Detroit Alpha	0.40
Henmon-Nelson	0.41
Davis-Eells Games	0.37
Cattell, Form A	0.42
Cattell, Form B	0.43

On the basis of these and related data, he concluded that he had discovered
no distinct tendency for lower socio-economic pupils to obtain higher I. Q.'s
when the presently used culture-controlled tests are given rather than the current conventional mental ability tests.

Coleman and Ward (1) compared Davis-Eells and Kuhlman-Finch scores
of children from high and low socio-economic status in three Tennessee cities.
In Nashville and Memphis, third- and fifth-graders were selected in schools
representative of the highest and lowest socio-economic areas in the cities.
The Knoxville sample was composed of 27 children of very high, and a like
number of very low, socio-economic status, selected on the basis of a modified
Warner socio-economic index. The results of the testing program are shown
below.

Table 3

KUHLMAN-FINCH AND DAVIS-EELLS MEAN I.Q. SCORES AND STANDARD
DEVIATIONS FOR EIGHT GROUPS OF ELEMENTARY PUPILS FROM THREE
LARGE CITIES (1)

	Kuhlman-Finch		*Davis-Eells*			
	M	*s*	*M*	*s*	*N*	*Grade*
Knoxville, First Grade						
High Socio-economic	108.59	8.1	103.07	15.1	27	1
Low Socio-economic	95.37	11.1	86.37	13.6	27	1
Nashville, Third Grade						
High Socio-economic	104.17	11.2	104.47	11.8	30	3
Low Socio-economic	91.35	12.2	90.62	12.4	26	3
Nashville, Fifth Grade						
High Socio-economic	107.90	12.9	113.85	11.3	28	5
Low Socio-economic	95.65	12.5	99.63	9.8	30	5
Memphis, Third Grade						
High Socio-economic	108.35	14.4	108.64	16.6	109	3
Low Socio-economic	100.05	12.5	96.62	13.7	117	3

The analysis of variance technique was used to test the hypothesis that differences in mean scores on the two tests would not be statistically different for the two socio-economic groups. The between-tests F ratio of 6.352 falls far short of the one per cent level of significance. The authors conclude that a hypothesis of the existence of real differences in reasoning ability between high and low socio-economic groups is at least as tenable as the stand taken by the Davis Group. Although the claims made for the Davis-Eells Games are not supported by this study, the authors point out that we really cannot know whether basically mean socio-economic differences exist until we develop tests "free" from cultural learnings. Certainly, the Chicago Group recognizes this psychometric limitation; witness their use of such terms as "culture-fair" or "culture-controlled."

The third investigation was concerned with Davis-Eells test performance of lower-class retarded children. Rosenblum, Keller, and Papania (5) compared the Games performance of 30 high-grade mentally handicapped (non-organic) school-aged boys with their success on three other mental tests. Table 4 presents the chief results.

Table 4

COMPARISONS OF DAVIS-EELLS GAMES WITH BINET, WISC, AND CMM (5, p. 52)

Test	Mean	SD	t
Games	64.65	8.02	
Binet	65.87	5.03	.88
WISC[1]			
FS[1]	66.53	6.46	1.57
V[1]	66.63	5.09	1.38
P[1]	72.67	10.09	4.31[2]
CMM[1]	66.47	7.07	1.24

[1] CMM stands for California Test of Mental Maturity; WISC for Wechsler Intelligence Scale for Children; FS for Full Scale; V for Verbal; P for Performance.
[2] Significance at .01 level.

The only significant difference found was in favor of the Performance I. Q. of the WISC versus the Davis-Eells Games. The authors conclude that for this kind of youngster, the Davis-Eells Games do not uncover a hidden intellectual potential — at least none not measured by presumably culturally biased tests such as the Binet, California, and Wechsler Children's Scale. Finally, the writers suggest some reasons for their results, including references to middle-class cultural overtones present in the Davis-Eells testing procedure as well as in all group and school-oriented tasks.

What can be learned from these investigations stimulated by the "Davis Hypothesis" and the relatively new Davis-Eells Games? First, these results, like those of most other really important psycho-educational ventures, provide a basis for cautious acceptance and interpretation of new instruments.

Such studies may give pause to the relatively undiscriminating users who en-visioned the "Games" as the final solution to the mental ability testing prob-lem. Yesterday, this same minority was advocating that we arbitrarily add five or 10 I. Q. points to the conventional intelligence test scores of young-sters from very underprivileged homes. Davis and his co-workers probably react to these few overenthusiastic supporters just as John Dewey did when he visited an anarchic class conducted under the label of progressivism. In-deed, the Chicago Group would be the last to think of the present "Games" as in the "ne plus ultra" stage. In short, we are still working with a hypothesis — not a proven fact or truth.

Second, we are all indebted to the Chicago Group for challenging present rationale and methods used in the construction and standardization of intelli-gence tests. Their novel approach, deviating from orthodox theories and techniques, represents a magnificent example of scientific penetration. These three studies constitute only a sample of the number of worthwhile investiga-tions provoked by the Davis Group techniques for the development of un-biased tests.

Finally, the tentativeness of the conclusions drawn in these studies sug-gests improved research designs, new instrumentation, and a continuance of the cautious acceptance of results from all sorts of intelligence tests.

REFERENCES

1. Coleman, W., and Ward, A. "Comparison of Davis-Eells and Kuhlmann-Finch Scores of Children from High and Low Socio-economic Status," *Journal of Educational Psychology*, 46 (December, 1955), 465–469.
2. Davis, A., and Eells, K. *Manual for the Davis-Eells Test of General Intelligence or Problem-Solving Ability*. Yonkers, N.Y.: World Book Co., 1953.
3. Eells, K., Davis, A., Havighurst, R. J., Herrick, V. E., and Tyler, R. W. "Intelligence and Cultural Differences." Chicago: University of Chicago Press, 1951.
4. Fowler, W. L. "A Comparative Analysis of Pupil Performance on Conventional and Culture-Controlled Mental Tests." Unpublished Ph.D. thesis, University of Michigan, 1955.
5. Rosenblum, S., Keller, J. E., and Papania, N. "Davis-Eells (Culture-fair) Test Per-formance of Lower-class Retarded Children," *Journal of Consulting Psychology*, Vol. 19, No. 1, 1955.

23

Aptitude Versus Achievement Tests
as Predictors of Achievement

Abraham S. Levine

Aptitude tests, including intelligence tests, usually contain a considerable amount of material which involves recall of information or skills. This, too, is a characteristic of achievement tests. What then is the difference between the two kinds of instruments? What is the proper use of each and how well can we expect one to function in the place of the other? Levine presents some comments pertinent to answering these questions.

Although commonly recognized to be primarily a matter of degree, an aura of confusion surrounds the alleged distinction between aptitude and achievement tests. The clarification of this ambiguity, or at least raising it to a higher level of confusion, represents one of the major objectives of this paper. The other principal purpose is to describe how one major type of achievement test may supplement conventional aptitude tests in practical prediction problems.

Why is there any confusion at all? After all, the conventional definitions of "aptitude test" and "achievement test" are clear enough. The trouble is that every aptitude test is in a sense an achievement test, since pure potential to learn is measured in some crystallized form that implies achievement. Conversely, virtually every achievement test, particularly of a printed nature, places a premium on ability to cope with abstractions which constitute the very nature of test items. A good score on an achievement test implies aptitude. Therefore, it would appear that the distinction between so-called "aptitude tests" and "achievement tests" is one of degree.

Degree of what? At first blush it would seem that "degree" refers to the level of achievement required for a successful encounter with the subject matter content of the test items. But standard aptitude tests of the college or graduate school level presuppose very high levels of attainment in bookish

From Abraham S. Levine, "Aptitude Versus Achievement Tests as Predictors of Achievement," *Educational and Psychological Measurement*, XVIII (Autumn, 1958), pp. 517–525. Reprinted with the permission of publisher and author.

skills; much higher in fact than is measured by a standard reading achievement test designed for the grade-school level.

Actually, the distinction between achievement and aptitude may be boiled down to two generic differences; on each of these differences hangs a type of achievement test. These two types of achievement tests are differentiated not so much by the nature of their subject matter content as by the use to which they are put, as will be elaborated later on.

The usual type of achievement test is administered after a specific course of instruction (e.g., French, Algebra, History) and used to measure the results of such instruction. An aptitude test, on the other hand, is usually administered before such instruction takes place and is used as a predictor of course achievement. Each course may require its own specific achievement test, but a common aptitude test may be used as a predictor of achievement in many different kinds of courses. This is the typical situation encountered in practice and the differences between an aptitude test and type 1 achievement test need not be belabored further.

The second type of achievement test is not so well known. This is an achievement test, which like an aptitude test, is also used as a predictor of achievement. The difference between such an achievement test and an aptitude test has many interesting psychometric implications, but basically it resolves itself into the degree to which a certain fundamental assumption is met. This assumption is the one on which all aptitude tests are predicated: *equal opportunity to learn*. The implications of this assumption will now be explored, and the discussion will be restricted to a consideration of the differences between aptitude tests and type 2 achievement tests.

If all the individuals of a particular population have had a more or less equal opportunity to learn certain kinds of material, then it is axiomatic that differences in achievement are attributable to differences in aptitude. A test is an "aptitude test" when this assumption is fulfilled. However, if gross differences in opportunity to learn is the case the same test may then be regarded as an "achievement test."

It would appear that if a test functioned as a pure aptitude test (i.e., opportunity to learn being equalized), this would provide a valuable tool with which to attack the heredity-environment problem. But it is difficult to find a population for which the basic assumption underlying an aptitude test is completely fulfilled. Therein lies one of the reasons for the perennial nature of the heredity-environment problem. Take, for example, the controversy which has raged over whether I.Q. can be raised by special training or by exposure to an enriched environment. Why should anyone be surprised if scores on certain kinds of tests are raised as a result of such kinds of environmental manipulation? After all, opportunity to learn has been increased. Has basic aptitude been raised? That is precisely the question which cannot be answered by tests which do not function as pure aptitude tests since the basic assumption is not fulfilled.

But the problem is even more involved since it can be argued that if for a particular hypothetical population "opportunity to learn" and "native ability" were both equalized individual differences in motivation operating through time would make for differences in test scores. These differences in test scores would be interpreted as aptitude differences. Therefore aptitude tests are in a sense tests of motivation as well as ability. Likewise "achievement tests" are measures of motivation since differential motivation will make both for differential learning and differential self-direction into different kinds of learning experiences. Thus scores on both aptitude tests and achievement tests reflect differences in interest. All of which serves to point up the protean nature of what tests measure. It is no wonder then that the basis for much argumentation is provided when empirical test data are forced into some bit of rigid conceptualization. Actually many psychometric concepts are inextricably interwoven at the empirical level and can be regarded only as convenient abstractions.

"Intelligence" may be what "intelligence tests measure," but what intelligence tests measure are crystallized correlates of ability. Achievement tests also measure crystallized correlates of ability. In both cases motivation serves as a catalyst in the crystallization process. The crystallized correlates which intelligence tests measure are merely more pervasive in scope than are the constituents of achievement tests. It does not matter much to which theory of human abilities you subscribe; some sort of pervasive factor generally emerges whether you call it "g," a second-order factor, or general reasoning.

Group factors, which are narrower in scope, also make themselves evident particularly if an extensive test battery is factored. The tests which are most highly saturated with these group factors may be called "special ability" tests but usually they measure the same sorts of things that achievement tests do, the difference often being mostly a matter of semantics. In mechanical aptitude tests, for example, the unique valid variance may best be named "mechanical experience." The mechanical comprehension tests of the Bennett type intercorrelate higher with standard intelligence tests and generally reflect less of this unique valid variance than do the more frankly mechanical information tests.

Intelligence tests, in addition to being more pervasive in scope, also measure correlates which for the most part crystallize earlier in life — at least in our culture. The printed group tests designed to be administered to high school students, college students, and adults contain primarily verbal and arithmetic reasoning items. We are exposed to a verbal environment as soon as we are responsive to such stimuli, and number concepts begin to impinge upon us no later than the beginning of our elementary school careers. It is significant that a test of arithmetic reasoning given to young adults is regarded as an aptitude test, but a test of algebraic and geometric reasoning is commonly regarded as a mathematics achievement test.

Garrett's differentiation hypothesis (1) that abilities tend to differentiate more as an individual matures fits squarely into the frame of reference being sketched in this paper. After all, most of our so-called intelligence tests measure largely verbal and quantitative reasoning. This kind of learning occurs relatively early. Special ability or achievement tests, on the other hand, measure the residuals of later learning which are not so ubiquitous in our culture and consequently not as highly correlated with each other as are verbal and quantitative reasoning tests.

From a practical point of view, what matters most about predictive-type tests are their external validities. This of course is just another way of saying that the most important thing about a predictor is how well it predicts. How does the foregoing discussion fit into this picture? Very simply: in predicting a criterion an appropriate achievement test will augment the validity obtainable from using the more general aptitude tests above. Consequently these two types of tests should be used in combination.

Before illustrating this thesis by a significant practical example it would be well to take a quick look at one of the current fashions in testing: the culture-free or culture-fair tests. These tests support their claim mostly by being scrupulously devoid of verbal and numerical symbols. Of course they intercorrelate appreciably with the more conventional verbal and arithmetic aptitude tests but less so than the verbal and arithmetic tests do with each other. These wordless and numberless tests do not predict school success as well as the usual kind of general academic aptitude test. The explanation for this disconcerting finding is that the culture-free or fair tests do not measure to the same degree the motivation to learn bookish sorts of things as do the more obviously bookish sorts of tests. It is interesting in this connection that the Binet test is more bookish at the higher age levels and also more predictive of school success than at the lower age levels.

Aptitude and achievement tests are both predictive of school success for about the same reasons. They both measure the end-products of the interaction between innate ability and motivated learning. (Innate ability is like ultimate reality in that it defies direct measurement; what is measured at best is like the shadows on the walls of Plato's Cave.) The motivated learning measured by achievement tests is generally more restricted in scope but more sharply aligned with the criterion to be predicted in a practical situation. Aptitude tests, on the other hand, predict a wider range of criteria. In a practical prediction problem, aptitude tests may be compared to the coarse adjustment on a microscope and achievement tests to the fine adjustment.

A better idea of how these two types of tests work in concert may be illustrated by an example from the annals of U. S. Navy psychometric research. In recent years, selection of electronics personnel has become a matter of critical concern since the nature of electronics duties require personnel of high caliber who must assimilate long and costly training before they begin to work for the Navy. The effectiveness of this selection largely depends on the efficiency of the tests used in assigning personnel to technical training schools with electronics oriented curricula. In general, the higher the validity or predictive efficiency of the tests, the lower the cutting score that can be set without any reduction in qualitative input into the school. Therefore an increase in the predictive efficiency of the selection tests has the effect of increasing the number of men who become available for the electronics schools without any corresponding increase in the attrition rate, which would otherwise result from lowering the selection standards.

The predictive efficiency of the two mainstays of the Navy's enlisted classification battery, the General Classification Test (verbal reasoning test) and the Arithmetic Test, together yield a multiple R of about .60 with final grades in Electronics Technician School. Despite such respectable validities obtained with the standard aptitude tests, a serious attempt was made to augment these validities because high-caliber enlisted men were in such short supply and their optimal utilization was of critical importance.

The Electronics Technician Selection Test, which was developed to meet this increasing need, is a successor to the "Eddy" Test developed during World War II for use in recruiting electronics personnel. The test contains five basic types of subject-matter or achievement items, namely, mathematics, general science, shop practice, electricity, and radio.

Research indicates that the new form of the Electronics Technician Selection Test represents an improvement over the older forms of the test and makes a substantial contribution to the verbal and quantitative aptitude tests for predicting performance in the Electronics Technician schools — a gain in validity from .60 to about .75. These findings are being implemented in the form of revised selection standards for Electronics Technician School which incorporates the use of this new instrument. It is estimated that the new test selection standards increases the number of men available for Electronics Technician training by about 20% without lowering the average quality of input or the percentage of men dropped from the school.

Additional research (3) has indicated the usefulness of this instrument for selecting men for training in several schools with electronics curricula. These results are being implemented and similar improvements in manpower utilization are being effected.

Generally speaking, achievement tests tend to supplement the aptitude tests by measuring the more specific valid variance in a criterion or particular group of criteria. They are generally valid for a smaller number of criteria than aptitude tests of the verbal and quantitative reasoning nature. If used in lieu of aptitude tests, they would have to be made even more specific and approach what amounts to job miniatures in order to yield validities as high as those obtainable by a combination of aptitude and more general achievement tests. This may be desirable as long as there is a single criterion or at least a small number of them to predict. However, when confronted with at least sixty different technical training schools to which recruits have to be assigned in the Navy, it is more economical to use a few aptitude tests supplemented by a small number of achievement tests each of which is appropriate for one or more rather critical occupational specialties.

When confronted with a single criterion it may be desirable to use a single selection instrument which combines the virtues of aptitude and achievement tests. For example, in attempting to predict success in graduate work in psychology, Levine (2) developed the Minnesota Psycho-Analogies Test. This test is predicated on the hypothesis that achievement in advanced psychology courses is to a large extent a function of a complex of general academic ability and previous psychological background. A test was developed to provide a composite measure of these factors. This test comprises items of the four-alternative multiple choice variety in analogy form. The first part of each item contains general vocabulary and information. The latter part of these items consists of a broad sampling of psychological terms, concepts and expressions which attempt to sample as widely as possible the content of all the major fields of psychology. The response alternatives are all psychological in content. Thus the first two terms of the analogy are of a general nature, usually non-psychological in content; while the third and fourth terms are psychological in character. An example of this type of item, with the correct response in italics is as follows: Orchestra: Violinist: Test: (1. Battery, 2. Item Analysis, 3. *Item*, 4. Validity).

With this instrument, a validity coefficient with course examinations as high as .74 was obtained. Generally speaking, wherever comparisons were possible, this instrument tended to be slightly more valid for predicting performance in psychology courses than a more general analogies test; i.e., the Miller Analogies Test.

SUMMARY

Differences between so-called aptitude and achievement tests tend to break down conceptually to differences in degree or relative emphasis. There appear to be two principal types of achievement tests: type 1 which is given at the end of a course of study to measure the outcome of instruction; and type 2 which is administered before instruction and used as an aptitude test, i.e., as a predictor. In practice, the basic difference between type 2 achievement tests and aptitude tests appears to be one of generality of subject matter content. The most predictive aptitude tests are the highly intercorrelated verbal and arithmetic reasoning types. Language and arithmetic skills are ubiquitous and therein lies the generality of the validity of these types of tests. Achievement tests are usually made up of more specialized subject-matter content. In a practical prediction problem, optimal forecasting efficiency can usually be obtained with a judicious combination of aptitude and achievement tests. Where many criteria are to be predicted, then the battery may best comprise verbal and quantitative reasoning tests plus a few tests which measure more specific subject matter content. The most efficient predictor of a lone criterion is often a specially devised single test which combines the general features of an aptitude test with the specific valid variance characteristic of appropriate achievement tests.

REFERENCES

1. Garrett, Henry E. "A Developmental Theory of Intelligence," *American Psychologist,* I (1946), 372–378.
2. Levine, Abraham S. "Minnesota Psycho-Analogies Test," *Journal of Applied Psychology,* XXXIV (1950), 300–305.
3. Thorndike, Robert L., and Hagen, Elizabeth. "Validation of the Electronics Technician Selection Test at Selected Class A Schools," U. S. Navy, Bureau of Naval Personnel, *Technical Bulletin,* 1955.

24

Standardized Achievement Tests:
Uses and Limitations

Robert L. Ebel

A number of objections to achievement tests have been proposed by different writers. Several of these have to do with teaching objectives and the extent to which objectives and teaching methods are regulated by test content. Ebel explores the most common objections to achievement tests and explains what he sees as the real validity of these points.

Standardized tests of educational achievement are essential educational tools, especially in the elementary school. They can be used to improve the effectiveness of the competent teacher or school administrator. They can help motivate and reward the child. They can provide a basis for constructive cooperation between parents and teachers in guiding the child's educational development. They can help the school staff and the community it serves assess the effectiveness of the school program.

A demonstration of how standardized tests can focus public attention on an educational need occurred recently in New York City. Results of a city-wide standardized reading test showed that the average reading ability of school children in New York was below the national average. A few years before, it had been above the national norm. While these findings were doubted, discounted, and rationalized by experts and spokesmen inside the schools and out, there was almost universal support for the vigorous action taken by the Board of Education to strengthen the program of reading instruction. Among other things, the number of specialists in remedial reading on the school staff was sharply increased.

This use of standardized tests as a basis for judging the effectiveness of a school program has been criticized by some educators. They point out that half the pupils or schools *have* to be below the norm and that remedial programs can never alter this situation. Further, they say, it is unreasonable and

From Robert L. Ebel, "Standardized Achievement Tests: Uses and Limitations," *The National Elementary Principal*, XL (September, 1961), pp. 29–32. Copyright 1961, Department of Elementary School Principals, National Education Association. Reprinted with the permission of publisher and author.

unfair to expect the same levels of achievement of all pupils and all schools. A pupil ranking well above average may, in fact, have less reason for self-satisfaction and complacency than a pupil ranking below average, if the high ranking pupil had educational advantages the other lacked.

There is merit in both these criticisms, perhaps more in the second than in the first, but it would be dangerous to accept them completely. No pupil, no teacher, no schoolboard, no community should be continuously satisfied with their educational achievements, and few are. Information provided by standardized tests of achievement helps them focus their dissatisfactions more purposefully and take remedial action more constructively.

The second criticism is sometimes used in general terms as a rationalization for below average performance. It contains enough truth to be a persuasive argument for unsound interpretations of test results and for inaction when action is needed. On the basis of intelligence tests and other measures, we know it is unreasonable to expect the same achievement of all pupils and all schools. Unfortunately, the usual effort to obtain a standard of reasonable expectancy of achievement from intelligence test scores is based, I think, on some misconceptions about intelligence, achievement, and the educational process.

The important point to remember is that most pupils and many schools could achieve considerably more than they have achieved. Further, it is probably true that the pupils and schools which are below average in achievement have both the greatest need and the greatest opportunity to improve.

Understanding the causes of inferior achievement is an important prelude to effective remedial action. No child's potential and no school's potential for educational achievement is unlimited. But this should never be used as an excuse for inaction.

If standardized tests are valuable tools, why do many schools lag in using them effectively? Lack of full awareness of the potential value of test information and lack of training in how to use that information may be partly responsible. But there are also three common misconceptions about educational testing which may account for much of the skepticism about the value of tests and the reluctance to use them more extensively.

IMPORTANCE OF TANGIBLE OUTCOMES

The first of these misconceptions is the belief that the most important outcomes of education are too subtle, too complex, too subjective to be measured effectively. Elementary school teachers are less guilty on this score than some college professors who take off on flights of fancy when discussing intangible but supposedly essential outcomes of education.

Teachers of young children know that the development of skills in the tool subjects and the establishment of solid foundations for understanding and interest in the major fields of human knowledge are concrete, specific, important objectives. But some of them may feel that tests, especially objective standardized tests, fail "to get at" the real essentials of achievement in these skill and foundation subjects. This mystical devotion to a hidden reality of achievement which is more essential than overt ability to perform has never satisfied the research worker. He wants to know the nature of this hidden reality and what evidence there is that it is important.

Danger of Overemphasis on Adjustment

The second misconception about educational testing arises from over-concern with the child's immediate happiness and self-satisfaction. Extreme supporters of this view often regard testing as an unfriendly, threatening, anxiety-generating process. They would shield the child from its stress and possible pain. I demur, and call as a first witness the physician.

Most of us learn to adjust to the physician's prescriptions, whether they are bad-tasting medicines, disinfectants that sting, shots that hurt, or even surgery. There is some emotional stress and discomfort, but the end result is usually increased health. To do what must be done a doctor needs courage, but this implies no lack of sympathy. What it does imply is farsighted concern for the ultimate welfare of the patient.

I have been appalled by the lack of this far-sighted attitude among some advocates of child-centered education. They talk as if the teacher's primary responsibility were to guard the child's ego against any bruises whatsoever. Let him achieve as much as he can without strain, they say, but be careful not to ask too much of him. Their excess of concern for protection of the child's present "security" may, however, encourage neglect of needed small readjustments until they accumulate into a crisis of major proportions.

Take the case of Sharon which illustrates a problem all too many schools and families have become unhappily acquainted with in recent years. Sharon was the third of four children in an upper middle-class family. Her early years at school were uneventful. Periodic descriptive reports indicated that she was adjusting well and making progress. If any standardized tests were given, the significance of the results was not reported to the parents.

Midway through the third grade, trouble developed. Sharon began to say she hated school and to seek escape by feigning illness. Investigation showed the basic problem was that Sharon couldn't read, at least not nearly as well as her classmates. They were beginning to refer to her as "dumb." The parents proposed that Sharon attend the reading clinic of a nearby university and perhaps get special individual instruction. The school staff counseled against such a step arguing that they could provide all the special help needed, now that the problem had been identified. Further, they said, much harm could be done if too much attention were paid to the problem. Better to treat it as casually and quietly as possible, they said.

Despite some misgivings, Sharon's parents agreed. For a while, things seemed to improve. Sharon was happier in school. She brought home reports of small triumphs, of special recognition and opportunities. The school reports, still couched in general, unthreatening phrases, indicated generally satisfactory progress. Then, near the end of Sharon's eighth-grade year, trouble developed again. Her teacher recommended that she repeat the grade because of her serious reading disability. The special attention she had received had apparently taught her to learn by listening, but she had not learned effective self-direction in reading.

After some plain-speaking conferences between teacher and parents, Sharon did not fail. She did go to summer reading camps. She went on to high school and took five years to finish college instead of four.

If the school had had a systematic program of standardized testing and had reported the results regularly, Sharon's reading disability would probably have been identified before it was translated into an emotional and social problem. And once the difficulty was identified, if the school had been more concerned with Sharon's future welfare than her current happiness, the problem might well have been corrected before it affected her subsequent schooling. In education, as in medicine and justice, an excess of present sympathy can postpone or even defeat the procedures necessary for an individual's future welfare.

Limited Value of Purely Local Objectives

The third misconception about standardized educational achievement tests results in their avoidance or de-emphasis on the ground that this teacher's objectives or that school's objectives are uniquely different from those for which the standardized test was presumably built.

We all recognize that it is desirable for both teachers and schools to have freedom to experiment with new materials and methods and that it is unwise for them to be bound tightly to a rigidly prescribed curriculum. It is good that they can capitalize on their own unique talents and opportunities. But it is also necessary that they recognize their responsibilities to develop the same basic skills and fundamental understandings which other teachers and other schools are seeking to develop.

What constitutes a good elementary education today in Bangor, Maine, is not radically different from what constitutes a good elementary education in Los Angeles, California. Even if the ideal elementary education in one locality should differ from the ideal in another, it would be unwise to build an educational program around only the local needs. For it is certainly true that many of those educated in one place will spend most of their lives in some other.

One of the essential values of a well-constructed standardized test is its reflection of expert consensus on nationwide objectives of achievement. Instead of asking how well the standardized test fits local objectives, the test selector should ask with how much competence the test constructors can speak concerning the common objectives of all schools. A teacher should not ask a standardized test to provide evidence on how well she has taught all the things she has tried to teach, but only on the things that all teachers ought to have taught. For those achievements which are truly and rightly unique to a particular school or teacher, locally constructed tests are the best answer.

Will the Test-Makers Dictate Curriculum?

Many of those who mistrust the nationally developed standardized tests of achievement frequently express fear that the test-makers will dictate the curriculum. There is some basis for this belief, but it should not be a source of anxiety. If the standardized test is taken seriously, it will certainly exert some influence on teaching. But if the test is constructed by competent experts, that influence should be more beneficial than harmful.

The content and emphasis of textbooks, courses of study, teaching methods, and tests of achievement should all be sanctioned by the same kind of authority — a consensus of expert judgements. If the test-makers try, as many of them do, to catch and reflect in their tests a consensus of the judgement of curriculum specialists, it seems unreasonable to charge them with attempting to dictate curricular developments. If standardized tests of achievement are supplemented by locally constructed tests, there is slight danger that the use of standardized tests will result in undesirable uniformity in curricula.

Expert Test Construction

A well-constructed standardized achievement test provides an independent, broadly based definition of *desirable goals* of achievement in *all* schools. This is one of its primary values. Two others are related to it. The first is expert, painstaking test construction. The second is independent, broadly based norms of achievement.

Those who prepare standardized tests, in consultation with subject-matter experts, usually are skilled in writing items. In addition, they pre-test the items to identify those which are too difficult or too easy or which fail to discriminate clearly between high and low achievers. Careful attention is also given to the balance of the test among content areas and item types.

The result of the expertness and care applied to the construction of a standard test of educational achievement is usually a technically better test than a local teacher or group would be likely to create. The task it presents are those the pupils should be able to handle. The scores it yields discriminate reliably different levels of achievement. It is usually convenient to administer and score and is efficient and economical in its yield of useful information.

The provision of national, regional, or statewide norms for score interpretation is a third valuable contribution of the standardized achievement test. To secure accurate norms for clearly defined and widely appropriate reference groups is not a simple matter. It is even more difficult to present these norms so that they will be easy to use and to interpret properly.

These norms enable the user of a standardized test to obtain an external, broadly based standard for judging the achievements of pupils. Norms are not universal standards. Nor are they self interpreting. An oversimplified approach to test norms can rob them of much of their potential usefulness. After the comparison of local achievements with external norms has been made and the difference noted, one must still ask, "Is this good or bad?" and

"Why do we seem to do so well, or poorly?" and "Under the circumstances, what should we do about the situation?" Standardized tests and their norms will not provide any automatic answers, but they can provide the basis for wise planning and for more reasonable decisions.

Schools exist to educate pupils, but it is the exceptional classroom teacher or school administrator who can report very precisely how much learning the pupils have acquired. Enrollment, attendance, and per-pupil cost can be specified accurately and in detail, but the acquisition of skills, knowledge, and attitudes is not readily stated in statistical terms. Educational achievement is not easy to measure, and existing tests leave much to be desired. But relatively few schools and teachers are obtaining and using even a small fraction of the information on educational achievement that existing tests could provide. I am persuaded that competent teachers and school systems can improve their effectiveness rapidly by making good use of existing standardized tests of educational achievement. Combined with other efforts, the systematic and skillful use of standardized tests should move any school toward higher levels of achievement.

FOR MORE INFORMATION

The bulletin *Selecting an Achievement Test* (5), published by the ETS, offers many helpful suggestions as to principles and procedures. Noll's book (7) should also be helpful, particularly Chapter 8 on "Measuring Achievement in the Elementary Grades."

For the teacher who has some solid background knowledge of educational measurement, Buros' *Fifth Mental Measurements Yearbook* (2) will prove a valuable source of information about published tests. For many of these tests, critical reviews have been written by specialists. While the reviewers are not infallible, most test purchasers find this volume highly useful. A comprehensive index to *Tests in Print* (3) also edited by Buros, is scheduled for publication this year.

Those concerned with selecting achievement tests will find valuable guides in *Technical Recommendations for Achievement Tests* (1). Another recent and highly useful bulletin is *Testing Guide for Teachers* (8). Somewhat older but still authoritative is the book by Traxler and others (9).

Two other general references may be useful. The first is a symposium on "The Place of Testing and Evaluation in Learning" (6). The other, also a symposium, presents the answers of six specialists in testing to "Eight Critical Questions About the Use of Tests" (4).

REFERENCES

1. AERA Committee on Test Standards, *Technical Recommendations for Achievement Tests.* Washington, D.C.: American Educational Research Association, 1955.
2. Buros, O. K. (ed.). *The Fifth Mental Measurements Yearbook.* Highland Park, N.J.: The Gryphon Press, 1959.
3. ———. *Tests in Print.* Highland Park, N.J.: The Gryphon Press, 1961.

4. Ebel, Robert L. "Eight Critical Questions About the Use of Tests," *Education*, 81 (October 1960), 67–68.
5. Educational Testing Service. *Selecting An Achievement Test*. Princeton, N.J.: the Service, 1958.
6. Harsh, Richard (coordinator). "Symposium: The Place of Testing and Evaluation in Learning," *California Journal of Secondary Education*, 35 (January 1960), 40–65.
7. Noll, Victor H. *Introduction to Educational Measurement*. Boston: Houghton Mifflin Company, 1957, 437 pp.
8. Technical Subcommittee of the Independent Schools Advisory Committee. *Testing Guide for Teachers*. New York: Educational Records Bureau, 1961.
9. Traxler, Arthur E., and others. *Introduction to Testing and the Use of Test Results in Public Schools*. New York: Harper and Brothers, 1953, 133 pp.

SUGGESTED READINGS

Anastasi, Anne. *Psychological Testing* (2nd ed.). New York: The Macmillan Company, 1961.

Parts 2 and 3 of this text present a detailed and critical analysis of many current tests of aptitude and achievement. Anastasi's sensitivity to the limitations of these tests is an especially important feature of the chapters.

Cronbach, Lee J. *Essentials of Psychological Testing* (2nd ed.). New York: Harper and Brothers, 1960.

In Part Two of this text the author presents a number of generalizations about ability testing, using specific tests as examples. He also deals with some test construction topics, such as factor analysis, which have been used rather widely in constructing ability tests.

Freeman, Frank S. *Theory and Practice of Psychological Testing* (3rd ed.). New York: Holt, Rinehart and Winston, Inc., 1962.

Chapters 7 through 20 deal extensively with basic concepts of aptitudes, with historical development of tests of these abilities, and with application of current instruments.

Lyman, Howard B. *Test Scores and What They Mean*. Englewood Cliffs, N.J.: Prentice-Hall, Inc., 1963.

This book provides a simple, yet direct approach to explaining the results of tests in terms of various scoring methods. The emphasis is on better use of tests through more accurate interpretation.

Stoddard, George D. *The Meaning of Intelligence*. New York: The Macmillan Company, 1943.

The entire text is an exhaustive review of the concept of intelligence, resulting in the development of a detailed presentation of basic components of this behavioral characteristic.

Wechsler, David. *The Measurement and Appraisal of Adult Intelligence* (4th ed.). Baltimore: Williams and Wilkins Co., 1958.

In the first sixty pages of this book the author presents a concise and critical analysis of the concept of intelligence and its measurement. His use of data in support of argument is clear and appropriate.

Assessing Typical Performance

Many psychometric devices are designed to get at modes of behavior which reflect affective responses to situations. These are in contrast to the ability tests, which are primarily oriented toward assessing cognitive or psycho-motor behavior. Even though emotional conditions may well bear significant influences on the operation being observed with ability tests, measuring emotional behavior is not the primary purpose of these tools. However, a group of devices have been devised, the primary purpose of which is to identify the affective responses one typically demonstrates toward various situations. Cronbach[1] has called these devices tests of typical performance. Included in this group are personality and interest inventories, projective techniques and attitude scales.

It is not the purpose of this unit to deal extensively with each of the types of instruments that could be classified in the area. Instead the articles to follow have been chosen to represent problems and issues which are common to a variety of tools. The basic issues center around methods of validation and consequent interpretation of these kinds of instruments. Consequently, these questions receive the greatest emphasis in the unit.

A persistent problem in evaluating the results of tests of typical performance is the extent to which scores signify a criterion status. Zubin, Eron, and Sultan deal with this point (Selection 26) in regard to projective techniques and their psychometric adequacy. It is hoped that through these presentations the reader may see parallel problems in the validation of all tests of typical performance.

To what extent do the results of an inventory indicate what the individual is, in contrast to what he wants to appear to be? If a test user is to place

[1] Cronbach, Lee J., *Essentials of Psychological Testing* (New York: Harper and Brothers, 1949), p. 13.

maximum confidence in scores, these figures must reflect a real characteristic of the test taker; that is, they must be resistant to casual manipulations by the test taker in his efforts to represent himself as feeling, believing, etc., differently than he actually does in out-of-test situations. The data provided by Corey and Wesman in Selections 27 and 29, respectively, raise some provocative questions in this regard.

Test situations are complex, involving many stimuli, and calling forth many kinds of responses from the testees. What, specifically, are the important variables reflected by the test, the variables that can serve as a springboard for test interpretation? Gross, in Selection 28, points to the fact that the test content is not the only — and may not even be the major — source of stimulation.

The content of this unit is designed to illuminate two basic problems: issues in the validation of tools for assessing typical performance, and the related topic, score interpretation. The reader should note especially the variety of problems which face the test constructor, as well as the issues which complicate effective application of this type of psychometric device.

25

The Dynamics of
"Structured" Personality Tests

Paul E. Meehl

The author presents some interesting comparisons between the conventional personality test (the Minnesota Multiphasic Personality Inventory, specifically) and less structured techniques such as the Rorschach. The reader should decide just how distinct the author sees these two methods as being and to what extent the distinction may influence the choice of one test over another.

In a recent article (6) . . . Lt. Max L. Hutt of the Adjutant General's School has given an interesting discussion of the use of projective methods in the army medical installations. This article was part of a series describing the work of clinical psychologists in the military services, with which the present writer is familiar only indirectly. The utility of any instrument in the military situation can, of course, be most competently assessed by those in contact with clinical material in that situation, and the present paper is in no sense to be construed as an "answer" to or an attempted refutation of Hutt's remarks. Nevertheless, there are some incidental observations contained in his article which warrant further critical consideration, particularly those having to do with the theory and dynamics of "structured" personality tests. It is with these latter observations rather than the main burden of Hutt's article that this paper is concerned.

Hutt defines "structured personality tests" as those in which the test material consists of conventional, culturally crystallized questions to which the subject must respond in one of a very few fixed ways. With this definition we have no quarrel, and it has the advantage of not applying the unfortunate phrase "self-rating questionnaire" to the whole class of question-answer devices. But immediately following this definition, Hutt goes on to say that "it is assumed that each of the test questions will have the same meaning to all subjects who take the examination. The subject has no opportunity of organizing in his own unique manner his response to the questions."

From Paul E. Meehl, "The Dynamics of 'Structured' Personality Tests," *Journal of Clinical Psychology*, I (October, 1945), pp. 296–303. Reprinted with the permission of publisher and author.

These statements will bear further examination. The statement that personality tests assume that each question has the same meaning to all subjects is continuously appearing in most sources of late, and such an impression is conveyed by many discussions even when they do not explicitly make this assertion. It should be emphasized very strongly, therefore, that while this perhaps has been the case with the majority of question-answer personality tests, it is not by any means part of their essential nature. The traditional approach to verbal question-answer personality tests has been, to be sure, to view them as self-ratings; and it is in a sense always a self-rating that you obtain when you ask a subject about himself, whether you inquire about his feelings, his health, his attitudes, or his relations to others.

However, once a "self-rating" has been obtained, it can be looked upon in two rather different ways. The first, and by far the commonest approach, is to accept a self-rating as a second best source of information when the direct observation of a segment of behavior is inaccessible for practical or other reasons. This view in effect forces a self-rating or self-description to act as surrogate for a behavior-sample. Thus we want to know whether a man is shy, and one criterion is his readiness to blush. We cannot conveniently drop him into a social situation to observe whether he blushes, so we do the next best (and often much worse) thing and simply ask him, "Do you blush easily?" We assume that if he does in fact blush easily, he will realize that fact about himself, which is often a gratuitous assumption; and secondly, we hope that having recognized it, he will be willing to tell us so.

Associated with this approach to structured personality tests is the construction of items and their assembling into scales upon *a priori* basis, requiring the assumption that the psychologist building the test has sufficient insight into the dynamics of verbal behavior and its relation to the inner core of personality that he is able to predict beforehand what certain sorts of people will say about themselves when asked certain sorts of questions. The fallacious character of this procedure has been sufficiently shown by the empirical results of the Minnesota Multiphasic Personality Inventory alone, and will be discussed at greater length below. It is suggested tentatively that the relative uselessness of most structured personality tests is due more to *a priori* item construction than to the fact of their being structured.

The second approach to verbal self-ratings is rarer among test-makers. It consists simply in the explicit denial that we accept a self-rating as a feeble surrogate for a behavior sample, and substitutes the assertion that a "self-rating" constitutes an intrinsically interesting and significant bit of verbal behavior, the non-test correlates of which must be discovered by empirical means. Not only is this approach free from the restriction that the subject must be able to describe his own behavior accurately, but a careful study of structured personality tests built on this basis shows that such a restriction would falsify the actual relationships that hold between what a man says and what he *is*.

Since this view of question-answer items is the rarer one at the present time, it is desirable at this point to elucidate by a number of examples. For this purpose one might consider the Strong Vocational Interest Blank, the Humm-

Wadsworth Temperament Scales, the Minnesota Multiphasic Personality Inventory, or any structured personality measuring device in which the selection of items was done on a thoroughly empirical basis using carefully selected criterion groups. In the extensive and confident use of the Strong Vocational Interest Blank, this more sophisticated view of the significance of responses to structured personality test items has been taken as a matter of course for years. The possibility of conscious as well as unconscious "fudging" has been considered and experimentally investigated by Strong and others, but the differences in possible interpretation or *meaning* of items have been more or less ignored — as well they should be. One is asked to indicate, for example, whether he likes, dislikes, or is indifferent to "conservative people." The possibilities for differential interpretation of a word like *conservative* are of course tremendous, but nobody has worried about that problem in the case of the Strong. Almost certainly the strength of verbs like "like" and "dislike" is variably interpreted throughout the whole blank. For the present purpose the Multiphasic (referred to hereinafter as MMPI) will be employed because the present writer is most familiar with it.

One of the items on the MMPI scale for detecting psychopathic personality (Pd) is "My parents and family find more fault with me than they should." If we look upon this as a rating in which the *fact* indicated by an affirmative response is crucial, we immediately begin to wonder whether the testee can objectively evaluate how much other people's parents find fault with them, whether his own parents are warranted in finding as much fault with him as they do, whether this particular subject will interpret the phrase "finding fault" in the way we intend or in the way most normal persons interpret it, and so on. The present view is that this is simply an unprofitable way to examine a question-answer personality test item. To begin with, the empirical finding is that individuals whose past history and momentary clinical picture is that of a typical psychopathic personality tend to say "Yes" to this much more often than people in general do. Now in point of fact, they probably should say "No" because the parents of psychopaths are sorely tried and probably do not find fault with their incorrigible offspring any more than the latter deserve. An allied item is "I have been quite independent and free from family rule" which psychopaths tend to answer *false* — almost certainly opposite to what is actually the case for the great majority of them. Again, "Much of the time I feel I have done something wrong or evil." Anyone who deals clinically with psychopaths comes to doubt seriously whether they could possibly interpret this item in the way the rest of us do (*cf.* Cleckley's (2) "semantic dementia"), but they *say* that about themselves nonetheless. Numerous other examples such as "Someone has it in for me" and "I am sure I get a raw deal from life" appear on the same scale and are significant because psychopaths tend to *say* certain things about themselves, rather than because we take these statements at face value.

Consider the MMPI scale for detecting tendencies to hypochondriasis. A hypochondriac says that he has headaches often, that he is not in as good health as his friends are, and that he cannot understand what he reads as well as he used to. Suppose that he has a headache on an average of once every month, as does a certain "normal" person. The hypochondriac says he often has headaches, the other person says he does not. They both have headaches once a month, and hence they must either intrepret the word "often" differently in that question, or else have unequal recall of their headaches. According to the traditional view, this ambiguity in the word "often" and the inaccuracy of human memory constitute sources of error; for the authors of MMPI they may actually constitute sources of discrimination.

We might mention as beautiful illustrations of this kind of relation, the non-somatic items in the hysteria scale of MMPI (10). These items have a statistical homogeneity and the common property by face inspection that they indicate the person to be possessed of unusually good social and psychiatric adjustment. They are among the most potent items for the detection of hysterics and hysteroid temperaments, but they reflect the systematic distortion of the hysteric's conception of himself, and would have to be considered invalid if taken as surrogates for the direct observation of behavior.

As a last example one might mention some findings of the writer, to be published shortly, in which "normal" persons having rather abnormal MMPI profiles are differentiated from clearly "abnormal" persons with equally deviant profiles by a tendency to give statistically rare as well as psychiatrically "maladjusted" responses to certain other items. Thus a person who says that he is afraid of fire, that windstorms terrify him, that people often disappoint him, stands a better chance of being normal in his non-test behavior than a person who does not admit to these things. The discrimination of this set of items for various criterion groups, the intercorrelations with other scales, and the content of the items indicate strongly that they detect some verbal-semantic distortion in the interpretation and response to the other MMPI items which enters into the spurious elevation of scores achieved by certain "normals." Recent unpublished research on more subtle "lie" scales of MMPI indicates that unconscious self-deception is inversely related to the kind of verbal distortion just indicated.

In summary, a serious and detailed study of the MMPI items and their interrelations both with one another and non-test behavior cannot fail to convince one of the necessity for this second kind of approach to question-answer personality tests. That the majority of the questions seem by inspection to require self-ratings has been a source of theoretical misunderstanding, since the stimulus situation seems to request a self-rating, whereas *the scoring does not assume a valid self-rating to have been given*. It is difficult to give any psychologically meaningful interpretation of some of the empirical findings on MMPI unless the more sophisticated view is maintained.

It is for this reason that the possible differences in interpretation do not cause us any *a priori* concern in the use of this instrument. Whether any structured personality test turns out to be valid and useful must be decided on pragmatic grounds, but the possibility of diverse interpretations of a single item is not a good *theoretical* reason for predicting failure of the scales. There is a "projective" element involved in interpreting and responding to these verbal stimuli which must be recognized, in spite of the fact that the test situation is very rigidly structured as regards the ultimate response possibilities permitted. The objection that all persons do not interpret structured test items in the same way is not fatal, just as it would not be fatal to point out that "ink blots do not look the same to everyone."

It has not been sufficiently recognized by critics of structured personality tests that what a man says about himself may be a highly significant fact about him even though we do not entertain with any confidence the hypothesis that what he says would agree with what complete knowledge of him would lead others to say of him. It is rather strange that this point is so often completely passed by, when clinical psychologists quickly learn to take just that attitude in a diagnostic or therapeutic interview. The complex defense mechanisms of projection, rationalization, reaction-formation, etc., appear dynamically to the interviewer as soon as he begins to take what the client *says* as itself motivated by other needs than those of giving an accurate verbal report. There is no good *a priori* reason for denying the possibility of similar processes in the highly structured "interview" which is the question-answer personality test. The summarized experience of the clinician results (one hopes, at least) in his being able to discriminate verbal responses admissible as accurate self-descriptions from those which reflect other psychodynamisms but are not on that account any the less significant. The test analogue to this experience consists of the summarized statistics on response frequencies, at least among those personality tests which have been constructed empirically (MMPI, Strong, Rorschach, etc.).

Once this has been taken for granted we are prepared to admit powerful items to personality scales regardless of whether the rationale of their appearance can be made clear at present. We do not have the confidence of the traditional personality test maker that the relation between the behavior dynamics of a subject and the tendency to respond verbally in a certain way must be psychologically obvious. Thus it puzzles us but does not disconcert us when this relation cannot be elucidated, the science of behavior being in the stage that it is. That "I sometimes tease animals" (answered *false*) should occur in a scale measuring symptomatic depression is theoretically mysterious, just as the tendency of certain schizophrenic patients to accept "position" as a determinant in responding to the Rorschach may be theoretically mysterious. Whether such a relation obtains can be very readily discovered empirically, and the wherefore of it may be left aside for the moment as a theoretical question. Verbal responses which do not apparently have any *self*-reference at all, but in their form seem to request an objective judgment about social phenomena or ethical values, may be equally diagnostic. So, again, one is not disturbed to find items such as "I think most people would lie to get ahead" (answered *false*) and "It takes a lot of argument to convince most people of the truth" (answered *false*) appearing on the hysteria scale of MMPI.

The frequently alleged "superficiality" of structured personality tests becomes less evident on such a basis also. Some of these items can be rationalized in terms of fairly deep-seated trends of the personality, although it is admittedly difficult to establish that any given depth interpretation is the correct one. To take one example, the items on the MMPI scale for hysteria which were referred to above as indicating extraordinarily good social and emotional adjustment can hardly be seen as valid self-descriptions. However, if the core trend of such items is summarily characterized as "I am psychiatrically and socially well adjusted," it is not hard to fit such a trend into what we know of the basic personality structure of the hysteric. The well known *belle indifference* of these patients, the great lack of insight, the facility of repression and dissociation, the "impunitiveness" of their reactions to frustration, the tendency of such patients to show an elevated "lie" score on MMPI, may all be seen as facets of this underlying structure. It would be interesting to see experimentally whether to the three elements of Rosenzweig's "triadic hypothesis" (impunitiveness, repression, hypnotizability) one might add a fourth correlate — the chief non-somatic component of the MMPI hysteria scale.

Whether "depth" is plumbed by a structured personality test to a lesser extent than by one which is unstructured is difficult to determine, once the present view of the nature of structured tests is understood. That the "deepest" layers of personality are not verbal might be admitted without any implication that they cannot therefore make themselves known to us via verbal behavior. Psychoanalysis, usually considered the "deepest" kind of psychotherapy, makes use of the dependency of verbal behavior upon underlying variables which are not themselves verbalized.

The most important area of behavior considered in the making of psychiatric diagnosis is still the form and content of the *speech* of the individual. I do not mean to advance these considerations as validations of any structured personality tests, but merely as reasons for not accepting the theoretical objection sometimes offered in criticizing them. Of course, structured personality tests may be employed in a purely diagnostic, categorizing fashion, without the use of any dynamic interpretations of the relationship among scales or the patterning of a profile. For certain practical purposes this is quite permissible, just as one may devote himself to the statistical validation of various "signs" on the Rorschach test, with no attempt to make qualitative or really dynamic personological inferences from the findings. The tradition in the case of structured personality tests is probably weighted on the side of non-dynamic thinking; and in the case of some structured tests, there is a considerable amount of experience and clinical subtlety required to extract the maximum of information. The present writer has heard discussions in case conferences at the University of Minnesota Hospital which make as "dynamic" use of MMPI patterns as one could reasonably make of any kind of test data without an excessive amount of illegitimate reification. The clinical use of the Strong Vocational Interest Blank is another example.

In discussing the "depth" of interpretation possible with tests of various kinds, it should at least be pointed out that the problem of validating personality tests, whether structured or unstructured, becomes more difficult in proportion as the interpretations increase in "depth." For example, the validation of the "sign" differentials on the Rorschach is relatively easier to carry out than that of the deeper interpretations concerning the basic personality structure. This does not imply that there is necessarily less validity in the latter class of inferences, but simply stresses the difficulty of designing experiments to test validity. A very major part of this difficulty hinges upon the lack of satisfactory external criteria, a situation which exists also in the case of more dynamic interpretations of structured personality tests. One is willing to accept a staff diagnosis of psychasthenia in selecting cases against which to validate the Pt scale of MMPI or the F% as a compulsive-obsessive sign on the Rorschach. But when the test results indicate repressed homosexuality or latent anxiety or lack of deep insight into the self, we may have strong suspicions that the instrument is fully as competent as the psychiatric staff. Unfortunately this latter assumption is very difficult to justify without appearing to be inordinately biased in favor of our test. Until this problem is better solved than at present, many of the "depth" interpretations of both structured and unstructured tests will be little more than an expression of personal opinion.

There is one advantage of unstructured personality tests which cannot easily be claimed for the structured variety, namely, the fact that falsehood is difficult. While it is true for many of the MMPI items, for example, that even a psychologist cannot predict on which scales they will appear nor in what direction certain sorts of abnormals will tend to answer them, still the relative accessibility of defensive answering would seem to be greater than is possible in responding to a set of inkblots. Research is still in progress on more subtle "lie" scales of MMPI and we have every reason to feel encouraged on the present findings. Nevertheless the very existence of a definite problem in this case and not in the case of the Rorschach gives the latter an advantage in this respect. When we pass to a more structured method, such as the T. A. T., the problem reappears. The writer has found, for example, a number of patients who simply were not fooled by the "intelligence test" set given in the directions for the T. A. T., as was indicated quite clearly by self-references and defensive remarks, especially on the second day. Of course such a patient is still under pressure to produce material and therefore his unwillingness to reveal himself is limited in its power over the projections finally given.

In conclusion, the writer is in hearty agreement with Lieutenant Hutt that unstructured personality tests are of great value, and that the final test of the adequacy of any technique is its utility in clinical work. Published evidence of the validity of both structured and unstructured personality tests as they had to be modified for convenient military use does not enable one to draw any very definite conclusions or comparisons at the present time. There is assuredly no reason for us to place structured and unstructured types of instruments in battle order against one another, although it is admitted that when time is limited they come inevitably into a very real clinical "competition" for use. The present article has been aimed simply at the clarification of certain rather prevalent misconceptions as to the nature and the theory of at least one important structured personality test, in order that erroneous theoretical considerations may not be thrown into the balance in deciding the outcome of such clinical competition.

REFERENCES

1. Benton, A. C. "The Interpretation of Questionnaire Items in a Personality Schedule," *Archives of Psychology*, No. 190, (1935).
2. Cleckley, H. *The Mask of Sanity.* St. Louis: The C. V. Mosby Co., 1941.
3. Hathaway, S. R., and McKinley, J. C. *Manual for the Minnesota Multiphasic Personality Inventory.* Minneapolis: University of Minnesota Press, 1943.
4. ———. "A Multiphasic Personality Schedule: I. Construction of the Schedule," *Journal of Psychology*, 10 (1940), 249–254.
5. ———. "A Multiphasic Personality Schedule: III. The Measurement of Symptomatic Depression," *ibid.*, 14 (1942), 73–84.
6. Hutt, Max L. "The Use of Projective Methods of Personality Measurement in Army Medical Installations," *Journal of Clinical Psychology*, 1 (1945), 134–140.
7. Landis, C., and Katz, S. E. "The Validity of Certain Questions Which Purport to Measure Neurotic Tendencies," *Journal of Applied Psychology*, 18 (1934), 343–356.
8. ———, Zubin, J., and Katz, S. E. "Empirical Evaluation of Three Personality Adjustment Inventories," *Journal of Educational Psychology*, 26 (1935), 321–330.
9. Leverenz, C. W. "Minnesota Multiphasic Personality Inventory: An Evaluation of Its Usefulness in the Psychiatric Service of a Station Hospital," *War Med.*, 4 (1943), 618–629.
10. McKinley, J. C., and Hathaway, S. R. "The Minnesota Multiphasic Personality Inventory: V. Hysteria, Hypomania, and Psychopathic Deviate," *Journal of Applied Psychology*, 28 (1944), 153–174.
11. ———. "A Multiphasic Personality Schedule: II. A Differential Study of Hypochondriasis," *Journal of Psychology*, 10 (1940), 255–268.
12. ———. "A Multiphasic Personality Schedule: IV. Psychasthenia," *Journal of Applied Psychology*, 26 (1942), 614–624.
13. Maller, J. B. "Personality Tests," in J. McV. Hunt (ed.), *Personality and the Behavior Disorders*. New York: The Ronald Press Company, 1944, 170–213.
14. Meehl, P. E. "A General Normality or Control Factor in Personality Testing." Unpublished Ph.D. thesis, University of Minnesota Library, Minneapolis, 1945.
15. Mosier, C. I. "On the Validity of Neurotic Questionnaires," *Journal of Social Psychology*, 9 (1938), 3–16.
16. Rosenzweig, S. "An Outline of Frustration Theory," in J. McV. Hunt (ed.), *Personality and the Behavior Disorders*. New York: The Ronald Press Company, 1944.
17. Strong, E. K. *Vocational Interests of Men and Women.* Stanford: Stanford University Press, 1943.

26

A Psychometric Evaluation
of the Rorschach Experiment[1]

Joseph Zubin, Leonard D. Eron, and Florence Sultan

The authors provide considerable data in an effort to determine which of the aspects of Rorschach testing are soundly supported by empirical results and which are not. The main discussions center around (1) agreement among judges as to the content of examinee responses, and (2) consistency of the examinee response patterns. The conclusions presented by the authors have definite implications for the validity of the test.

In this paper we will discuss the evaluation of the Rorschach technique as an *experiment* and not as a *clinical tool.* In evaluating the Rorschach experiment one must bear in mind that it has not remained static during the course of the last thirty years. Rorschach himself in his posthumous paper added a new dimension — shading. Others have added different dimensions, and have altered directions for scoring and inquiry.

Most users of the Rorschach regard it as a test or as a technique, while only a few have retained Hermann Rorschach's original view of it as an experiment. In what way does an experiment differ from a test? A test is the end result of a previously conducted series of experiments in which behavior sampled by the test is examined for its reliability and for the validity with which it predicts extratest behavior. On the other hand, an experiment usually attempts to examine the tenability of a hypothesis emanating from some scientific model of behavior. What is the model of behavior with which Rorschach dealt and what hypothesis emanating from that model was he trying to test? One looks in vain in his work for explicit statements of this sort. If he had lived in the present decade he might have formulated his

From Joseph Zubin, Leonard D. Eron, and Florence Sultan, "A Psychometric Evaluation of the Rorschach Experiment," *American Journal of Orthopsychiatry,* XXVI, No. 4 (October, 1956), pp. 773–782. Copyright, the American Orthopsychiatric Association, Inc. Reproduced by permission of publisher and authors.

[1] This investigation was supported in part by Research Grant M 586 (C2) from the National Institute of Mental Health of the National Institutes of Health, Public Health Service, and by Foundations' Fund for Research in Psychiatry.

model for personality somewhat like this: Personality reflects one's perception of the world and one's perception of oneself. A hypothesis emanating from this model of personality is that by studying the way one perceives the world and the way one perceives his own self, one can arrive at an understanding of the individual personality. In order to study the perceptual characteristics of the individual, some neutral medium or nonsense material, uninfluenced by life experience, had to be utilized. At first, one of Rorschach's friends cooperated with him in using geometrical shapes, but these did not yield very much. After his return from Russia he conceived of the inkblots as a medium for studying perception. Whether he was influenced by Leonardo da Vinci's "instructions to the painter" in this regard is not known. To formalize Rorschach's hypothesis: We perceive in inkblots in accordance with our personality characteristics.

After thirty years of Rorschach work the tenability of this hypothesis is still in doubt. Lag in scientific validation is, however, not peculiar to our field; clinical hunches are always ahead of scientific validation, but without scientific validation, one hunch is no better than any other hunch. How is the clinician to prevent himself from following a will-o'-the-wisp hunch? Without a scientific methodology to help him, the clinician would be at the mercy of whatever hunch blows his way. Galton long ago had this to say about the relative value of clinical impressions versus scientific evaluations:

> General impressions are never to be trusted. Unfortunately, when they are of long standing they become fixed rules of life, and assume a prescriptive right not to be questioned. Consequently, those who are not accustomed to original inquiry entertain a horror and a hatred of statistics. They cannot endure the idea of submitting their sacred impressions to cold-blooded verification. But it is the triumph of scientific men to rise superior to such superstitions, to desire tests by which the value of beliefs may be ascertained, and to feel sufficiently masters of themselves to discard contemptuously whatever may be found to be untrue (5, p. 10).

Must the Rorschach remain beyond the pale of measurement? The dilemma of the clinician, especially the more recently trained one, is quite clear. On the one hand, his most cherished conventions, learned in graduate school and indoctrinated during internship, are under challenge; yet he must have subjective faith in them. Otherwise, much of his current usefulness in the clinic is under a shadow. The dilemma of the psychometrician arises from the fact that the Rorschach *is* apparently clinically useful (6,000 psychologists and an equal or even larger number of psychiatrists and social workers can't be entirely wrong!), but as yet he has found no way of demonstrating its usefulness scientifically.

In a recent study one of us (10) enumerated the past failures of the Rorschach. They are: 1) failure to specify a generally accepted method of administration; 2) failure to provide an objective scoring system; 3) failure to provide a method for testing reliability — no acceptable alternate form; 4) failure to provide indications of general validity.

How are these difficulties to be corrected? What can be done to salvage this undeniably valuable clinical tool as a scientific instrument? How can we refine and calibrate the traditional Rorschach schema so that the *sine qua non* of a true measuring rod, reliability and validity, can be demonstrated consistently, without sacrificing clinical utility and meaningfulness? The use of rating scales affords an opportunity to combine qualitative clinical judgments and a more or less rigorous quantification. It is possible for the ratings to be as subjective and global as necessary, so long as the criteria are verbalized, permitting communicability of the method, and in this way allowing subsequent raters to utilize the scales with comparable results.

In order to develop a system of scales for appraising Rorschach responses, a survey was made of all the various types of evaluations which Rorschach experts have utilized in developing personality interpretations from subjects' protocols. This analysis led to the development of approximately 50 different 5-point scales. It is not maintained that all of these factors are of equal importance in any given protocol, nor do they exhaust all the possible nuances of a Rorschach response. However, after a careful pre-examination of several hundred records of both normal subjects and patients of various classifications these are the factors which emerged as both significant and measurable.

The scales have been divided into three general classes, corresponding roughly to the traditional Rorschach scoring of location, determinants, and content. Each response is scored on every scale. For example, when location is being considered, every response is scored for Whole response, Large Detail response and Small Detail response, W, D, and Dd, the rating awarded on each of these depending on how much each of these locales contributed to the response. If a subject calls card 1 a bat because of the whole outline, specifying the wings and feelers and protuberances, the response would get the highest possible rating for W, since this was the most important location, and in addition, would receive lesser ratings for D and Dd, depending on how much these areas contributed to a determination of the final response, bat. That aspect of the response which orthodox Rorschachers have categorized as determinants, we have broken down into two categories: 1) that which we call the determinants proper, referring to the actual stimulus correlates of the response (the physical attributes of the area selected); and 2) the way in which these determinants are elaborated into the characteristics of the perceived object. The physical properties of the blots, which constitute the actual determinants of the response, have been analyzed into three aspects: color, either chromatic or achromatic; intensity, referring to the amount of luminous flux reflected from the area; and heterogeneity, which is the result of variations in color and intensity. These determinants, color, intensity, and heterogeneity, may be interpreted in isolation or elaborated in a variety of ways so that the actual perception takes on the characteristics of hue, surface quality, shape, solidity, distance, movement, etc.

Since these scales actually yield quantitative data, ordinary statistical procedures which have been utilized with success in intelligence testing and personality inventories can appropriately be applied in an evaluation of the objectivity, reliability and validity of Rorschach's test. Table 1 includes a few sample scales.

Table 1

Some Reliable Scales for Evaluating Rorschach Responses

40a. *Degree of Self-Reference (Se). Split-half r = .81*

The personal reference must be stated specifically in order to receive more than a 0 rating.

  0. Impersonal response.
  1. Slight degree of self-reference, e.g., objects seen which are in some way connected with the trade or occupation of the subject.
  2. Some degree of self-reference: object recognized as similar to one experienced by the subject.
  3. Marked self-reference: members of the subject's family, objects involved in important or traumatic experiences of the subject.
  4. Completely self-referred: subject sees himself as a child, some part of himself, eyes looking at him, gorilla coming at him.

49. *Definiteness of Content[1] (Def). Split-half r = .89*

The definiteness or specificity of content may vary from vague, amorphous objects like "shapes in the clouds" or "things you might see in a kaleidoscope" to such specific responses as: "Michelangelo's Moses," "a gossiping old woman wearing a ridiculous hair-do."

  0. Vague, formless, lacking in specific content: reflection of something with nothing else specified, mist, splotches, clouds of no particular shape.
  1. Highly generic and indefinite: "a spread eagle effect," "an animal or something like that."
  2. Less generic: a fishlike animal, an insect, "some sort of pumping instrument," a tree, responses on which two possibilities are mentioned (a dog or a lion).
  3. Specifically designated objects: a praying mantis, an old man, huge pink rats, etc.
  4. Specifically designated and definite objects: Mark Twain, a Spanish dancer with mantilla and flowing cape, Arc de Triomphe.

56. *Congruousness of Response (Cg). Split-half r = .98*

By congruousness we mean the degree to which various elements in a given response hang together. It is reasonable to assume that this in turn is a measure of the subject's clarity of association. Most simple responses are *a priori* congruent, so that it is only in fairly complex responses that the question of incongruency arises. For example, "black bear" or "white bear" is a congruent response, while "grass bear" is completely incongruent. Rorschach had obtained such a response from a schizophrenic patient who had fused two percepts, green grass and the shape of a bear, into one. Contaminated responses of this type may be expected from certain schizophrenics, but there are degrees of incongruency and not all responses are as thoroughly "contaminated" as "grass bear."

  0. Completely incongruous response: two different concepts, completely unrelated to each other, arising in the same area of the blot are telescoped or fused into one: "grass bear."
  1. Intrinsically incongruous but some associative connection present: "a lamb-camel," "a Madonna-candelabra," "a penis-vagina."

2. Incongruousness between distinct elements in the response: two men shaking hands and a drop of blood falling between them; unable to detach distinct concept.
3. Whimsical or fanciful responses: a bull with a sense of humor, characters of the Alice-in-Wonderland type, monsters, centaurs, freaks, sports, when object can be either animal or human.
4. Completely congruent response.

---

[1] In the orthodox Rorschach scoring the lower categories in the scale are noted as F−, C−, etc. A minus can arise from two sources, lack of correspondence between determinants and interpretation content, or vagueness of content. The above scale has been introduced in order to differentiate between these two sources of minus scores.

The first step in evaluating objectivity of scaling is to determine if the scaling itself can be done reliably; that is, to see if two independent raters, given the same responses, can rate them with a reasonable degree of agreement. This has been demonstrated by a study in which the protocols of 44 superior individuals were analyzed independently by two raters after a short period of training in the use of the scales. Responses were selected at random from the records and typed on individual sheets of paper. All ratings on any one scale were made at one session. The agreement between judges was excellent. Degree of agreement ranged from perfect agreement on 70 per cent of the response ratings on one scale to perfect agreement on *all* the responses on ten scales; the median perfect agreement on all the scales was 94 per cent. The number of response ratings on each of the scales on which this agreement was based ranged from 43 to 56. Table 2 shows the median per cent of perfect agreement for the various scales grouped according to type. It is obvious that two independent analysts *can* rate the same responses with a considerable degree of agreement, and thus interscorer reliability of the scales is unquestioned.

Another kind of reliability is concerned not so much with the system of scoring as with the consistency of the performance of the subject. It would be expected that if an individual perceives in Rorschach space the same way

Table 2

INTERSCORER AGREEMENT ON RORSCHACH SCALES

Category of Scales	No. of Scales	Per Cent of Response Ratings on Which Agreement Was Perfect	Median Perfect Agreement
Location	3	82– 96%	86%
Determinants	3	83– 95%	93%
Elaborations	21	81–100%	93%
Content	22	70–100%	95%
Total	49	70–100%	94%

as he perceives in real life space, these characteristic habits of perception would consistently mark his performance. Thus, some degree of agreement should emerge when ratings on one half of an individual's responses are compared with ratings on the other half. Our method of psychometric scaling of responses permits the use of the Pearson Product Moment Correlation in evaluating split-half reliability, since it yields continuous data, more or less normally distributed, which is not the case, of course, with traditional scoring procedures. A number of methods of dividing protocols into two halves were utilized because we were aware that, since the structures of the individual cards themselves are so different, good agreement could not reasonably be expected if, for example, the first five cards were compared with the second five. In one series of reliability estimates, responses to cards 1, 2, 4, 7, and 10 were compared with cards 3, 5, 6, 8, and 9. In another, cards 1, 2, 3, 4, 5, and 8 were compared with cards 6, 7, 9, and 10. Total responses to these cards, as well as initial responses only, were utilized. We also calculated separate reliabilities for colored and uncolored cards by comparing cards 2 and 10 with 3 and 8; and 4 and 5 with 6 and 7. However, what appeared to be the best method was that of alternative responses, so that for subject 1, response 1, card 1 was assigned to series A; response 2, card 1, to series B; response 3 to series A, and so on continuously through the protocol. Subjects were alternated so that half started with response 1, card 1, in series A and the other half with that response in series B. For some of our scales the reliabilities are quite high, but for the majority of them the relationship is not high. Table 3 presents the perceptual scales for which the uncorrected correlation is above .30, the minimum correlation that may be regarded as

Table 3

SPLIT-HALF RELIABILITIES OF VARIOUS RORSCHACH PERCEPTUAL SCALES

Category of Scale	Total No. of Scales	Product-Moment Correlation	Spearman-Brown Correction
Location	3		
W		.76	.86
Dd		.30	.46
Determinants	3		
Color		.32	.48
Heterogeneity		.51	.68
Elaborations	21		
Hue		.52	.68
Texture		.48	.65
Shape		.67	.80
Three dimensions		.69	.82
Three dimensions projected onto two planes		.62	.77
Vista		.45	.62

significantly different from zero at the .05 level of confidence. Of 27 correlations, 10 meet the criterion. While this shows there is some relationship, none have a correlation above .80 which would permit somewhat reliable individual prediction. Table 4 presents the content scales for which the uncorrected correlation is above .30. These scales fare somewhat better. Of 26 scales, 20 meet this criterion, and 9 have correlations above .80.

Table 4

SPLIT-HALF RELIABILITIES OF VARIOUS RORSCHACH CONTENT SCALES

Category of Scale	Total No. of Scales	Product-Moment Correlation	Spearman-Brown Correction
Dynamic content	6		
Self-reference		.81	.89
Formal content	10		
Human		.59	.74
Animal		.42	.59
Plant		.60	.75
Inanimate		.45	.62
Anatomy		.45	.62
Whole Part		.64	.78
Sex		.57	.73
Definiteness		.89	.94
Gender		.47	.64
Psychological characteristics	7		
Perseveration		.48	.65
Elaboration		.71	.83
Description		.83	.91
Mood		.94	.97
Affect		.98	.99
Congruousness		.98	.99
Communality		.55	.71
Subject's attitude	3		
Self-estimate of adequacy		.98	.99
Interpretive attitude		.97	.98
Awareness of interpretive attitude		.96	.98

It is interesting that the content scales, that is, those scales which measure the nature of the objects reported by the subject and his characteristic ways of thinking about them, show consistently higher reliability than the scales which measure so-called perceptual habits. Thus, those scales which measure the degree of self-reference, the specificity of the content, the tendency toward blot description, the mood of the response, the affect of the subject, the communality of the response and the self-estimate of its adequacy, have split-half reliabilities which can be considered high even for intelligence and aptitude tests. On the other hand, those scales which measure the type of perceptual response with which Rorschachers have been traditionally concerned; location, use of color, form, texture, vista, movement, etc., have reliabilities which, barring a few exceptions, are so low as to indicate they measure little that is consistently characteristic of the individual.

Herein may be the reason for the clinical utility of the Rorschach method, despite the lack of experimental evidence for its validity. If you forget about perceptual scoring and limit yourself to the evaluation of the content of the protocols, the way you would evaluate any other interview — through a content analysis — the Rorschach can be clinically useful. It is simply a standard interview behind the veil of inkblots. The perceptual factors have nothing to do with it. Scales for evaluating content as well as factor analyses of these scales seem to work because it is the content that matters. Although our present study deals only with reliability, the validity of content scoring has been established by Sen (7), Elizur (3), and Watkins and Stauffacher (9). One should be careful not to confuse content analyses with content scoring like H, A, etc. Content scales of this type which we included among our own scales did not have sufficiently high reliability for predictive purposes. By content analysis we mean the underlying contextual rather than perceptual dimensions of the protocols. These include the attitudinal factors (dominance, evaluative attitude, mood, etc.) and thinking processes (perseveration, elaboration, congruity, communality, etc.). There were 25 such scales and 15 of them were found to have reliabilities above .47. Furthermore, 10 of these 21 scales had reliabilities in excess of .70. It is these attitudes and characteristics of thought which indicate whether the subject is schizophrenic or normal, just in the same way that the clinical interview might reveal these factors. The advantage of the Rorschach inheres in the fact that it is a standard interview.

In a previous study it was shown that the following general conclusions may be made about the efficacy of the Rorschach:

(1) Global evaluations of the Rorschach seem to work when the Rorschach worker and the clinician work closely together.
(2) Atomistic evaluation, as well as global, of the content of the Rorschach protocols (as distinct from the perceptual scoring) seem to work.
(3) Atomistic analysis of the perceptual factors is a failure.
(4) Factor analysis of atomistic scores of both the perceptual as well as the content variety seem to work (10, p. 313).

What is the simplest, most parsimonious method for explaining these findings? The answer, we believe, is that Rorschach's test is no more or less than an experimental interview and, like any interview, it should be evaluated for its content.

What about Rorschach's hypothesis? Is it disproved? No, it is still indeterminate, because we still have no way of testing it. We frankly do not know the stimulus correlates of perception in inkblots, nor even of perception in the visual world. When we do learn how perception takes place in the visual world we may then be able to test whether color means emotion and form means control, etc. Part of the difficulty arises from the fact that our scoring of responses is so unreliable. Baughman's recent work (1, 2) has shown that much of the conventional scoring of even popular responses is attributed to determinants erroneously. The experimental removal of these determinants by alteration of the stimulus does not alter the responses. Meantime, we do know that the content elicited by the Rorschach technique is helpful in diagnosing the mentally ill. Rather than wait for the psychologists concerned with perception to catch up, clinicians ought to forge ahead and examine the interview itself as a technique. Models for the interview have been provided by Skinner (8), by Fries (4), and by Zubin (11), and many sagacious insights into the interview process were made by Freud and by Sullivan. Gill, Newman and Redlich (6) have recently analyzed the initial interview with profit. This is the road along which Rorschach workers too should travel if they would improve their technique.

SUMMARY

When we adopt the view of the Rorschach technique held by its creator, namely, that it is an *experiment,* it becomes necessary to make explicit the model which Rorschach conceptualized and the hypotheses emanating from that model which he was trying to test. We believe that Rorschach con-ceived of personality as the habitual or systematic way of responding to life situations — or, as the style of life characterizing the individual. We also believe that he conceived of the perceptual behavior of the individual as controlled by perceptual habits or systematic preferences. His basic model consisted of paralleling personality characteristics with perceptual charac-teristics. Since perceptual behavior in real space is difficult to control and measure, he substituted inkblot space for real space, under the assumption that the perceptual characteristics of the individual in real space will be paralleled in inkblot space. On the basis of his preliminary observations, he and his followers derived a series of hypotheses from this model which presumably could be tested — relation of form perception to control, color to emotionality, chiaroscure to sensitivity and depression, etc. He furthermore rejected the content of the responses as being significant for personality, because it reflected recent experience only, or superficial aspects of behavior. These hypotheses thus far have not been subjected to rigorous experimentation, because we still do not know how perception takes place in the real world, nor do we yet know the stimulus correlates of the dimensions of space per-ception. Nevertheless, many attempts at testing these hypotheses, both clinically and experimentally, have been undertaken during the past 30 years. The net result may be summarized as follows: Clinical global evalua-tions of the protocols have often been regarded as successful, especially by clinicians, and found to be useful in the evaluation of personality. Experi-mental approaches have rarely yielded positive results. One stumbling block that faced the experimentalist was the lack of objectivity in scoring. In order to make a crucial test of the hypotheses provided by Rorschach, psychometric scales have been developed for each of the dimensions that Rorschach and his followers found useful in analyzing protocols. The degree of agreement reached in rating responses on these scales was quite high. The consistency of the ratings for the same individual was found to be high for scales rating content of thought and content of percept, but not for the scales rating the perceptual characteristics of the individual. Others who have studied the *validity* of these and similar scales also found that the content scales show high validity, but that the perceptual scores failed to do so. Since the perceptual scales are lacking in reliability and validity, while the content scales satisfy these two requirements, it is concluded that the *content* of the protocols and not the perceptual factors in the individual is the basis for whatever success the Rorschach has achieved. Thus, the Rorschach takes its rightful place as a systematic controlled interview, whose value lies in the content analysis that can be achieved of its protocols, and not as a test. Rorschach's hypotheses about the relation between perception and personality will have to wait until we develop more knowledge about perception itself. Until then, viewing the Rorschach technique as a systematic, controlled interview and basing its evaluation on content analyses of the protocols is the method to be recommended, because it is the only one that can now yield reliable and valid results.

REFERENCES

1. Baughman, E. E. "Rorschach Scores as a Function of Examiner Differences," *Journal of Projective Techniques*, 15 (1951), 243–249.
2. ———. "A Comparative Study of Rorschach Forms with Altered Stimulus Characteristics." Unpublished Ph.D. dissertation, University of Chicago, 1951.
3. Elizur, A. "Content Analyses of the Rorschach with Regard to Anxiety and Hostility," *Rorschach Res. Exch.*, 13 (1949), 274–281.
4. Fries, C. C. *The Structure of English*. New York: Harcourt, Brace & Co., 1952.
5. Galton, F. *Proceedings of the Royal Institute*, 9 (1879), 9–10.
6. Gill, M., Newman, R., and Redlich, F. C. *The Initial Interview in Psychiatric Practice*. New York: International University Press, 1954.
7. Sen, A. A. "A Statistical Study of the Rorschach Test," *British Journal of Psychology*, 3 (1950), 21–39.
8. Skinner, B. F. "Verbal Behavior." William James Lecture, Harvard University, 1948 (mimeographed edition).
9. Watkins, J. G., and Stauffacher, J. C. "An Index of Pathological Thinking in the Rorschach," *Journal of Projective Techniques*, 16 (1952), 276–286.
10. Zubin, J. "Failures of the Rorschach Technique," *Journal of Projective Techniques*, 18 (1954), 303–315.
11. ———. "The Interview Technique as a Clinical Tool," *Experimental Abnormal Psychology*, 1953 (mimeographed edition).

27

Professed Attitudes and Actual Behavior

Stephen M. Corey

A common problem in using clinical reports as a basis for pre-
dicting behavior is that a discrepancy may exist between what a
person says about a given topic and how he actually behaves in
reference to that topic. Corey provides some interesting informa-
tion about professed attitudes, as assessed by an attitude scale, and
actual behavior. The reader may wish to ponder the findings in
reference to the validity of certain kinds of self-report inventories.

INTRODUCTION

Granting the significance from certain points of view of verbal opinions as such, they are of limited practical value unless they presage behavior. It is of interest to determine what a subject says his attitude is in regard to communism, the church, or foreign missions, but of greater moment socio- logically is the way he acts in relation to these institutions. Most psychologists and sociologists are implicitly, at least, in agreement on this point as is made evident both by their definitions of social attitudes and by the statistical data advanced in defense of published scales. Droba (7), Allport (1), Bain (2), Cantril (3), Faris (8), and others have reported large numbers of definitions which have in common an insistence that a social attitude of a particular sort predisposes one to *behave* in a particular manner. Words such as "preparatory for" or "indicative of" behavior are common in these defini- tions.

In view of this general agreement as to what a social attitude is, it is possible to state one criterion of the validity of social attitude questionnaires — namely, the relationship between questionnaire scores and overt behavior. In other words, if a social attitude is a determiner of overt behavior, social attitude questionnaires may be considered valid if they make possible predic- tions of overt behavior. Under some circumstances behavior might be con- sciously engaged in to give a false impression of an attitude, but in the long run the only evidence for the insincerity of such an expression would be

From Stephen M. Corey, "Professed Attitudes and Actual Behavior," *The Journal of Educational Psychology*, XXVIII (April, 1937), pp. 271–280. Reprinted with the permission of Abrahams Magazine Service, Incorporated, and the author.

more behavior under different circumstances. In the last analysis, the way a person acts over a period of time is a reliable and valid indication of his attitudes.

If this concept of attitude questionnaire validity is granted, it is rather surprising that so few investigations have been undertaken to determine the relationship between verbal opinions and overt behavior. As might have been predicted in light of what we know about the history of the testing movement in general, the investigators who have developed the social attitude questionnaires have apparently been much more concerned with reliability than with validity. Consequently, very reliable instruments called attitude scales are commonly employed in psychological and sociological investigations, but the validity of these scales, in the sense of the writer, has either been taken for granted or has been demonstrated by administering the questionnaires to groups commonly believed to represent varying attitudes with respect to the institutions, objects, or practices in question. A number of years ago Bain (2) called attention to this lack of dependable evidence for validity and contended that while in most cases a relationship between verbal and overt behavior is assumed, ". . . this relationship must be determined . . . before the study has any great value."

There are a considerable number of investigations which imply the validity of attitude questionnaires. The implication, however, is not quantitative in any statistical sense but is based on common sense evidence. For example, Smith (20), found that her "Attitude Toward Prohibition" scale, when administered to college students, Y.W.C.A. workers, Methodists, and business men, yielded scores in keeping with the attitude one might expect these groups to hold. Our very expectations, however, are in most cases based upon verbal opinions rather than observations of overt behavior so that some degree of relationship would be inevitable. It would be more significant could we know for these same groups the degree in which their attitude scale scores were indicative of their actual drinking practices.

Rogers (17) reported analogous results after administering a questionnaire involving attitudes toward war to students taking advanced R.O.T.C., basic R.O.T.C., and a control group taking neither. Practically every question was reacted to differently by the three groups — the men in the advanced R.O.T.C. courses expressing attitudes significantly more sympathetic to war while those in the control group were most antipathetic. These results are a bit more pertinent in that by and large the men in the advanced R.O.T.C. units were, by their very interest in such an activity, manifesting overt behavior indicative of some sympathy for militaristic activities.

Porter (15) found that the amount of military training and attitude toward war correlated $+ .30 \pm .03$ for a group of 562 college men. This datum implies validity for the questionnaire used inasmuch as the men expressing the most militaristic attitudes had elected to continue military training for the longest period. This need not necessarily mean, however, that the military training resulted in changed attitudes because no retest was administered involving any appreciable number of subjects (4). The test was readministered one year later to only 19 men who had undergone military training during this period and, paradoxically enough, their final scores indicated a slight shift toward pacificism. The number of cases involved was obviously too few to permit of any generalizations.

Sims and Patrick (19) administered Hinckley's "Attitude Toward the Negro" scale to northern and southern university students and reported that the latter were significantly more antagonistic to Negroes. These results are in harmony with those reported by Garrison and Burch (10), Hinckley (11), Likert (13), and others and seem as well to coincide with our common sense notions. Reinhardt (16), on the other hand, using Bogardus' "Social Distance" method, found that students in North Dakota were more prejudiced toward Negroes than were students in West Virginia. While Reinhardt's groups were very small his results imply a criticism of the validity of attitudinal investigations based upon statements of verbal opinions. Katz and Allport (12) also found that Syracuse University students from the North were more resentful of Negroes than were their classmates from the South.

Droba (6) administered his "Attitude Toward War" scale to some one thousand college students and found that men who had seen war service were slightly more militaristic than those who had not. This result would constitute an argument either for or against the validity of the questionnaire depending upon whether the investigator thought that military experience was conducive to the development of militaristic or pacifistic attitudes. Because both points of view have been advanced the argument is circular. Droba's report is of particular interest in view of Porter's (15) statement that for his subjects military training in college resulted in at least a noticeable trend toward pacifism. The 21 Socialists who were included in Droba's study were decidedly more pacifistic than members of either the Republican or Democratic parties. This is in agreement with rather commonly accepted beliefs about Socialists.

Stalnaker (22), using Thurstone's technique, investigated the attitudes developed toward intercollegiate athletics by various groups, and found, in general, what might have been predicted. Athletes and parents were in general most sympathetic and faculty and administrative officers were most antagonistic. An interesting check upon the common sense evidence for the validity of Stalnaker's questionnaire might be systematic observation of the behavior of some of his subjects when intercollegiate athletics were involved.

These investigations, and there are others like them, do present some indirect evidence almost of an anecdotal sort for the validity of attitude questionnaires. They indicate that in general and roughly speaking certain groups express attitudes such as might be expected under the circumstances. In but one or two instances, however, was actual overt behavior compared with attitude scale results and in no case was the amount of the overt behavior accurately estimated. On the contrary, attitude scales scores, based upon verbal opinions, were compared with what is generally expected of certain groups, which expectations are also in large part based upon verbal opinions.

There is another group of investigations which come a bit nearer the heart of the matter. These are not quantitative in any complete sense, but the actual behavior with which attitudinal statements are compared was estimated more objectively than was the case in the studies summarized above. Zimmerman (25), for example, investigated the attitudes of Minnesota farmers toward coöperative buying and selling and then related their verbally expressed attitudes to the number of years' experience each farmer had had in the coöperative movement. He reported a high degree of curvilinear correlation between these two variables. In Zimmerman's study those groups most favorable in their attitudes toward coöperative buying and selling had been actively engaging in such practices for the longest time. The attitude expressed by these Minnesota farmers had validity in terms of the definitions of attitudes most commonly advanced. It was definitely indicative of behavior.

Stouffer (23), in his comparison of statistical and case history methods of attitude research found a correlation of +.86 between "Attitude Toward Prohibition" scale scores and attitudes as inferred from autobiographies describing the subjects' experiences with liquor. This relationship is indicative of the validity of the attitude scales, in the sense the writer is using, only if it is assumed that the autobiographical sketches were descriptive of actual experiences. Such descriptions are subject to many of the same limitations with regard to their validity as are attitude questionnaires.

Stagner and Drought (21) checked the validity of their scale measuring the attitude of children toward their parents in much the same fashion — by comparing attitude scale results with autobiographical materials. Again, it may be said that both of these sources for inferring attitudes are subject to the same inherent limitations. In the Stagner-Drought study some of the biographical materials appear to have been supplied by individuals other than the subjects, which would enhance their value for the purpose of validating the attitude scales.

These three studies indicate rather definitely that the attitudinal opinions did accord, first, with what might be expected from knowing certain aspects of the subjects' behavior (Zimmerman) and, second, with their own description of their past behavior (Stouffer, Stagner, and Drought). No study has been made, so far as the writer is aware, in which it was possible to get a rather accurate quantitative estimate of degree of attitude as expressed in statement form and in addition an equally reliable measure of behavior, bearing upon the same institution or practice, with which comparisons might be made. The present investigation is of this sort. It is a comparison of scores made on an attitude questionnaire pertaining to honesty in the classroom with actual cheating in the classroom.

SUBJECTS AND METHODS

The subjects were 67 university students taking an introductory course in educational psychology. Each Friday, for five weeks, an objective true-false examination was administered covering the week's work. These tests ranged in length from 40 to 45 items. The papers were given back to the students for grading at the next class meeting. In the meantime, they had been scored accurately but no marks were placed upon them. The difference between the true score and the score the student reported for himself was the basic cheating index. The students were told to mark the statements with symbolic "pluses" and "minuses" so that cheating, providing the intent was present, was very easy. No attempt was made to supervise the students' scoring of their own papers.

Objections to this technique are rather obvious. It might be contended that university students would very quickly suspect some ulterior motive in such a procedure, and behave a bit contrary to their custom. Certainly, if even a small group was of the opinion that its honesty was being measured, the news would soon get around. Under the circumstances, the only check possible upon the circulation of such a rumor would be the tendency for cheating to decrease from week to week. The data presented in Table 1 indicate that there was no such decrease. While there was variation in the amount of cheating from week to week, the amount of dishonesty in grading the last test was almost as great as that on the first. Apparently the students' practices in regard to cheating were not complicated by fears that their dishonesty was regularly detected. The chief determining factor seemed to be, as will be indicated later, the difficulty of the test.

Table 1

MEAN NUMBER OF POINTS REPRESENTING
CHEATING ON EACH OF FIVE TESTS

Test	
1	2.38
2	.40
3	1.35
4	2.54
5	2.18

The attitude questionnaire used has been described elsewhere (5). It was constructed somewhat after the Thurstone (24) technique with modifications suggested by Seashore and Hevner (18). The questionnaires were scored after the fashion described by Likert, *et al.* (14). The corrected reliability of the questionnaire was $+.907 \pm .02$[1] when signed and $+.913 \pm .02$ when unsigned. By a system of secret identification marks it was possible to obtain both signed and unsigned questionnaires from each student in such a manner that the unsigned papers could later be identified. Although the differences between the two questionnaires were not statistically significant (5), those that were unsigned consistently indicated a more sympathetic attitude toward cheating. Because such seemed to be inherent evidence of their greater validity the unsigned scales were used in all of the computations reported below.

[1] All sigmas are approximate and were obtained from nomographs.

Measures of Cheating. As has been suggested, the basic cheating score was the gross difference between the score secretly given by the instructor and that given to himself by the student. For example, the student who reported a grade of 43 for himself after the paper had been scored by the instructor with a resulting grade of 35, was given a cheating score of 8 for that examination. The reliability of this cheating index was none too satisfactory. When a Pearson product-moment reliability coefficient was computed between gross cheating scores on the first two and last two tests and stepped up by use of the Spearman prophecy formula the result was $+.65 \pm .07$. Because of the asymmetry of the data this coefficient was checked against a similar index resulting from the use of Sheppard's method of unlike signs. There was no appreciable difference between the two coefficients.

Another cheating index was computed by getting the relationship between this gross cheating score and the proximity of the student's actual score to the maximum possible on that particular examination. This index made it possible to control in a measure the variable factor of temptation to cheat. For example, if a student's true score on a forty-five point test was 25, and if he raised his score to 35 by changing 10 questions, his cheating index corrected for "temptation to cheat," so to speak, would be .5; or 10 (the amount he cheated) divided by 20, (the difference between his true score and the maximum possible score). Similarly, a student might have the same "corrected" cheating index whose true score on a forty-five point examination was 35 but who reported for himself a grade of 40. The latter student cheated but half as much, but the temptation to do so was not so great.

FINDINGS

Range of Scores. The maximum score on the attitude questionnaire was 250 and the minimum 50. Because of the scoring method each statement on the fifty-item questionnaire was given a maximum point value of 5, which indicated sympathy for the practice of cheating, and a minimum value of 1, indicating antipathy for cheating. The mean obtained score for the 67 students was 133.48 with a standard deviation of 21.84. The maximum actual cheating score in terms of the number of points a student so inclined might add to his actual score for all examinations was 225, or the total number of items on all 5 tests. The mean cheating score for all 5 tests was 9.03, with a standard deviation of 12.66 — slightly less than 2 points per test. The distribution of the actual cheating scores was markedly skewed to the right. Twenty-four per cent of the subjects did not cheat on any of the 5 tests. One student, on the other hand, raised his score an average of 12 points (about 25 per cent) on each test.

Correlation Between Gross Cheating Score and Attitude Questionnaire Score. The Pearson product-moment coefficient of correlation between gross cheating scores and attitude questionnaire scores was practically zero. The obtained coefficient was $+.024 \pm .12$ SD which when corrected for attenuation became +.032 ± .12 SD. In other words, the attitude questionnaire used — a highly reliable one — gave no hint as to how students would behave. Verbal opinions regarding cheating on examinations were unrelated to actual cheating practices. Because of the lack of symmetry of the distribution of the cheating scores, the zero scores were eliminated and a coefficient computed between attitude questionnaire scores and the cheating score for those fifty-two students who cheated. The resulting coefficient was +.014 ± .13 SD.

No correlation ratios were computed for two reasons (9), first, the number of cases was too small to make such an index very significant, and, secondly, the correlation table did not indicate clearly any degree of non-linear relationship despite the implication that such might be the case in view of the data presented in Table 2 below.

Another method of expressing the lack of relationship between the unsigned attitude questionnaire scores and the gross cheating scores is by indicating the mean cheating scores for students ranking in the different quarters of the attitude questionnaire. These data are set forth in Table 2. The lack of symmetry of the distributions is again illustrated in the unusually large standard deviations. The difference between cheating scores for students in the highest and the lowest attitude questionnaire quarters is less than its standard deviation. The differences in cheating scores between the middle two and either the lowest or highest questionnaire quarters were equally insignificant statistically.

Relation Between Cheating and Temptation to Cheat. Defining "temptation to cheat" as it was above, namely, the difference between the true score on the test and the maximum possible score, and correlating this index with the actual cheating score yielded a Pearson coefficient of +.46 ± .09 SD. Whether or not a student cheated depended in much larger part upon how well he had prepared for the examination than upon any opinions he had stated about honesty in examinations. This is also brought out in the mean cheating score for test 2 as given in Table 1 [see page 249]. This particular test was by far the easiest of the series and consequently presented the least temptation to cheat.

Table 2

CHEATING SCORES FOR STUDENTS SCORING IN DIFFERENT QUARTERS
OF THE ATTITUDE QUESTIONNAIRE

	Quarters of the Attitude Questionnaire		
	Lowest	*Middle Two*	*Highest*
Mean cheating score	6.67	9.91	8.63
Standard deviation	11.60	12.15	11.8
Number of cases	17	34	16

When scores on the attitude questionnaire were correlated with cheating scores with temptation to cheat eliminated as a factor[2] the coefficient was $+.13 \pm .12$ SD, an insignificant and unreliable relationship. This coefficient seemed to imply further lack of validity on the part of the attitude questionnaire used.

Conclusions. The data presented in this study show that overt behavior, as measured by the amounts students will change their test papers when allowed to do their own grading, is not related to attitudinal scores derived from a highly reliable questionnaire measuring verbal opinions toward cheating on examinations.

DISCUSSION

It is impossible to say in advance of investigation whether the lack of relationship reported here between attitude questionnaire scores and overt behavior is generally true for measures of verbal opinion. Were that the case, the value of attitude scales and questionnaires would for most practical purposes be extremely slight. It would avail a teacher very little, for example, so to teach as to cause a change in scores on a questionnaire measuring attitude toward communism if these scores were in no way indicative of the behavior of his pupils.

It is difficult to devise techniques whereby certain types of overt behavior can be rather objectively estimated for the purpose of comparison with verbal opinions. Such studies despite their difficulty, would seem to be very much worthwhile. It is conceivable that our attitude testing program has gone far in the wrong direction. The available scales and technics are almost too neat. The ease with which so-called attitudinal studies can be conducted is attractive but the implications are equivocal.

REFERENCES

1. Allport, G. W. "Attitudes," *Handbook of Social Psychology.* C. Murchison (ed). Worcester, Mass.: Clark University Press, 1935. Chapter 17.
2. Bain, R. "Theory and Measurement of Attitude and Opinion," *Psychological Bulletin,* Vol. XXVII (1930), 357–379.
3. Cantril, Hadley. "General and Specific Attitudes," *Psychological Monographs,* Vol. XLII (1931–1932), 109 pp.
4. Corey, Stephen M. "Attitude Differences Between College Classes: A Summary and Criticism," *Journal of Educational Psychology,* Vol. XXVII (1936), 321–330.
5. Corey, Stephen M. "Signed *versus* Unsigned Attitude Questionnaires," *Journal of Educational Psychology,* Vol. XXVIII (1937), 145–148.
6. Droba, Daniel D. "The Effect of Various Factors on Militarism-Pacifism," *Journal of Abnormal and Social Psychology,* Vol. XXVI (1931–1932), 141–153.
7. ———. "The Nature of Attitude," *Journal of Social Psychology,* Vol. IV (1933), 443–463.
8. Faris, Ellsworth. "Attitudes and Behavior," *American Journal of Sociology,* Vol. XXXIV (1928), 271–281.

[2] This elimination of the factor "temptation to cheat" was not effected by the partial correlation technique. Rather, each gross cheating score was divided by the difference between the true score and the maximum possible score on that examination.

9. Garrett, H. E. *Statistics in Psychology and Education.* New York: Longmans, Green & Co., Inc., 1926, 211.
10. Garrison, K. C., and Burch, J. S. "A Study of Racial Attitudes of College Students," *Journal of Social Psychology*, Vol. IV (1933), 230–235.
11. Hinckley, E. D. "The Influence of Individual Opinions on Construction of an Attitude Scale," *Journal of Social Psychology*, Vol. III (1932), 283–296.
12. Katz, Daniel, and Allport, F. H. *Students' Attitudes.* Syracuse, N.Y.: Craftsman Press, Inc., 1931, 408 pp.
13. Likert, Renis. "A Technique for the Measurement of Attitudes," *Archives of Psychology*, Vol. XXII, (1932–1933), 55 pp.
14. Likert, Renis, *et al.* "A Simple and Reliable Method of Scoring the Thurstone Attitude Scales," *Journal of Social Psychology*, Vol. V (1934), 228–238.
15. Porter, Eliot. "Student Opinion On War." Unpublished M. A. thesis, University of Chicago, 1926.
16. Reinhardt, J. M. "Students and Race Feeling," *Survey*, Vol. LXI (1928), 239–240.
17. Rogers, H. W. "Some Attitudes of Students in the R.O.T.C.," *Journal of Educational Psychology*, Vol. XXVI (1935), 291–307.
18. Seashore, R. H., and Hevner, Kate. "A Time-saving Device for the Construction of Attitude Scales," *Journal of Social Psychology*, Vol. IV (1933), 366–372.
19. Sims, V. M., and Patrick, J. R. "Attitude Toward the Negro of Northern and Southern College Students," *Journal of Social Psychology*, Vol. VII (1936), 192–204.
20. Smith, Hattie N. "A Scale for Measuring Attitude about Prohibition," *Journal of Abnormal and Social Psychology*,Vol. XXVI (1931–1932), 429–437.
21. Stagner, Ross, and Drought, Neal. "Measuring Children's Attitudes Toward Their Parents," *Journal of Educational Psychology*, Vol. XXVI (1935), 169–176.
22. Stalnaker, J. M. "Attitudes Toward Intercollegiate Athletics," *School and Society*, Vol. XXXVII (1933), 499–504.
23. Stouffer, S. A. "Experimental Comparison of a Statistical and a Case History Technique of Attitude Research," *American Sociological Society Publications*, Vol. XXV (1931), 154–156.
24. Thurstone, L. L. "Attitudes Can Be Measured," *American Journal of Sociology*, Vol. XXXIII (1928), 529–554.
25. Zimmerman, C. C. "Types of Farmers' Attitudes," *Social Forces*, Vol. V (1927), 591–596.

28

Effects of Verbal and Nonverbal
Reinforcement in the Rorschach

Leonard R. Gross[1]

In the testing situation, substantial emphasis is placed on standard conditions for all persons being tested. To what extent is the examiner a significant part of test conditions in an unstructured testing situation? Gross provides some interesting data on this point. Are projective test results due to examinee responses to the test material or to the examiner?

While there is some awareness of the dynamic interactions between examiner (E) and subject (S), the problem of just how and to what extent test results are influenced by these interactions [has] not been fully explored. It has been demonstrated that Rorschach responses can be influenced by orientational sets stemming from pretest practice (3), pretest suggestion (1), and conscious instructions (2), as well as by E differences (4), but there are also reasons to believe that the E's actions throughout the testing situation may affect Rorschach performance (6).

It would be desirable to show that different cues given by the E are responded to without conscious awareness by the S, resulting in a changed Rorschach protocol. This study attempted to reinforce general human content on the Rorschach, using the verbal reinforcer *good* and the nonverbal reinforcer *nodding*. The Ss were randomly selected psychiatric patients.

On the basis of previously mentioned studies it can be hypothesized that: (a) the verbal reinforcer *good* will increase the frequency of the reinforced responses over that of a control group; (b) the nonverbal reinforcer *nodding* will increase frequency of the reinforced responses over that of a control group; and (c) the verbal stimulus will be more effective than the nonverbal stimulus in increasing the reinforced responses.

From Leonard R. Gross, "Effects of Verbal and Nonverbal Reinforcement in the Rorschach," *Journal of Consulting Psychology*, XXIII (February, 1959), pp. 66–68. Reprinted with the permission of the American Psychological Association.

[1] The author wishes to acknowledge his indebtedness to W. J. Eichman and B. M. Smith of the Roanoke, Virginia, Veterans Administration Hospital for their guidance and assistance.

METHOD

The Ss were selected from the psychiatric section of a university hospital on the following bases: (a) no history of organic brain damage, (b) a minimum of tenth grade education, and (c) no previous Rorschach experience. They were randomly selected from both the inpatient and outpatient services and placed in one of three groups in the following prescribed order: verbal reinforcement group (VR), nonverbal reinforcement group (NVR), or control group (C).

The Ss were excluded from the study if they did not meet both of the following criteria: (a) give at least one response involving general human content (humans, human-like creatures, human anatomy) during the first two cards, and (b) give three responses per card for all ten cards.

Out of the 46 Ss tested, 6 did not meet the criterion of three responses per card, and 10 failed to produce one human response within the first two cards, leaving a total of 30 Ss, with 10 Ss in each group. The mean age of all the Ss was 34, with a range of 17 to 53. The sexes were evenly divided. The diagnoses were mixed and included neurotics, character disorders, and psychotics. The mean level of education for the 30 Ss was the twelfth grade with 11 Ss having some college education. There were no significant differences in educational level among the three groups.

The Ss were presented with the complete set of Rorschach cards in the standard procedure for the free association with one variation in the Beck instructions, i.e., the inclusion of a sentence requesting three responses per card.

In the VR group, the E said "good" after each general human response. In the NVR group, the E nodded his head once after each human response. In the C group, the cards were administered with the attempt not to offer any cues.

Posttest interviews revealed that none of the Ss verbalized any awareness of the nature of the study.

RESULTS

The mean number of general human responses were compared for the three groups. As a result of heterogeneity of variance, a square root transformation was applied to the raw scores of the individual Ss. The means and variances of the transformed scores as well as the raw scores are found in Table 1. The analysis of variance of the transformed scores for the effect of reinforcement yielded an F significant at the .06 level. The groups were compared with each other by means of individual t tests. One-tailed t test was used as the direction was previously specified. The VR group gave more human responses than the C group at the .05 level of significance. The NVR group yielded more human responses than the C group at the .02 level of significance. The VR and NVR groups did not differ significantly from each other.

Table 1

RAW AND TRANSFORMED SCORES OF THE THREE GROUPS

Group	Raw Scores		Square Root Transformation	
	Mean	*Var.*	*Mean*	*Var.*
VR	8.7	11.34	2.86	.32
NVR	10.3	27.12	3.09	.59
C	6.3	6.77	2.39	.33

DISCUSSION

The results suggest that nodding or saying "good" will increase the frequency of preselected content responses in a Rorschach situation.

The first two hypotheses that the verbal reinforcer *good* and the nonverbal reinforcer *nodding* will increase the frequency of the reinforced responses appear to be substantiated. The third hypothesis that the verbal stimulus will be more effective than the nonverbal stimulus in increasing the reinforced response is rejected. The latter result is in conflict with previous studies using nonverbal cues (5). A possible explanation is that the use of a flashing light as a nonverbal reinforcer in other studies was not perceived as part of the testing situation, while nodding was.

The most obvious implication of the results is that one cannot discount even minimal or unconscious cues of the E when analyzing a Rorschach protocol. It follows that interpretations of test responses and test behavior should not be considered separately but in light of the total situation. Both the E's behavior and the S's conception of the testing situation are of import.

While the results in this study are suggestive of some of the variables involved in the complicated interaction between tester and testee or interviewer and interviewee, it remains for future research to make experimentally clear other variables operating in such situations. It is probable that other aspects of Rorschach responses can be reinforced in a similar manner, but exactly which responses occur in sufficient number to be reinforced as well as how much of a variation in E behavior is necessary to produce a change in a response level has not been answered. Another question is just how important are the variables that can be affected. It seems that if classical scoring methods are used these variables can have considerable effect on the dynamic picture.

SUMMARY

The main interest was interpersonal relations in a clinical situation. The study was designed to test the general hypothesis that E-S interaction is an important variable in test results. Thirty psychiatric patients were randomly selected and administered the free association of the Rorschach with the standard instructions modified so as to elicit three responses per card. The Ss were then presented with either verbal reinforcement *good,* nonverbal reinforcement *nodding,* or no reinforcement, whenever they gave a general human content response. It was found that both the VR and NVR groups gave significantly more of the reinforced responses than the C group. There were no significant differences between the two types of reinforcement. The findings suggest that cues given by the E can affect response categories. The necessity for avoiding interpretations of test protocols *in vacuo* was discussed.

REFERENCES

1. Abramson, L. S. "The Influence of Set for Area on Rorschach Test Results," *Journal of Consulting Psychology*, 15 (1951), 337–342.
2. Henry, Edith M., and Rotter, J. B. "Situational Influences on Rorschach Responses," *Journal of Consulting Psychology*, 20 (1956), 457–462.
3. Leventhal, H. "The Influence of Previous Perceptual Experience on the Variance of the Rorschach W and Z Scores," *Journal of Consulting Psychology*, 20 (1956), 93–98.
4. Sanders, R., and Cleveland, S. E. "The Relationship Between Certain E Personality Variables and S's Rorschach Scores," *Journal of Projective Techniques*, 17, (1953), 34–50.
5. Taffel, C. "Anxiety and the Conditioning of Verbal Behavior," *Journal of Abnormal and Social Psychology*, 51, (1955), 496–501.
6. Wickes, T. A., Jr. "Examiner Influence in a Testing Situation," *Journal of Consulting Psychology*, 20, (1956), 23–26.

29

Faking Personality Test Scores
in a Simulated Employment Situation

Alexander G. Wesman

In many situations where tests are used, the test taker has a considerable stake in the results of his examination. For example, test findings may determine whether an applicant gets a badly needed job. In such situations, the individual tries hard to make the test result in the way he thinks will best place him in the desired light. How sensitive are personality tests to this type of distortion? Wesman provides some interesting evidence on this question.

It has been the experience of most industrial psychologists that personality and interest inventories are ineffective when used for selection purposes (1, 2, 3, 4, 6, 7, 8). Ordinarily, many of the items can be seen through by most applicants, and the appropriate response given. The stereotypes which many employment officers seek (e.g., aggressive, self-confident salesmen) are also the stereotypes which the applicant expects the employer to be seeking. He is therefore all too likely to respond accordingly.

The data reported herein were collected in the course of a teaching demonstration. The author wished to impress a group of extension students at a large university with the untrustworthiness of personality inventories in employee selection. He gave the Bernreuter Personality Inventory to a group of 85 students with about the following instructions:

> I want you to pretend that you are applying for the position of salesman in a large industrial organization. You have been unemployed for some time, have a family to support, and want very much to land this position. You are being given this test by the employment manager. Please mark the answers you would give.

The following week, at the start of class, the same inventory was again distributed to the class, with the following instructions:

From Alexander G. Wesman, "Faking Personality Test Scores in a Simulated Employment Situation," *Journal of Applied Psychology*, XXXVI (April, 1952), pp. 112–113. Reprinted with the permission of the American Psychological Association and the author.

You are now applying for the position of librarian in a small town. You need the employment to support your family and meet financial obligations. Please mark the answers you would give.

Both administrations of the inventory occurred before there was any discussion of the field of personality measurement. The 73 students who took the test twice were a very heterogeneous group in age, academic background, industrial experience, and test sophistication. On the latter variable, they ranged from a young lady taking her first course since high school, with

Table 1

STUDENTS' SCORES ON A SELF-CONFIDENCE SCALE IN
TWO SIMULATED EMPLOYMENT SITUATIONS

	Self-Confidence Scale	Employment Situation	
		Salesman	Librarian
	Raw Score*		
Minus Values	260–241	1	
	240–221	2	
	220–201	18	
	200–181	27	7
	180–161	11	3
	160–141	2	6
	140–121	4	3
	120–101	2	6
	100– 81	1	8
	80– 61	2	3
	60– 41		3
	40– 21		
	20– 1		
Plus Values	0– 19	2	3
	20– 39		3
	40– 59		1
	60– 79		2
	80– 99		3
	100–119		4
	120–139		4
	140–159		1
	160–179		4
	180–199		2
	200–219		1
	220–239		2
	240–259		3
	260–279		1
	280–299	1	
	Total	73	73

* Minus scores represent greater self-confidence.

almost complete innocence of the test field, to a young man about to receive a Ph.D. in measurement, with several years of professional experience behind him.

Table 1 presents the score distributions obtained from these two administrations of the inventory for one of the measured traits, Self-Confidence (Scale F-1) (5). The table speaks eloquently for itself. If one saw these distributions without foreknowledge of how they were obtained, he could only conclude that they represented two quite different groups of people. The first column, "Salesman," is apparently composed of people who are, with three exceptions, above average in self-confidence. The second group, "Librarian," seems to contain almost as many below-average people on this trait as above-average (34 and 39, respectively). Those at the *fifth* percentile of the first group are more self-confident than the "applicants" at the *fiftieth* percentile of the second group. It is hard to realize that these "two" groups are really one and the same, except that the positions for which they are pretending to apply are different.

The demonstration is, of course, artificial. These are not true applicants. They are students pretending that they are applicants. Unquestionably, some of them are more test-wise (and stereotype-wise) than the average real applicant. Nonetheless, the demonstration seems to the author sufficiently dramatic to point up the susceptibility to faking of personality inventories in the industrial situations. Teachers who have not already used similar demonstrations with their students will find this approach rewarding.

REFERENCES

1. Benton, A. L., and Kornhauser, G. I. "A Study of 'Score Faking' on a Medical Interest Test," *Journal of the Association of American Medical Colleges*, 23 (1948), 57–60.

2. Bordin, E. S. "A Theory of Vocational Interests as Dynamic Phenomena," *Educational and Psychological Measurement*, 3 (1943), 49–65.

3. Cofer, C. N., Chance, June, and Judson, A. J. "A Study of Malingering on the MMPI," *Journal of Psychology*, 27 (1949), 491–499.

4. Ellis, A. "The Validity of Personality Questionnaires," *Psychological Bulletin*, 43 (1946), 385–440.

5. Flanagan, J. C. *Factor Analysis in the Study of Personality*. Stanford: Stanford University Press, 1935, p. 103.

6. Hunt, H. F. "The Effect of Deliberate Deception on Minnesota Multiphasic Personality Inventory Performance," *Journal of Consulting Psychology*, 12 (1948), 396–402.

7. Longstaff, H. P. "Fakability of the Strong Interest Blank and the Kuder Preference Record," *Journal of Applied Psychology*, 32 (1948), 360–369.

8. Paterson, D. G. "Vocational Interest Inventories in Selection," *Occupations*, 25 (1946), 152–153.

UNIT FOUR •

ASSESSING TYPICAL PERFORMANCE

SUGGESTED READINGS

Anastasi, Anne. *Psychological Testing* (2nd ed.). New York: The Macmillan Company, 1961.

In Part 4 of this text the author presents a rather detailed description and analysis of personality, interest and attitude inventories. Her emphasis is on relating basic methods of test construction to the utility of these tests in the practical setting.

Andersen, Harold H., and Anderson, Gladys L. *An Introduction to Projective Techniques.* Englewood Cliffs, N.J.: Prentice-Hall, Inc., 1951.

Although some years have passed since the publication of this text, the bulk of its content is of current interest. The majority of the tests discussed are still widely used and the procedures described are still accepted techniques. This source is recommended for persons who wish only to get a concise introduction to clinical testing.

Meehl, Paul E. *Clinical vs. Statistical Prediction.* Minneapolis: University of Minnesota Press, 1954.

This relatively small book contains a series of lectures delivered by the author on the general topic of measurement and its application in the clinical setting.

Super, Donald E., and Crites, John O. *Appraising Vocational Fitness* (rev. ed.). New York: Harper and Row, Publishers, 1962.

Chapters XV through XIX deal with the nature of personality variables and their measurement. These chapters present excellent reviews of the literature, and are thorough in their structuring of viewpoints based on empirical evidence.

The Teacher as Evaluator

The classroom teacher is the most active test maker of all. Besides the millions of standardized tests given annually in the schools, millions more teacher-made tests are constructed and applied. Probably no single factor weighs heavier in the evaluation of student progress than these teacher-made tests. Because of this, the quality of the teacher's work as an evaluator assumes considerable importance.

The reader, through experience as a test maker or test taker, no doubt realizes that a wide variation in quality is evident in classroom testing. However, the awareness of the problem does not necessarily suggest a solution. The purpose of this unit is to present information which can be used as the foundation for attacking the problems of evaluation in the classroom.

The pitfalls which ensnare teachers in their efforts to construct tools for assessing achievement are primarily these: tests do not square with the objectives which are stated (or implied by method) for the course, test items are not capably constructed, and the results of tests are inadequately interpreted.

This unit attempts to get at each of the above problems. Thelen, in Selection 30, writes adroitly on the matter of objectives and what they mean for measurement. Are there objectives, the achievement of which can be observed, but which are not reflected in the typical classroom test? Thelen probes this issue with considerable skill.

A long-standing controversy has gone on between persons who favor the essay test and those who feel that objective tests can achieve many, if not most, of the goals claimed as the province of the essay test. Although the most active period of research on the relative status of the two types of tools was some years ago, a considerable battle continues at the nonempirical level.

Ashburn's views, in Selection 34, are representative of a number of studies conducted at the time the controversy was most heated. His findings still have relevance.

The versatility of the objective item is one of its great advantages, but many authors feel that in a typical situation this characteristic is not exploited. The ideas provided by Mosier, Myers, and Price in Selection 31 not only provide guidelines for good test item writing, but also show how objective items may be applied to many purposes beyond mere assessment of factual knowledge. As an example, in Selection 33, Palmer has applied objective tests to the area of English, which is known for its wide use of essays as a basis for evaluation. The student may wish to list the objectives of English instruction and compare Palmer's test with the full range of these course goals.

Much writing has centered around the teacher's report to parents. Richardson's comments (Selection 32) are recommended for their conciseness and summary quality on this topic. Her emphasis is the well-taken point that parents should receive more than a single kind of information about their child's work. This implies that assessments of achievement be based on more than a single type of information.

Briefly then, this unit is devised to help teachers become better test builders. Accordingly it emphasizes three basic points: the outcomes of instruction to be evaluated, how to construct tests which more effectively assess these outcomes, and what to report to parents.

30

The Triumph of "Achievement" over Inquiry in Education

Herbert A. Thelen

In his article, Thelen raises a significant question regarding the objectives of instruction and the apparent objectives reflected by many examinations. Ideally, the objectives of instruction should determine the objectives represented on the measuring devices. Before a teacher makes an examination, he may wish to give thought to the points presented by Thelen.

Principals, teachers, parents, professors, or practice teachers who try to improve instruction in the classroom soon find themselves in a trap.

It is a fascinating trap built by people who know better. The fact that they built the trap very much against their will does not make the trap any less a trap. But it does show that one can get swept along by forces at work in the larger society.

In big, broad terms, the trap is the conflict between the Organization Man, who continually seeks to reassure himself of his place in society, and the Inquiring Man, who seeks to better himself and his society. In narrower terms, the conflict is between the way we try to teach children and the way we measure what they have learned. In middle-sized terms, the conflict is between education and achievement as school goals.

CLOSE-UP OF A TRAP

I should like to begin by describing the trap — by reporting on the conflicts and contradictions that make up the trap. So I shall talk about practices, not sentiments or theories.

My testimony comes mostly from thoughtful teachers who think wistfully about the possibility of improving their own courses. They are tired of just

Reprinted from Herbert A. Thelen, "The Triumph of 'Achievement' over Inquiry in Education," *The Elementary School Journal*, LX (January, 1960), by permission of The University of Chicago Press and the author. Copyright 1960 by The University of Chicago Press, with the Department of Education of The University of Chicago. Pp. 190–197.

covering the ground, by which they mean exposing the pupil to a prescribed body of already organized ideas. They would like to get some inquiry going. They would like to see pupils study because there is something important to learn, something important to the pupils, that is.

As these teachers see it, the chief obstacle to making this shift is the way achievement is now defined by the public and measured by tests. The teachers perceive that their pupils are realistic enough to know that their job is to pass tests; this is what academic aspiration means; this is what achievement means to pupils and to the public.

Of course, some of these teachers say, "We don't mark exclusively on tests. We take other things into account." But these "other things" are subjective and unconfidently known. At best, they merely blur the harsh outline of test results.

And here we can point to the heart of the conflict. Teachers try to set up learning experiences based on one set of views while they measure achievement based on a different set of views. The disparity can be disconcerting to pupils, parents, and concerned citizens as well as teachers. Let's look at some aspects of the conflict.

Pupils feel that testing puts them in competition with one another. But the teacher wants them to co-operate, not compete. In class discussion and class projects, the teacher seems to want class members to share ideas. But on tests, pupils see their classmates as rivals who are required to get the better of one another.

There are even conflicting economic connotations here. In testing it is usually assumed that there are not enough A's to go around; in teaching it is assumed that everyone can have an A — if he earns it.

Our tests teach pupils that academic status, not learning, is the goal of education. If learning were the goal, achievement would be measured as the difference between pre-tests and post-tests on the material of the course. Since pre-tests are seldom used, the teacher has no way of knowing how much the pupil learned. The mark testifies to final status, not to what was learned during the course.

Pupils work for marks rather than in response to the challenge of the subject. The purpose of learning is to gain status, symbolized in a mark, rather than to master the discipline of the subject. Good marks mean promotion and the regard of adults. Snap subjects and "soft" teachers are the sensible route to good marks. Moreover, acceptance or capitulation by the teacher to the mark-getting routine tends to free him from his professional obligation to make study meaningful in its own right.

Pupils study the teacher rather than the subject. Often the main object of inquiry in the classroom is the sort of question the teacher is likely to ask, the bases he uses for marking, his biases and enthusiasms. This experience, over the years, has no doubt helped mold the Organization Man, who studies the boss for the same reasons that he once studied the teacher. In good teaching, the demands the pupil faces come from the problem situation, not from the teacher.

Learning becomes a kind of academic hit-and-run. The class hits the test and runs on to a new unit. Once knowledge is tested, it can be safely forgotten. This notion directly contradicts the idea of education as a "deepening and enriching" experience. The unit plan, originally designed to organize learning into significant wholes, has become a package plan, with each package wrapped up by a unit test.

Pupils learn that specific information is an end in itself rather than the means to broad understanding of universal principles. The easiest way to make a reliable test is to use a large number of independent, specific, and separate items. This discovery about testing dealt a severe blow to the educational goal of understanding. The educated citizen is the quiz kid, not the wise man. And cramming for examinations, whether in school or on TV shows, is the basic learning process.

Pupils learn from experience with tests that all questions have clear-cut answers certified by authority. Such "thought questions" as the teacher uses are asked just to keep conversation going. Compared with "getting the facts," the process of reasoning from data to probable conclusions is at best an intriguing parlor game. The teacher, himself conditioned by tests, may strive to be a walking encyclopedia rather than a guide to inquiry. We present to children a world in which all the lovely mottled grays of the adult world are squeezed into black-and-white certainties.

Post-Sputnik pressures, aided by the nationally standardized test, are rapidly turning the school into a processing plant rather than a place for inquiry. In this processing plant, the teacher's role is that of a technician, not a professional. The professional, like the learner, must be aware of alternatives in a situation, choose among them, and test the consequences of his choice. The technician, like the rote learner, treats all situations alike, using prescribed rules and memorized procedures.

The range of choices that require mature judgment of the teacher is rapidly narrowing, and with this change the climate for inquiry is becoming less favorable. If we no longer trust the teacher, our confidence might be restored if we gave him better preparation, especially in his major subject. Detailed specifications for content, method, and activities were appropriate for war-time crash programs by the armed forces charged with the task of turning out technicians in quantity, but crash programs of this nature will not produce enlightened citizens and creative leaders.

The pupil is being taught to escape from freedom for the sake of material reward and social approval. Freedom can exist only if self-knowledge is valued. Our procedures for measuring achievement do not help the pupil find out who he is or discover his strengths and weaknesses as a person. Our tests only tell us how well the pupil is conforming to a specified 1960 super-technical model.

But we do have a conscience. Having conditioned the pupil, through awards and other forms of social approval, into submissiveness, we then propose to put him in a liberal arts college to develop his human spirit!

Our 1960 super-technical model is defined by tests that give the pupil feedback about his growing strengths, his self-concept, and his abilities. These are expressed in terms that we prescribe, not necessarily in the areas where growth and development are taking place.

In teaching, we hunt for growth areas because it is through them that the pupil puts forth effort and gives attention. In testing, we have to disregard categories of information of unique importance to particular individuals, partly because we have to test everybody with the same instrument and partly because we simply do not know the ways in which children at various stages of growth relate to ideas and subject disciplines. Thus we teach the pupil that his own life and interests are irrelevant to education.

What do our present practices in measuring achievement contribute to education? Tests can be used to supply extrinsic motivation. This kind of motivation is considered undesirable by those who regard pupils as human beings rather than as manpower for technological enterprises.

Tests can also be used to spot children who need help. Many pupils have received remedial help because an appropriate screening test revealed their need. Most of us would agree that it is desirable to use tests in this way.

Tests can be used to guide teaching. But tests are generally given too late to serve this purpose. By the time the test results are known, the class has already moved on to a new unit. To help guide instruction, the teacher may, of course, devise short questionnaires of his own and use them at frequent intervals.

As diagnostic tools for helping the pupil understand himself and set his life goals, tests have little value for at least two reasons. First, what is past is past. We do not go back. We are satisfied to say how much the pupil learned, but not to help him master presumably important learnings. Second, achievement tests are not constructed to tell much about a pupil's unique strengths. This fact about our tests is an unfortunate one, since the pupil's strengths are all that he and the teacher have to build on.

ALTERNATIVES

Having described school practices in destructive, cynical, or perhaps honest, terms, I now ask: Do we have to be content with this kind of evaluation?

The answer is no, and many test-makers would be the first to agree. Their responsibility for the present state of affairs is no more and no less than the responsibility of atomic physicists for Hiroshima. The bomb was dropped because of a complex alignment of social forces. The triumph of "achievement" over education is a sign of the times rather than the intention of educational evaluators. Moreover, like atomic energy, evaluation is taking an increasingly important place in our lives.

But the proper use of evaluation will not come about through the single-handed efforts of evaluators, teachers, or any other one group. Evaluation will contribute to education rather than to narrow goals in achievement only after widespread effort by many groups. As far as each school is concerned, the problem involves the attitudes, expectations, and goals of the entire community.

How can we return to the goal of education?

First, we could try to measure the pupil's growth as a whole, unique person, with his own goals, his own way of viewing people and the world. Individuals differ in their way of life. By *way of life* I mean the pattern of attitudes, abilities, and habits by which an individual lives and develops his strengths. If we could determine each child's general pattern, we could follow him as a whole person and help him make choices appropriate to the effective development of his way of life. We could be concerned with how he is organizing subject matter in his subjective world and the relationship between this world and his behavior in all situations.

But such evaluations can be achieved only if we start with children. We will not succeed if we start by asking: What does chemistry teach? What does history teach? We shall have to ask: How is the pupil assimilating the discipline of chemistry? Of history? How well is he mastering the method of the chemist? Of the historian? What do his learnings in chemistry and history mean for his way of life? This last question is the proper concern of the teacher, and it is a very different concern from the one that now motivates schools and communities.

My second suggestion recognizes that it is the purpose of education not only to develop individual powers but also to prepare effective citizens. Our schools have the responsibility of helping children live as self-realizing people, not in a vacuum or a hermitage, but in a complex society. In short, we recognize that children are going to have to take roles in a real world. They are going to manage others; interpret the world around them; make discoveries; create social, political, and economic alternatives; ferret out facts; and persuade, promote, criticize, analyze, guide, console, and teach.

Education is at least partly an inquiry into the kinds of roles boys and girls may be fitted for. We must not seal off pathways before children's tendencies are thoroughly demonstrated, and we must always allow for unexpected changes in tendencies. But we can ask, as the Strong Vocational Interest Blanks ask in regard to occupations: What kinds of roles are children developing potential for? And we could keep records through the school years of profiles that show the child's aptitudes and readiness for certain roles.

RECOMMENDATIONS

The first thing we must do is to free the schools from the pressures that keep them from their proper job of educating boys and girls. We must reduce the pressures, so fashionable at present, for achievement, for covering ground, for mass production of pseudo-experts.

Let the schools concentrate on doing something for our children. Let the others — college faculties and employers — worry about what they are going to do about our pupils after the schools have done all they can. In other words, let's stick to our proper job of saying what has happened to our pupils and what goals they are moving toward. Let each college decide whether the student is ready to embark on its study program. Let the industrialists decide whether they want to hire him. Let the parents decide whether they are satisfied with him. These are their decisions, not ours.

Many of us in the schools know that our marks have always been monstrous. They try to signify two things that cannot be measured together.

They try to measure the pupil's standing, judged against standards we have assumed (often erroneously) the higher school or college desired.

Marks also try to measure what the child has done compared with what he might be capable of doing. The criteria for measuring the pupil's standing must be the same for all pupils. Yet the criteria for measuring capability or growth of powers must differ from one pupil to the next.

The confusion over marks is a symptom of the larger confusion over the mission of the school. Let us commit ourselves to the educational job defined earlier, and let us find appropriate means for describing the results.

My second recommendation has to do with both the means and the measurement of education. Let us confront the pupil with the events, the ideas, the attitudes, and the practices that he must cope with. Let us help him cope with them, and from time to time let us assess his growth in the ability to cope.

In teaching let us use situations that are vital and lifelike, though not necessarily a slice of natural life. The situations we provide should have the validity of significant human activity. They should release the essentially dramatic quality of purposeful human endeavor. In testing, perhaps the simplest way of stating the recommendation is to say that more *complete* situations should be used.

I would like to see us experiment with sound movies. The pupil views a situation on the screen, tells what he would do in the situation, and justifies his response.

I would like to see us make much more use of role-playing. Certainly one of the major goals of the disciplines of history, anthropology, and psychology is to develop the individual's ability to put himself in the place of people who lived at other times and other places. In role-playing, we can watch the pupil as he tries to feel and understand situations from another's point of view. As we watch, we should be as interested in the child's actions and expressions as in his words. I would like to see these techniques used in our assessment of the pupil's powers as manifested in performance, not in puzzles.

I do not see any reason why we cannot use situations in the community to probe development. We have had a lot of talk about democracy. All right, let the pupil see a club or a board of directors in action. Let him come back and tell us about it. Let's note what he observes, what he responds to, what is important to him. Isn't this the sort of information we need to plan further activities and to assess educational growth?

I would like to get at the ideas to which the pupil is committed. What ideas are important to him? What causes is he nurturing? Is he developing any life goals? Any compelling purposes? Are his intellectual interests expanding?

To discover answers to these questions, we must occasionally give the pupil opportunities for free choice. In planning his work, we can offer him six or eight kinds of activities from which to choose. Which does he select? Why?

I maintain that this is relevant and interpretable information and that it has the feel of life. But let's let him choose among activities, not just among phrases written on a piece of paper.

The Doctor and the Detective

John H. Watson, M.D., wrote what may well be the longest and the most complete case study on record. His subject was Sherlock Holmes, the detective. In *A Study in Scarlet*, Watson attempts, after some weeks of acquaintance, to assess Holmes, and he writes out a report card in the best achievement tradition.

He certifies Holmes' knowledge of literature, philosophy, and astronomy to be nil. Politics — feeble. Botany — strong on poisons but weak on practical gardening. Geology — recognizes mud stains from various parts of London. Chemistry — profound. Sensational literature — knows "every detail of every horror perpetrated in the last century." Anatomy — "accurate, but unsystematic." Good violinist, expert amateur athlete, "good practical knowledge of British law." And Watson, with rare insight into his own evaluative processes, labels the report card "Sherlock Holmes — *his limits*" (italics mine).

But with all this observation, which is quite accurate, Watson misses the essence of Holmes, and Sherlock has to tell him, finally, what his powers and abilities are and what social role organizes these powers and abilities into an effective personality and contributor to society.

What Watson missed, because he had never seen Holmes perform in an appropriate situation, was his intuition for unraveling crimes, his ability to apply special knowledge to problems, his conscious use of rules of deduction, his habit of observation. And the report card could never have led Watson to predict Holmes' role of "consulting detective."

Watson, I am afraid, embodies the achievement point of view in our schools. He represents the traditional, academic, propaedeutic view of education, which asks after achievement in its own categories but fails to comprehend, and therefore to educate, the child.

Sherlock is unique, as human personality is unique; and he represents that part of every man which must be understood within its own frame of reference and commitments. The categories useful for understanding Sherlock are not the categories most useful for understanding Watson.

Watson talks about his own education in language that is typical of certification and achievement. He "took his degree" and proceeded "to go through the course prescribed for surgeons."

Holmes never talks about his education. But he does talk about problems to be solved, inquiries to be conducted, and methods of thought that he values. For the most part, Holmes educated himself. His studies were "very desultory and eccentric, but he . . . amassed a lot of out-of-the-way knowledge which would astonish his professors." And the habit of inquiry — which the university could not stamp out — survived.

Can we say as much for our pupils?

31

Suggestions for the Construction
of Multiple-Choice Test Items

Charles I. Mosier, M. Claire Myers, and Helen G. Price

Effective use of objective tests depends first upon the skill of the item writer. Mosier et al., suggest important techniques of item construct which they illustrate with applications. Objective testing has often been associated with assessing factual knowledge. The reader should note the suggestions for applying objective tests to outcomes of instruction beyond mere factual content.

In writing items in a particular area it is possible, but not very profitable, to use the inspiration technique. One reads until he is inspired to write an item, jots it down, and then reads some more. Those concepts that fall readily into item form get tested over and over again; those more difficult to test go untested. This procedure is likely to result, among other things, in very spotty coverage of the subject-matter area. In writing items, as in other activities, planning is essential.

The present paper presents three work tools for the construction of multiple-choice items: definition of the subject-matter area to be covered and systematic sampling of it; a check list of the kinds of questions which can be asked; and a summary of criteria for multiple-choice items.

Although these materials were developed for use in examining for public personnel selection, they are applicable, with minor changes, in the other fields of test construction.

To cover a subject-matter area adequately, whether in educational testing, merit system examining, or aptitude testing, the first step should be a definition of the area or areas to be tested. Even in a limited field, all possible questions cannot be asked; it is necessary to resort to a sampling of the field. If, however, the individual's performance on the sample is to represent his performance in the entire field, it is a truism that the sample must represent the field; the sample to be representative cannot be left to chance,

From Charles I. Mosier, M. Claire Myers, and Helen G. Price, "Suggestions for the Construction of Multiple-Choice Test Items," *Educational and Psychological Measurement*, V (Autumn, 1945), pp. 261–271. Reprinted with the permission of publisher and authors.

but should be planned. The definition of the field states the limits which must be reached; it does not prohibit going beyond those limits. If items are written outside the boundary of the definition, they can usually still be used; if no items are written on an area within the field, that part of the area has not been sampled. A picture may help to visualize this.

The entire circle [in Figure 1] represents the particular subject-matter area, e.g., knowledge of elementary and intermediate statistics. Each subdivision represents a set of related concepts within the broader field. For example, *1* might be the concepts relating to frequency distributions; *2* those relating to central tendency; *3* those relating to dispersion, etc. Unless the total area is defined by correctly drawing the total circle, e.g., closing the circle in the lower right quadrant, the existence of the sixth subdivision escapes our attention.

Figure 1

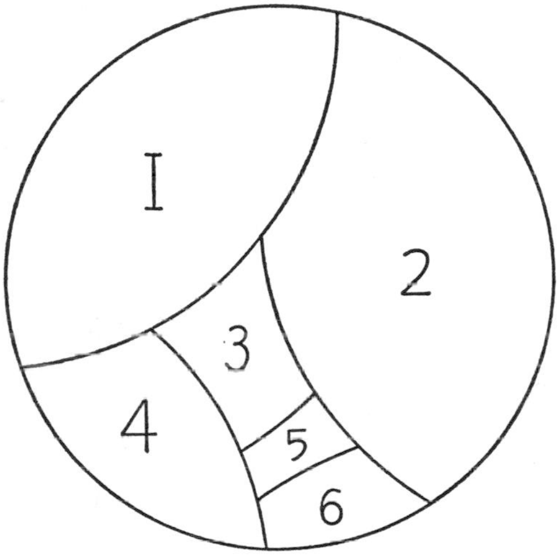

It is essential, if one is to test adequately for a knowledge of the principles and techniques in statistics, that he be prepared to include test items in each of the areas. It is not necessary to include one from every area in every examination; one should not, however, include three from section *1* and none from section *6* unless he is prepared to say that the concepts in *1* are very important and those in *6* are inappropriate to the purposes of the particular examination.

After the area has been outlined, the next step is the identification of its significant subdivisions. This can be accomplished by listing the important concepts, topics, principles, or subdivisions of the field or of the various types of skills which contribute to the total. This list represents the specifications for the set of items. It should not, generally, be a list of the items to be written, but of the sub-areas to be covered, with each area to be sampled by several items. Preparing such a list assumes either an authoritative outline already set up, or an over-all familiarity with the field. The chapter headings in a text or the paragraph headings within a chapter constitute one source of such a listing. Once made the list is important: first, as an index to the resulting assembly of items; second, as a guide to future item construction; and third, as a more elaborate definition of the types of items contained in the subject-matter area. Table 1, showing an outline of statistics, is presented as an illustration, not necessarily as a model.

Once the list of concepts, principles, skills or topics to be tested has been completed, appropriate sources or sections of the source should be used in constructing the items.

It is useful to distinguish between the concept, or the skill, being tested and the kind of question asked to test that concept. A further distinction which should be made is between the kind of question asked (e.g., what, why, who?) and the form of the test item used to ask the question (e.g., true-

Table 1

OUTLINE OF STATISTICS

1. General
     Interpretations
     Life Tables
     "Severity Rate"
     Simple computations
     Sources and bibliographies
     Tabular presentation of results
     Terms and symbols
     Planning surveys
     Compound interest formula

2. Frequency Distributions
     Class intervals and limits
     Bimodality
     Symmetry
     Skewness
     Frequency polygon
     Kurtosis
     Percentiles
     Normal curve properties
     Binomial expansion

3. Charts, Graphs and Index Numbers
     Ogive
     Moving average
     Straight-line equation
     Semi-log paper
     Interpolation and extrapolation
     Pictograms and circle diagrams
     Gantt, Lorenz, ratio, and time
       charts
     Graphic computation
     Index numbers

4. Central Tendency
     Mean
     Median
     Mode
     Harmonic mean
     Geometric mean

5. Dispersion
     General
     Sigma
     Average deviation
     Quartile deviation

6. Correlation
     Interpretation and use
     Scatter diagram
     Pearson
     Other coefficients
     Regression lines
     Partial and multiple
     Coefficient of alienation
     Standard error of estimate

7. Non-Linear Regression
     Trend lines
     Population curves
     Eta and Blakeman's test

8. Sampling
     Methods: random, weighted
     Sampling errors
     Interpretation, S.E., and C.R.
     Combination of samples
     Probability theory

false, multiple-choice, completion). We are concerned here primarily with multiple-choice items and the *form* of the test item will not be considered further. In Table 2 is a check list of some of the kinds of questions which may be asked together with illustrative examples based on the concept of central tendency.

Table 2

TYPES OF QUESTIONS

1. Definition
a. What means the same as . . . .
b. What conclusion can be drawn from . . . .
c. Which of the following statements expresses this concept in different terms?
   Example: The value which is determined by adding all of the scores and dividing by the number of cases is known in statistics as the:
   (1) arithmetic mean;
   (2) median;
   (3) mode;
   (4) harmonic mean;
   (5) average deviation.

2. Purpose
a. What purpose is served by . . . .
b. What principle is exemplified by . . . .
c. Why is this done . . . .
d. What is the most important reason for . . . .
   Example: The mean is obtained for the purpose of providing:
   (1) a single number to represent a whole series of numbers;
   (2) the central point in a series;
   (3) a measure of group variability;
   (4) an indication of the most frequent response given;
   (5) an estimate of the relationship between two variables.

3. Cause
a. What is the cause of . . . .
b. Under which of the following conditions is this true . . . .
   Example: From which of the following measures of central tendency will the sum of the deviations equal zero?
   (1) the mean;
   (2) the mode;
   (3) the median;
   (4) an arbitrary origin;
   (5) any measure of central tendency.

4. Effect
a. What is the effect of . . . .
b. If this is done, what will happen?
c. Which of the following should be done (to achieve a given purpose)?
   Example: The arithmetic mean of 55 cases is 83.0. If 3 of the cases, with values of 82, 115, and 130 are deleted from the data, the mean of the remaining 52 cases will be: (1) 81.50; (2) 77.05; (3) 83.00; (4) 84.50; (5) 94.08.

5. Association

What tends to occur in connection (temporal, causal or concomitant association) with . . . . (Cont. on p. 276)

Example: If the distribution of scores is skewed positively, the mean will be:
(1) lower than the median;
(2) the same as the median;
(3) higher than the median;
(4) relatively unaffected;
(5) the same as the mode.

6. Recognition of Error

Which of the following constitutes an error (with respect to a given situation)?
   Example: The mean should not be used as the measure of central tendency when:
(1) the distribution of scores is significantly skewed;
(2) there are a large number of cases;
(3) a non-technical report is to be prepared;
(4) the data are continuous;
(5) other statistical formulae are to be computed.

7. Identification of Error

a. What kind of error is this?
b. What is the name of this error?
c. What recognized principle is violated?
   Example: In computing the mean of a distribution from grouped data, the sums of the deviations above and below the arbitrary origin were found to be 127 and 189, respectively. The final value for the mean was in error. Of the following possibilities, that one which is most likely to have caused the error is that the computor:
(1) failed to note the correct sign in adding the mean of the deviations to the assumed origin;
(2) used an assumed mean higher than the true mean;
(3) omitted some of the cases in tabulating the data;
(4) divided by the wrong number of cases;
(5) multiplied by the wrong class interval value.

8. Evaluation

What is the best evaluation of . . . (for a given purpose) and for what reason?
   Example: When the number of cases is small, e.g., less than 20, and the magnitude of the values is likewise small, the use of an assumed mean in the computation of the mean can best be evaluated as:
(1) less efficient than computation from actual values;
(2) likely to distort the value obtained by the introduction of a constant error;
(3) more accurate than the use of actual values;
(4) neither better nor worse than computation by other methods;
(5) applicable only if the distribution is reasonably symmetrical.

9. Difference

What is the important difference between . . . .
   Example: Of the following statements, that one which characterizes the essential difference between the mean and the median as measures of the central tendency of a distribution is that:

(1) the magnitude of each score does not contribute proportionately to the computation of the median but does for the mean;
(2) the median is a point whereas the mean is a distance;
(3) the mean is less affected by extreme values;
(4) the median is easier to compute;
(5) the median is more generally used.

10. Similarity

What is the important similarity between . . . .
Example: The mean and median are the same in that they are both measures of:
(1) central tendency;
(2) distance;
(3) position;
(4) variation;
(5) relationship.

11. Arrangement

In the proper order, (to achieve a given purpose or to follow a given rule) which of the following comes first (or last or follows a given item)
Example: In computing the mean for data already grouped in class intervals the most efficient first step is to:
(1) determine the arbitrary origin and enter the deviation values;
(2) find the midpoints of the class intervals;
(3) multiply the frequency in each interval by the midpoint of the interval;
(4) add the column of scores;
(5) find the reciprocal of the total number of cases.

12. Incomplete Arrangement

In the proper order, which of the following should be inserted here to complete the series?
Example: In deriving the formula for computing the mean from grouped data using an arbitrary origin the following steps were taken:

a. $X' = \dfrac{X - A}{i}$;

b. $\Sigma X = i\Sigma X' + NA$;

c. $\dfrac{\Sigma X}{N} = A + \dfrac{i\Sigma X'}{N}$.

The step which is implied between steps (a) and (b) is:
(1) solving (a) for X;
(2) summing (a) over the N cases;
(3) multiplying by i;
(4) adding A to both terms of (a);
(5) dividing by N.

13. Common Principle

All of the following items except one are related by a common principle:
a. What is the principle?
b. Which item does not belong? (Cont. on p. 278)

c. Which of the following items should be substituted?

Example: All except one of the following items (arithmetic mean, median, mode, and quartile) are measures of central tendency; of the following statistics, that one which could be substituted in the series for the item improperly included is the:

(1) harmonic mean for quartile;
(2) average deviation for mode;
(3) range for quartile;
(4) standard deviation for quartile;
(5) 50th percentile for median.

14. Controversial Subjects

Although not every one agrees on the desirability of ———, those who support its desirability do so primarily for the reason that:

Example: Although not every one agrees that the mean is the best measure of central tendency, those who advocate its general use base their recommendation on the fact that the mean:

(1) has the smallest sampling error;
(2) is easiest to compute;
(3) is most readily understood;
(4) is the most typical score;
(5) is not affected by extreme values.

Frequently a concept can be tested by a variety of questions; for some concepts only one kind of question is appropriate; for still others, several are applicable, but one or two are clearly most appropriate. To secure adequate sampling in the construction of items on any concept, the concept should be checked against the list and as many items written as seem appropriate, each asking a different kind of question. By writing items which test knowledge of a concept through several kinds of questions, it is frequently possible to sample the area at several levels of difficulty, ranging from the simplest to the most difficult.

The construction of a number of different items on each concept included in the outline of the subject-matter field provides a more effective means of meeting the objective of those who feel that internal weighting is essential to give the appropriate emphasis to the more important concepts. The proponents of internal weighting argue that since certain concepts are more important, extra credit should be given for the questions on those concepts. If the desirability of such extra credit is granted, the weighting is more easily and more reliably accomplished by including extra questions than by doubling the credits for a single question, thereby doubling the effect of measurement errors in the question. The availability of several different questions on each concept makes it possible to include more than one for any that are considered more important. These considerations apply whether items are being constructed for a single examination or for a central file.

The check list, *Types of Questions*, in Table 2 is not intended to be all-inclusive nor is it intended to prescribe the language to be used in asking any particular kind of question. Rather it is a guide to assist in formulating questions and a check to help insure that all of the appropriate kinds of questions will be asked.

Once the concept to be tested and the kinds of questions to be asked have been determined, there remains the task of framing objective questions which will accomplish the intended purpose.

The task can be stated simply: To phrase a question in such terms that (a) all prospective examinees understand the task set; (b) those who have the requisite degree of knowledge will give the intended answer; and (c) all who do not will give another answer. Fashioning such an item is more difficult than formulating the problem. The criteria in Table 3 are set up as aids in constructing such items. They are by no means original; they have been assembled from various sources and are summarized here for convenience. The criteria in the table were formulated for use in merit system examining; each one, however, with slight changes in wording or in emphasis is applicable in other examining settings. These criteria should be applied to each item written; the item should not be considered as complete until the writer is satisfied that it meets each criterion.

Table 3

CRITERIA FOR CONSTRUCTING MULTIPLE-CHOICE ITEMS[1]

I. General Validity
1. Can we readily predict that those candidates who know the answer would, on the average, be better qualified for the purpose at hand than those who do not?
2. Is the item thought provoking, rather than calling merely for scraps of information?

II. Item Content
1. Is the content of the item important enough to justify a question — not so specialized that only a few highly selected experts could know the answer?
2. Does the subject matter of the item appear to be reasonably related to some type of activity appropriately covered by the test?
3. Are the subject matter and the phrasing of the item such that no emotional antagonism will be aroused on the part of the public and the candidate? How would the item look in a newspaper unfriendly to the merit system? (Although this criterion is primarily formulated for merit system examiners, it has application in education testing; there is no need to antagonize students unduly in testing them.)
4. Is the content of the item something which can be learned without having actually been on the job itself?
5. Does the subject matter mirror a consensus of current authoritative beliefs and opinions, rather than the opinion of one individual?
6. Could general terms be used to make the item usable in more than one testing situation. If the principle is applicable only in one situation, has this fact been flagged by specific reference in the item?
7. Does the item call for a knowledge of concepts, reasons, and relationships, rather than for mere factual information, whenever the former is appropriate? (Cont. on p. 280)

[1] These criteria, stated in terms of merit system examining, can be made applicable to other testing situations by appropriate changes in wording.

8. Could any part of the item, such as modifying phrases, qualifications, etc., be omitted without significantly influencing the distribution of responses?

III. Item Structure
   A. Premise
   1. Is a definite task clearly and unambiguously set, so that all candidates work on essentially the same problem? Is it sufficiently clear that an informed candidate could give the correct answer from the premise if it were written as a completion item with no choices given?
   2. Is the idea stated clearly and directly, with the answer an important part of the statement — not buried at the end of a preposition in a parenthetical "which clause"?
   3. Does the premise, combined with each choice, constitute a complete unit of thought, both ideologically and grammatically?
   4. Does the premise, combined with the right answer, constitute a definite and true concept? Is the premise phrased to require something more (the correct choice) for completeness?
   5. If the question is stated negatively, can it be restated in positive terms? If not, has the attention of the candidate been directed toward the negative phrasing of the question?
   6. Is the premise phrased to ask for the best rather than the correct answer whenever possible?
   7. Is the premise stated so complexly that the item becomes a test of whatever is taken to understand a complex premise rather than a test of knowledge or reasoning? If so, is this what was intended?
   8. Does the premise avoid all unnecessary content which might give away the answers to other items?
   9. If there are other answers conceivably as good as the intended answer, is the premise limited by the phrase, "of the following"?

   B. Correct Answer
   1. Is there one and only one correct answer to the problem as set by the premise? If the intended answer is merely the best of those given, is this indicated clearly in the premise?
   2. Do competent authorities agree on the correct answer?
   3. Could the candidate distinguish the correct answer from the incorrect answers without having read the premise? If so, the item is in need of revision.
   4. Does selecting the correct choice require a real or reasoned understanding of the concept rather than mere recall or recognition?
   5. Is there no possibility that a candidate may select the correct response simply because it is the only one containing the same words or phrases as the premise or because of other external characteristics?

   C. Distracters
   1. Are the distracters such that a person likely to be inferior on the job will think they are correct? Is each distracter so plausible that someone not knowing the correct answer will choose it?
   2. If there are popular misconceptions in the field, are the distracters designed to attract candidates holding those misconceptions? Can familiar or stereotyped phrasing in the distracters be used to make

them sound plausible? Can words or phrases similar to those in the premise be deliberately planted in the distracters to give them added plausibility? Can this increased plausibility be achieved without distracting too many of the qualified candidates as well? Are specific determiners, such as "always" or "never," avoided?

3. Are [the] distracters, as well as the intended answer, related to the premise, both ideologically and grammatically?
4. Are there no distracters so nearly correct that well qualified persons are likely to accept them and be able to defend their answers?
5. Can the question be answered by someone who knows, not that the intended answer is correct, but that the incorrect choices are obviously wrong? If so, does the item remain at the difficulty level originally intended?
6. Do all the choices constitute possible answers to a single direct question implied in the premise?
7. Are the distracters of about the same length and complexity as the correct answer? If not, are there at least two which are parallel with the intended answer?
8. Do pronouns refer clearly to one and only one antecedent?
9. Are the choices parallel in grammatical form and in meaning?
10. Are there repetitions in the choices which could be avoided by putting the repeated thought into the premise?

After the concept has been identified, the question asked in a premise which is clear and the intended choice written, the next task is that of writing distracters. The ideal distracters are those wrong answers actually given by representatives of the group for which the item is intended (not by some other group), in response to the question asked as a completion item. Since item writers do not normally have ready access to such answers, it is up to them to project themselves into the situation and say, "If I were one of the group to whom this test is to be given and were asked this question as a completion item and didn't know the answer, what response would I give?" On the success with which the item writer can thus project himself into the situation of such candidates and predict their responses rests the value of the item from a technical standpoint.

In presenting a completed item the item writer is, in effect, saying: "This item is to be included in a test and given to a group of examinees, some qualified and some not qualified with respect to a particular objective. If we could accurately separate the qualified individuals from the unqualified, and examine the responses of each group, we would find the keyed answer given by a relatively high proportion of the qualified group and by a low proportion of the unqualified. Each of the four distracters, on the other hand, should be given by a high proportion of the unqualified group and by a low proportion of the qualified." If, after finishing an item, one cannot in all honesty make this prediction, the item should be worked on further. If this prediction can be made, it still needs empirical verification by observing the actual responses of the two groups, "qualified" and "unqualified," as defined by an acceptable criterion.

32

Reporting to Parents

Sybil Richardson

What should parents know about the child's work in school? How should this information be reported? Richardson presents some interesting suggestions for reporting school progress, suggestions which deserve careful consideration. If Richardson's points are accepted, what specific items of information must a teacher collect regarding a child? How will these items be conveyed to the parent?

In the past, the written report card was often the only communication between teachers and parents. Today, even though many parents and teachers meet in individual and group conferences, the written report is still used. What and how to report seems to be a greater problem than ever, for, while teachers have become sensitive to the discouraging effects of poor marks on children, many people continue to hold traditional expectations regarding marks or grades. Parents often have unwarranted confidence in the precision with which grades in school can indicate a child's effort or foretell his success in adult life. On the other hand, teachers know that parents do need to understand their child's capacities and limitations if they are to plan wisely with and for him.

Today's teachers, consequently, when reporting to parents:

Give attention to many aspects of the child's growth. (To mention only academic achievement implies that other kinds of growth are not important or are not taken into account.)

Use language that is simple, easy to understand, meaningful.

See that the child himself has goals for the year and that he helps in the evaluation of his own progress toward them.

Describe desired behaviors specifically. (Instead of such comprehensive areas as "reading" or "social adjustment," written reports today provide for the child to be rated on several distinct skills which the teacher can evaluate and the parent can observe.)

From Sybil Richardson, "Reporting to Parents," *The Instructor*, LXIX (June, 1960), p. 9. Reprinted with the permission of publisher and author.

Recognize that the report card is seen by the child. (To call attention, on a report card, to irremediable problems is not good. If such conditions require comment, the report card should be supplemented by individual conferences or by letter.)

Consider the child's progress from a three-way vantage: whether or not he is improving on his own record, how he compares with the others in his particular group, and how he stands in relation to larger numbers of children of the same age. (Comparisons, of course, can be harmful to a child's self-respect and continued effort. When parents and teachers appreciate a child's uniqueness, they give him many opportunities to discover his own strengths and needs.)

In reporting to parents, the teacher draws upon standardized-test results, cumulative records, and other information. Isolated bits of information are subject to error and must be considered in relation to the child's total growth. Specific test scores, therefore, are not too helpful. Parents do need, however, to know the kinds of tasks required in the tests, the abilities which these are thought to represent, and the comparative bases on which these tests were selected and applied. With this background, parents are enabled to understand the child's general *capacities* and *needs* and the *trends* of his growth. This is essential.

Reporting methods are more successful when the children themselves play an active part in evaluating their progress. Children should be helped to understand the immediate goals toward which they are working and to evaluate their day-by-day progress toward these goals. In the long process of arriving at self-understanding, children are helped to understand their limitations while maintaining self-respect and a feeling of adequacy.

Parents, too, have a role in reporting children's progress. Sometimes teachers send a note home as a guide to cooperative reporting. Thinking about such questions as: "Does your child enjoy reading at home?" or "What did he say about our study trip?" helps parents to note evidences of the progress their child is making.

Parents can help by discovering gaps in children's learning which need to be bridged. At home, too, new interests may come to light which may be followed through in the classroom.

33

Sense or Nonsense? The Objective
Testing of English Composition

Orville Palmer

*Skill in the fundamentals of English expression is often thought
to be measurable only by means of essays. Palmer presents some
interesting arguments regarding this problem. The reader should
first think about the characteristics of "good writing," then determine whether all these characteristics are assessed by the methods
Palmer describes.*

In the pages of *Commentary* magazine not long ago appeared an attack
on objective English tests written by an experienced and respected New
York City English teacher. Two paragraphs of the article ran as follows:

College teachers want students who can write. High school teachers would
like to supply demand. Both groups think they should require more writing
of the student, and naturally both want the student to be properly tested.
Between the two groups stands the [College Entrance Examination] Board,
dividing and ruling.

At every organized or unorganized discussion of problems of high school
and college teaching and testing, these sentiments are loudly and often eloquently voiced. Everybody agrees that writing should be tested by writing.
Then the representative of the Board rises to face the drumfire (there should
be a special bonus paid for such unswerving devotion to a thankless task).
He unreels his statistics. He explains, parries, soothes, confuses. At the end
of the fray he escapes to Princeton, no doubt exhausted but victorious over
the clear consensus of the meeting, to continue for another year the process of
awarding driving licenses on the basis of skill in reading stop signs and
identifying Buicks [i.e., to continue the testing of English compositional
ability through IBM-machine-scored examinations (1)].

I quote the paragraphs primarily because they point up succinctly two
opposing points of view. It would be absurd, of course, to pretend there is

From Orville Palmer, "Sense or Nonsense? The Objective Testing of English
Composition," *The English Journal*, L (May, 1961), pp. 314–320. Reprinted with
the permission of the National Council of Teachers of English and Orville Palmer.

not controversy; a running warfare between the proponents of objective and essay-type testing has been going on now for some four decades. The author of the quotation stakes out his position plainly and persuasively. His position is one yet widely held by English teachers. I take strong issue with such views and shall state my own position as clearly and logically as I can in the pages that follow.

The author of the article in question is seriously mistaken, I believe, both in his premises and in his conclusions. He writes with a sovereign contempt for years of research in the field of English testing by able and dedicated teachers who do not share his prejudice against any kind of proof based on numbers or statistics. In any attempt to find out what kinds of tests work better than others in picking out students who write well or poorly, the use of statistics is mandatory, whether we like it or not. Unfortunately, many English teachers know very little about the field of tests and measurements, cheerfully admit it, and even take a perverse pride in their ignorance of and immunity to any educational research involving statistical proof. They have pledged their loyalty to a cluster of attitudes and opinions centered in what I tend to call "the mystique of the essay examination" — which reminds me for all the world of General de Gaulle's "mystique of French grandeur": six parts wishful thinking, two parts fact, and two parts pure fantasy.

But this "mystique of the essay examination" — which I consider to be an albatross around the neck of the profession — is another subject, as is the quoted paragraphs' attempt to set up the College Board as a scapegoat, as the villain responsible for the present lamentable situation in American composition teaching. Of course, their author does the good gray Board too much honor. The College Board rules nobody and dictates little or nothing. If there are, as I am informed, 90,000 high school English teachers today in America, probably 85,000 of them are scarcely aware of the Board's existence. If they supply semi-literate freshmen to the colleges, should the blame properly be laid at the doorstep of the College Board? There seems excellent reason to doubt it.

Yet the myth of the Board's baneful influence dies hard, even though scarcely one fact can be adduced to support it. Let me give you an example of the Board's real influence on English teaching in America. The last Board English examination which contained questions involving formal grammar was administered in 1950. Did American English teachers stop teaching the parts of speech in 1951? No English teacher has as yet come forward and admitted dropping the teaching of grammar for this reason.

The College Board's experience with English tests should be of interest to every English teacher for several reasons pertinent to the present discussion. The Board has now been engaged in English testing and research for sixty years. Of that period, the thirteen years between 1947 and 1960 in particular have seen the Board engaged in an astonishingly broad and no-where-equalled body of English research and experimentation about which the profession as yet has scarcely any awareness or knowledge. The College Board has used objective (i.e., multiple-choice) tests for more than thirty years, and objective English tests for slightly more than a decade.

Over the past few months the present writer has reviewed as meticulously and dispassionately as possible the many reports and studies, the analyses, and the examinations themselves which represent this long and cumulative Board activity in English testing, unparalleled in America. The following paragraphs are based upon these materials, upon the experience of those many members of past and present College Board English committees, upon the experience of College Board officers, and upon the work of my colleagues at Educational Testing Service who have constructed, administered, graded, and analyzed literally hundreds of English tests of all sorts — objective *and* essay, and in the aggregate far more essay examinations than objective examinations — and whose work over an unbroken period of six decades surely constitutes a major contribution to English composition testing theory and practice. A major contribution, undoubtedly. A widely appreciated and disseminated contribution? Unfortunately not. For most of the English teaching profession, the Board's six decades of English testing and research activity doubtless constitute the equivalent of William James's tree that crashed to earth in the middle of an empty desert — unseen and unheard.

What does this major contribution to English composition testing theory and practice state in essence? Essentially this: Sixty years of Board English testing have amply proved that essay tests are neither reliable nor valid, and that, whatever their faults, objective English tests *do* constitute a reliable and valid method of ascertaining student compositional ability. Such a conclusion was very painfully and reluctantly arrived at. It struck at the heart of beliefs cherished by the teaching profession, and especially the English teaching branch of the profession. It made a villain and a fraud of one of pedagogy's oldest servants of all work. And it put in his place a monstrous testing device that asked the student to do virtually nothing except draw tiny marks on a sheet of paper, marks that would later be counted and tabulated by a soulless machine. Could there be virtues to such a testing monster? The College Board experience suggests that there may be at least seven virtues to well constructed objective English tests.

VIRTUES OF OBJECTIVE TESTS

A *first*, and elementary, *virtue* of any good objective English test, to judge from the Board's experience, is this: the students' task is set out clearly and explicitly, and the student is given an adequate amount of time in which to work. This sounds so reasonable, so simple-minded, that it may be wondered why it is mentioned here. The unfortunate truth is that it is one of the last things learned by English teachers. It was not learned in a day by the College Board. The first College Board English test — a three-hour essay examination — was administered in June 1901, and was typical of all the early Board tests in that it was highly speeded and made extraordinary demands of the examinees. For example, in the 1904 English test, students were asked to write three two-page compositions in an initial ninety-minute period. In 1907, much wiser, the Board English examiners made a striking concession to the realities: they reduced the requirement for each of the several compositions from two pages to two paragraphs. Yet, even today, a half century later, how many English teachers are there who deliberately or in ignorance set highly speeded examinations, a situation almost guaranteed to make any important examination a traumatic experience? How many English teachers still ask a class "to discuss in detail" the life and works of a famous author — in fifty minutes?

A *second virtue* of the good objective English test is that it demands sound reasoning and thorough comprehension rather than a smattering of information, verbal glibness, and whatever it is that English teachers have in mind when they use the word *originality* or the phrase *original thinking* — and which proves to be about the last thing one can expect to find in a student theme or examination booklet. It may be felt that I am confused in my terms, for the familiar argument has it that objective English tests call only for facts and information, and that taking them is only a superficial matter of picking choices. On the contrary, a good objective English test is anything but superficial. No *objective* College Board English Composition Test has ever required memory of a single "fact" or bit of information, although the Board English *essay* tests between 1901 and 1916 asked for little else. It was 1916 before the Board painfully came to the conclusion that any test which could be answered adequately through a careful cramming of facts followed by an assiduous serving up of the memorized information was a bad test. The outcome was a new battery of tests, the famous "Comprehensives," which could not be so answered. This was forty-five years ago; yet how many English teachers still set examinations which invite their students to parrot back lecture notes or crammed-up highlights of textbooks? How many essay tests elicit only shopworn cliches in halting basic English, and nothing more?

A *third virtue* of standardized and nationally administered objective English tests is that they do not fluctuate in difficulty from year to year. This is a matter of simple fairness to students, for one thing. By 1930 the College Board had realized the necessity for parallel English test forms, to avoid favoring candidates one year with an easy test, and penalizing other candidates the next with a difficult test. Yet, thirty years later, few English teachers see any need for course final examinations which are equivalent in difficulty from one year to the next.

A *fourth virtue* of good objective English tests is that they furnish a reliable score, a score far more reliable than any grade or mark derivable from an essay examination. By 1930 the Board had realized that an examination unreliably graded was worse than no test at all, for its results were apt to be so inaccurate as to be dangerously misleading. Laboriously and carefully all through the Thirties it evolved an elaborate essay reading system, one both time-consuming and expensive, in an attempt to achieve a satisfactory reader reliability. Only once did it achieve a grading reliability of .90, which is probably the least we should settle for in a crucial examination. Today, twenty years later, the overwhelming majority of English teachers choose not even to think about reading reliability, though there has been no lack of studies showing how inconsistent, shaky, and unreliable even the most careful essay reader is. Here again it is necessary to be as categorical as possible. The typical superficial, hasty marking of themes and essays is one of the most unfair and shabbiest aspects of that continuing scandal, the marking and grading system (or systems) of American schools and colleges.

There is a *fifth*, and related, *virtue* of objective English tests, which has to do with student reliability, or, more accurately, unreliability. English teachers hardly need to be told that there exists a great deal of variability in student writing from one theme to another and from one essay to another. The most brilliant student may do well on one essay topic and badly on another. An objective test greatly reduces this inconsistency or variability.

A *sixth virtue* of objective tests is this: they are more valid than essay examinations. By this I mean simply that objective English test scores correlate higher with such criteria as course grades in English and teachers' rating of student writing ability than do essay test scores. (Contrariwise, a set of essay papers, independently read and marked, all too often will correlate poorly or even negatively with such criteria.)

By the late 1930's, College Board officers were thoroughly convinced of two shortcomings of essay tests: they were not valid and they were not reliable. But it was not until 1947 that the Board proved conclusively to itself that objective English tests are superior to essay tests from a measurement standpoint. A final-form English examination administered in that year contained three kinds of test materials: a section of multiple-choice usage items, a brief essay, and a rewriting exercise. A study based upon this test matched the performance on these three sections of a selected group of students with two criteria: high school English course grades and teachers' ratings of their students' writing ability. The section of objective usage items had a significantly higher correlation with each criterion than either the essay or the rewriting exercise. Since most of the students had taken the College Board Scholastic Aptitude test also, it was possible to study, as well, the Verbal section of the SAT as an indicator of writing ability. Very quickly it developed that the SAT-V (composed entirely of multiple-choice questions) had a higher correlation with each criterion than any section of the English test or even the English test as a whole.

But this 1947 English test was a relatively crude and simple affair. Perhaps better, more refined testing measures would give different and contradictory results? Subsequent Board tests amply confirmed the findings of the 1947 examination. As a result, the Board's English Composition Test from 1948 on has been a predominantly objective examination. Many English teachers were unhappy about the appearance in the test of objective, indirect measures for ascertaining writing ability. To give them the sort of evaluation instrument they demanded, the Board administered experimentally in 1951, 1952, and 1953, and as a regular Board examination in 1954, 1955, and 1956, a carefully constructed two-hour essay test called the

General Composition Test. Though it was carefully structured and carefully read, this ambitious and costly project failed, for three reasons: reader reliability was low, validity was unsatisfactory, and its practicality was dubious because of the excessive time and effort required to grade it.

More specifically, matched against high school course grades in English and teachers' estimates of students' writing ability, the GCT ran a poor third to both the largely objective English Composition Test and the wholly objective SAT-V.

The phrase "excessive cost" brings up the *seventh virtue* of objective tests. They cost far less to score than do essay tests. No one is more aware of this than the College Board which has spent, and continues to spend, large sums of money on the grading of essay examinations. The point need not be dwelt on unnecessarily; many testing experts would agree that, in the selection of a test, the cost of grading ought not to be a major or deciding factor. A good test should be worth whatever it costs to administer and grade, whatever its nature.

Problems in Objective Testing

So much for the more obvious virtues of objective English tests. There is, of course, another side to the matter. Objective tests may have defects and limitations as well as virtues. No one knows this better than the College Board. Between 1947 and the present, the Board's Examiners in English utilized no fewer than six types of free-response exercise and seventeen varieties of objective questions in the ECT, in a search for superior testing measures of writing ability. In deciding upon these six kinds of free response exercise, the Examiners considered or pretested some thirty to forty kinds of essay-type questions. In sifting or creating a wide variety of objective exercises and developing the best of them, the Examiners utilized thousands of freshman students in dozens of Board and non-Board colleges as "guinea pigs." In effect, this massive experimentation constituted a screening or winnowing of almost every known type of free-response and objective English exercise. Of the nine item types in current use in the Board's English Composition Test, four made their initial appearance as recently as 1958 and 1959. No fewer than fourteen objective and free-response exercises utilized in final-form examinations since 1948 have been withdrawn from use. And the winnowing continues.

More and more the tasks set the examinee in the Board's English Composition Test reflect and parallel the major problems faced by students when they are actually engaged in writing and revising themes. It is quite probable that the Board English examinations of the future will combine the best features of both objective and free-response tests as we now know them.

One point should be interjected here and emphasized as strongly as possible. Nowhere and at no time has the College Board uncovered evidence suggesting the imminent obsolescence of a long and arduous apprenticeship in actual writing, both in secondary school and in college. Nor has it found any evidence even suggesting that objective tests and workbooks offer a red carpet or royal road to writing competence. Certainly no objective English test yet seen by this writer is an adequate or proper substitute for actual writing practice. Most decidedly, theme writing is not yet obsolete.

Since much has been said about the virtues and little about the short-comings of objective tests, it should in fairness be added that most of the objective English tests in use today leave much to be desired. Unless a user is wise, he may very easily end up short-changed in both scope and validity. Many objective English tests appear to be built after the formula for a popular patent medicine: you put in two cents' worth of spelling, five cents' worth of punctuation problems, eight cents' worth of capitalization, fifteen cents' worth of simple usage problems, and so on. English tests assessing ability in spelling, punctuation, capitalization, and simple grammar have been with us for several decades. Some of them never were very good; after fifteen or twenty-five years of use, almost wholly unrevised and unaltered, they now are both threadbare and bankrupt, if I may mix a metaphor.

Nonetheless, it seems entirely probable that the next decades will bring us more rather than fewer standardized objective English tests. Undoubtedly, they will be immeasurably better than most of the current nationally used — and much abused — tests. These objective English tests of the future will possess a validity greater than any present test or test battery basically because they will measure writing ability more directly than has been done up to the present. The most recent College Board English Composition Tests might well become the prototype for such tests.

A few examples of exercises used in these recent tests might be given: the Board's interlinear exercise requires an examinee to revise carefully and thoughtfully a corrupted piece of prose. I happen to be one of those people who strongly believe that the art of writing is in large part the art of revision. Therefore, I look upon the interlinear exercise as one of the best direct measures of writing ability yet evolved. Another, and objective, item type presents the examinee with one good sentence and requires him to rewrite it in an indicated, different way, thereby testing his mastery of sentence structure. A third and quite new exercise is based on the sentence outline and asks the examinee to produce a logical sentence outline, using a number of furnished sentences. Other types of questions test diction, grammar, and related matters.

It is to be devoutly hoped that the all-purpose, scattergun objective English test, with its smattering of this and dab of that, will follow the dodo into oblivion. In its place there should be rigorously designed and carefully developed objective and semi-objective English tests tailored to fulfill specific functions. An all-purpose English test, when all is said and done, is almost as absurd as an all-purpose cooking recipe. To expect one brief objective English test to perform a variety of tasks, such as discovering weaknesses in individual students, classifying large numbers of students into homogeneous groupings, helping standardize a school's English work, measuring a year's achievement in English, and motivating student learning, is to expect the unobtainable. A bargain basement test bought from a store equipped with plain pipe racks is not likely to perform prodigies of measurement. It is all too easy to buy an inadequate, misfit test. It is pathetically easy to cobble together at the eleventh hour an even poorer and less useful one. It is high time American English teachers learned to recognize good tests, use good tests, and construct good tests of their own.

REFERENCE

1. Brown, Spencer. "Gateway to the Colleges," *Commentary*, XXVII (June 1959), 472–483.

34

An Experiment in the Essay-Type Question

Robert R. Ashburn

This article is far from being a recent publication. The study was done, however, at a time when the controversy between objective and essay tests was at its strongest. To what extent are the findings generalizable? Would the general results be expected to vary from one subject area to another, from one cognitive act to another?

The experiment described in the following pages was suggested by a discussion in a meeting of the lecturers in the General Humanities course at West Virginia University. The examiner was attempting to make all the tests in the course of an objective type. A number of the lecturers insisted that the essay question should be used because of their belief that it tests certain abilities that can not be measured by other types of questions. It was decided that some essay questions should be used, but in order to check their value it was thought best to ask three persons to read the answers to each question.[1]

From Robert R. Ashburn, "An Experiment in the Essay-Type Question," *The Journal of Experimental Education*, VII (September, 1938), pp. 1–3. Reprinted with the permission of the publisher.

[1] The author wishes to express to the faculty members of West Virginia University who took part in this experiment his sincere appreciation of their effort and splendid cooperation. In this article, however, he will cloak their identity under the names of Professors R, S, T, U, V, W, X, Y, and Z.

The first question, given to the Thursday discussion sections of Humanities I, was:

Discuss the ideas of geography held by Dante: (1) as to the universe in general, and, (2) as to Hell in particular. (Time: 15 minutes)

The second question, given to the Friday discussion sections of Humanities I, was:

Discuss the plot of Dante's *Divine Comedy*. (Time: 15 minutes)

Three members of the faculty, all authorities on Dante, were asked to read the answers to the questions and to assign to each a letter grade according to the University grading system, in which the highest grade is A and the lowest is F.

When the papers were returned there seemed to be, at first glance, a high degree of agreement. The average grades given by Professors R, S, and T were D, D+, and D, respectively. The number of papers assigned failing grades (E or F) by Prof. R was twenty-four; by Prof. S and Prof. T, twenty-one and twenty-three, respectively. A closer study of the grades, however, revealed some interesting things. While each reader gave approximately the same number of failing grades, they were not assigned to the same papers. They agreed in giving a failing grade to only eight papers, five of which were completely blank. Of the sixty-five students taking the test, forty-four were assigned a failing grade by one or more of the readers, but of these forty-four there were thirty-six who received a passing grade from one or more of the readers. The paper rated by Prof. R as the fourth best, as indicated by his grades, was rated thirtieth by both Prof. S and Prof. T. The paper rated the best by Prof. S was considered fifteenth and seventeenth by Profs. R and T, respectively. There were three cases of grades of A and D being assigned to the same paper by different readers and two cases of B and F being given to the same paper. The correlation between the grades assigned by Prof. R and Prof. S to the same sixty-five papers, according to the rank-difference method, was .65 ± .05; between the grades of Prof. R and Prof. T, .67 ± .05; and between the grades of Prof. S and Prof. T, .69 ± .04.

When the results of the grading became known two objections were raised: first, the two discussion groups had had different questions and it was difficult to compare the papers of one group with those of the other; second, the questions were not carefully worded. To meet these objections and to make the experiment as fair as possible it was decided to give two essay questions on the final examination, when all the students would be together, and to appoint two committees of three faculty members each, to prepare the questions, one on some phase of history and one on some phase of English literature.

The history committee submitted the following question:

Compare or contrast in approximately 400 words life in a medieval castle and life in a medieval town in regard to the following points:

(a) security or the lack of it.

(b) sanitation or the lack of it.

   (c) training of boys for knighthood or industry.

   (d) recreations or diversions.

The English committee submitted the following:

Name seven types of medieval characters presented in the *Prologue* to *The Canterbury Tales* and discuss two of them.

The examiner called the attention of the committee to the fact that the first part of the question called for pure factual information which could easily be tested in objective form and suggested, since the use of the essay question was based on the belief that it tests something that can not be tested by other methods, that the naming of the seven types of characters be included elsewhere in the examination and the essay question be restricted to discussing two types of medieval characters found in the *Prologue*. The committee immediately asked for time to reconsider.

When the report of the English committee was finally returned it was accompanied by a minority report. One member of the committee could not agree with the others on what constitutes a good essay question. The majority report, which was accepted by the examiner, proposed the following:

Answer any two of the following questions, in paragraphs or short compositions of 150–200 words each. Wherever possible, support the statements you make by reference to the parts of *The Canterbury Tales* which you have read.

   (1) What was Chaucer's plan and purpose in *The Canterbury Tales?*

   (2) Show that Chaucer had a sense of humor.

   (3) Show that the *Prologue* affords a good picture of medieval society.

   (4) Are the characters in the *Prologue* and the *Tales* individuals or merely types?

As before, the members of each committee were asked to read the papers independently and assign a letter grade to each. On the history question, the average grades given by Prof. U, Prof. V, and Prof. W were C−, D, and C−, respectively. Of the seventy-five students taking the examination, eleven received a failing grade from Prof. U, twenty-four from Prof. V, and nineteen from Prof. W. Twenty-nine different students received a failing grade from one or more of the readers. Of these twenty-nine, twenty-one received a passing grade from one or more of the readers. Only two papers received the grade of F from all three readers. One of these was a blank paper. There were two cases of the grades A and C− being assigned to the same paper by different readers, one case of B and E, and two cases of C and F. The correlation between the grades assigned by Prof. U and those assigned by Prof. V was .72 ± .04; between the grades of Prof. U and Prof. W, .71 ± .04; between the grades of Prof. V and Prof. W, .61 ± .05.

On the Chaucer question, the average grades given by Prof. X, Prof. Y, and Prof. Z were C−, D, and C−, respectively. Seventeen papers received a failing grade from Prof. X, twenty-nine from Prof. Y, and sixteen from Prof. Z. Of the seventy-five papers, thirty-three received a failing grade from one or more of the readers. Of these, twenty-two received a passing grade from one or more of the readers. In regard to the grade of F, the English committee agreed much better than the history committee, unanimously assigning this grade to nine students. There were, however, five blank papers on the Chaucer question as compared with one on the history question. There was one case of the grades A and D being assigned to the same paper by different readers, one case of A and C, and three of B and E. The correlation between the grades assigned by Prof. X and Prof. Y was .77 ± .03, between those of Prof. X and Prof. Z, .81 ± .03, and between those of Prof. Y and Prof. Z, .84 ± .02

At this time it was becoming increasingly obvious that the members of the faculty do not have the *same* standard in grading essay tests, and the question was raised: Does each one, separately, have a consistent standard? In an attempt to find a partial answer to this question, the committees were asked to read again the papers of the final examination after a period of two weeks. The members of the history committee refused point-blank, saying that they were already convinced that they could not grade essay tests with any degree of accuracy. The members of the English committee, however, agreed to the proposal.

Even before the results of the second reading of the Chaucer question were reported, reasons were advanced why there would be little improvement in agreement. Prof. X stated that he had been misled by certain remarks of the examiner and had not graded right the first time, but he believed he was doing it properly the second time. Prof. Y said that he was conscious of being in a better humor for the second reading and, moreover, he had more time and was reading with more care. Prof. Z read with much more care, going over all the papers in inverse order to check his own grading. He also pointed out certain pertinent facts: there was no agreement as to what to do when a student failed to follow instructions; some of the readers had marked on the papers and this hindered his forming an independent judgment; some of the papers were written with pen and others with pencil and this made it difficult to appraise their relative worth.

On the second reading, only one member of the committee agrees with himself better than with his colleagues. This is Prof. Y. The agreement between the first and second readings in the cases of Prof X and Prof. Z is about the same as that between the readings of the different members of the committee. According to the grades assigned by Prof. X, the papers had deteriorated in the two weeks that they had lain on the examiner's desk. His average grade drops from C− to D+. He finds that five students have passed on the first reading that now deserve to fail. There are some outstanding examples, however, of papers that have improved with age. The paper which he indicates by his grade as *the* best on the second reading rated sixteenth the first time. The correlation between the grades of his first reading and those of his second reading is .84 ± .02.

Prof. Y, who is in a better humor, finds the papers generally improved. Five students pass who failed before, but he finds two F papers that he missed the first time. The correlation between the grades of his first and second readings is .88 ± .01.

Prof Z, like Prof. X, thinks the papers worse, finding ten more failures than in the first reading. Some papers, however, have improved. He assigns the grade of A— to a paper that he had given D before, thus raising it from the obscurity of the fifty-fourth paper to the distinction of the fifth best.

Although all three readers used greater care in the second reading, the lack of agreement is greater. The correlation between the grades assigned by Prof. X and Prof. Y is .70 ± .04 as compared with .77 ± .03 the first time; between those of Prof. X and Prof. Z, .72 ± .04 as compared with .81 ± .03 on the first reading; between those of Prof. Y and Prof. Z, .82 ± .03 as compared with .84 ± .02 on the first reading.

One would scarcely venture to draw any very definite conclusions on the basis of this one experiment, but it seems pertinent to call attention to the following facts:

(1) The essay questions used in this experiment were more carefully prepared than is usual in many course examinations.

(2) The answers were read with more care than is usual in many course examinations.

(3) In the cases covered by this experiment:

    (a) about 6 per cent of the students fail.

    (b) about 44 per cent pass.

    (c) the passing or failing (not merely the difference of a letter grade but the difference between credit and no credit) of about 40 per cent depends, not on what they know or do not know, but on *who* reads the papers.

    (d) the passing or failing of about 10 per cent depends, not on what they know or do not know, but on *when* the papers are read.

SUGGESTED READINGS

Ahman, J. Stanley, and Marvin D. Glock. *Evaluating Pupil Growth*. Boston: Allyn and Bacon, Inc., 1963.

Part Two of this book deals specifically with improvement of teacher-made tests. The emphasis given to objectives as a basis for measurement is especially important.

Green, John A. *Teacher-Made Tests*. New York: Harper and Row, Publishers, 1963.

The entire book is devoted to methods of construction and analysis of teacher made tests. The reader may find the chapters on item writing most useful.

Stanley, Julian C. *Measurement in Today's Schools* (4th ed.). Englewood Cliffs, N.J.: Prentice-Hall, Inc.

This entire text is oriented toward illuminating the use of tests by teachers. Chapters 6, 7, 8, 9 and 11 are especially important to the weekly measurement activities of teachers.

Travers, Robert M. W. *How to Make Achievement Tests*. New York: Odyssey Press, Inc., 1950.

The book is a worthwhile exposition of constructing tests which will successfully assess progress toward objectives of instruction.

Wood, Dorothy Adkins. *Test Construction: Development and Interpretation of Achievement Tests*. Columbus, Ohio: Charles E. Merrill Books, Inc., 1960.

This text, like Green and Travers, is a simply written guide to the construction and use of classroom type tests.

Use of Tests in Counseling and Guidance

The chief work of counselors lies in helping students with their educational and career plans and personal problems. Obviously, this means using different approaches with different students. With many counselees, taking educational and psychological tests becomes a logical way to explore the problem confronting them. The appropriate use of tests in no way minimizes the significance of other approaches to studying students. Interview techniques, school reports, observations of teachers, anecdotal records, and the like — all constitute other important sources of information for the guidance counselor. When psychological testing is used in the counseling process, counselors must answer such questions as how to go about testing? when? what tests? and how to use the results most intelligently?

Many counselor educators maintain that test results, as well as other counseling information, are used primarily to help the counselor and the counselee originate and examine hypotheses concerning the counselee's future behavior. Thus, the admissions officer at Indiana University uses an expectancy table to find an applicant's likely freshman grade-point-average based on his rank in his high school graduating class and his performance on some college aptitude test. The admissions officer then formulates a hypothesis about the applicant's future behavior in the university. On the other hand, some admissions officials may not be so statistically oriented and may elect to study the applicant's aptitude test scores on a more "clinical" basis. One of the most interesting and profound questions in this field is the matter of statistical versus clinical prediction. A fair amount of research exists for the counselor to examine.

Another important aspect of testing in counseling has to do with the extra-measurement use of tests. This concept, provocatively discussed by Kirk in Selection 36, broadens the scope of purposes for guidance testing. Other questions considered in this unit include the validity of multiple-choice tests in the identification of talent, and the use of, multi-factor test batteries in guidance. The counselor-in-training, regardless of his "school affiliation" — client-centered, eclectic, non-client-centered, or whatever — cannot afford the luxury either of using or not using tests until he has critically examined all rival claims. Once this study has been accomplished, it is most likely that the budding counselor will no longer view the use of tests as a dichotomous issue.

35

Testing for Guidance and Selection

William W. Turnbull

The following selection is a clear explication of the techniques and rationale of standardized test construction. Turnbull summarizes both valid and invalid criticisms of objective tests. The guidance counselor will find straightforward accounts of test relevance in college admissions and the predictive power of admissions tests.

Although there have been many lengthy replies to the critics of standardized testing in counseling and guidance work, this short but cogent article encompasses the best in logic and presentation. The reader should critically compare this selection with Ballinger's "Of Testing and Its Tyranny" (Selection 4). What are your own conclusions on this important issue?

In the last few years educational testing has suddenly attracted the attention of writers, editors, and the general public. Articles on the pros and cons of standardized tests appear in popular magazines and in the newspapers. People write books about testing and then go on television shows to debate the subject.

This is hardly surprising in view of the fact that students are taking more tests and parents are worrying more about how tests are used. There are perhaps as many as 150 *million* standardized tests given in American schools and colleges each year. There are aptitude tests, achievement tests, interest tests, personality tests. Usually the scores are used for some combination of guidance, selection, placement, evaluation, or research — although there are those who fear that too many score reports are used mainly to fill file drawers.

Most of the attention and most of the controversy has by-passed the commoner uses of tests in education. In the main, standardized tests are given to pupils by their teachers for the purpose of finding out something about the achievement of individuals in reading, mathematics, or other school subjects and for the added purpose of relating the accomplishments of the

From William W. Turnbull, "Testing for Guidance and Selection," *Phi Delta Kappan*, XLIV (May, 1963), pp. 372–378. Reprinted with the permission of publisher and author.

class or school to those of similar classes or schools elsewhere. This quiet within-school use of achievement tests causes relatively few fireworks. The arguments usually center on the use of tests in guidance and especially in selection, with special reference to testing for admission to college.

Why the surge of interest in using tests for these purposes? A somewhat cynical view is that tests for guidance and selection are the lamentable fruits of American susceptibility to fads, gadgets, and scientific-sounding quackery. A more flattering suggestion is that they are the inevitable product of the American regard for individualism (erstwhile rugged) and the democratic ethic of justice for all. There may be some truth in both views. And I fondly believe that some part of the increased use of standardized tests is traceable to the simple fact that they are better than they used to be. But I suspect the principal reason for the new interest lies not in our national character or in the quality of the tests but rather in the changing circumstances of our educational system and to a lesser extent, of our society.

Among the new educational circumstances, two are fundamental: the fact that the individual student has more (and more difficult) educational choices open to him today, and the fact that institutions have more decisions to make about students — admitting them, placing them at the proper level, and assessing their later progress.

The student's greater range of choices reflects the increasing diversity of education in this country. The choice of a secondary school curriculum to follow, the selection of courses within that curriculum, the choice of a college to attend, the choice of a major, the decision as to whether or not to seek admission with advanced standing — all these are increasingly complex decisions within which the alternatives are often varied. The student, his parents, and his advisors all need dependable information about his individual characteristics that make one choice better than another for him. If other sources of this information were adequate, clearly there would be no need for standardized tests. Since no source of data (including tests) tells the whole story, however, it seems desirable to look for whatever additional useful information the tests can provide in relation to important decisions about the student's educational future.

Common Misconceptions of the Role of Tests

In passing, it may be worth commenting on two common misconceptions about the role of standardized tests in education. The first is that they are somehow associated with standardized students, that their function is to force everyone into the same mold. Granting that it would be possible to contrive such a misuse of some kinds of examinations (not necessarily standardized tests), it is nonetheless true that in the great majority of schools the standardized tests are in fact of major help in the desisions aimed at getting the student into the educational program best suited to his individual abilities. Thus they are a force for maximizing rather than minimizing attention to unique human talents.

The second misconception is that tests are the cause of "pigeonholing" students. Again, it must be granted that some misguided guidance has overtones of pigeonholing, but good guidance is a matter of keeping open to the student the maximum number of opportunities that are realistic for him. This is a matter of guidance philosophies, however, and the tests are instruments rather than causes of whatever philosophy is applied. The choices the student must make are products of the educational and social system in which he is operating. The function of whatever tests are used is to help him make those choices as intelligently as possible.

Just as the individual student has choices to make, so too does the institution. At a rock-bottom level, for example, the instructor of a course in which the student is already enrolled is obligated to choose either to pass him or to fail him. The more complex choices are those that must be made by an institution — typically a college or university — to which great numbers of students are applying. The applicants often come in greater numbers than can be accommodated and they hail from a tremendous variety of schools. These are the inevitable consequences of an educational system that combines high mobility, freedom of choice to apply anywhere, and differential prestige or popularity among colleges. In this situation, from the standpoint of the college, a standardized test taken by all applicants provides a useful common currency with which to supplement the local currencies represented by the grades assigned by the several school systems. Standardized tests on which all students are graded alike are a predictable by-product of our decentralized system of secondary education with its bewildering diversity of course titles and grading practices. By the same token, it is the existence of impartial external standards with common meaning that makes our decentralized system viable.

In a day when some colleges must turn away large numbers of applicants, it is natural that a good deal of pressure and anxiety should come to surround the process of admission to higher education. By the time the student approaches the end of his high-school years, it's a little late for him to do anything about some of the information the college will take into account — his over-all school record, for example, or the estimate his teachers and principal have formed of his ability. The one remaining bit of evidence, for good or ill, which he feels he still may be able to turn to his advantage or which may work against him, is his entrance exam score. Thus all of the hopes and fears that stem from the difficulty of entering some universities become associated with the tests they require for admission. This concern about the pressure that tests "introduce" into the college-going process affects parents even more than students. (The square of the anxiety of the student is less than the sum of the anxieties of mama and papa.) The fact is, of course, that the tests become the focus of the pressures and anxieties that stem from the need of some colleges to admit selectively. Taking the tests away would not take the pressure away but would deflect it to other aspects of the selection procedure such as school grades and recommendations.

TESTING THE RELEVANCE OF TESTS

Because educational tests enter into important decisions, it is proper to inquire into their adequacy from the standpoint of their accuracy and their relevance to the decisions to be made. It is equally proper, of course, to ask these same questions of other important sources of information, either for guidance or for selection: grades, interviews, or recommendations.

As far as accuracy (reliability) is concerned, present day aptitude and achievement tests stand up very well in comparison with any other source of data available. This is not to say they are as accurate as one might like them to be; nothing is. The problem of reducing error has been faced with some success, but the problem of eliminating error is unlikely to be solved. One noteworthy characteristic of standardized tests is that their accuracy can be determined and expressed rather precisely. This occasionally leads people to deplore the fact that the accuracy level is not perfect. For such data as school grades, no comparable index of accuracy (or inaccuracy) is ordinarily available. Consequently, the unwary may forget that these indices also have their built-in wobbles due to chance. The same comment applies to interviews and references. The workings of chance affect these indices much more importantly than they affect test scores.

Accuracy is one thing, relevance another. It is possible, for example, to measure the height of all college applicants with great accuracy but the relevance of this statistic to any important educational experience in college (outside the province of the basketball coach) is probably nil. The relevance of a test can be judged in various ways. For example, with reference to an achievement test one would want to know how a group of skilled teachers in the subject rate the test questions as to importance and adequacy of coverage. Second, one might well ask whether the people who make high scores on the test are also those whose teachers rate them at the top as far as mastery of the content and principles of the course are concerned.

TEST RELEVANCE IN COLLEGE ADMISSIONS

Both aptitude and achievement tests have proved themselves to have a high degree of relevancy to the problem of college admissions. There are several reasons for this. In the following paragraphs I shall describe briefly the procedures used at Educational Testing Service in the preparation of the multiple-choice aptitude and achievement tests of the College Entrance Examination Board in order to maximize relevancy.

In the first place, the exams are designed painstakingly to reflect the readiness of students to undertake a college program. In the case of the achievement tests, content is determined by a group of school and college people who are actively teaching the particular subject to high-school or college students. Working closely with test specialists, they prepare the questions and discuss each one minutely to make sure it is clear and deals with important concepts within the range that a high-school student can be expected to have covered. In the case of scholastic aptitude tests, the questions are prepared mainly by test specialists who work with a national committee of authorities on the subject of aptitude for college work.

After the questions have been prepared, criticized, and revised, they are given to several hundred students like those who will eventually encounter them in a College Board exam. This try-out is designed to provide three bits of information about each question: 1) How hard is this question? The percentage of students choosing the right answer provides a good indication of this. A typical exam is made up of questions ranging from those few that nearly everyone answers correctly to a few that very few students solve correctly. 2) How discriminating is this question? In general, a good question will be answered correctly by a substantially higher proportion of good students than poor ones. Therefore, the students are separated into high and low groups according to their over-all grasp of the subject and, for each individual question, a separate tally is made of the percentage of "highs" and "lows" who choose the right answer. Unless the "highs" choose correctly with much greater frequency than the "lows," the committee will want to review the question to see why it is tripping up competent students. It may contain some ambiguity or it may lie outside the experience of even the very good students. In any case, some revision is probably in order. 3) How clear is this question? The data on percentage of "highs" and "lows" answering correctly may provide an important clue to clarity vs. ambiguity, as we have just seen. To pursue this matter further, a similar tally is made for each of the wrong answers included in the multiple options. If a substantial number of good students select a particular "wrong" answer, the committee responsible for the test will want to look for lines of reasoning that could lead a good student to such a choice and will probably either clarify the question before it is used in an actual exam or discard it altogether.

The "pretest" results are an invaluable source of information about how *students* — not teachers — read and respond to the questions. But they provide no automatic bases for changing the questions. It is up to the committee in each case to use its own judgment in deciding whether or not a question is appropriate for use. Thus it is important that the committees be composed of teachers and scholars of the highest degree of competence in the area of the examination.

The final evidence as to relevance must be sought in relation to the test as a whole, of course, rather than in relation to individual test questions. If students who are known to their teachers to have an excellent grasp of a subject generally make high scores on an achievement test in that subject, while those whose knowledge is slight or superficial make low scores, the test obviously has a promising degree of relevance. In the case of aptitude tests, the evidence sought is usually the relationship between the test scores and later academic success in college. By making systematic comparisons of these kinds, using different varieties of tests in different educational settings, we have been able to learn a good deal about the kinds of tests that do or do not do a good job.

THE PREDICTIVE POWER OF ADMISSIONS TESTS

It is difficult to express the degree to which the tests "work" in this sense — their predictive power — without either oversimplifying or burying the reader under a mound of statistics and charts. Suppose, however, we look at an incoming college class and focus particularly on the half who were above average on the tests they took when they applied for admission. If the tests worked quite well, about 70 per cent of these students will rank in the top half of their class, as determined by their academic grades. Thirty per cent of them will be in the lower half of the class. This is a long way from perfect prediction[1] but, in human affairs, perfect prediction would be an unrealistic and probably undesirable goal.

The results of the admissions test do, then, have a degree of utility. In general, the scores derived from a single day's testing with well constructed measures are almost as useful to a college admissions officer — almost as relevant to the decision he must make — as are the grades the student has made in school. The school grades are, however, more often the best *single* source of evidence. If grades and test scores are used in combination, the results are better than if either source of evidence is used alone. And references, interviews, and the like may further fill out the picture of the student.

Why are the grades better than the test scores? Probably because they measure the student's accomplishments over three years' time or more, in a task that is quite similar to the one he will face in college. Grades reflect qualities not present in the tests, such as staying power and willingness to accept and complete assignments. Most of all, they reflect repeated observations by many teachers over time, so that they come to have some stability.

Turning the question around, how is it that a set of test scores representing the work of a single day (or even half-day) on the part of the student, tells almost as much as the grades he has achieved over a period of years? The answer seems to be threefold. First, grades mean different things in different schools whose standards are unequal. Although the college knows the meaning of a Scholastic Aptitude Test score of 550 no matter where the student comes from (unless he is, for example, from a foreign country), it does not know the meaning of a B-plus grade average unless it knows the school. The more varied and unfamiliar the school systems from which the applicants come, the more reliance the college may have to place on standardized test scores. Second, secondary school grades may over-represent some elements that are of diminished importance in college — qualities like punctuality, neatness, and a desire to please the teacher. The test is blind to these virtues. Third, school grades ordinarily are somewhat less precise or accurate than test scores. Although this lack of precision detracts somewhat from their utility, their high degree of relevance saves the day.

In any case, the grades and scores in combination appear to make an excellent team, each compensating for defects in the other and providing, in combination, a reasonably good picture of the student.

The tests are far from infallible, obviously. They can undoubtedly be improved and a great deal of effort is going into this task. Critics of present-

---

[1] The 70-30 odds would be produced by a correlation of .60 between test scores and grades — representative of the results obtained where the student body is not unusually homogeneous with respect to test scores. The correlation would have to drop to .31 in order to lower the odds to 60-40 — a performance that would be considered poor in even a highly typical institution.

day tests perform a service when they identify weaknesses in the examinations and especially when they propose constructive alternatives. On the other hand, they may serve only to confuse the public and obscure real problems when they level their criticisms against false or trivial issues. I should like to comment briefly on what seem to me to be overdrawn and generally invalid criticisms and then go on to what I believe to be valid and important points of criticism, more germane to the improvements needed in testing for guidance and selection.

Ambiguity — A Catchy but Unsupportable Criticism

The inherent ambiguity of objective test questions is one of the catchy but unsupportable criticisms — unsupportable except in the general sense that all language, all communication is inherently ambiguous in some degree. The argument is advanced in its least cogent form when the critic cites questions that are alleged to be ambiguous (and it is beyond dispute that ambiguous questions exist), and concludes that tests containing any such items must be bad tests. This is a little like arguing that any poet guilty of an occasional bad line is a poor poet, or that a library with any poor books is a bad library. Luckily, it is possible to limit the incidence of ambiguous questions severely by securing the services of excellent teachers to write them and by employing the pretesting methods already described. Although it is inevitable that some questions that are ambiguous will appear on final exams, the over-all scores based on a great many questions (often a hundred or more of them) will be affected very little. The inclusion from time to time of an ambiguous question is, to be sure, one of the factors that lowers the accuracy of test scores, but it is not a major one.

Proving That the Bumblebee Can't Fly

A second direction sometimes taken within the same general argument is that good students are more likely to see the ambiguities than poor students. Thus the best students will be put to the greatest number of guesses and their scores will suffer accordingly. As a consequence, the highest scores will go to the second-rate students. The critics who urge this "proof" that the tests can't work seem to me to be in the same boat as the aerodynamicists who can prove that the bumblebee can't fly. It happens that the evidence is to the contrary. If the contention were correct, we would expect that in college the students who had scored highest on their entrance exams would be surpassed by the deeper, more analytical students whose troubles with ambiguous items presumably had penalized them on the tests. In fact, however, when the college record is examined, it invariably turns out that *in general* the students who made the highest test scores have done better work in college than those whose entering scores were a little lower.

The last sentence was qualified by insertion of the words "in general." The critic who sees this qualification sometimes responds with, "Aha! How about the exceptions? Don't you care about them?" The exceptions are of course important. As long as we lack prescience about all that fate has in store for each college student, however, we will always have exceptions to any set of predictions based on past indications of competence. The question becomes: At the present time, by what system of examinations now known to us can we keep the exceptions as low in number as possible?

At this point, the critic frequently cites reasons for his belief that essay exams would, in fact, possess superior relevance for college admissions and hence reduce the number of mis-measured people. It is true that good essay exams rate high with respect to relevance. They are, in effect, miniatures of college examinations. The problem with them as college entrance measures is that they must be extremely long (covering several hours per field) in order to compensate for their lack of accuracy or precision as measuring devices. Part of the inaccuracy stems from the limited power of essay questions to sample broadly within a field, part arises from the fact that a student's performance varies from one theme to the next, and part is due to the inconsistency of scorers. If several hundred readers must collaborate in grading the papers, a student's score on a particular piece of work is likely to depend as much on which reader happens to mark it as on its intrinsic merit. As a result, essay exams of a length at all comparable to that of the objective exams produce more exceptions, more cases of mis-measurement, than we now experience — as repeated attempts to improve the system have demonstrated. If we were to give a couple of weeks to college entrance examinations, it might well be possible to improve the over-all record of successful measurement by using substantial amounts of essay material, provided we could make sure that several readers marked the work of each student. But the expense to the candidate would be enormous, even assuming that the necessary graders could be found.

One or two other criticisms sometimes voiced may also be noted as having little basis in fact. One is an implication that the tests are produced by "testers" behind a curtain of secrecy — that if only teachers and scholars could pierce the veil they would be appalled at what they would discover. The fact is that there are few activities in education that are so open. Hundreds of school and college teachers write and review achievement examinations, and the aptitude tests are prepared under the aegis of a national committee of review.

A final unsupported criticism implies that the college entrance exams are fastened tyrannically on the schools, which are resentful but powerless. In fact, the schools have played an increasingly important role in determining the nature of the examination program — witness, for example, their substantial representation in the College Entrance Examination Board. The most succinct and impartial answer to this charge, however, may be seen in the following tabulation of teachers' opinions gathered by the National Education Association Research Division and published in December, 1962 (1):

> Are nationwide testing programs, such as merit scholarship examinations and college entrance examinations, exerting an influence on the instructional program of your school?

	All Teachers	Elementary School Teachers	Secondary School Teachers	Men Teachers	Women Teachers
Yes, and influence is desirable	41.0%	34.9%	49.3%	46.2%	38.6%
Yes, and influence is undesirable	5.4	4.5	6.6	8.8	3.8
No, there is no influence	32.3	35.6	27.8	29.3	33.6
Undecided	21.3	25.0	16.3	15.7	24.0

These replies would seem to offer substantial reassurance to those who fear that nationwide standardized tests are distorting the aims or hampering the progress of teachers in the schools.

WHAT ARE THE VALID CRITICISMS?

What, then, are some of the more important and more valid criticisms of testing as it is carried on today? One is that too many tests contain too many items that are trivial. Granted that such questions may be unambiguous and otherwise impeccable: they deal with a fact of marginal importance. Tests of trivia beget learning of trivia. Our techniques for guarding against ambiguity are much better developed than our techniques for ensuring an emphasis on the central issues of an academic field. In the past decade or two, I believe, the better tests have in fact included a much higher proportion of questions depending on a grasp of broader principles, on the ability to apply facts in the solution of new problems, on skill in analysis, or on capacity for artistic or literary appreciation. Although we have made a good deal of progress in this respect, I think there is still room for improvement.

A second valid criticism is that our total information-gathering system, whether for guidance or college admission, gives us only rudimentary information about student motivation, initiative, originality, values, and a host of other important qualities. The criticism is sometimes leveled (improperly, in my judgment) against one or another source of data that was not intended and should not be expected to provide the information. For example, one will look in vain to the Scholastic Aptitude Test for an indication of a student's integrity. But if the criticism is improper with respect to a given instrument designed to do a specific (and different) job, it is still valid with respect to the entire data-gathering mechanism. Until we have a more accurate way to assess these qualities systematically, the conscientious guidance director or admissions officer will lack important information that would help him do his job and would be of real significance to the student in planning for his own future.

At present, our best source of enlightenment about the "intangibles" is the school record and recommendations. Compared with the effort that has gone into improving tests, the systematic work done on increasing the accuracy and usability of the non-test data has been astonishingly small considering the central importance of the record accumulated over the school years. If it should prove feasible to devise tests that can tease out information about a student's goals, attitudes, "workage vs. loafage," and the like, the need to improve the school's evaluation of these characteristics, based on repeated observation, would of course be diminished. For the immediate future, however, it seems likely that a concentrated effort on systematizing and communicating the relevant information that already exists in the schools would help to fill a major gap in school-to-college mechanisms of articulation.

Perhaps the most serious criticism of the present use of tests in guidance and selection is the lack of established standards of competence among the users. Real improvements in this regard seem to be flowing from the efforts to improve guidance under provisions of the National Defense Education Act and from such continuing programs as the workshops for college admissions officers sponsored by the College Entrance Examination Board. Comparable efforts are needed for teachers and administrators, however, if the general level of sophistication in interpreting tests is to reach a satisfactory level. It may be that the general inclusion of appropriate courses in tests and measurements in teacher training programs would go far toward remedying the situation. Whatever the course of action, in view of the importance of the decisions affected in part by test scores, a strenuous effort to improve the understanding of those who must use them now seems very much in order.

Thus it is quite apparent that improvements are needed in the instruments and processes connected with guidance and selection. It is healthy to have continuing scrutiny and evaluation of the tests. At the same time, we should not concentrate so narrowly on the deficiencies of the system that we fail to see any of its virtues. And the evaluations based on *a priori* logic should be tested against practical observation and especially against experience accumulated over significant periods of time. Since the Scholastic Aptitude Test of the College Entrance Examination Board has been used for over 36 years, it is instructive to look at some of the more significant changes in college admissions patterns that appear to have been associated in some degree with its use. In the ETS Annual Report for 1961–62 (2), Henry Chauncey has pointed out ". . . that, during the lifetime of the SAT, more opportunities for higher education have been opened up for more students than ever before in this country. In the 1930's, the availability of the SAT provided the additional method needed for identifying able students sufficiently well to justify the award of very large national and regional scholarships. Since then, the SAT and other tests similar to it have contributed to the effective selection of scholarship students in many colleges throughout the country.

"Another interesting development is the change that has occurred in the undergraduate bodies of colleges that have used the SAT over the last two or three decades. In the Ivy League colleges, for instance, the undergraduate body of the 1920's was a homogeneous group with respect to socio-economic background and a heterogeneous one with respect to intellectual ability. Today the picture is almost reversed — undergraduates in these colleges come from widely varying socio-economic backgrounds and possess a generally high intellectual ability.

"A third development worth noting is the fact that at colleges where the SAT has been used as part of the admissions process for the last twenty or thirty years, the academic failure of enrolled students has been reduced to a minimal level.

"Surely more than coincidence is involved in the fact that these developments occurred during the lifetime of the SAT. Obviously, many other elements have also contributed to expanding opportunities for higher education, to better identification and encouragement of able students, to better guidance, and to reduction of the academic failure rate at many colleges. The SAT, however, has played its part. And the net effect has been the lifting of many of the earlier restrictions to higher education in this country."

Thus there is much in the record that suggests we have made important progress. And there is every reason to believe that, given the continued close involvement of the academic community, both the procedures and the tests used in guidance and selection can be steadily improved in the future.

REFERENCES

1. *NEA Research Bulletin*, Vol. 40, No. 4 (December, 1962).
2. "Report of the President," Educational Testing Service *Annual Report 1961–1962*, 44–46.

36

Extra-Measurement Use of Tests in Counseling

Barbara A. Kirk

The following selection emphasizes a much neglected value of tests in counseling — the extra-measurement or qualitative uses of tests. Kirk explains how tests provide limitless materials for introducing ideas, for establishing and exploring hypotheses, and for clarifying insights. By means of a fuller utilization of tests and test results, counselees have opportunities for greater self-understanding. Specifically, Kirk presents three extra-measurement contributions of tests: (1) clinical diagnosis, (2) self-assessment, (3) interactive facilitation.

Although most counselors and guidance workers believe that testing furnishes one very valuable type of information, some modern counselors maintain that test results are of little or no value. The proponents of relevant testing in the counseling process have long relied on the value of quantification and the relation of the counselee's scores to appropriate norms. Now, a forceful case is made for an important second dimension — the qualitative — in the utility of test information in counseling. These extra-measurement uses of tests in counseling enhance the amount of client information available for decision-making and adjustment.

The use of tests for purposes of measurement has been extensively investigated over a number of decades. During and following World War I, tests came into extensive service for population description and comparison, in the assessment of a variety of traits. Then, and most importantly, measurement devices were applied to problems of placement and prediction. From their application in mass terms, instruments were developed which had validity and reliability to a degree commensurate with their utilization for selection, placement, and counseling of the *individual*. Testing became a fundamental technique for processes of educational and vocational counseling and constituted a major step forward from vocational guidance based primarily upon occupational information.

From Barbara A. Kirk, "Extra-Measurement Use of Tests in Counseling," *Personnel and Guidance Journal*, XXXIX (April, 1961), pp. 658–661. Reprinted with the permission of publisher and author.

In the current status of the field of educational and vocational counseling, testing is an integral and indispensable technique. What part does it play? Are only tests which have acceptably high levels of validity and reliability, and for which probabilities can be adequately calculated, of value to individuals who are faced with educational and vocational choices and decisions? Without in any sense gainsaying the value of quantification and the relation of individual scores to normative standards, the contribution of standardized tests to the counseling process must be viewed qualitatively to appreciate their full yield. There are three contributions in particular which may be emphasized, although to the resourceful counseling psychologist, this list should not be considered exhaustive. The three areas under consideration here might be called clinical diagnosis, self-assessment, and interactive facilitation, and represent the values directly to the counselor, to the counselee, and to the interaction between them.

Before describing the three primary extra-measurement uses of tests in counseling, it might be well to indicate for whom these uses are appropriate. The interpretation of test results, either quantitative or qualitative findings, as has been elsewhere indicated, is a highly skilled activity of the fully qualified, experienced clinical or counseling psychologist. The counselor, teacher-counselor, or dean is commonly dependent upon a school psychologist or consulting clinical or counseling psychologist for evaluation of test data. An article by the staff of the University of Maryland Counseling Center, "A Check-list for Recording Test-Taking Behavior" (1), attempts to study the reliability of observations of such behavior. It shows how complicated and difficult making such observations can be. Because of the inherent difficulty in soundly interpreting behavior on tests or in a test-taking situation, such reports must be regarded as tentative within counseling and not fully accepted until proven out in the counseling process. Of the extra-measurement use of tests subsequently delineated, *Clinical Diagnosis* is the prerogative of the clinical and/or counseling psychologist whose analysis may be of assistance to the counselor; *Self-Assessment* is an area open to all counselors who are either competent with counseling techniques or who have the good judgment and restraint to permit a counselee to work out his problems himself to the full extent of his capacity; *Interactive Facilitation* again applies to the use of test data by competent counselors.

Clinical Diagnosis. This is undoubtedly the best known and the most common extra-measurement use of tests in both clinical and counseling practice. We are concerned here with observation of test-taking behavior, of intellectual and emotional functioning, and of demonstrated habits and attitudes. From such observations, conclusions can be obtained by the clinician for habitual and characteristic performance. The presentation of a standard situation gives unique opportunity to observe individual modes of reaction, deviations from usual behavior, and particular trends and quality of intellectual and emotional functioning. Usually tests implicated for this purpose are those which are individually administered, allowing for intensive observation of a sample of some type of performance. On mental ability tests, kind of approach to mental tasks is demonstrated, i.e., trial and error, problem solving, insight gaining. There is also opportunity to learn quality and kind of functioning in relation to such traits as memory, judgment, comprehension, reasoning, abstraction. Furthermore, malfunctioning may be seen and distinguished from healthy mental functioning. Also observable are personality traits such as confidence, persistence, security, dependence, defensiveness, etc. The observations and clinical determinations of the psychologist are accurate, subtle, deep, and enlightening to the degree of his particular skill, competence, and experience. Here, and only here, can determination be made of true intellectual capacity as distinguished from and discrepant from performing capacity.

Similarly, tests of manual dexterity, manipulation, and so forth, can provide information of great value about attitudes toward work and habits of work. What are the counselee's standards, and what is his approach? Does the counselee improve with practice and continue on to an ever-better performance? On the other hand, does he tire with a prolonged task and tend to reduce his energy output and decrease his motivation? Is he careful, meticulous, accurate, or does he tend to try to rush or be inaccurate and careless? Does he have pride in his performance and to what degree?

Not only is observational material obtainable from individually administered tests, but approach to paper-and-pencil tests, administered in a testing room with other counselees, also is revealing. Consideration for the examiner and other test-takers, dependency on the examiner, fear, demandingness, efficiency, and organization are some of the behaviors which may be most helpful in understanding and counseling the counselee.

Subjective examination and analysis of test content of other than individual ability tests is also a major aid to clinical diagnosis over and beyond and apart from the quantitative test result. We are accustomed to analysis of content of projective test responses for broad and deep understanding of the individual. Other tests also, when their content is analyzed, can make similar contribution. Whether it be an item review and analysis on an inventory-type personality test, or a paper-and-pencil mental ability test, or study habits and attitudes questionnaire, each has something of real significance to offer. Greatly impoverished is the counselor and the counseling when this rich source of knowledge is overlooked.

Analysis of content wherever we implicate it may afford bases for hypotheses and clues for exploration. Even though they do not provide the "answers," they may each and all supply a part of the jigsaw puzzle which when put together gives us the formulation or diagnosis.

Self-Assessment. This refers to self-assessment only as part of the process of counseling and not independent of it.

A vitally important contribution of tests, both measurement-wise and extra-measurement-wise, is that of gain in self-knowledge for the purpose of self-evaluation and thus development of insights. Even a biographical form, with the opportunity to put together information about oneself, both historically and cross sectionally, can give a counselee sufficient objective self-perception and clarification of problem and goal to facilitate the solution of his problem or determination of a choice or a decision.

To an even greater extent, this function can be served by the range of tests which compel self-inspection and self-inquiry. All of the inventory-type personality tests are of this character. Similarly, tests of general college adjustment; tests of attitudes and values; and tests of study habits, attitudes, methods, and techniques serve this purpose. The very "taking" of such tests as these, with the necessity for recording a response, compels thought and self-investigation, which activity in itself is both part of, and accelerative of, the process of counseling. Subsequently bringing to the counseling interview the counselee's conscious reaction to any or many of such items may lead to further insights and to reconstruction of many aspects of the self-concept.

The counselee can benefit from his own content analysis. For example, a counselee, in responding to adjustment or personality inventory tests, begins to recognize that he replies to items in a way which indicates to him that he must be rather passive. His passivity may thenceforth become a concern in his counseling. In self-assessment, the counselee has found clues to explore and pursue in his counseling.

Tests of the sort called special aptitude tests may often be most informative in the area of occupational information. Not only do such tests present situations and problems which occur in the occupation in question, as, for example, law, medicine, teaching, nursing, etc., but also give the counselee an opportunity to relate for himself his own attitudes and inclinations to the occupational demands. An example might be that of a counselee considering the possibility of preparing for teaching who, on responding to a teaching attitudes inventory, learns of the practical disciplinary problems in the classroom and who can thus visualize himself in such situations and try them on for size. Tests which reveal special knowledge in other than professional fields may provide some of the same direct view of occupational characteristics. In this category may be considered such tests as sales aptitude and comprehension, comprehension of mechanical principles, knowledge of supervisory principles. Even vocational interest tests, such as the Kuder, may be directly helpful to a counselee in this fashion since they describe the function or content of occupations rather than simply list them.

Interactive Facilitation. Here we are concentrating on the use of tests specifically within the interview framework for assisting in both the counseling relationship and communication and in furthering the counseling itself.

For the inarticulate uncommunicative person, testing may offer the means not only of immediate communication but may also be an impetus factor toward overcoming long-standing habits. For those who find it difficult to communicate orally in an interview, a Sentence Completion Test, for example, where thoughts are communicated in written form, may be most helpful in that they can then be talked about directly in the interview. If the counselee has been able to say in writing what he cannot say directly to the counselor, he has at least communicated and has expressed his willingness for the counselor to know what he has said and thus to begin to use it to help him to talk. A Thematic Apperception Test will perhaps draw on a counselee's unconscious attitudes and feelings, forming the basis for his communication on a deeper level than he has formerly been capable of in an interview.

We have indicated that both counselor and counselee can gain from tests very valuable information about the counselee's behavior and traits, again despite the fact that from a quantitative point of view validity and reliability coefficients might be less than desired.

In a sense the testing situation can be likened to a laboratory in which one learns about oneself in a real life situation and then can gain perspective upon it from counseling discussion. After test taking, both the counselor and counselee have the opportunity in the counseling relationship to share the impressions which come from the testing experience. Any of the information and impressions so derived can be used as an interview aid, as a method of entering into exploration and discussion. For example, with personality inventory-type tests, it may be very useful in the counseling process for the counselee in the interview to evaluate with the counselor the presence or absence of a tested trait and the degree to which he feels it pertains. For the counselor, tests provide limitless material for introducing ideas, for exploring hypotheses, for presenting interpretations, for clarifying, for reinforcing insights. In communication regarding the counselee's reactions to the tests, their items, and his performance, the counselee has opportunity for greater self-understanding, leading to resolution of problems. Working in this way utilizes the resources of the counselee in involving him actively in the counseling process.

Reference

1. Staff, Counseling Center, University of Maryland. "A Check-list for Recording Test-Taking Behavior," *Journal of Counseling Psychology,* 7 (1960), 116–119.

37

The Multifactor Tests: Summing Up[1]

Donald E. Super

One of the most useful series of articles dealing with multifactor tests appeared in the Personnel and Guidance Journal, September, *1956 through September, 1957. These articles were later brought together in a reprint series. The author, Dr. Donald Super, looks discerningly in this summary article at eight multifactor batteries. He reviews briefly his reaction to each test and then sets forth his conclusions regarding the usefulness of the batteries for counseling.*

Which of the eight test batteries does the author believe ready for use in counseling? which ready for research use only? which not suitable for use at the time (about 1958) Super wrote on the topic? Has the author changed his mind about the suitability of any of these multifactor test batteries as evidenced by statements in his 1962 book, Appraising Vocational Fitness by Means of Psychological Tests? *The reader may also wish to compare Super's judgment with that of reviewers presented in the* Mental Measurement Yearbook *series.*

In the opening paper in this series, the question asked was: "To what extent have the multifactor batteries lived up to the great promise which, as recently as ten years ago, they were deemed to have?" Another way of phrasing this question would be to ask: "How useful are these batteries to the practicing counselor?" In the survey of current thinking on this matter, that first paper brought out the fact that these tests which looked so promising only a few years ago are now viewed with considerable dissatisfaction and disillusionment by several leading test specialists. As the test authors submitted their manuscripts for this series describing the multifactor batteries, we therefore examined the materials critically, asking how well they met the desiderata of guidance tests. Opinions and data, especially data, were re-

From Donald E. Super, "The Multifactor Tests: Summing Up," *Personnel and Guidance Journal,* XXXVI (September, 1957), pp. 88–91. Reprinted with the permission of publisher and author.

[1] The writer is indebted to his colleague, Dr. Elizabeth Hagen, and to Professor George Speer of the Illinois Institute of Technology for their critical reading and helpful suggestions.

viewed in order to judge the *timelessness*, the *multipotentiality*, the *ability to yield descriptions of individuals*, and particularly the *predictive power* of the various test batteries. This final paper in the series attempts to summarize the conclusions reached, conclusions concerning the usefulness of these tests in counseling practice and concerning the need for further research.

The Batteries in Brief

The Differential Aptitude Tests make use of types of items which have proved promising in earlier tests, which are relatively timeless, and which in some instances deliberately sacrifice factorial purity for predictive validity. Because of this last fact the tests are in some instances not as independent of each other as tests in multifactor batteries tend to be. The picture of a person which they yield is therefore somewhat unsatisfactory for the study of mental structure, but it gains in lifelikeness: mechanical reasoning may be even less a "primary mental ability" than the scores that pass as such, but since it has predictive value it is a useful construct. The battery has been in use long enough, and it has been and is being studied persistently enough by its authors and by others, that a great deal of data have been accumulated concerning its predictive validity. It has been shown that several of the tests in the battery provide good predictors of success in academic courses in high school: the battery serves at least as a superior and somewhat refined intelligence test. Furthermore, two tests which have little predictive value for academic courses do have some predictive value for certain non-academic courses.

To some extent, then, the DAT is serving its purpose as a multifactor battery. The counselor must remember, however, that the predictive value of the tests varies considerably from one situation to another, making local validation studies necessary. Furthermore, the criterion which is being predicted must be understood, for one implication of the varying validities for the same subjects is that grades are given on differing bases by different teachers. The DAT may be characterized as currently the best battery for use in educational guidance in high school, although keeping this advantage over other batteries will depend on the ultimate wisdom of the decision to use a combination of pure and impure tests and on better analyses of the criteria of educational success. Its occupational norms and validity data are still too limited, however, for it to be used with confidence for differential vocational prediction or counseling. Conclusion: ready for use in educational counseling.

The General Aptitude Test Battery emphasized factorial purity in its construction, but at the same time made use of item types which had been shown to have validity in other tests. They are thus relatively timeless in content. They are multipotential in that they cover a very wide variety of factors, including manual and finger dexterity. The profile provides a good basis for describing the psychological make-up of a person. At the same time, the stress on occupational norms and validity has given the battery a practical usefulness which is still unique.

The user must remember, however, that much of the material on the occupational interpretation of the battery is based on job analysis rather than on actual validation, for the number of occupations for which Occupational Ability Patterns have been established and cross-validated is only a fraction of those for which OAP's have been suggested. Only a fraction of these have been established by testing prior to employment to make the validities predictive rather than merely concurrent. The GATB may nevertheless be characterized at this stage as the most useful existing multifactor test battery for vocational counseling. Whether or not it maintains this advantage will depend upon the validation and cross-validation of more of the OAP's with larger numbers, local validation studies, and upon the use of predictive rather than concurrent criteria. Conclusion: ready for use in vocational counseling.

The Guilford-Zimmerman Aptitude Survey meets the usual requirements of a factorial battery rather well. Like the majority of multifactor tests, it provides what seems to be a refined and rather good measure of intelligence, and in addition a measure of spatial visualization which is valid for success in science and in art courses. But, in its case, as in the case of the majority of multifactor batteries, work to date has consisted largely of studies of factorial independence and purity. This narrow although important focus has resulted in a dangerous disregard of predictive validity, and even in a disregard of the criticisms made of the data presented with the battery as a justification for its recommended use. At present, one is warranted in concluding only that the GZAS is a promising battery, which may prove useful to counselors if and after substantial data on its educational and occupational predictive validity are collected and reported. Conclusion: ready for research use only.

The Holzinger-Crowder Unifactor Tests is another promising looking multifactor battery, more promising than some because its tests seem to have more differential validity for the academic subjects than do some such tests. This may be because the battery attempts to cover fewer factors, concentrating on the more strictly intellectual abilities. But this good beginning remains to be firmly established by more large-scale and local studies of the battery's predictive validity for both educational and occupational success. It may well prove less useful for non-academic predictions than some other batteries, because of the stress on intellectual ability. Conclusion: ready for research use only.

The Factored Aptitude Series, we have seen, has some merit in its conception and construction, but has so consistently filtered information concerning its validity through a screen of advertising that one can only be suspicious of the sweeping claims made for it. These suspicions are not allayed by the fact that a recent study showed that the publisher's list of claimed users of the battery was a "significant overstatement" (Philip Ash: "Claimed and Reported Use of an Industrial Aptitude Test Battery." Paper read at the Annual Meeting of the American Psychological Association. San Francisco, 1955). The recommendation can only be a *caveat emptor.* Conclusion: not suitable for use.

The Segel-Raskin Multiple Aptitude Tests seem to resemble the Differential Aptitude Tests in that they stress factorial purity less than face validity, but they differ from that battery in that they rest their case for validity, so far, largely on theory and content. That is to say, the authors believe that their tests and test items make sense. There is as yet too little evidence of the educational validity of the battery: the limited data presented are, in light of experience with the more extensive validation of other batteries, simple and clear to the point of probable deception. When more studies are completed and when the data are reported in more detail, it is quite likely that the relationships will not seem as clear as they do in the limited report presently available. As for occupational validity, there is now no evidence to justify the battery's use. This is a battery worthy of watching, and perhaps of experimenting with, but not ready for use in counseling. Conclusion: ready for research use only.

The Flanagan Aptitude Classification Tests are ambitious in their conception and in their claims. The latter fact has bothered some experts, for the occupational validity data so far accumulated and reported are indeed nothing more than a very small beginning. But this fact must be viewed against the author's plans as steps in a program rather than as the ultimate justification of the battery. Some of the authors of multifactor tests have published batteries, made claims of certain types of validity, and recommended their tests for use in educational and vocational counseling. When they have recognized the need for further validation they have tended to do this with a certain lack of enthusiasm or conviction, as though paying lip service to an idea of which neither their tone nor their subsequent actions suggest genuine acceptance. Some other authors have shown more interest and belief in validation, but have let this work proceed somewhat haphazardly and incidentally, even to the point of relying largely on test users to supply the data. But Flanagan is one of a small minority who reports plans to validate a battery. He plans to do so in the most appropriate and painstaking way, proposes to carry out this plan himself, and has made small beginnings along these lines since the publication of his manual.

The practicing counselor must remember that *most* of the recommended use of the FACT battery is based on expert judgment, not on the proved validity of these specific tests. This is true also of the GATB, and even of the DAT (in view of the confused picture of educational validity from which the counselor must make some kind of sense). But the collective judgment of a group of experts as made available in these batteries is better than the isolated judgment of any one counselor using one of the other batteries released for vocational counseling solely on the basis of content and construct validity. The FACT battery therefore seems to merit the same type of cautious use as the GATB and the DAT, with the same expectation that the author will continue to collect and make available additional and improved empirical data as a basis for prediction and counseling. Conclusion: for research and perhaps for limited use in vocational counseling.

The SRA Primary Mental Abilities Tests are a modified version of the first American multifactor battery. The original battery made a major contribution to research in the structure of mental abilities and to test construction: the work represented by the tests discussed in this series owes a good deal to the Thurstones' pioneering. But the pioneer who blazes the trail and builds the first log cabin does not necessarily build a good house for the city which later develops around the site of his cabin. The SRA PMA Tests have proved most disappointing, and the authors' lack of interest in validation, combined with their disregard of the criticisms which have for some time been made of this battery, do not make one optimistic for its future. Conclusion: not suitable for use.

Conclusions

For Counseling. It is with some hesitation that I write these concluding paragraphs, for fear that even the most cautiously stated conclusions concerning the practical usefulness of specific tests or batteries will be misinterpreted and misapplied. For example, acquaintances occasionally ask whether I plan to write a briefer and simpler version of my measurement textbook, omitting the research material and concentrating on use and interpretation; the only reply which I can honestly give is that an understanding of the kind of material reviewed in that book is essential to the intelligent use of tests. Conclusions without a knowledge of their bases are dangerous, for the basis changes with the accumulation of data: the counselor must be able to relate new data to old and to revise his conclusions as he encounters new data. The present conclusions are therefore drawn with the hope that the reader will recognize that he must have his own basis for drawing conclusions, and that these conclusions will need modification with time.

Two multifactor batteries may be judged to be ready for use in counseling. These are the *Differential Aptitude Tests*, for which educational norms and predictive data are available, and the *General Aptitude Test Battery*, for which occupational norms and predictive data are on hand. In both instances considerable caution is called for in interpretation, for the validity data in the first case are confused and conflicting, and in the second they are limited and much less adequate than they seem prior to careful study of their nature. The pessimism of some reviewers is partly warranted by the fact that the proved value of these batteries is to a considerable extent no different from that of intelligence tests, but good intelligence tests are useful for a number of purposes, and these batteries include superior tests of intelligence. Since they also include tests of factors which are relatively independent of intelligence and which do have some special predictive value, they are not as disappointing as some interpretations of the findings might suggest.

Batteries which practicing counselors will want to watch, because they may in due course prove to be as good as, or perhaps better than, the above series are briefly commented on below. But first a word concerning judging the readiness of a battery for practical use. The reviewing of these test materials suggests that counselors might well be wary of the widespread tendency of test authors and publishers to play up *content*, *construct*, and *concurrent validity*. The counselor's job is, after all, to help evaluate prospects of success.

For Research. The fact that the DAT and the GATB are considered ready for use in counseling does not, of course, mean that they no longer need to be validated. The DAT needs to be validated against more carefully selected and analyzed criteria of educational achievement, and against occupational criteria in greater variety and numbers; multiple correlation and discriminant function techniques need to be applied in order to ascertain just what each test contributes to prediction. The GATB needs to have more of its OAP's validated and cross-validated against occupational criteria, using a predictive research design and larger numbers.

Two of the available multifactor test batteries have not stood the test of time or the scrutiny of science. These are the SRA *Primary Mental Abilities Tests* and the *Factored Aptitude Series:* the counselor and the researcher may be well advised to dismiss them from further consideration.

But some other tests seem well worth further study and may in due course be made into superior counseling tools by appropriate research. In this category the *Holzinger-Crowder Unifactor Tests* and the *Segel-Raskin Multiple Aptitude Tests* look promising, and perhaps also the *Guilford-Zimmerman Aptitude Survey,* as prospective competitors of the DAT, and the *Flanagan Aptitude Classification Tests* seem like batteries which might develop into rivals of the GATB. They may become competitors and rivals, that is, *if* and *after* more research on predictive validity is completed, analyzed, and published.

38

The Use of Information in Counseling

Ralph Berdie, Wilbur Layton, Edward Swanson, and Theda Hagenah

The following selection from Testing in Guidance and Counseling *is written by counselors with extensive experience in providing testing instruction to school counselors. The basic theme is that test results aid the counselor either by suggesting hypotheses about the counselee that require further verification or by furnishing evidence that helps verify hypotheses derived from other kinds of client information.*

From *Testing in Guidance and Counseling* by Ralph Berdie, Wilbur Layton, Edward Swanson, and Theda Hagenah. Copyright © 1963. McGraw-Hill Book Company. Used by permission. Pp. 133–145.

The authors give some attention to the relative accuracy of clinical and statistical predictions. A highlight of this selection is the presentation of some actual case studies. These should help the prospective counselor as he learns to work with tests of ability, achievement, special aptitudes, interest, and personality. What kinds of information other than test results do you think are especially helpful in the counseling process? What about the reliability and validity of these other types of data?

. . . .

IMPROVING STATISTICAL PREDICTIONS

Our thesis has been that test scores and other counseling information are used to help the counselor and the counselee originate and study hypotheses concerning the counselee's future behavior. The predictions about which we have been talking are in a sense hypotheses of this sort. When a counselor has a student take a college aptitude test and then through the use of a prediction table or prediction equation arrives at an estimate of the student's probable success, he is formulating a hypothesis about the pupil's future behavior. He could originate or review the hypothesis without the test data or without other pertinent data, but the more relevant and accurate the available data, the greater the probability that the hypothesis will correspond to the actual outcome.

Most of the hypotheses and most of the predictions made by counselors are not quantified. Seldom does a counselor make use of statistical methods of prediction; usually his predictions are formulated in a more intuitive or subjective manner. A counselor may use a statistical prediction when he is attempting to help a student understand his probability of success in a given college. When he is attempting to help a student understand his possibility of success in an occupation or his probability of liking that occupation, he is less likely to use a statistical prediction and more likely to use the intuitive, or what has been called a clinical, prediction.

The relative accuracy of clinical and statistical predictions has been carefully studied. Traditionally counselors have assumed that the best conclusions can be attained through careful consideration of whatever statistical predictions are available, manipulation and correction of these predictions on the basis of information that cannot be or is not included in the statistical prediction, and use of the statistical prediction as adjusted for other conditions. For example, a counselor working with a pupil considering college attendance has a series of test scores and a prediction table indicating that this particular pupil has 84 chances out of 100 of achieving at least a C average during his freshman year in college. The counselor knows, however, that the pupil will live at home while attending college and will have to commute to the campus and that the student will have to work on an outside job to help meet his expenses. He considers the ten hours a week the student will spend traveling back and forth between home and school and the twenty hours a week the student will spend on his job and decides that, in light of these considerations, the pupil's true probability for success in college is not 80 out of 100, but closer to 50 out of 100. Consequently, the counselor has adjusted the statistical prediction to account for information not included in the prediction tables.

This approach seems so reasonable that for decades nobody questioned its validity. Sarbin (3) was the first person to study the accuracy of predictions derived statistically and predictions derived from clinical manipulation of statistical predictions. He studied a number of college freshmen who had taken college aptitude tests and using regression equations, predicted the probable grade averages of these freshmen. He also had the college counselors who had access to the statistical predictions make clinical predictions as to the academic success of their counselees, and he compared the statistical predictions and the clinical predictions to the actual success of the student. Consistently the statistical predictions were somewhat superior to the clinical predictions, even though the latter were based in part on the statistical predictions.

The problem of statistical versus clinical prediction and the research related to this problem have been reviewed by Meehl (2), and in general Meehl's conclusions tend to confirm and expand on Sarbin's results.

In the case of the pupil cited above, the kind of information the counselor incorporated into the prediction, information about commuting and working, well might have been incorporated into a prediction table, and separate prediction tables could be prepared on the basis of test scores for students who live at home and who live on campus and for students who work varied numbers of hours a week. By using such tables, predictions most likely would be more accurate than those based on test scores alone or those made without access to prediction tables. The need for more comprehensive means of arriving at statistical predictions is obvious.

Ideally, the counselor would have before him tables presenting the probability for all events for all categories of students in all situations. These probabilities would be based on observations of actual outcomes. A counselor and a pupil would be able to look at such a table and to observe that of all pupils similar to this one who entered a certain curriculum in a given school, a given proportion succeeded, a given proportion failed. Little of the counselor's or pupil's time would have to be spent finding out the probability of success, and more time could be spent counseling and helping the student use the new information. Such probability figures are not available now and perhaps will not be for a long time. Counselors and pupils will have to continue to use whatever probability information is available and "semiprobability" information arrived at experientially, subjectively, intuitively, and vicariously.

The conscientious counselor constantly and systematically will strive to gather and organize observations in order to provide bases for making probability predictions. For example, a counselor in a high school which sends large numbers of its graduates to four different colleges will observe during the years that different types of pupils appear to succeed differentially in these colleges. Pupils with outstanding mathematical aptitude do particularly well in College A, but this aptitude does not seem to help them in College B. On the other hand, many students who are socially advanced and verbally fluent do well in College C, but students similar to these who enter College A frequently fail. The counselor uses this information in counseling pupils, and if the counselor's observations are accurate, this information is helpful. The counselor will find the information increasingly useful, however, if he finds a way for categorizing students according to his predictive observations and actually relates these categories to success in the four colleges. In this way, he would be able to say to himself and to his counselees that of every 100 students with ability such as theirs, a given proportion succeed in College A, a given proportion succeed in College B, and so on. Occasionally the counselor will find that his tabulations fail to bear out his intuitive impressions, and consequently he will be able to avoid predictions based on false premises. Equally important, however, are the opportunities of quantifying observations, easing communication, and attaching an estimate of error to the data.

USING DIFFERENT INFORMATION

The best way to learn how to use information in counseling is to use it, but practical learning experiences can be supplemented by reviewing the experiences of others. We will be helped by examining some of the experiences and problems of persons working with psychological tests of academic ability, educational achievement, special ability, vocational interest, and personality, and with other kinds of information about pupils.

The Case of Martin. Martin Brown was a thin, rather shy boy completing his senior year in high school when he came to the university counselor. Speaking easily and smiling readily throughout the interview, he said that he wanted to attend the university, but did not know what to take. He thought some aptitude tests would help him.

Martin had a part-time job and decided to attend the university only after his employer had discussed several times with him the advantages of a college education and had convinced Martin of the desirability of going to college. In high school he had liked but not done well in mathematics, so in order to learn more, he had repeated his algebra course in an evening school. When he talked to the counselor, he was taking a correspondence course in engineering, since he thought he would like to be an engineer, though he realized this was a very difficult course and thought perhaps he first ought to take a general course in college. In high school he had done well in but not liked typing and bookkeeping. He had thought of going into business.

Martin's father was a mechanic and did not care what his son became, as long as he did not become a mechanic. The father thought his own occupation dirty and was especially concerned about the amount of time his wife spent keeping his clothes clean. Martin and his father spent much time keeping the boy's motorcycle and car in repair.

Martin said his health was good and his hobbies included hunting and fishing. While in high school he had worked part time in a supermarket, in a machine shop, and as a gardener. His high school counselor, on the basis of his high school tests, had suggested that he consider being an electrician or plumber.

The university counselor talked with the high school counselor and learned that Martin had obtained his highest grades in shop courses. His high school percentile rank was 62 because of his good grades in these courses, but throughout his school career his academic achievement had been low. In the sixth grade his grade level in reading was 4.7 on the Metropolitan Achievement Test, and on this test his average grade level was 4.9. In the eighth grade, the Stanford Achievement Test placed him at the sixth-grade level. On the Cooperative English Test taken in the eleventh grade, his score placed him in the lower 1 per cent of university freshmen. On the Kuhlmann-Anderson Test taken in the sixth grade, his IQ was 89. In the ninth grade his percentile scores on the Differential Aptitude Tests, using ninth-grade norms, were: verbal reasoning — 6, number ability — 28, abstract reasoning — 40, spatial relations — 40, mechanical reasoning — 16, and clerical speed and accuracy — 1. His score on the American Council on Education Psychological Examination in the eleventh grade placed him in the lower 2 per cent of high school juniors who had become university freshmen.

In spite of this consistent information, the university counselor had Martin take the Ohio Psychological Examination on which he obtained a score placing him in the lower 2 per cent of university freshmen. On the Cooperative Mathematics Test he fell in the lower 3 per cent of engineering students, and on a retest of the Differential Aptitude Tests his percentile scores were, using norms based on university students in a two-year general college course: verbal reasoning — 10, number ability — 69, abstract reasoning — 35, spatial relations — 43, mechanical reasoning — 14, clerical speed and accuracy — 9, and language usage-spelling — 1. The counselor did not know that Martin had previously taken this battery of tests when he gave them, and later, when the original scores became available, the counselor had no way of taking into account the practice effect on the retests. The counselor assumed that the retest scores provided overestimates of Martin's true abilities, but he suspected there would be relatively little practice effect on the Differential Aptitude Tests after a three-year interval.

On the Kuder Preference Record, Martin obtained percentile scores of 95 on musical, 93 on clerical, 89 on artistic, and 53 on computational. All other percentile scores were below 50. On the Strong Vocational Interest Blank, he obtained A's on the scales for farmer, carpenter, policeman, and office man, and scores of B+ on scales for printer, mathematics and physical science teacher, industrial education teacher, vocational agriculture teacher, senior certified public accountant, and banker. On the Minnesota Multiphasic Personality Inventory, the scores were generally elevated, indicating personal conflict and psychological discomfort, but none of these scores were high enough to indicate an extreme problem.

All of the information collected influenced the course of counseling. The

Kuhlmann-Anderson Test, the American Council on Education Psychological Examination, the Differential Aptitude Tests, and the Ohio test — all suggested that Martin did not have enough ability for a highly academic university course. His extra-high school experience in some mathematics and engineering courses tended to verify this judgment. The achievement tests and high school grades provided supporting evidence.

The interest tests and the information Martin revealed in the interviews about his family background, his hobbies, and his aspirations suggested that he might find ultimate satisfaction in jobs not requiring vocational preparation in a college. During two or three interviews, Martin realized that his own motivation to attend college was not high, but that he was being overly influenced by his employer. The university counselor agreed that it might be worthwhile for Martin to attempt a university course of a general and elementary nature for at least a few months if he wished. Although he did not actively encourage Martin, at the same time he attempted to help Martin realize that he might later discover that the plan was not the best one for him.

Martin returned to the counselor after one quarter at the university and said he was satisfied with his experience, but he wished to leave the university and hoped to work. The counselor and Martin discussed again the implications of the information, and Martin decided to accept a job offered by the owner of a neighboring nursery. This employer had been favorably impressed by Martin's friendliness, serious attitude, and common sense. The counselor assisted Martin in selecting adult education courses that would help to prepare him for advancement in this work, and later reports showed satisfactory progress both in his job and in his courses.

Almost all of the information collected was used during counseling. The counselor and Martin both considered test scores, work history, family background, high school experiences, reports from the high school counselor, and scores on achievement, special aptitude, and vocational interest tests. Without the other information, the scores on the academic aptitude tests could have been used only in a negative way. Martin could have been told or warned that his probability for success in the university was small. The other information, however, allowed the counselor to approach the problem more constructively and to help reduce future frustration and disappointment.

Other pupils similar to Martin may wish to embark on courses of action which, according to all the counselor's information, will lead to failure. The counselor's function is not necessarily to prevent the pupil from taking a particular road, but rather to help the pupil become aware of more promising alternatives in case the road selected does lead to failure. One of the most important jobs of the counselor is to help the pupil realize that being unable to meet certain requirements does not necessarily mean the pupil is a failure; rather, it may mean that the pupil has tried one alternative to learn if it is the correct one, and having discovered that it is not, he has succeeded in learning that some other alternative should be chosen.

The Case of Marietta. Marietta was a junior when she saw her school counselor. The counselor knew that Marietta came from a large family living on a farm, that she was quiet, submissive, and shy, and that in school she had never shown any outstanding academic promise. She was not active in extracurricular affairs and according to her classroom teachers, had not done well in classes. The counselor invited Marietta to her office to discuss her plans. Marietta said that she had not done well in school and that she did not have the ability to do better. She planned to work as a telephone operator for a while after graduation from high school and hoped then to be married.

Marietta had been tested in the statewide testing program, and the report to her high school indicated that she had a percentile rank of 70 on the American Council on Education Psychological Examination, using norms which compared her with entering college freshmen. Her scores on the Cooperative English Test, Form Z, lower level, were a percentile rank of 10 on Mechanics of Expression and 11 on Effectiveness of Expression, with a first percentile rank on total English score. The English norms also were based on entering college freshmen. The other test data available to the counselor described a girl of below-average ability who had never performed well on tests.

When the counselor reviewed Marietta's case, she wondered if an error could have been made by the statewide testing agency in reporting her college aptitude score to the school. She wisely wrote to the director of the agency, called Marietta's scores to his attention, and asked that they be checked. A check in the central files indicated that the ACE percentile rank should have been reported as 1, rather than 70; the Mechanics of Expression percentile rank on the English test should have been reported as 7, instead of 10; and the Effectiveness of Expression percentile rank should have been 1, instead of the 11 that was reported. The original percentile rank on the total English test was correct.

The counselor's treatment of Marietta's case illustrates well the care with which a counselor should review all available information, especially when one or two items of data are incongruent with other data. Tests must be administered to students by counselors who are human and who are subject to human error in spite of all the effort made to reduce these errors to a minimum. Tests are processed and prepared for scoring by persons similarly prone to error. Many times tests are scored and reports are prepared by IBM machines and other electrical equipment. In spite of the efficiency of IBM machines and modern scoring devices, none are yet 100 per cent accurate, and no system has ever been devised which allows all errors to be detected and corrected before scores are reported to counselors. Consequently, the counselor must look at every test score, just as he looks at all other information, with a small question mark and realize that error possibly may explain some of the information at hand.

USING INFORMATION IN PLANNING

The following case of two brothers, who in many ways were different from each other, illustrates how information is used in counseling high school students. One of these brothers most likely will attend college after he graduates from high school; the other may attend college, but is equally likely to obtain post-high school training some place other than in college. The boys have different abilities and different expressed interests, and perhaps different measured interests, different aptitudes, and different backgrounds of information. To work effectively with these boys, their counselors and teachers must have information about them continually through high school.

The Nestor boys were students in a small city high school and were sons of an insurance salesman who himself had graduated from that school. Donald, seventeen years old, was in the twelfth grade and was planning to attend college, while Lloyd, fifteen years of age, was quite undecided about his plans, but expressed more interest in activities involving mechanical apparatus than in academic pursuits.

When Donald was in the eleventh grade, he had been inspired to become an engineer, influenced in part by advice given to him by a local industrialist during a "college and career day." His only work experience which he had enjoyed, had been in selling, and he had no experience even indirectly related to engineering. His school grades had been evenly divided between A's and B's with the exception of four grades of B, D, D, and C in mathematics. The test scores for the two boys are presented in Figures 1 to 3.

Instead of discouraging Donald from seriously considering engineering, his school counselor called to his attention other occupations that would allow him to use his abilities to his best advantage. In the twelfth grade the counselor spoke with him several times, twice with Donald and his parents together. The outcome was that Donald decided engineering was inappropriate and that he should enter college and take a two-year general course. During that time he could decide if he should subsequently take a college or university course in business administration or if he should leave college at the end of two years and obtain his occupational training on the job, perhaps in something related to selling.

At this time Lloyd was too young to approach a definite decision, but in light of his expressed interest, the counselor helped Lloyd and his parents plan how he could take advantage of every opportunity that might provide additional experience in mechanical and related work. The counselor also worked with Lloyd and his English teacher to improve his reading skills.

When pupils enter high school, they have to choose the general direction in which they will go. Will they take the academic road leading toward college, the road leading toward trade schools and apprenticeship training, the road leading directly toward employment, or the road leading to what, for lack of a better term, might be called a general education? Admittedly, none of these is an unalterable choice, and the choice made at the beginning of the high school period should be regarded as tentative and subject to later change. Nevertheless, the appropriateness of this choice determines in part the efficiency with which a pupil will be able to use his years in high school.

The age at which pupils are ready to make choices varies greatly, and a few pupils are in a position to make definite and permanent decisions while relatively young. On the other hand, many are not ready for these decisions until after they complete high school. Arriving at educational and vocational decisions is a process extending through long periods of time (4, 5), and there is no point in time at which it occurs. This means that the planning of pupils' programs must take into account the fact that decisions may change, that room must be left for new plans, and that life programs cannot be mapped rigidly even by the most skillful counselor.

By the time a pupil arrives at a choice point when action must be taken, he and his teachers should have a good idea of what his abilities and aptitudes are, what the general nature of his interests is, and what informational background he has.

CHOICE POINTS

The information we have been discussing is used repeatedly by counselors as they assist pupils in evaluating choice points. A few of these major points are of a kind that occur only once or only a few times. Other choice points occur repeatedly. For instance, specific courses must be considered and

Figure 1

DONALD'S TEST PROFILE

University of Minnesota
Office of the Dean of Students
Student Counseling Bureau
Summary Profile

Name: Nestor, Donald   Class: Senior   Sex: Male   Age: 17

Date	Name of Test	Percentile	Norm Group
3/49	American Council on Education Psychological Examination (high school edition)	89	High school: 9th grade
1/52	American Council on Education Psychological Examination (college edition)	83	Minnesota college freshmen
3/49	Differential Aptitude Test		High school:
	Verbal	89	9th grade
	Numerical	50	9th grade
	Abstract	45	9th grade
	Spatial	38	9th grade
	Mechanical	38	9th grade
	Clerical	21	9th grade
	Spelling	75	9th grade
	Sentence	92	9th grade
3/49	Cooperative Mathematics	50	9th grade
3/49	Cooperative Social Studies	93	9th grade
3/49	Cooperative Natural Sciences	91	9th grade
3/49	Cooperative English		
	Mechanics	90	9th grade
	Effectiveness	94	9th grade
	Reading Comprehension	91	9th grade
1/52	Cooperative English — Total	90	Minnesota college freshmen

Figure 2

DONALD'S INTEREST PROFILE
STRONG VOCATIONAL INTEREST BLANK — MEN

Name: Nestor, Donald   Age: 17   Date: January, 1952

Group	Occupation	Score
I	Artist	C +
	Psychologist	B −
	Architect	C
	Physician	C
	Osteopath	C
	Dentist	C
	Veterinarian	C
II	Mathematician	C
	Physicist	C
	Engineer	C
	Chemist	C
III	Production Manager	C +
IV	Farmer	B −
	Aviator	C +
	Carpenter	B −
	Printer	B
	Math Physical Science Teacher	B −
	Industrial Arts Teacher	B −
	Vocational Agriculture Teacher	C +
	Policeman	C +
	Forest Service Man	C
V	Y.M.C.A. Physical Director	A
	Personnel Director	A
	Public Administrator	A
	Y.M.C.A. Secretary	B +
	Social Science High School Teacher	B +
	City School Superintendent	B +
	Minister	B
VI	Musician	C
VII	C.P.A.	A
VIII	Senior C.P.A.	B
	Accountant	B −
	Office Man	B
	Purchasing Agent	B −
	Banker	B
	Mortician	C +
	Pharmacist	B −
IX	Sales Manager	A
	Real Estate Salesman	A
	Life Insurance Salesman	A
X	Advertising Man	B −
	Lawyer	B −
	Author-Journalist	C +
XI	President — Manufacturing Concern	B −

Interest Maturity, 50
Occupational Level, 43
Masculinity-Femininity, 52

Figure 3

LLOYD'S TEST PROFILE

University of Minnesota
Office of the Dean of Students
Student Counseling Bureau
Summary Profile

Name: Nestor, Lloyd   Class: Sophomore   Sex: Male   Age: 15

Date	Name of Test	Percentile	Norm Group
3/51	American Council on Education Psychological Examination (high school edition)	55	High School: 9th grade
3/51	Differential Aptitude Test		
	Verbal	55	9th grade
	Numerical	62	9th grade
	Abstract	48	9th grade
	Spatial	92	9th grade
	Mechanical	95	9th grade
	Clerical	12	9th grade
	Spelling	14	9th grade
	Sentences	21	9th grade
3/51	Cooperative Mathematics	48	9th grade
3/51	Cooperative Social Studies	53	9th grade
3/51	Cooperative Natural Sciences	61	9th grade
3/51	Cooperative English		
	Mechanics	22	9th grade
	Effectiveness	41	9th grade
	Reading Comprehension	18	9th grade

evaluated repeatedly in terms of pupil attitude and interest and chosen accordingly. Sometimes decisions must be made regarding the assignment of students to sections of courses, and when students are classified according to aptitude and achievement backgrounds, decisions again must be made.

Every week and perhaps every day the teacher will make and help the pupil make decisions that should depend on the information we are discussing. Class assignments and projects will be selected on the basis of the information about the pupil. Methods of motivating pupils will be selected more efficiently if the pupil's own interests and aptitudes are considered. Remedial measures can be provided for pupils who are retarded in specific areas or deficient in basic skills. The effectiveness of any attempt to individualize classroom instruction and high school planning depends on the use of objective and reliable information about individuals.

Choice points often appear outside the classroom. High school counselors and teachers help pupils select cocurricular activities appropriate in terms of interest, personality, and aptitudes. Some pupils who have meager musical backgrounds can be encouraged to participate in musical activities, not with the hope that they will become star performers, but rather in order to enrich their own backgrounds so that they can derive greater satisfaction from life. Other pupils with just as meager backgrounds but perhaps with inadequate musical aptitude will be encouraged to participate in other kinds of activities, because for these pupils music may be far too great a failure experience.

Some pupils begin to make their post-high school plans as early as the ninth grade and even before that, but most delay definite planning until the beginning of the twelfth grade. Some evidence suggests that for some students plans made early are more valid than plans made late (1), but many high school pupils simply are not mature enough to make plans before the twelfth grade. Regardless of when these plans are made, however, the more information considered, the more realistic and appropriate they will be. The student projecting himself into the future and thinking of marriage, of occupations, or of community responsibilities should know his own strengths and limitations if such plans are not to eventuate in frustration.

One of the major purposes of collecting and providing the kind of information we have discussed is to help the student know himself.

References

1. Dyer, D. T. "The Relation Between Vocational Interests of Men in College and Their Subsequent Occupational Histories for Ten Years," *Journal of Applied Psychology*, 23 (1939), 283.
2. Meehl, P. E. *Clinical versus Statistical Prediction.* Minneapolis: University of Minnesota Press, 1954.
3. Sarbin, T. R. "The Logic of Prediction in Psychology," *Psychological Review*, 51 (1944), 210–228.
4. Super, D. E. *The Psychology of Careers: An Introduction to Vocational Development.* New York: Harper & Row, Publishers, 1957.
5. Super, D. E., et al. *Vocational Development: a Framework for Research.* New York: Teachers College, Columbia University, Bureau of Publications, 1957.

39

The Importance of Understanding Talent

John C. Flanagan, John T. Dailey, Marion F. Shaycoft, William A. Gorham, David B. Orr, and Isadore Goldberg

No selection of readings on the use of tests in counseling would be complete without reference to Project Talent. The United States pays a high price for its failure to capitalize fully on talented youth. This massive and long term research project has been launched to see how talents can be better identified and brought to a point of high productivity and usefulness.

Although the following brief selection will give the reader some flavor of Project Talent, the prospective school counselor will profit by reading the entire small volume, Design for a Study of American Youth. *The thoughtful student will wish to follow the subsequent reports emanating from Project Talent since they will be designed to provide more effective plans for the identification, development, and use of all the talents of our young.*

. . . .

The academicians defend their subject matter areas in a loud and firm voice. No less loud and firm are the voices of those who advocate more and better guidance for children. Much is claimed for guidance. Its advocates insist that if every school were staffed with "an adequate number of well-trained guidance counselors" (though criteria for determining quantity or quality are lacking) we would have less juvenile delinquency, better adjusted children, more intelligent career and scholastic choices, and so on. But to what extent do school guidance activities make a difference in the lives of young people? From where do the influences which shape the lives and careers of young people really come — from classroom teachers, counselors, parents, or the neighbors next door? We do not have the facts to answer such questions. Nor do counselors have scientifically devised tools to appraise vocational fitness. Batteries of tests for some few specific occupations do exist. Some are adequate, some are not. But taken together, these do not begin to cover the occupations found in American industry, business, and the professions.

From John C. Flanagan *et al.*, *Design for a Study of American Youth* (Boston: Houghton Mifflin Company, 1962), pp. 29–33. Reprinted with the permission of publisher and authors.

Speakers in state legislatures and at school board meetings frequently demand the abolition of small schools on the assumption that "the larger the school, the better its education." How do they know? Such speakers rely on the arguments of partisans rather than on the evidence of investigators. We still don't have facts that would answer with precision what effect the size of the school has on the effectiveness of education. Nor do we have evidence to answer a host of other questions. Take these two: To what extent would an increase in appropriations for instruction result in an increase in teaching quality? And, what is the effect of home background and parent occupation on a child's learning?

Although the air in the educational community is thick with expressions of opinion, only rarely is objective proof available to show that one practice is better than another; one policy more productive than a second.

Research studies, designed to make the schools more effective, are under way in many graduate schools and are being sponsored here and there by professional or special-interest groups. But much research in education is limited to surface problems and too few cases. Research also suffers from short-span inquiries.

No single research effort, regardless of scope or duration, can provide all, or even a substantial part, of the information needed for the development of talent in a country as large as ours. Without anticipating what is to follow, we can say now that Project TALENT involves the largest number of school children ever to take part in a research study — and that they will be involved for more than two decades — thus providing the vast dimensions required for an investigation of such complex problems.

· · · ·

How Can an Individual Make the Best Use of His Talents?

What does it avail a person if he has a unique pattern of aptitudes and if these are developed — if he doesn't use them? Use of talent is a test of talent. Production is the pay-off. But what forces release our productivity? And how can the levels of productivity be raised so that what we do is more than ordinary or routine, and reaches the quality of creativeness and brings us lasting satisfactions?

Now we are at the last of the three underlying questions about talent — that is, how can the individual best use his talents? Enough research has been done to suggest that there exist forces within us and outside us that can operate on our will to perform and increase our power to create. The research literature on motivation, productivity, and creativity is growing. We shall have occasion to refer to it — in later reports coming from Project TALENT. Some of it is significant and revealing.

For the moment, it will be more revealing to become acquainted with a high school student we shall call Robert. Robert is one of nearly 440,000 students taking part in our research activities. We are not using his real name so we can tell you freely a good deal about him.

When Robert took the Project TALENT tests, he was 16 years old and at the end of his junior year in high school. He reported that he gets up at

5 o'clock every morning to deliver papers. With this and other jobs, he works about 16 to 20 hours a week, earning all his spending money. When he gets home after school, he puts in some time on chores, amounting to about 10 hours a week. Athletics take up 12 hours a week. He also spends part of his spare time building and repairing electrical and electronic apparatus.

He has had four semester courses in science, two in a foreign language, six in social studies, six in English, and six in mathematics. His grades in mathematics have been mostly C's and D's, while his grades in other subjects have been mostly B's and C's. He spends only one to four hours per week on his homework. It appears to be crowded out by other activities and interests (26 to 30 hours of work and 12 hours of athletics each week).

Robert says he likes to hunt, swim, and explore. He does not like to read novels, but he enjoys science fiction and technical books. He states that he would like to work at a government rocket proving ground because he likes working with electricity and electronics.

We have additional facts about Robert which only a battery of aptitude tests similar to that of Project TALENT could reveal. (Figure 1 shows the profile of his test scores.) He had a perfect score on our aeronautics and space information test. He had exceptionally high scores on tests which measured his accumulation of facts on physical sciences and mechanics, his ability to visualize in two dimensions, and his creativity. These high scores suggest that Robert has considerable aptitude in the general field of science. He has probably acquired information about science and mechanics outside the classroom — just as he has confirmed his strong interests in science through spare time tinkering and science-fiction reading.

Our tests also spotlighted an almost hidden fact about Robert. He made a very good score on a math information test, showing that he has considerable general knowledge about mathematics even though his performance in school math work has been below average, as shown by his C and D grades. On the Project TALENT math achievement test his score exceeded those of 78 per cent of the high school juniors in the study — not outstanding, but better than his grades would suggest.

Robert's English test scores were very low. Since a passing grade in English is still one of the requirements for admission to colleges and engineering schools, he does not, to the traditional-minded teacher, look like good college material. What are Robert's college plans? He reported to Project TALENT that he might not go to college, although he would like to. He may have to borrow money to do so. If he is able to raise the money, he would like to major in physical science.

Such are the facts Project TALENT obtained about Robert. How can Robert's school and parents use these facts to help him make the best use of his talents?

Teachers could do much to assist in developing Robert's considerable talents in science if they gained an appreciation of the nature of these talents. Once they gain this appreciation (in this instance, from the test scores), they can direct Robert to further education in the physical sciences, since that is what his interests and aptitudes point to. But low math and English grades

Figure 1

ROBERT'S PROFILE CHART

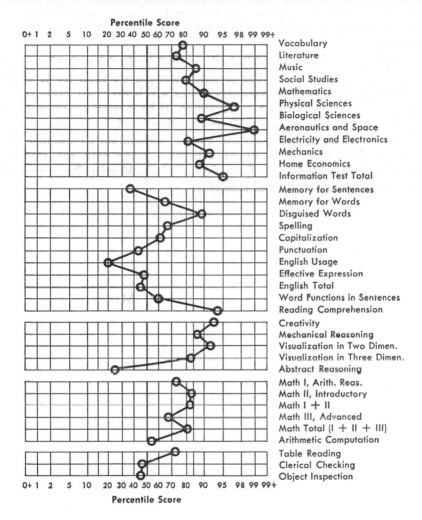

stand in the way. His teachers, therefore, should try to point out to him, the relation of better achievement in math and English, his poor subjects, to physical sciences, his main interest. This encouragement may motivate Robert to study math and English harder. Motivation for Robert can also operate in another way. It is quite possible that the pull of his strong interest in the field of electronics may, itself, induce him to work harder on math and English — that is, if he sees the relationship between these subjects and the job he wants in the future.

Within a year after his graduation from high school, we shall know more about what happened to Robert. We shall ask him to give us facts about his post high school experiences. We shall know whether he has, in fact, enrolled in a college and has chosen the physical sciences as his major interest. Within five years we shall know what kind of employment he has accepted; within ten years we shall know much about his success; and within twenty years we shall know even more about the way in which Robert has used his talents.

Throughout our follow-up of Robert, we shall try to determine how he has utilized his latent talents in the physical sciences; we shall try to identify the educational and occupational experiences which may have encouraged or discouraged his productivity or his creativity. If he is relatively unproductive, we shall try to find the reasons. If, on the other hand, he becomes a highly productive, perhaps creative, person, gaining recognition as scientist or inventor, we shall learn from Robert's record — along with the records of thousands of other students — facts that will help Martha, Peter, and John toward greater productivity and creativity.

SUGGESTED READINGS

Flanagan, John C., *et al. Design for a Study of American Youth.* Boston: Houghton Mifflin Company, 1962.

This small book, the first of a series of reports by the staff of Project Talent, sets forth the design for the study, the construction of the tests and inventories, their administration, data analysis, and the next steps. Student personnel workers will find this study impressive and their knowledge of it will enable them to act as intelligent consumers of the results of this significant, long-term investigation.

Froehlich, Clifford P., and Hoyt, Kenneth B. *Guidance Testing.* Chicago: Science Research Associates, Inc., 1959.

In this book, the authors consider the different methods available to counselors and teachers for studying their clients and students. Various types of tests and simple statistical techniques are reviewed. The remainder of the work presents the nature and recording of observations, the interview technique, home-school communications, self-reporting, and sociometry.

Goldman, Leo. *Using Tests in Counseling.* New York: Appleton-Century-Crofts, Inc., 1961.

This work is invaluable for prospective school counselors. The author discusses in a very readable yet thorough manner the major problems of test selection, administration, interpretation, and reporting. Especially worthwhile is the evaluative treatment of statistical versus clinical approaches in test interpretation.

McLaughlin, Kenneth F. *Interpretation of Test Results.* Washington, D.C.: U.S. Department of Health, Education, and Welfare, Office of Education, Bulletin No. 7, 1964.

This bulletin was prepared by the Guidance and Counseling Programs Branch of the U.S. Office of Education in connection with Title V of the National Defense Education Act of 1958. It explains the proper use and limitation of regularly administered tests. The listing of some seventy-five selected references is a good one and should be quite helpful to school counselors in their constant search for more meaningful uses of test results.

Meehl, Paul E. *Clinical versus Statistical Prediction.* Minneapolis: University of Minnesota Press, 1954.

Guidance counselors inevitably encounter this problem: Shall we make use of mathematical manipulations of data or should we rely upon the subjective interpretation of our data through skilled judgment? This discussion will serve as a useful guidepost in helping to solve the dilemma. It is not easy reading, but the reward of increased understanding is well worth the effort.

Super, Donald E., and Crites, John O. *Appraising Vocational Fitness by Means of Psychological Tests* (rev. ed.). New York: Harper and Brothers, 1962.

In many respects, this is the "Bible" for the test user — the counselor in school, college, or community agency, and the personnel worker in government, industry, and business. This book has found a distinctive place in educational experiences which seek to provide the student with a real knowledge and understanding of the tests he may use, and some skill in employing these instruments. Especially appropriate are Chapters XXI and XXII and Appendices A and B.

Womer, Frank B., and Frick, Willard B. *Personalizing Test Use: A Counselor's Casebook*. Ann Arbor: Bureau of School Services, The University of Michigan, 1964.

This booklet is a very practically written resource for persons specifically interested in utilizing test results to aid the adjustment of students to their present and future school programs. Twenty-five cases are presented. Most or all of these were contributed by active school counselors.

Test-Taking Behavior

A topic of considerable importance, but one which is often ignored in test analysis, is the matter of nontest influences that affect student performances on the test itself. It is generally assumed that differences in scores among individuals are primarily due to differences in the trait being assessed, but various other problems enter into the determination of responses. Some individuals bring with them to the test situation predispositions to respond in certain ways, for example, to be agreeable, or to choose the second alternative among those provided in a multiple-choice test. Cronbach has dealt with this issue rather extensively, and his second major article on the topic is reported here in Selection 40.

However, a question arises at this point. If students bring with them a predisposition to respond in a given way, can this mode of response be altered by the nature of the test content itself? Likewise, is it possible that if a student does not bring with him a certain response set, he can acquire one from the testing situation? The entire problem is one of determining just which aspect of a test is the one a test taker responds to in producing the score that he eventually gets. This is the problem dealt with by Chase in Selection 41.

Another question deals with the way people respond to the environment in the test situation. Test administrators are admonished to regulate conditions so as to eliminate distractions. In Selection 42, Super, Braasch, and Shay show just how important this is, while Bernstein illustrates another environmental influence on test results — the presence of the examiner (Selection 44).

"First impressions are most often correct" is a saying out of student folklore. Reile and Briggs investigate the validity of this mode of test-taking behavior in Selection 43, with interesting results.

This unit, then, points to at least five different conditions that influence the behavior of students in a testing situation. These conditions are in some cases tied to test content; in other cases, they are probably quite independent of test content. The reader may wish therefore to examine the question of just what part the testing situation should play in eliciting the behavior to be observed. The structure of the test, including the test taker's environment, may be less common from person to person than testers would like to believe.

40

Further Evidence on Response Sets
and Test Design

Lee J. Cronbach[1]

In an earlier article, Cronbach stated the basic propositions of response set. In this article he elaborates his original report, and suggests ways of dealing with the problem. The reader may wish to consult Rorer, Psychological Bulletin, LXIII (March, 1965), 129–156, for a criticism of Cronbach's presentation.

When a person takes an objective test, he may bring to the test a number of test-taking habits which affect his score. Personal ways of responding to test items of a given form (e.g., the tendency to say "agree" when given the alternatives "agree" — "uncertain" — "disagree") are frequently a source of invalidity. In 1946, the writer (1) assembled evidence demonstrating that these "response sets" are present in a wide variety of tests. Since that time, much new evidence has come to light, and it is now possible to examine more completely the nature of response sets. While much of the material to be reported is new, evidence has also been drawn from scattered publications which were overlooked in the earlier review. Material on response sets is to be found in a great many sorts of studies, discussed under many names. Particular attention should be drawn to the early reports of Lorge (15) and Goodfellow (6) on this topic.

As our earlier report demonstrated, response sets have been identified in tests of ability, personality, attitude, and interest, and in rating scales. Among the most widely found sets are acquiescence (tendency to say "True," "Yes," "Agree," etc.), evasiveness (tendency to say "?," "Indifferent," "Uncertain," etc.), and similar biases in favor of a particular response when certain fixed alternatives are offered. Other sets include the tendency to work for speed rather than accuracy, the tendency to guess when uncertain, the tendency to check many items in a checklist, etc. Response sets become most influ-

From Lee J. Cronbach, "Further Evidence on Response Sets and Test Design," *Educational and Psychological Measurement*, X (Spring, 1950), pp. 3–31. Reprinted with the permission of publisher and author.

[1] This study was assisted by funds from the Bureau of Research and Service, College of Education, University of Illinois.

ential as items become difficult or ambiguous. Individual differences in response sets are consistent throughout a given test, as shown by split-half coefficients. Response sets dilute a test with factors not intended to form part of the test content, and so reduce its logical validity. These sets may also reduce the test's empirical validity. Response sets tend to reduce the range of individual differences in score.

The pattern of this discussion is as follows: First, many studies are cited which bolster the conclusion that response sets are widely found, and are particularly influential when a test is difficult. These new sources confirm earlier findings and do not modify them. The significant new material in this section relates to two multiple-choice tests, and confirms the hypothesis that this form of test is nearly free from response sets. The second section of the report deals with the nature of response sets. Questions considered are: Can performance be altered by special directions or training to avoid response biases? Are response sets consistent traits, so that a person shows a similar set on different tests? Are response sets correlated with other aspects of personality? These studies deal particularly with the question whether response sets are due to a transient mind-set and are therefore only a nuisance in testing, or whether they may provide data on important variables. The third and final section reviews methods used to control the influence of response sets on validity, and discusses what test constructors can do to design better tests.

EVIDENCE THAT RESPONSE SETS EXIST

It is scarcely necessary to marshal further evidence that reliable individual differences in response sets exist. Yet the widespread use of test forms which permit response sets indicates that their existence is not adequately appreciated. It is not only the old tests — Seashore, Bernreuter, Thurstone attitude, Strong — that suffer from response sets. New tests appear continually, especially tests of attitude and personality, whose forms invite response sets. The writer has routinely requested graduate students to analyze their data for response sets whenever their research employed tests with fixed response categories (A-U-D, Yes-No-?, etc.). *Never has such an analysis failed to disclose individual patterns of response, statistically consistent from item to item.*

The most effective simple design to demonstrate response sets is to obtain a score for each person on the suspected response set. Thus, Lorge tested the existence of "gen-like," or acquiescence on the Strong test, by counting how many items each person marked "L." The split-half or Kuder-Richardson reliability of the response-set score can then be computed. Table 1 condenses the evidence obtained by this and other techniques, evidence which, together with that previously assembled, shows conclusively that response sets are to be found in a great many tests.

One study requires a separate report, because it is based on a factorially-designed test in which items are intended to be homogeneous. Kenneth Eells supplied the writer with tests "Cards" and "Figures," from Thurstone's

Tests of Primary Mental Abilities, which had been given to pupils in a Midwestern city as part of a study by the University of Chicago Committee on Cultural Factors in Intelligence Tests, under a grant from the General Education Board. Both of these tests present a geometric figure at the left of the row, and follow it with figures just like the given one save that they have been rotated through 90°, 180°, or 270°, or are mirror-images of one of these rotations. Directions are to "mark every card (figure) that is like the first card (figure)." It was observed that some pupils seem to search for all correct answers, whereas others are content to identify one or two seemingly correct answers, and then go on to the following row. Papers were drawn at random from those given to all pupils in two large junior high schools. Papers were discarded where any row had been omitted, or where the total score on Cards was high (46 or more out of 54 possible). This avoids spuriously high apparent reliability for the response-set score. The test had been given with double time, and the test was in effect unspeeded for the pupils studied. Two response-set scores were obtained for each pupil: Cards R + W, and Figures R + W. This score indicates a tendency to mark many items in a row. It implies thoroughness and persistence in marking, and perhaps acquiescence. The correlation of the two R + W scores is .54 ($N = 109$). On the whole, those who mark fewer items appear to be poorer students, but no estimate of response sets, independent of ability, could be obtained. For the selected cases, the correlation of R + W cards with R − W Figures was .44, and that of R + W Figures with R − W Cards was .33. These data are interpreted as showing that in addition to the space factor (ability to discriminate similar forms), performance on this test is influenced by a response set. Many students are found who mark few or no incorrect figures (R + W = R − W) but who fail to mark all the correct alternatives. Since some of the reliable response-set variance is uncorrelated with the space factor, the entrance of response sets reduces the factorial purity of the test. Certainly tests which aim at measurement of a single factor must be designed to eliminate response sets.

Response Sets in Multiple-Choice Tests. The only major form of fixed-alternative test which has so far been found free from response sets is the multiple-choice item. In order to determine whether response sets can be extracted from a typical test of this type, the writer has studied the *Henmon-Nelson Test of Mental Ability, Form A,* for Grades 3–8. The data for this study were supplied by Eells, from the study which provided the Thurstone data discussed above. Thousands of test papers were available, since every child in several grades in a midwestern city had been tested. The sample for this study was chosen indiscriminately, from papers of upper-lower and lower-middle-class children. In administering the test experimentally, Eells allowed an extended time of 20 minutes beyond the standard time of 30 minutes. Papers not completed even in the extended time were discarded in the present analysis.

The Henmon-Nelson is a suitable test for investigating response sets because items were prepared with care, are fairly well arranged as to difficulty, and are designed so that the correct answer appears about equally often in each of the five response-positions. The hypothesis is that some students may persistently tend to select choices early in the group of five. This would raise

Table 1

Studies Reporting Response Sets

Investigator and Reference	Name and Nature of Test	Response Called for	Response set	Finding
Bennett, Seashore, Wesman (1)	Differential Aptitudes, Clerical	Checking errors	Speed vs. carefulness	Good students may earn falsely low scores due to set to work accurately at slow speed.
Brotherton, Read, Pratt (2)	Questionnaire on word meanings	Checking fixed categories on six-point scale	Definition of terms	Substantial differences in meaning are found from person to person and group to group. Questionnaires involving *many, few, several,* etc., "are invalid and unreliable."
AAF (7)	Tests of plotting, scale reading, etc.	Solving many items, with time limit	Speed vs. carefulness	In one test, reliability of Rights .76, Wrongs .56. But intercorrelation only −.48. Factor analysis shows "carefulness" often the most prominent factor in Wrongs scores.
Humm and associates (11)	Humm-Wadsworth temperament	Yes-No	Acquiescence	High No-Count reduces validity of scores.
Knoell*	Spelling	Check words correctly spelled, and respell those given incorrectly; also spell from dictation	Acquiescence, tendency to omit	Factorization of twenty scores, for tests of same and different types, applied to sixth-graders in Indian schools, shows four factors having low intercorrelations. These are: (1) general ability to spell, (2) ability to recognize correct spellings, (3) tendency to mark many items "right," (4) tendency to omit dictated words. Av. loadings in the respective factors for correct-spellings-marked-correct are .06, .46, .93, −.04. Loadings for incorrect-words-checked-correct are −.82, .25, .74, .02. For difference of these scores, .86, .13, −.04, −.10. In twelfth-graders, acquiescence factor does not appear but recognition of correct spellings remains distinct from general ability.
Lorge (15)	Strong interest	L-I-D	Acquiescence, evasiveness	Reliability for number of L's in two testings is .8; for number of I's, .84.

Lorge (15)	Thurstone attitude	Checking "agrees"	Acquiescence, evasiveness	Reliability for number of checks in two testings is .88; for number of ?'s, .95.
Mathews (16)	Interests	L-l-i-d-D	Acquiescence	Reliability of tendency to "like" many items is .75–.79. Responses are altered when choices are in order D-d-i-l-L. Responses at extreme left and fourth from left tend to be used. Shift is greatest on items where students have least pronounced views.
Philip (19)	Judgment of proportion in color mixtures	Absolute judgment on 11-point scale	Tendency to use certain portions of scale	Some individuals scatter their judgments more broadly over the scale than others. Each individual uses certain "foci" along the scale more often than other responses. Stimuli at the foci and ends of the scale are more often judged correctly than others. "Subsidiary cues" have greatest influence when discrimination is difficult.
Rubin (20)	Seashore pitch	H-L	Tendency to judge H	Score on High items only has K-R reliability .827; on Low only, .790. Correlation High x Low only .265, so two types of item do not measure same factor. Bias increases with difficulty. Bias score (H-L) has reliability .725.†
Singer and Young (21)	Judgments of pleasantness of stimuli	Rating on continuous scale	Tendency to rate P	"When definite affective reactions not aroused, subjects show habitual ways of using rating scale." Differences stable over two weeks.
Thorndike (22)	Pressey Interest-Attitude	Checking worries, interests	Checking many items	Frequent individual differences, reliable by split-half method. Low checking threshold leads to low emotional maturity score.
Vernon (24)	Interest items	Checking likes	Checking many items	Twenty per cent of variance appears in this general factor, running through all items regardless of content.
Wesman (26)	Spelling	Check all misspelled words	Acquiescence	Incorrect spellings correlate higher with total test than correctly-spelled items.

* Part of incomplete study, to be published later.
† Computed by the writer with Rubin's help.

their scores on items where the correct answer is choice "1" or "2," but lower than on items keyed "4" or "5." The psychological basis for the hypothesis is the possibility that some students read every alternative and discriminate carefully, where some merely read through the item to find a plausible answer, mark it, and go on to the next item.

The procedure was the usual one: to obtain a "bias" score for each individual and determine its reliability. If the score is reliable, the response set is proved to exist. The response set score for the present hypothesis consists of "number of errors appearing to the left of the correct answer" minus "number of errors to the right of the correct answer." Before rescoring papers for bias, papers of high scoring pupils (those having a score above 60 out of 90 items correct) were discarded. This was done to *increase* the likelihood of finding a response set, since response sets have no opportunity to show themselves when the pupil gets most items correct. For a group of 66 papers, bias scores ranged from 24 to −12. The person with the bias score 24 had made 39 errors to the left of the true answer, and only 15 errors to the right of the true answer. Such a preponderance is hard to explain as other than a habit of marking items. For the cases studied, however, the split-half reliability of the bias score was only .095, corrected. Such a low correlation indicates that the postulated response set is of no consequence for this group. A second sample of 84 cases having raw scores of 40 or below in extended time (these pupils had IQ's near or below 80) were studied separately, in order to increase the probability of finding a response set. For these pupils, the reliability of the bias score was .42, corrected. Evidently for a group of pupils taking a difficult multiple-choice test, reliable response sets can be found. Bias has a slight relation to raw score; the mean raw score for these poor pupils was 24.5 for those with negative bias, and 29 for those with positive bias. For some reason, very poor students tended to mark alternatives to the right of the correct answer proportionately more often than slightly better pupils.

An attempt was made to demonstrate such biases as "preference for position 1." No statistical evidence for such sets could be obtained, although an occasional case does suggest that such biases may occur. One boy, for example, never in 90 items marks the fifth choice as correct, and another student places 30 of his marks on position "1."

A second study was made with a modified version of the *Ohio State University Psychological Examination,* using data made available by N. L. Gage and Dora Damrin. The shortened test they used consists of 90 five-choice vocabulary items, unspeeded. This test was administered to unselected juniors and seniors in several high schools. When papers for all 171 pupils were scored for tendency to place answers before rather than after the correct position, the odd-even reliability of the bias score was found to be .20. When only the lowest 65 students (as judged by the total number right on the test) were used as a sample to determine the reliability of the bias score, the reliability rose to .29. This was a group of students for whom the test was extremely difficult; the highest score for the group was 22 right out of 90. It should be noted that this test is normally used for predicting college success among superior high-school students; the highest score in this limited subdivision of our sample is only chance expectation. When an even more restricted sample was used — the lowest 26 cases, all of whom fell below a raw score of 15 items correct — the reliability of the bias score rose to .54. The mean bias score changed as the quality of students became poorer. For the total group, the mean bias score was −6.5; for the second group, −7.7; and for the very lowest group, −9.7. Here, also, the poorest students apparently tended particularly often to mark errors to the right of the correct answer.

Both of these studies demonstrate that response sets are a minor factor, since so great a selection of cases was required in order to demonstrate any evidence of bias. Probably other multiple-choice tests where all subjects mark all items suffer little from response sets. Confirming studies on other multiple-choice tests are desirable, but the generally satisfactory experience with forced-choice tests should encourage their continued widespread use.

STABILITY OF RESPONSE SETS

While there is ample evidence that response sets are consistent throughout a single test, it is important to determine whether they are characteristics of the individual stable from time to time, or are transient sets which can only be regarded as errors in testing rather than personality characteristics.

Some evidence that response sets are stable appears in scattered studies. Thorndike (22, p. 33) reports that on a speeded Air Force test, scores obtained at the same sitting correlate no more than scores obtained several hours apart. If a speed-accuracy set is operating, it is not a set which shifts from hour to hour. Singer and Young (21) found that a tendency to rate varied stimuli as "pleasant" was highly stable, correlations as high as .90 being found under certain conditions over time intervals of two weeks.

Whereas these and similar studies tend to stress the stability in response sets, we ordinarily think of mental sets as easily changed by suitable directions. If the response set is viewed as a way of interpreting an ambiguous situation, as when the word "like" is left for the subject to define, any change in directions should re-define the stimulus elements and alter individual response sets. Several studies show that this can be done.

Rubin (20) several years ago demonstrated the existence of bias in the *Seashore Pitch Test*. He gave the Revised Test B twice to 245 college students, and found that the group as a whole used 13,958 "H" responses and only 10,542 "L" responses, in judging whether the second tone was higher or lower. According to the key, there were actually an equal number of differences in each direction. A similar mean bias was found by Rubin in data of Farnsworth.

In two ingenious studies Rubin then established that temporary sets are a major element in bias. First he gave a "guessing" test, in which subjects imagined a tossed coin, and wrote down the way they imagined it would fall. One group was given directions as follows: "Imagine a coin which has an H for *High* on one side, and an L for *Low* on the other side." In the other group this was reversed: "Imagine a coin which has an L for *Low* on one

side, and an *H* for *High* on the other side." There was a significant preponderance of the first-mentioned response on the first guessed item (i.e., the
former group tended to say "*H*"; the second group to say "*L*"). There was a
significant preponderance of the second-named response on the third guess
of the series. Rubin then applied the same reversal to the Seashore test
directions. Two hundred seventy-two students were told, "If the second tone
is lower than the first tone, print *L*; if higher, print *H*." Only 56.8 per cent of
the errors were lows marked "*H*," compared to 60.0 per cent when much the
same group were given the original directions (but note that some bias remained).

A miniature experiment performed by graduate students as a class exercise
gives further indication that response sets are easily altered. Lynn Hender-
son and Esther Williams administered the revised *Seashore Pitch Record B*
to ten students, repeating the Record to make a total of 100 items. At the
next class meeting, each student's scored paper was returned to him for brief
study. His attention was drawn specifically to the nature of bias by having
him count whether he tended to mark "*H*" more often than "*L*." He was
informed that in each group of ten items, just half were correctly answered
"*High*." The writer conducted the discussion, talking about bias for about
fifteen minutes and suggesting strongly that bias could be eliminated with
effort and that pitch scores would be improved as a result. Papers were collected as soon as bias had been examined, to reduce the possibility of learning specific answers. Students were never informed, and few suspected, that
the same record was used for both items 1 to 50, and 51 to 100. After the
discussion, the 50-item record was readministered, the papers collected, and
the record readministered again, yielding a 100-item post-test. This is
admittedly an inadequate experiment, especially in the absence of a control
group to measure the effect of practice and suggestion, separated from training regarding bias. The results are nevertheless striking (Table 2). Bias was
notable on Tests IA and IB, largely eliminated on IIA and IIB. Total scores
generally rose, especially on IIB. The amount of gain in score corresponds
somewhat to the amount of initial bias, except for case 7, whose gain is
presumably an effect of practice or motivation. This finding is not statistically
significant.

This study, small as it is, seems to show that bias can be eliminated by
direct coaching which makes the subject aware of his own bias. If the Pitch
Test measured pitch threshold alone, increased insight into habits of responding would not affect scores. The study does not prove that training in bias
raises pitch scores, but it strongly suggests that this is true. Wyatt (28) also
reports training subjects to avoid bias as a means of improving discrimination.
Surely, on the basis of these data, it can be recommended that Seashore test
papers should be checked for bias, and that where the person shows a marked
bias in either direction scores should be regarded as probably giving too low an
estimate of the person's ability to discriminate pitch.

Another report that altering directions affects response sets is made by
Goodfellow (6). He finds that in psychophysical judgments the predisposition to report a stimulus as absent was reversed when the directions were

Table 2

RESULTS OF PITCH TESTS BEFORE AND AFTER DISCUSSION OF BIAS

Student	Score on Successive Tests				Bias on Successive Tests*				Total Score		Total Bias	
	IA	IB	IIA	IIB	IA	IB	IIA	IIB	I	II	I	II
1	41	44	42	46	−2	−8	−4	0	85	89	−10	−4
2	45	39	41	43	−2	10	2	−2	84	84	8	0
3	40	42	44	45	−8	−4	8	−2	82	89	−12	6
4	35	41	35	33	2	−6	2	2	76	68	−4	4
5	38	36	29	32	4	−4	−2	4	74	61	0	2
6	31	37	31	48	−14	2	2	0	68	79	−12	2
7	30	32	42	39	0	0	−4	−2	62	81	0	−6
8	24	31	32	36	4	2	0	0	55	68	6	0
9	24	27	33	32	−24	−26	−10	−8	51	65	−50	−18
10	26	21	30	28	−12	−6	0	0	47	58	−18	0
Median	33	36½	34	37½	−2	−4	0	0	71	73½	−7	0
Mdn. absolute value					4	5	2	2			9	3
Mean	33	35	36	38					68	74		

* Bias score equals number of items marked High minus number marked Low.

worded: "Remember that in approximately one-half of the trials the correct answer will be yes."

The resemblance between response sets inferred from statistical data and "learning sets" found experimentally by Harlow (9) should be pointed out. In studies of monkeys, and also of children, he established definite evidence of generalized learning to solve problems. The monkey enters an ambiguous situation, namely, a discrimination apparatus where the proper choice among two alternatives leads to a food reward. In this situation, a personal communication from Harlow informs us, the monkey demonstrates a preference for one or another of the choices offered (e.g., for the red object rather than the blue). This preference may serve to increase errors (if, for instance, the square object has been keyed as correct, regardless of color). If the monkey is put through one learning series after another, in which a different cue differentiates the right and wrong choices in each series, the monkey quickly learns to learn. His learning curve on later series is strikingly steep. "With each successive block of problems the frequencies of errors attributable to these factors [one of which is initial preference or response set] are progressively decreased. . . . The process might be conceived of as a learning of response tendencies that counteract the error-producing factors."

Harlow has therefore shown that response sets are present in the new, ambiguous situation, and that under his conditions they are extinguished. In contrast, the test-taking sets of adults appear not to be extinguished by usual experiences, even though they increase the probability of error. The difference appears to be that in Harlow's experiment there is an immediate frustration attached directly to the wrong (preference-determined) response. In school tests the penalty is delayed, and is usually attached to the total test performance rather than to the specifically wrong responses. False approaches to problems, such as biases, can be eliminated; sound sets, such as reading each item carefully, can be learned. But direct and immediate teaching will be more effective than such incidental punishments as low total scores.

GENERALITY OF RESPONSE SETS

To some degree, a person shows consistent response sets from situation to situation. Table 3 summarizes studies bearing on this question. When similar situations are presented, response set scores are significantly correlated. But there is no evidence that response sets are consistent over widely different situations, and Singer and Young's evidence indicates that this is not true. But one does not measure response sets alone. Response sets show only when the response to a situation is in some way unclear. Singer and Young point out that habits of using their rating scale are operative only when "affective arousal is weak or absent." Perhaps affective arousal is weak for one person on tones, for another on odors. This would reduce the response-set correlations.

Response sets might be mere incidental sources of error in measurement, or they might reflect deeper personality traits. Evidence from many sources now combines to show that response sets reflect "real" variables.

Johnston (13) gave the *Bernreuter Inventory* and the *Hunter Attitude Scale* to two groups of teachers. These groups were chosen on the basis of ratings by their principals, so that one group consisted of "autocratic" teachers, and

Table 3

CORRELATION OF RESPONSE SETS ON VARIED TESTS

Investigator	Tests	Response Set	Findings
Lorge (15)	Bernreuter, Thurstone attitude, Strong	Acquiescence	Average intercorrelation of number of Yes's: .24.
		Evasiveness	Average intercorrelation of number of I's or ?'s: .43.
Singer-Young (21)	Two series of tones	Tendency to rate "pleasant"	r's .58, .67.
	Two series of words	Tendency to rate "pleasant"	r's range .44 to .59.
	Two series of *different* stimulus-types	Tendency to rate "pleasant"	r's range −.24 to .36.
AAF (7)	Wrongs score on four tests of plotting, etc.	Carefulness vs. speed	r's range .14 to .41.

one consisted of teachers who were markedly "democratic" in classroom practice. Johnston found that these groups differed significantly in response sets. On the Bernreuter, the autocratic group gave an average of 52.6 "Yes," 62.3 "No," and 10.8 "?" responses. The three totals for the democratic group were 55.9, 66.8, and 4.7 respectively. There were 42 teachers in the former group, and 43 in the latter. The difference in "tendency to use question marks" (evasion?) was significant (P < .01). There was a similar difference on the Hunter scale. The mean number of statements marked "Undecided" rather than "Agree" or "Disagree" was 15 in the autocratic group and 10 in the democratic group (P < .01).

Mersman (17), in a small study of vocational interests, compared the Bernreuter responses of college students planning to be lawyers, musicians, and engineers. There were seventy-five cases in each group. Upon analyzing the number of responses of each type in each group, he found the following means:

	Yes	No	?
Lawyers	53	62	10
Musicians	56	58	11
Engineers	54	64	7

The differences between engineers and musicians are significant (1 per cent level).

Evidently groups differentiated on external criteria also differ in response sets. Where this is so, part of the response-set variance must represent some real variable. For example, use of question marks may indicate anxiety and evasiveness of personality, rather than a transient set alone. Lorge (15) finds that the tendency to say "Yes," "No," and "?" (estimated from several tests) correlates as follows with scores on the Flanagan-Bernreuter keys:

	Yes	No	?
Confidence	.27	−.15	−.03
Sociability	.00	.27	−.26

Possible significance of response sets for empirical prediction is suggested by a study which finds that tendency to respond "?" is correlated negatively with success in selling life insurance (14). While the relationship found was not statistically significant, the difference between the mean number of question marks in the good and poor groups (8.4 vs. 12.8, CR 1.57) is large enough to suggest further investigation along this line.

IMPROVEMENT OF TEST DESIGN

The heterogeneous bits of evidence pieced together here and in our previous report have established several generalizations.

1. Any objective test form in which the subject marks fixed response alternatives ("Yes"-"No," "True-False," "a"-"b"-"c," etc.) permits the operation of individual differences in response sets. The influence of response sets in the multiple-choice tests is, however, of minor importance.

2. Response sets have the greatest variance in tests which are difficult for the subjects tested, or where the subject is uncertain how to respond.

3. Items having the same ostensible content actually measure more than one trait, if response sets operate in the test. This is true even for tests which, scored as a whole, are "factorially pure."

4. Slight alterations in directions, or training in test-taking, alter markedly the influence of response sets. But if the situation is not re-structured by the tester, individual differences in response set remain somewhat stable when similar tests are given at different times.

5. Response sets are to a small degree correlated with external variables such as attitudes, interests, and personality. This shows that they are in part a reflection of "real" and stable traits. To this degree, response-set variance may be valid variance in some investigations.

6. Tests are usually constructed to measure a trait defined by the content of the test items. If the form of the items permits response sets, two persons having equal true scores on the content factor will often receive different scores on the test. Response sets therefore ordinarily dilute the test and lower its validity.

Paragraphs (5) and (6) crystallize the paradox response sets present. Some of the response-set variance is potentially useful, some of it is an interference with measurement. The problem for the tester is to capitalize on the effect of response sets where they are helpful to validity, and to eliminate their influence where it is undesirable. It is therefore important to decide which view is to be taken in any given situation. The writer has attempted to formulate rationally the response-set problem in factorial terms. The analysis has been unsuccessful, primarily because response sets do not obey the fundamental additive law of factor theory. One cannot define a person's test score as a weighted addition of his content-factor and response-set-factor scores, since response sets have an influence on his performance on each item proportional to his doubtfulness. That is, the weight for the response-set factor in any item is not a constant for all persons, but is a function of each person's score in the content factor. Since the problem is not at present formulated analytically in a way which clarifies our thinking, we are confined to a general description of the relations.

Considering only biases such as acquiescence and evasiveness, response-set variance may be conceived as containing the following elements, combined in some proportion:

1. Chance variance; resulting from purely random excess of choice of one or another alternative.

2. Internally consistent but momentary response tendencies; sets operating throughout one testing, but shifting on a retest at another time.

3. Stable response tendencies; sets operating consistently even when the same test is given at different times.

Evidence of the existence of Type 3 variance has been consistently found whenever investigators have sought it. Evidence for Type 2 variance is lacking, but it may be postulated on the grounds that no observed trait is expected to be perfectly stable. And of course chance variance is always with us.

Response-set variance of Type 1 is not important; it is simply another manifestation of error variance, and its influence can be reduced by lengthening the test. Variance of Type 2 is unquestionably harmful, unless one happens to be doing research on evanescent sets or moods or some other fluctuating variable (for example, a study of mood changes concomitant with fatigue). Type 2 variance cannot correlate with stable variables, and therefore lowers the validity coefficient of the test. Moreover, Type 2 variance is present in many items and probably increases the coefficient of equivalence (split-half or Kuder-Richardson reliability) of the test. Therefore, even if the test given on a particular day were lengthened indefinitely, we could not raise its empirical validity to 1.00 because scores are partly saturated with an invalid factor. Type 3 variance is potentially useful, but to understand its action we must divide it between

3a. Valid variance, the portion of 3 that correlates with the criterion the test is intended to predict, and

3b. Invalid variance, the portion of 3 that does not correlate with the criterion.

We may always expect a portion of Type 3b, since the response set could correlate perfectly with the criterion only if the criterion is itself a set or a personality trait causing the set.

Variance of Type 3a does exist, since in some studies the response-set score did correlate with some external variable. Moreover, research in a good many fields is turning to personality variables which may be close cousins to response sets. Guilford anticipates that the "carefulness" factor, which is a response-set, may prove to have validity as a component of a battery for aircrew selection. In studies of prejudice or liberalism, an investigator may find evidence on negativism useful. And this is possibly one source of bias toward "No" and "Disagree" in taking tests. Variance of Type 3b reduces validity, and limits the maximum possible validity the test can have even if trials on different days are combined. Variance of Type 3a may increase validity if it is added into the score in one way, or it may lower validity if it is added in differently. Thus the studies of true-false tests (5) show that students tend to say "True" when in doubt, and the duller students, who are in doubt most often, say "True" most often. This raises their score on true items, lowers it on false items. Hence the potentially valid portion of the response-set variance lowers the discriminating power and validity of true items, and enhances the validity of the false items.

Finally, it should be noted that there is no possibility of separating the four types of response-set variance in data from a single test; they come entangled in a single performance, and we must therefore consider the effect of the response-set variance as a unit. This total is made up of a random element (Type 1), a real but invalid element (Type 2, 3b), and a potentially valid element (3a) which may in practice raise or lower the validity of the test score. Of these three categories, only 3a, the valid variance, is likely to be entirely absent, and the size of the correlations of response sets with external variables suggests that 3a is not likely to be the principal component of the variance. Therefore:

a. The probable effect of response-set variance is harmful, since elements 2 and 3b are usually present, and these elements reduce the extent to which the test is saturated with the content factor it is supposed to measure.

b. Even if valid variance is present, its effect may be to lower validity of some items or of the total score. But under certain circumstances, it may be treated in such a way that it raises the validity coefficient.

c. Only under exceptional circumstances, when a test is designed to study the very personality characteristics which are reflected in the response set, does the response set appear to be a potentially helpful source of variance.

Because the operation of response sets upon score is complex, a detailed illustration seems worthwhile. A spelling test is planned, using the directions: "Some of these words are correctly spelled and some incorrect. Mark every item, + if correct, o if incorrect." If the test is intended to indicate whether the student will identify errors in his own writing outside of school, this form of item has an appealing resemblance to the criterion task. Now suppose we have 6 students. A, B, and C know 40 words out of 60, are doubtful on the remainder. D, E, and F know 30 words. (This oversimplification of "knowing" a word avoids difficulty in this explanation.) A and D have no response set. Of the 60 words, just half are wrongly spelled, and when A and D are doubtful, they mark just half of the unknown words o. B and E are a little undercritical in nonschool writing; they fail to notice some errors. But in taking a school test, they suspect the teacher of planting errors where there are none, and so mark o 60 per cent of the time when they are doubtful. C and F are undercritical in all their writing, and in taking the test they are also willing to accept errors; they mark o only 30 per cent of the time when in doubt. The scores then may develop as follows:

	A	B	C	D	E	F
Bias (Proportion of + responses to o responses)	50/50	40/60	70/30	50/50	40/60	70/30
Words known	40	40	40	30	30	30
Guesses correct by chance:						
guessed + ...	5	4	7	7½	6	10½
guessed o	5	6	3	7½	9	4½
Most probable score	50	50	50	45	45	45
Maximum possible correct guesses:						
guessed + ...	10	8	10	15	12	15
guessed o	10	10	6	15	15	9
Maximum possible score ..	60	58	56	60	57	54
Minimum possible correct guesses:						
guessed + ...	0	0	4	0	0	6
guessed o	0	2	0	0	3	0
Minimum possible score ..	40	42	44	30	33	36

In this, as in other problems, the tendency is for bias to restrict the range of scores, not to alter the mean score. Where an unbiased person may, with lucky guesses, earn a very high score, the biased person has a much smaller probability of reaching the same total. Bias which reflects "true criticalness" operates in the score no differently from bias which is only a special set used in taking a test. If the items are divided so that 70 per cent of the words are correctly spelled, C and F are given an advantage, even over A and D. If more than half the spellings are incorrect, B and E will tend to earn higher scores than those who know an equal number of words (and are equal on the criterion).

In an unbiased test, where all alternatives have an equal weight in the total test, response sets do not add to the variance of scores, but have a damping effect, reducing the range of points people may earn from a combination of guessing and partial knowledge. If one alternative is present more than another, response sets form part of the variance of the test scores.

Methods of Eliminating Response-Set Variance. The writer concludes that as a general principle, the tester should consider response sets an enemy to validity. Even when seeking to measure a trait resembling a response set, one can have confidence in the meaningfulness of the score only after showing that variances 1, 2, and 3b are small in proportion to 3a. Therefore, in most tests and certainly in those not intended to measure personality, we should keep response sets from affecting the test score by one of the following methods: designing test items which prevent response sets, altering directions to reduce response sets, or correcting for response sets.

(a) *Test design.* — Since response sets are a nuisance, test designers should avoid forms of items which response sets infest. This means that any form of measurement where the subject is allowed to define the situation for himself in any way is to be avoided. (We must make an exception for tests where his way of interpreting the test is treated as a significant variable. But even so, the above analysis suggests limits to the possible validity of tests like the Rorschach which capitalize on ambiguity.)

Item forms using fixed response-categories are particularly open to criticism. The attitude-test pattern, where the subject marks a statement A, a, U, d, or D, according to his degree of agreement, is open to the following response sets: Acquiescence, or tendency to mark "A" and "a" more than "d" and "D"; evasiveness, tendency to mark "U"; and tendency to go to extremes, to mark "A" and "D" more than "a" and "d". Probably not all three of these sets will operate to a significant degree in any given test, but it is better to eliminate the sets at the outset than to spend effort later trying to measure the effect of the sets and root them out. Test designers generally have argued for retaining the five-point scale of judgment, or the more indefinite seven-point, ten-point, or even continuous scales. Such scales are open to marked individual differences in definition of the reference positions, with the more complex scale offering more chance for personal interpretation. The usual argument for the more finely divided scale of judgment on each attitude item is that it is more reliable and that subjects prefer it. If the latter advantage is significant, the finer scale may be retained and scored dichotomously. The argument that the finer scale gives more reliability is not a sound one, since this is precisely what we would expect if all of the added reliable variance were response-set variance and had no relation to beliefs about the attitude-object in question. There is no merit in enhancing test reliability unless validity is enhanced at least proportionately. It is an open question whether a finer scale of judgment gives either a more *valid* ranking of subjects according to belief, or (what we are beginning to recognize as even more important) scores more *saturated* with valid variance. With raters trained to interpret the scale uniformly, so that response-set variance is removed, the finer scale may be advantageous.

The writer therefore renews his earlier recommendation that the following forms of item be avoided in tests where high validity is more important than speed-of-test construction: true-false, like-indifferent-dislike, same-different, yes-?-no, agree-uncertain-disagree, and mark all correct answers. What does this leave? Foremost, it leaves the forced-choice or best-answer test. Our attempt to find a response set in the multiple-choice test was almost completely unsuccessful. A set was extracted, and that a set with little reliability, only when the test was applied to subjects for whom it was unreasonably difficult. Further studies of multiple-choice tests are still in order, but experience to date justifies the assumption that they are generally free from response sets. One confirmation of the argument that forced choices should be used comes from a study by Owens (18). He found that substituting forced-choice for the "yes-no" response of the conventional neurotic inventory significantly reduced the number of false positives, i.e., it increased empirical validity. The forced choice has long been used successfully in many fields. Tests of mental ability now use it almost to the exclusion of other forms. Spelling, arithmetic, and grammar tests can certainly be cast in "recognize the right (or wrong) choice" form, rather than checklist forms and others open to response sets. Thurstone used it successfully in his paired-comparison approach to attitudes, and the same approach has long been found satisfactory in psychophysics. The Kuder interest test is well known, and Kuder has recently developed a new test of personality in the same forced-choice form. Paired comparisons may serve well in employee rating, and the Army has found the forced-choice valuable in obtaining officer ratings. Apparently forced-choice items can be used for nearly all purposes now served by the inadequate item forms.

Another important consideration is test difficulty, regardless of item form. The influence of response sets rises with difficulty, and therefore measurement of differences between students who find the test difficult is particularly invalid. This is, first, a reason for not using a test on subjects for whom it is quite difficult. Second, however, it suggests basing measurement on scales of adaptable difficulty. Thus, with the Kuhlmann-Anderson mental-test series, one selects the scales which have a difficulty appropriate for the subject, and if the first tests tried prove to be too difficult, the tester can move to an easier set of items to obtain more accurate measurement. Tests of this type, which are common in psychophysics, would be hard to use in group measurement; but experimental trial of such test designs is worth considering. If the *Seashore Pitch Test*, for example, were redesigned, one might have a preliminary section of twenty (?) items, ranging from very hard to very easy. This could be scored as soon as completed, and if the score were high, the subject would be given a difficult 50-item test (perhaps with all differences five cycles or two cycles). But a subject who performed near the chance level on the preliminary test would be given a final test of items with large differences (perhaps 20 to 30 cycles). A set of several overlapping scales would be required, all standardized on the same group. Such a test could not test large groups inexpensively, but could be quite accurate in testing individuals.

(b) *Modification of directions.*— If, in any test, we expect a particular response set to arise, we can revise the directions to reduce the ambiguity of the situation. Another way of accomplishing the same end is to give students general training in test-wiseness. For example, if they know that in most true-false tests about half the items are false, they will tend to avoid excessive acquiescence. If they know that the correction formula is based on chance, they will know that the odds are in their favor when they respond to items where they are uncertain.

It appears to the writer that, in most tests, subjects should be directed to answer all items, even though this tends to increase the random error variance. In many situations, this source of error is less damaging than the constant errors introduced by differences in tendency to guess, checking threshold, or diligence in searching for correct answers. Wesman (25) reports partial evidence that grammar items, where the subject marks each error he notices in given sentences, become more reliable when the subject is directed to mark every sentence-part "correct" or "incorrect," rather than just checking the "incorrects" (but evidence on validity is lacking).

Whisler (27) raised the question of response-habits in Thurstone-type attitude scales. He found that some subjects marked six or more items in a 22-item scale, and for them the reliability (parallel-test) of the attitude score was .89. But for the subjects who marked five or fewer items that they agreed with, the reliability was .62. Whisler thought that the subjects who checked more items were more careful in using the scale, or that their attitudes were more integrated. Hancock (8) followed Whisler with an experimental alteration of directions. First, he directed subjects to mark all the statements they accepted, then the five with which they most agreed, and, finally, the three of that five which they most strongly accepted. The shift of directions produced some alteration in scores. Generally, the standard deviation (in scale value) of scores increased when fewer items were counted. For those with attitudes favorable to an occupation, the more items they checked, the closer their score was to the indifference position. Unfortunately, there is not enough evidence in the Hancock report to give a basis for selecting any particular number of checks as preferable. If the number of items checked affects mean, sigma, and reliability, there can be little justification for permitting the number to vary. It appears desirable to require every subject to mark a fixed number of alternatives, selecting the statements with which he most agrees. Limited experience with this procedure suggests that the subject should check around one-fourth of the statements.

(c) *Correction for response sets.*— When response sets are entering scores on a test, we may control or correct for the effect by special scoring keys. One widely used method is the control score. If a "response-set score" can be obtained, we may identify all cases with extreme response sets and drop such cases from the sample, admitting that measurement for them is invalid. The most familiar examples appear in the control scores of the Minnesota Multiphasic. Many other tests also permit us to derive such scores as bias or acquiescence, or number of items marked. In some tests it may be acceptable to report two scores for every subject; all the essential data in the hypothetical spelling test discussed earlier could be reported in one score "number right" and a second "number marked as incorrect." But simultaneous consideration of patterns of scores is awkward.

Humm has long used the No-Count as a control score on his Temperament Scale. A comment in the Supplemental Manual for that test is of interest

> It was observed that subjects whose scores in the Scale were at variance with the results of case studies by psychiatrists, psychologists, and social workers were found more often among those with an ultra-high or an ultra-low proportion of no-responses, than was the case where no-responses were in the middle ranges. Individuals who answer the questions of the scale with a high number of no-responses tend, consciously or unconsciously, to obscure their real temperaments. On the other hand, individuals with a low number of responses may exaggerate their temperamental characteristics.

Eliminating cases with extreme control-scores has the disadvantage of throwing out numerous subjects, but it is vastly better than treating the subjects as if the scores were valid. Sometimes a simple solution is to readminister the test with more careful directions, as Bennett and others illustrate (1). But more complex correction procedures are possible. In this, Humm and his co-workers were also pioneers.

Two procedures have been developed for cases where No-Counts are extreme. The first is the "profile score." For an initial sample of 181 cases, Humm had a criterion score on each component the test claimed to measure. The profile score is the best estimate of the criterion score from the uncorrected score and the No-Count. This procedure, regressing from an external criterion rather than merely partialling out No-Count in terms of the zero-order r between No-Count and raw component score, allows for the very reasonable assumption that part of the No-Count variance represents significant elements in personality.

The second correction, reserved only for cases where profile scores are inadequately revealing, yields the "regression score." This "stated the standard deviational distance of the given component score from the mode of scores in that component attained in scales showing the same No-Count. The regression score takes no account of validity. It does not, therefore, consider how well the Component Score measures the 'true' component strength." This, of course, partials out all the response-set portion of the score variance.

Humm and Humm (12) report that their procedures raise the validity of interpretations, for those papers where correction is required. Similar methods could no doubt be applied to other tests, and in the K-correction of the

Multiphasic, a similar treatment is illustrated. Such refined statistical improvements are worth making only when one intends to treat a test quite seriously. It would scarcely be worthwhile to build a correction score for acquiescence into the Bernreuter test, in view of the many other bases for doubting its validity. But where great statistical labor in the form of factor analysis has already entered such a test as Guilford's series, application of a control score for response sets may be worth serious consideration.

Correction for response sets is a problem in suppressor variables (10, pp. 140–142). We wish to retain valid response-set variance (Type 3a), but we wish to remove from the score the variance of Type 3b and 2. If an independent estimate of the Type 3a variance, or of the combined undesirable variance, could be obtained by a pure measure of the response set itself, this estimate might be used as a suppressor variable.

Capitalizing on Response-Set Variance. If response sets are thought of as possibly contributing to validity, one may weight the response sets in a way that maximizes their contribution. Cook and Leeds (3) correlate each possible response on an attitude scale for teachers with a criterion, and assign positive or negative scoring weights accordingly. One item is as follows, where the numbers in parentheses are weights:

	1	2	3	4	5
It is sometimes necessary to break promises to children.	Strongly agree	Agree	Undecided	Disagree	Strongly disagree
	(0)	(4)	(−1)	(4)	(−1)

The criterion used was a dependable estimate of the ability of teachers to establish rapport with children, which the scale was supposed to predict. It will be noted that the scoring weights are "illogical," since there can be no stronger response to "It is *sometimes* necessary. . . ." than to disagree (response 4), which amounts to saying "It is *never* necessary." The weights for responses 4 and 5 reflect the difference in response set (not in logically considered opinion) between teachers in the superior and inferior criterion groups. The defense of the Cook-Leeds procedure, and the comparable method used in Strong's Interest Blank, is that it yields considerable validity. The limitation is that invalid variance (Types 2 and 3b) is weighted just like valid variance. A particular "good" teacher who has a set to respond very emphatically will be penalized by the weights. The majority of "good" teachers, who avoid extreme responses, will be reliably discriminated by the key. One difficulty with the sheer empiricism represented here is that the weights serve their practical purpose but give little insight into the nature of the variables tested. The only basis for extending or improving the test is trial-and-error, developing many more items of all sorts and trying them to see how the weights come out.

Sometimes, instead of employing correction scores to refine the total test score, one may modify the original test scores. Thus Flanagan (23, p. 9) suggests scoring Rights and Wrongs separately, and using each score in the multiple-correlation when trying to predict a criterion. This procedure permits one to weight "carefulness" variance separately from "ability" variance. Work with true-false tests suggests that scores Rights-on-True-Items and Rights-on-False-Items will have different validity and may be assigned different weights in the predictor score (5). Probably this notion could be extended further, in empirical prediction.

SUMMARY

This paper summarizes extensive evidence demonstrating that such response sets as bias in favor of a particular alternative, tendency to guess, working for speed rather than accuracy, and the like, operate in conventional objective tests. Not only are such sets widespread, but they reduce the validity of test scores. The response set can be altered readily by alteration of the directions or by coaching. Some studies show that response sets are somewhat correlated from one test to another (but not if the tests differ greatly in content), and that they are correlated with important external variables. While response-set variance may under certain circumstances enhance logical and empirical validity, it appears that its general effect is to reduce the saturation of the test and to limit its possible validity.

The following recommendations for practice, most of which were previously suggested, are reinforced by the present findings:

1. Response sets should be avoided with the occasional exception of some tests measuring carefulness or other personality traits which are psychologically similar to response sets.

2. The forced-choice, paired-comparison, or "do-guess" multiple-choice test should be given preference over other forms of test item.

3. When a form of item is used in which response sets are possible,

a. Directions should be worded so as to reduce ambiguity and to force every student to respond with the same set.

b. The test should not be given to a group of students for whom it is quite difficult.

c. A response-set score should be obtained, and used to identify subjects whose scores are probably invalid.

4. Where response sets are present, attempts should be made to correct for or to capitalize on the response set by an appropriate empirical procedure.

In view of the overwhelming evidence that many common item forms invite response sets, and in view of the probability that these sets interfere with accurate measurement, it will rarely be wise to build new tests around item forms such as A-U-D, Yes-No-?, and "check all correct answers." It is to be hoped that the tests forthcoming in the future will be designed to increase their saturation with the factors the test is seeking to measure.

REFERENCES

1. Bennett, George K., Seashore, Harold G., and Wesman, Alexander G. *Differential Aptitude Tests, Manual.* New York: The Psychological Corporation, 1947.
2. Brotherton, D. A., Read, J. M., and Pratt, K. C. "Indeterminate Number Concepts: II. Application by Children to Determinate Number Groups," *Journal of Genetic Psychology,* LXXIII (1948), 209–236.

3. Cook, Walter W., and Leeds, Carroll H. "Measuring Teacher Personality," *Educational and Psychological Measurement,* VII (1947), 399–410.

4. Cronbach, L. J. "Response Sets and Test Validity," *Educational and Psychological Measurement,* VI (1946), 475–494.

5. ———. "Studies of Acquiescence as a Factor in the True-False Test," *Journal of Educational Psychology,* XXXIII (1942), 401–415.

6. Goodfellow, Louis D. "The Human Element in Probability," *Journal of General Psychology,* XXXIII (1940), 201–205.

7. Guilford, J. P. (ed.). *Printed Classification Tests.* AAF Aviation Psychology Program Research Reports, No. 5. Washington, D.C.: Government Printing Office, 1947.

8. Hancock, John W. "An Experimental Study of Limiting Response on Attitude Scales," in H. H. Remmers (ed.), *Further Studies in Attitudes,* Series III. *Studies in Higher Education,* XXXIV. Lafayette, Ind.: Purdue University, 1938, 142–148.

9. Harlow, H. F. "The Formation of Learning Sets," *Psychological Review,* LVI (1949), 51–65.

10. Horst, Paul. *The Prediction of Personal Adjustment.* New York: Social Science Research Council, 1941.

11. Humm, Doncaster G., and Wadsworth, Guy, Jr. *The Interpretation of the Humm-Wadsworth Temperament Scale.* Los Angeles: D. G. Humm, 1943.

12. Humm, Doncaster G., and Humm, Kathryn A. "Compensations for Subjects' Response-Bias in a Measure of Temperament," *American Psychologist,* II (1947), 305.

13. Johnston, Aaron Montgomery. "The Relationship of Various Factors to Autocratic and Democratic Classroom Practices." Unpublished doctoral dissertation, University of Chicago, 1948.

14. Kahn, D. F., and Hadley, J. M. "Factors Related to Life Insurance Selling," *Journal of Applied Psychology,* XXXIII (1949), 132–140.

15. Lorge, I. "Gen-like: Halo or Reality?" *Psychological Bulletin,* XXXIV (1937), 545–546.

16. Mathews, C. O. "The Effect of the Order of Printed Response on an Interest Questionnaire," *Journal of Educational Psychology,* XX (1929), 128–134.

17. Mersman, Ivo. "Personality Traits as Related to Vocational Choice." Unpublished Master's thesis, University of Chicago, 1948.

18. Owens, W. A. "Item Form and 'False-Positive' Responses on a Neurotic Inventory," *Journal of Clinical Psychology,* III (1947), 264–269.

19. Philip, B. R. "Generalization and Central Tendency in the Discrimination of a Series of Stimuli," *Canadian Journal of Psychology,* I (1947), 196–204.

20. Rubin, Harry K. "A Constant Error in the Seashore Test of Pitch Discrimination." Unpublished Master's thesis, University of Wisconsin, 1940.

21. Singer, William B., and Young, Paul T. "Studies in Affective Reaction: III. The Specificity of Affective Reactions," *Journal of General Psychology,* XXIV (1941), 327–341.

22. Thorndike, R. L. "Critical Note on the Pressey Interest-Attitudes Test," *Journal of Applied Psychology,* XXII (1938), 657–658.

23. Vaughn, K. W. (ed.). "National Projects in Educational Measurement," *American Council on Education Studies,* Series I, No. 28 (1947), 8–12.

24. Vernon, P. E. "Classifying High Grade Occupational Interests," *Journal of Abnormal and Social Psychology,* XLIV (1949), 85–96.

25. Wesman, Alexander G. "Active versus Blank Responses to Multiple-Choice Items," *Journal of Educational Psychology,* XXXVIII (1947), 89–95.

26. ———. "The Usefulness of Correctly Spelled Words in a Spelling Test," *Journal of Educational Psychology,* XXXVII (1947), 242–246.

27. Whisler, L. D. "'Reliability' of Scores on Attitude Scales as Related to Scoring Method," in H. H. Remmers, (ed.), *Further Studies in Attitudes,* Series III. *Studies in Higher Education,* XXXIV. Lafayette, Ind.: Purdue University, 1938, 126–129.

28. Wyatt, Ruth F. "Improvability of Pitch Discrimination," *Psychological Monographs,* LVIII (1945), No. 267.

41

Relative Length of Option and Response Set in Multiple-Choice Items

Clinton I. Chase

Considerable interest has been given to the influence of person-ality characteristics on examinees' styles of responding to test items. However, very little attention has been given to characteristics of the test itself as an influence on response style. Does the way one responds to preliminary test items affect how one will respond to subsequent items? The following article provides a basis for some hypotheses in this matter.

Studies of the influence of response set on test scores, as reviewed by Cronbach (1, 2), have led to the conclusion that in multiple-choice ex-aminations set is relatively unimportant. However, the great bulk of re-search has dealt with a set to select a given position among the various responses provided. What about other factors in determining a set to re-spond? This paper reports the influence of relative length of an option as a condition of set.

The first question then is how long must an alternative be before a set appears to select it over shorter ones, when the basis of response to the item is other than knowledge. The second question, which is the principal in-terest of the paper, is based on the first. Wevrick (3) has shown that a re-sponse set can be made to appear by putting the correct option repeatedly in one position in easy items. In other words, the location of correct alternatives in one item appears to influence the probability of selecting a given response position in a successive item. If, then, in difficult items a set does exist to choose the longer alternative among several shorter ones, what would be the influence on this set of preceding the difficult items with easy ones in which a shorter alternative is always correct? That is, can responses to previous items influence a length-of-response set just as previous items in-fluenced position set in Wevrick's study? As noted, principal interest of the investigation centers around the second problem; however, the first question must be dealt with before the conditions for the second one can be explored.

From Clinton I. Chase, "Relative Length of Option and Response Set in Multiple-Choice Items," *Educational and Psychological Measurement*, XXIV (Winter, 1964), pp. 861–866. Reprinted with the permission of publisher and author.

Method I

To investigate the first problem the following procedure was used. A multiple-choice test was built with four responses provided for each item. There were 25 items in the test. In ten items the long alternative was at least three times longer by word count than the other responses — a word ratio of one-to-three. These were called Type A items. In ten other items, Type B, the long alternative had a word ratio which ranged from two-to-three to one-to-two. The position of the long alternative, as well as the correct response, was determined by random numbers. These items all dealt with advanced topics in psychology, and were administered to a beginning class in Educational Psychology. Instructions were given to try every item, whether or not the student thought he knew the right answer.

Since motivation is an important consideration in getting subjects to try to solve all items, rather than carelessly marking responses, five rather simple items were spaced throughout the test, beginning with the first item. When the subjects found that they did know some items, it was hoped that this would motivate them to make a serious attempt at other items. The principle of partial reinforcement would support this belief, since extinction of the response of trying items would not set in as rapidly with periodic success. However, these simple items were not entered into the test analysis.

The test was administered to 48 undergraduate students in their regular discussion section of beginning Educational Psychology. The ratio of males to females was about four to five. The test was not timed.

Results I

The results of the test were analyzed for the items containing the long alternatives only — Type A and Type B items. First these items were scored for correct responses to see if knowledge were the basis of response. The average number correct was 5.95. In 20 items five should be chosen by chance. The difference is not a significant one. Apparently students were responding on a basis other than knowledge. Next, Type A items were scored one point each time a long alternative was chosen; Type B items were scored in the same manner. The two distributions of the scores so obtained were compared with a theoretical distribution based on the binomial expansion where $p = .25$, since the test contained four options for each item. Chi square was used to test the hypothesis that the obtained scores did not differ from the theoretical distribution. Since the chance selections beyond five are so small, all categories from five to ten were combined into one group for the purpose of computations. The results of the analysis are given in Table 1 for Type A items and in Table 2 for Type B items.

The results reveal a definite set to select the long alternative in Type A items but no such set appears in Type B items. There the variation in response is within chance range. To determine the reliability of the observed long-response set a split-half approach was used. The resulting coefficient, with the Spearman-Brown extension for the whole test, was .86, indicating a reasonable consistency in the responses made to these long alternatives.

Table 1

A COMPARISON OF OBSERVED AND EXPECTED SELECTIONS OF TYPE A
ALTERNATIVES IN FOUR-OPTION MULTIPLE-CHOICE ITEMS

Number of options	0	1	2	3	4	5–10
Number of persons expected to select given number of options	2.69	9.02	13.54	12.00	7.01	3.74
Number of persons who actually selected given number of options	0	1	3	11	14	19

$x^2 = 88.97$ significant beyond 1 per cent level.

Table 2

A COMPARISON OF OBSERVED AND EXPECTED SELECTIONS OF TYPE B
ALTERNATIVES IN FOUR-OPTION MULTIPLE-CHOICE ITEMS

Number of options	0	1	2	3	4	5–10
Number of persons expected to select given number of options	2.69	9.02	13.54	12.00	7.01	3.74
Number of persons who actually selected given number of options	3	17	13	9	4	2

$x^2 = 9.97$ nonsignificant at 5 per cent level.

The above data support the conclusion that when students are responding to difficult questions, relative length of an alternative in a given item is a predisposing factor in the selection of that alternative if the long option is at least three times longer, by word count, than other options. However, the set does not appear for alternatives that are relatively shorter than this.

METHOD II

It was now possible to investigate the next problem, which is: does the long-response set continue to appear on difficult items after subjects have repeatedly selected short alternatives on easy items preceding these difficult test questions? In other words, if a student is presented with multiple-choice items each of which contains a long alternative, but he successively recognizes a short option as the correct response, will he still evidence a long-alternative set when confronted with a difficult item in which he does not recognize the correct response?

To investigate this matter a second test was made. Items were all of the Type A construction, the long alternative in each item being at least three times as long as other alternatives. This long option was randomly placed in the items so as to avoid position preferences of test takers.

Most of the items were designed to be easy, coming directly from the most obvious points of recent lectures the subjects had attended in Educational Psychology. Interspersed among 16 easy items were six difficult problems. Thus, every difficult item was preceded by several easy items. In the easy items the long option was never the correct answer, although in difficult items the correct answer was randomly placed among both short and long options.

The test was administered to 49 students from the same class as the first sample. The answer sheets were scored in three ways: once for right responses for easy items, once for right responses for difficult items, once for long alternatives for difficult items. The scores obtained on the rights for easy items averaged just short of 100 per cent, so scoring long alternatives for these simple items was not necessary, since the possibility for their selection was negligible. Students clearly chose the short, correct response.

Results II

The analysis of scores showed the following results. The difficult items, which on the previous test had shown the long-alternative response set, no longer evidenced this condition. In fact, as Table 3 reveals, the long responses were chosen fewer times than chance expectancy. An avoidance response appeared to be evidenced in this situation. Correct responses, which had been randomly distributed for these difficult items were below chance level, but not significantly so.

Table 3

A COMPARISON OF OBSERVED AND EXPECTED SELECTIONS OF TYPE A ALTERNATIVES IN FOUR-OPTION MULTIPLE-CHOICE ITEMS THAT HAVE BEEN PRECEDED BY ITEMS WITH SHORT OPTIONS CORRECT

Number of options	0	1	2	3–6
Number of persons expected to select given number of options	8.72	17.48	14.52	8.29
Number of persons who actually selected given number of options	18	19	9	3

$x^2 = 15.81$ significant beyond the 1 per cent level.

Discussion

The above data suggest that the tendency for a long-alternative response set occurring in the face of difficult items depends upon the nature of responses to test questions that precede these difficult items. If all items are difficult and subjects are responding essentially on a random basis, a definite long-alternative set appears. However, if these difficult items are preceded by easy items that contain long alternatives, and in these easy items subjects select short responses as correct, then the set to choose the long alternative in difficult items disappears. In fact these long options are selected less often than chance. It therefore appears that the existence of a set to choose long alternatives in difficult items depends upon the nature of items around these difficult ones.

In a given classroom examination a student usually knows the correct response to many items. If he then faces a difficult question, it cannot be said that he will be disposed to select the long alternative if one is provided, but rather his response will be influenced by his choices in previous test questions. Therefore, without knowing the nature of previous items in a test, one can not say in what way a long alternative will influence the probability of selecting the various options to an item in the standard classroom examination.

SUMMARY

This investigation was designed to study response set that may be associated with relatively long alternatives to multiple-choice items. First, a difficult, four-option test was made with ten items, each of which contained one long response that had three times as many words as any of the three short responses, and a second ten items containing long alternatives which had a word length ratio with short items that ranged from two-to-three to one-to-two. Also, five easy items were interspersed among the difficult ones for motivational purposes.

The test was administered to 48 undergraduate students in beginning Educational Psychology. A set to choose the long alternatives existed in items where the long options were three times longer than other options, but no set appeared in items where the long alternative was proportionately shorter than this.

The next step in the study was to determine if choosing short alternatives in easy items just prior to a difficult item would influence the set to choose the long alternative in this difficult item. Accordingly, a four-response multiple-choice test was built with several easy items preceding every difficult item. All items contained a three-to-one ratio long alternative to maximize set possibilities, but in the easy items the long response choice was never correct. This test was given to a second sample of 49 students from the same course as before.

In this second test the long-alternative set in difficult items vanished, in fact an avoidance set appeared. These results seem to indicate that whether long alternatives are selected in a chance response situation depends upon the nature of items around them. Therefore, it cannot be generalized that students will have a set to choose the long alternative in a given difficult item when that item is situated among others that are less difficult.

REFERENCES

1. Cronbach, Lee J. "Further Evidence on Response Set and Test Design," *Educational and Psychological Measurement*, X (1950), 3–31.
2. ———. "Response Set and Test Validity," *ibid.*, VI (1946), 475–494.
3. Wevrick, Leonard. "Response Set in a Multiple-Choice Test," *Educational and Psychological Measurement*, XXII (1962), 533–538.

42

The Effect of Distractions
on Test Results

Donald E. Super, William F. Braasch, Jr., and Joseph B. Shay

*Test manuals always emphasize the importance of quiet test
settings with all distractions controlled. Super, et al., provide some
interesting evidence regarding the impact of distractions on test
results.*

Current practices in test administration specify that the place of testing
be free from distractions. For example, Bingham (1) states that the examiner "will secure suitable quarters, free from disturbances and interrup-
tions" but does not define a "disturbance" nor an "interruption." In practice
psychometrists realize that the complete elimination of stimuli is impossible
to attain and so direct their efforts to reducing distractions to a minimum.
That certain disturbances might have a favorable effect on the test situation
has been pointed out by Terman and Merrill (3). According to their observations, familiar sounds "are reassuring to a child who is inclined to be a
bit timid." The authors also report that in their experience excellent testing
may be done "under very inadequate physical conditions." Apparently the
effect of specified distractions on test results needs to be more adequately
determined, with the distractions described in sufficient detail for their
nature to be clear and with an experimental design which permits the
drawing of verifiable conclusions.

The purpose of this experiment was, therefore, to study the effect of
certain commonly encountered distractions on test results. On the basis
of clinical observations the hypothesis was established that group test scores
would not be appreciably affected by commonly occurring distractions.

PROCEDURE

The tests used were the Minnesota Vocational Test for Clerical Workers
and the Otis Quick-Scoring Mental Ability Test, Gamma Am. The direc-

From Donald E. Super, William F. Braasch, Jr., and Joseph B. Shay, "The Effect
of Distractions on Test Results," *The Journal of Educational Psychology*, XXXVIII
(October, 1947), pp. 373–377. Reprinted with the permission of Abrahams Magazine
Service, Incorporated, and the authors.

tions as given in the manual were used with the following changes: on the clerical test, Part II, Name Comparison was given first, and on the Otis the time limit was reduced to twenty minutes. This latter change meant that an IQ could not be calculated, but the nature of the experiment required only that the raw score be obtained.

The subjects were two groups of graduate students, ages twenty-two to thirty-eight, taking a course in testing. There were thirty in the distracted group and twenty-six in the control group. The division of the class into sections had been made earlier on a random basis for instructional purposes. The Names part of the clerical test was used to determine the equality of the groups as it is a measure of the two abilities measured by the other tests (general intelligence and speed of discrimination); no distractions were planned during its administration.

Since the tests were administered during the regular laboratory period the impression given by the examiner was that they were a demonstration of group test administration and that the results were to be analyzed to ascertain the effect of administering the Names Test before rather than after the Numbers Test.

The instructions for the distractions during the various tests were as follows:

1. Minnesota Clerical Names Test
   None

2. Minnesota Clerical Numbers Test
   a) At the end of the second minute of testing the trumpeter will play the scale up, then down, will pause thirty seconds, then play the scale back up. The trumpeter will be in the next room and stand facing the closed connecting door.
   b) At the end of the fourth minute Mr. Hummel will burst into the room, stop short, look around, tiptoe to the examiner in an exaggeratedly quiet manner, whisper hoarsely, "How long are you going to be here?" and then exit on tiptoe, leaving the door slightly ajar.

3. Otis Test of Mental Ability
   a) While marking the answer to the third question, Miss Furstman will break her pencil point with a loud snap. She will then make a mild exclamation as she drops the pencil, slide the chair back with a scraping noise, get up and walk with ostentatious care to the examiner for another pencil.
   b) At the end of the fourth minute Mr. Hummel and Mr. Appel will walk down the stairs from the fourth floor, arguing loudly on Schwellenbach's suggested ban of the Communist Party. The discussion near the door should last for about one minute. The examiner will have placed himself on the far side of the room so as to arrive at the door at about the time the two men are ready to move on.
   c) At the end of ten minutes the trumpeter will play six bars of "Home Sweet Home," falter, recover, and go on to finish the melody. The trumpeter will give the impression that the melody is being played by a novice. The location will be the same as described in 2a) above.

d) At the beginning of the test, the examiner will set the timer to ring at fifteen instead of twenty minutes. When the bell rings the examiner will pick up the timer, look at it, look at his stopwatch, and announce, "Go on with the test."

The inclusion of musical distractions was not incongruent since the music department uses nearby rooms for practice.

None of the distractions went unnoticed during the test period. One minute after the Minnesota Numbers Test started, the playing of a piano in the room below could be heard. This did not attract as much attention as the trumpet which caused a number of students to look up, some to snicker, and one to inquire facetiously, "Was that intentional?" The examiner shook his head.

The entrance of the examiner's "friend" caused a few of the students to look up.

The pencil-breaking incident at the beginning of the Otis caused some murmuring among the students in the immediate vicinity.

The argument in the hall was aided by passing students who joined in the discussion, thinking it genuine, and added to the commotion in a realistic way. Several of the subjects looked up and one or two looked out of the door at the disputants.

The trumpeter's second effort resulted in many of the students looking up and a good deal of snickering.

A general reaction of annoyance at the mis-timing of the Otis was expressed by unintelligible muttering.

After the test a few comments on the quality of the trumpeting and the fact that the examinees had been "cheated out of two seconds" were made. A discussion of the experiment the following week confirmed the belief that none of the class was aware of the real intent of the experiment.

RESULTS

The tests were scored according to standard procedures and the results were tabulated by age and sex for each group. No differences approaching statistical significances were found for either age or sex, so combined data were used for comparisons.

Table 1 gives the means, standard deviations, and critical ratios for each of the tests. None of the differences were statistically significant even at the 10 per cent level.

The greatest mean difference obtained was for the Minnesota Names Test which was administered without distractions. The difference of 12.7 points is not statistically significant, since a critical ratio larger than that of 1.6 could be expected in ten cases out of one hundred. Critical ratios larger than .676 and .75 can be expected in more than forty cases out of one hundred.

The conclusion reached is that the distractions were not sufficiently disturbing to affect the performance of the group.

Table 1

	Mean	SD	C/R
Names Experimental Group Control Group	148.2 135.5	24.54 34.86	1.6
Numbers Experimental Group Control Group	132.7 138.1	30.62 27.68	0.676
Otis Experimental Group Control Group	55.4 52.1	8.43 9.29	0.75

SUMMARY

This experiment was designed to determine whether or not some of the more commonly occurring distractions have an effect on group test results.

Two groups of graduate students were given the Minnesota Vocational Test for Clerical Workers and the Otis Test for Mental Ability. Several commonly occurring distractions were staged for one group during the Numbers part of the Clerical Test and during the Otis Test. None of the subjects was aware of the nature of the experiment.

No statistically significant differences were found. The conclusion was drawn that commonly occurring distractions do not affect test results.

REFERENCES

1. Bingham, W. V. *Aptitudes and Aptitude Testing.* New York: Harper & Brothers, 1937.
2. Ligon, E. M. "Administration of Group Tests," *Educational and Psychological Measurement,* 2 (1942), 387–400.
3. Terman, L. M., and Merrill, M. A. *Measuring Intelligence.* Boston: Houghton Mifflin Company, 1937.

43

Should Students Change Their Initial Answers on Objective-Type Tests?: More Evidence Regarding an Old Problem

Patricia J. Reile and Leslie J. Briggs

In the test-taking folklore of students, there is an adage that says, "Your first impression is generally the right one." Reile and Briggs delve into this problem in an effort to supplant folklore with fact.

THE PROBLEM

Students have frequently asked instructors or counselors whether it is advantageous to change answers on objective-type tests providing time permits a second consideration of at least some of the items. Many students have received the reply that first impressions are best; others have been told that a second consideration of an item is likely to be better than the first. In one sample (8), a majority of students questioned on the issue believed that it is better not to make such changes, possibly indicating they had been previously so advised. This issue, of course, should be decided on basis of facts rather than upon opinions.

Previous reports relating to the present question actually deal with two different problems. The first problem of most immediate practical import (to the students, at least) is the determination of whether revisions in answers tend to raise or lower the total score on the test. Several investigators (1, 6, 7, 8) have been unanimous in concluding that scores on multiple-choice and true-false tests are increased more than they are lowered by the incidence of changed answers. The amount of such gains has variously been related to the type of test, the relative achievement of the student, the instruc-

From Patricia J. Reile and Leslie J. Briggs, "Should Students Change Their Initial Answers on Objective-Type Tests?: More Evidence Regarding an Old Problem," *The Journal of Educational Psychology*, XLIII (February, 1952), pp. 110–115. Reprinted with the permission of Abrahams Magazine Service, Incorporated, and the authors.

tions given, and to the proportion of items changed. It has been agreed that (1) most of the changes are made on items upon which the student is uncertain originally; and (2) bright students change relatively few of the easy, 'most visible' items, although they recognize more readily than do the duller students the need for a second consideration of items requiring niceties of discrimination. A second problem relating to this topic has been investigated by Jarrett (5), who was interested primarily in determining whether revisions in answers arise from chance-determined factors or from the operation of sub-threshold response tendencies. He concluded in favor of the latter.

The purpose of the present study is to return to the original problem, thus seeking additional data regarding the effect of revised answers upon total scores and letter grades earned, and to further analyze the results according to sex, grade earned, and serial position of items changed. An account of the nature of all revisions will be presented first, followed by a test to discover whether the net result of changing responses is a gain or a loss to the student. The results should furnish a more substantial basis for guidance of students in respect to this aspect of the skill of test-taking. It should be noted that this study does not purport to determine whether first impressions are best, since conceivably students may often record their second or third impressions as the first overt answer to the item.

PROCEDURE

Answer sheets were examined for one hundred twenty-four students who took a final examination in a course in General Psychology in January, 1950, at the University of Hawaii. The examination items were of the four-answer type. Students recorded their answers to each item by marking an 'X' in one of the four columns in the answer sheet corresponding to the four alternatives offered for each question. A maximum time of two hours was allowed for the completion of the 130-item test. Most students had ample time to reconsider and change items if they so desired. No special instructions were given, since it was considered not desirable that the students should be aware that the answer sheets would be used for other than grading purposes.

The procedure of analysis was to identify, on each answer sheet, the answers which had been changed. These were indicated by erasures or by cross-outs. Careful recheck of the answer sheets under high illumination seemed to indicate a high degree of accuracy in locating such changes. Next, the changed answers were classified into three major categories: (1) items changed from the right answer to a wrong answer; (2) items changed from a wrong to the right answer; and (3) items changed from one wrong answer to another wrong answer. It was discovered that nine hundred seventy-three of the total one thousand one changed answers were included by these three categories. Obviously, responses in categories 1 and 2 affect the score on the examination, whereas items in category 3 do not.

Results and Discussion

Over-all trends. The sixty-seven male students, as seen in Table 1, made a total of four hundred sixty-two revisions in their answers, of which one hundred two or 22 per cent represent changes from right to wrong answers, tending to lower scores that much, whereas two hundred forty-four or 53 per cent represent answers changed from wrong to right, resulting in a net increase in the scores. The remaining one hundred sixteen items were changed from one wrong answer to another; these may be significant pedagogically, but they have no influence on the scores and they represent a waste of time and effort. Similar results are shown for the female students and for both sexes combined.

Table 1

NUMBER, PERCENTAGE, AND TYPE OF REVISED ANSWERS MADE BY
124 STUDENTS ON A MULTIPLE-CHOICE EXAMINATION IN
GENERAL PSYCHOLOGY[1]

Number of Students		Category 1 Right to Wrong		Category 2 Wrong to Right		Category 3 Wrong to Wrong		Total Number of Revisions
		N	%	N	%	N	%	
Males	67	102	22	244	53	116	25	462
Females	57	122	24	232	45	157	31	511
Total	124	224	23	476	49	273	28	973

[1] Total number of responses: 16,120. Total number of changed responses 1,001. The twenty-eight changed responses not included in the three categories above were: Right to Right; 17. (Indicated by erasure and re-mark.) Two revisions; final answer incorrect, 8. Two revisions; no final answer, 2. One revision; no final answer, 1.

In order to test the hypothesis that there is no net change in score brought about by making revisions, chi-square values were computed for each sex separately and for the sums for both sexes. They indicate that the data depart from the hypothetic 50–50 distribution of responses into categories 1 and 2 at the 1 per cent level of confidence. The practical conclusion is that these students gained much more than they lost by making the changes in their answers on these items.

The agreement between the present results and those cited above suggests that one might expect similar results from still further sets of examination papers which might be studied.

Sex Differences. Whereas the mean number of revisions for all students was 7.8, the mean for the women was 9.0 as compared to 6.9 for the men. Thus, the women changed answers more frequently than the men but they profited from this slightly less than did the men. The data suggest that the males were better students. It seems a possibility that the women in the sample changed more responses and improved their scores less than the men because they were poorer students rather than because they were women.

Item Position. Fewer revisions were made upon items placed near the end of the test than upon items appearing near the beginning. This presumably could have been due to decreasing difficulty of the items, to different subject matter covered, or to increasing 'fatigue' or increasing carelessness toward the end of the test. It must be recognized, of course, that some changes on items placed near the beginning of the test may have actually been made near the close of the test period.

Number of Revisions in Relation to Letter Grade Earned. Table 2 summarizes the three major types of changed responses according to the letter grades earned. For the men there was a clear inverse relationship between grade earned and proportion of items changed from right to wrong. This trend was somewhat less consistent throughout the grade range for the women, but the relationship appears again in the totals for both sexes. Conversely, the proportion of items changed from wrong to right is greater for persons earning high grades than for persons earning low grades. As might be expected, changes from one wrong answer to another wrong answer is more characteristic of students earning low grades than of those placing higher. In summary, it appears that the poorer student makes more revisions, but the proportion which turn out to be unfortunate for him is greater than is true for the better student. Nevertheless, at all grade levels, the percentage of wrong to right revisions tends to exceed the percentage of right to wrong!

Although the purpose of this section has been to study the general effect of revisions upon scores throughout the letter grade range rather than to determine how many grades may have changed by revisions, twenty papers

Table 2

Number, Percentage, and Type of Revised Answers Made by
124 Students on a Multiple-Choice Examination in
General Psychology, Arranged According to Grade Earned[1]

Grade	Number of Students	Category 1 Right to Wrong		Category 2 Wrong to Right		Category 3 Wrong to Wrong		Average Number of Revisions per Student
		N	%	N	%	N	%	
A	9	8	18	26	58	11	24	5.0
B	30	40	18	142	64	39	18	7.4
C	47	87	23	176	47	108	29	7.9
D	30	68	26	106	40	88	34	8.7
F	8	21	28	26	35	27	36	9.3

[1] All percentages are listed to the nearest whole number. Therefore, adding percentages in the table horizontally will not always equal exactly 100.

were selected, sampling each sex in proportion to its incidence in the class, for comment. Of the twenty papers, fourteen were not affected in terms of letter grade by their revisions. The remaining six of the twenty gained a letter grade by their revisions.

SUMMARY AND CONCLUSIONS

For one hundred twenty-four students who took a multiple-choice final examination in General Psychology at the University of Hawaii, the answer sheets were examined in order to determine the effect upon test scores of changing initial answers. In general, the students gained significantly more than they lost in raw score, and many gained a higher letter grade by making such revisions. Only one student dropped one letter grade for this reason. Women students made more revisions than did men, but women profited less thereby. Students in the D and F range profited less from their revisions than did A and B students though the former made more revisions.

Although the hypothesis that there is a 50–50 distribution of revisions between the right-to-wrong and the wrong-to-right categories has been rejected for this group at the 1 per cent level of confidence, a finding that is in agreement with results of previous studies, confirmation of the results should be sought from examination papers written by still other groups of students in different courses with various instructors before the results should be interpreted and applied generally. On the other hand, the results constitute a warning to teachers and others who advise students that first impressions are the best in reference to examination performance.

REFERENCES

1. Berrein, F. K. "Are First Impressions Best on Objective Tests?" *School and Society*, 50 (1939), 319–320.
2. Crawford, Claude C. *The Technique of Study*. Boston: Houghton Mifflin Company, 1928. (Referred to in the article by 8.)
3. Edwards, Allen. *Statistical Analysis*. New York: Rinehart and Company, Inc., 1946.
4. Hedemann, Nancy. (Unpublished study of true-false and multiple-choice tests conducted at the University of Hawaii.)
5. Jarrett, R. F. "The Extra-Chance Nature of Changes in Students' Responses to Objective Test-Items," *Journal of General Psychology*, 38 (1948), 243–250.
6. Lehman, H. C. "Does It Pay to Change Initial Decisions in a True-False Test?" *School and Society*, 28 (1928), 456–458.
7. Lowe, M. L., and Crawford, C. C. "First Impression vs. Second Thought in True-False Tests," *Journal of Educational Psychology*, 20 (1929), 192–195.
8. Matthews, C. O. "Erroneous First Impressions on Objective Tests," *Journal of Educational Psychology*, 20 (1929), 280–286.
9. Porter, J. P. (Unpublished study cited by 6.)

44

The Examiner as an Inhibiting Factor
in Clinical Testing

Lewis Bernstein[1]

*In most testing situations it is assumed that the test content is
the stimulus to which the examinee is responding. Bernstein inves-
tigates the possibility of the test taker's responding also to the
examiner. What hypotheses do the results of this study suggest for
weighing the effect of other features of the test taker's environment?*

This study attempted a simultaneous investigation of two factors in test
administration, and their interaction. The factors studied were oral vs. written
administration of the TAT, and the effects of the presence or absence of an
examiner under each of these methods of administration.

In the two studies which have previously investigated oral vs. written administration of the TAT (3, 8), the oral condition was administered individually, and the written condition was administered in group form. For
example, Eron and Ritter (3) administered the written condition to groups of
six, with two subjects sharing one set of TAT cards. In addition to the unknown effects of the group situation, we have the further contaminating
factor of the interaction of the two subjects using the same set of cards.
Furthermore, the individual oral administration was according to standard
directions, with no time limit, while the written group administration imposed a time limit of five minutes per card. It must be pointed out, however,
that the conditions of Eron and Ritter's study were necessary since they were
interested in determining whether the group method could economically be
used in gathering normative data. However, the two forms of administration are not strictly comparable for determining the relative usefulness of
written vs. oral stories in a clinical situation. It would appear, then, that
there remains a need for comparing oral vs. written TAT stories, both administered individually.

From Lewis Bernstein, "The Examiner as an Inhibiting Factor in Clinical Testing,"
Journal of Consulting Psychology, XX (August, 1956), pp. 287–290. Reprinted
with the permission of the American Psychological Association and the author.

[1] The author is indebted to Dr. Richard H. Dana for his assistance in the collection of
the data. Thanks are also due to the following persons who served as raters: Paul R.
Binner, A. Frank Knotts, Mrs. Nancy M. Robinson, and Robert A. Spicer.

As to the need for investigating the effect of the presence or absence of the examiner on test protocols, Sells (7) has reported that Rorschach responses appeared quite uninhibited in the group test (with relative absence of the examiner), but controlled in the individual administration. He goes on to state that ". . . one important hypothesis requiring careful study is that the presence of an examiner in the clinical test may inhibit the reporting of highly emotional content" (7, p. 25).

In this study, then, by using a 2×2 factorial design (1), we were able to investigate these two factors, as well as their interaction, which potentially could be of even more significance than the individual factors themselves.

METHOD

The subjects were 67 female college students — the entire sophomore class of the University of Colorado School of Nursing. The subjects were randomized into four groups: (a) Oral, examiner absent; (b) Oral, examiner present; (c) Written, examiner absent; (d) Written, examiner present. There were two examiners — one was the subjects' psychology instructor, the other completely unknown to any of the subjects prior to the experiment.[2]

Subjects in all conditions were shown into a private office and were told they would find directions for what they were to do and the necessary materials on the desk. On each desk was a set of TAT cards turned face down with card one on top. The cards were the third revision, and included all twenty pictures recommended by Murray (6) for use with adult females. The following directions for all subjects were typewritten on individual cards:

> This is a task which you should find interesting. On the table before you is a set of pictures which you are to look at one at a time, and make up as dramatic a story as you can for each one. Tell what has led up to the event shown in the picture, describe what is happening at the moment, and then give the outcome. Since this is a test of how good your imagination can be, try to tell as much as possible about what the characters are feeling and thinking.
>
> When you get to Card No. 16, you will find it is a blank card. Imagine a picture for this card, and then go ahead and give a story about this imagined picture.
>
> Be sure to number your stories to correspond to the numbers on the cards.
>
> (Be sure to dictate the number of the card before dictating your story.)
>
> No further instructions will be given.

All subjects who were to be assigned to the oral conditions were given group instruction on the use of the dictaphone prior to being shown into the office in which they were to work. Each desk was equipped with either a pad of paper and pencils or a dictating machine, depending on the experimental condition. The only difference between the examiner-present and examiner-absent conditions was that in the examiner-present situation, one of the examiners sat across the desk from the subject throughout the session.

[2] The small number of examiners in this study does not fulfill the requirements of representative design, as suggested by Hammond (5), and the conclusions will therefore be limited to the two examiners in this study until the number of examiners has been increased.

Each story was coded and typed on a duplicating stencil so that comparable sets of stories could be presented to the raters. Stories were rated on Eron, Terry, and Callahan's scale for emotional tone (4); on Eron's scale for outcomes (2); and on Terry's scale for level of response (9). Only one variable was rated at a time and all the stories for a given picture were rated together. All stories were independently rated by two judges. Pearson *r* reliability coefficients were .88 for emotional tone, .82 for outcomes, and .83 for level of response.

Results

Table 1 shows the differences in the means for the three scales under each of the four conditions of administration. For each scale the examiner-absent condition yielded a significantly higher mean than the examiner-present condition, whether the stories were oral or written (with the exception of the written stories for level of response). There were no significant differences between oral and written stories for any of the scales, whether the examiner was present or absent.

Table 2 shows the results of the analysis of variance for each scale. In each case, the only significant *F* was for the examiner-absent vs. examiner-present condition. There was no significant interaction between the two testing factors studied.

Discussion

It has been demonstrated, within the limits of this experiment, that there is no appreciable difference between TAT stories given orally or written by

Table 1
Differences in Means for All Scales

Variable	Oral, Examiner Absent (N = 17)	Oral, Examiner Present (N = 16)	Written, Examiner Absent (N = 18)	Written, Examiner Present (N = 16)	Mean Difference	*t*
Emotional Tone	−17.06	−11.13			5.93	3.01**
	−17.06		−17.33		.27	.15
		−11.13		−10.25	.88	.49
			−17.33	−10.25	7.08	4.19***
Outcomes	−8.71	+3.69			12.40	3.82***
	−8.71		−6.61		2.10	.67
		+3.69		+3.69	.00	.00
			−6.61	+3.69	10.30	4.68***
Level of Response	68.47	58.50			9.97	2.98**
	68.47		63.61		4.86	1.83
		58.50		60.00	1.50	.50
			63.61	60.00	3.61	1.60

Note. — For each of the examiner-present conditions the scores for the two examiners were combined since there were no significant differences on any scale between the two examiners.

** Significant at the .01 level of confidence.

*** Significant at the .001 level of confidence.

Table 2

SUMMARY OF ANALYSIS OF VARIANCE

Variable	Source of Variation	df	Mean Square	F
Emotional Tone	Oral vs. Written	1	.55	.017
	Exam. abs. vs. Exam. pres.	1	708.99	21.193***
	Interaction	1	6.30	.188
	Within groups	63	33.45	
	Total	66		
Outcomes	Oral vs. Written	1	14.55	.228
	Exam. abs. vs. Exam. pres.	1	2140.59	33.541***
	Interaction	1	23.81	.373
	Within groups	63	63.82	
	Total	66		
Level of Response	Oral vs. Written	1	51.53	.761
	Exam. abs. vs. Exam. pres.	1	748.81	11.062**
	Interaction	1	177.67	2.625
	Within groups	63	67.69	
	Total	66		

Note. — In each case the hypothesis of homogeneity of variance is tenable.
** Significant at the .01 level of confidence.
*** Significant at the .001 level of confidence.

the subjects in this experiment, as far as emotional tone, outcomes, and level of response are concerned. However, with the examiner absent the stories are sadder, have sadder outcomes, and show greater involvement on the part of the subject. These findings clearly support Sells' suggestion that the presence of an examiner may inhibit highly emotional content (7). It was noted by the examiners in the present study that subjects frequently looked up to see if the examiner was being attentive; and in the written condition, many subjects put their completed stories under the pad of paper, as if to assure that the examiner could not read them.

However, the mere physical absence of the examiner may not be the important variable. It seems more likely that what may be operative is the subject's expectancy for immediate evaluation. For example, Terry (8) reported a significantly higher level of response for individually administered TAT stories than for those given by written group-administration. Although the examiner was relatively absent from the group administration, she noted that "After completion of the first story all subjects were reminded of the directions if they had omitted any part of the story, such as the ending, or what had happened before to the characters" (8, p. 14). What may have happened here is that the subjects, after having had their first story evaluated by the examiner, expected that further evaluation might follow. On the other hand, this expectancy was apparently not created in the group administration of the Rorschach reported by Sells (7). In the present study, the examiner did not read or hear any of the stories given in the examiner-absent condition until the subject had left the examining room. In other words, it is tentatively proposed that the creation of an expectancy for immediate evaluation, even if further evaluation does not in fact occur, changes the testing-field situation for the subject from one of examiner-absent to examiner-present. It is planned to study this possibility in future experiments.

SUMMARY

Sixty-seven female college sophomores were randomized into four groups for administration of the TAT under the following conditions: oral, examiner absent; oral, examiner present; written, examiner absent; and written, examiner present. The resulting 1,340 stories were rated for emotional tone, outcomes, and level of response. Analysis of variance indicated that the only significant difference in the stories on each scale was a function of the presence or absence of the examiner, with the examiner-absent condition yielding higher means on each of the scales. There were no apparent differences between written and oral stories, nor was there any significant interaction between the two variables studied.

The data support the hypothesis that the presence of an examiner in a test situation acts as an inhibiting factor for strongly emotional material. It was suggested that the variable operative may not have been the mere physical presence or absence of the examiner, but rather an expectancy created in the subject for either immediate or more remote evaluation of his productions.

REFERENCES

1. Edwards, A. L. *Experimental Design in Psychological Research.* New York: Rinehart & Company, Inc., 1950.
2. Eron, L. D. "A Normative Study of the Thematic Apperception Test," *Psychological Monographs* (Whole No. 315), 64, No. 9 (1950).
3. Eron, L. D., and Ritter, Anne M. "A Comparison of Two Methods of Administration of the Thematic Apperception Test," *Journal of Consulting Psychology,* 15 (1951), 55–61.
4. Eron, L. D., Terry, Dorothy, and Callahan, R. "The Use of Rating Scales for Emotional Tone of TAT Stories," *Journal of Consulting Psychology,* 14 (1950), 473–478.
5. Hammond, K. R. "Representative vs. Systematic Design in Clinical Psychology," *Psychological Bulletin,* 51 (1954), 150–159.
6. Murray, H. A. *Manual for the Thematic Apperception Test.* Cambridge, Mass.: Harvard University Press, 1943.
7. Sells, S. B. "Problems of Criteria and Validity in Diagnosis and Therapy," *Journal of Clinical Psychology,* 8 (1952), 23–28.
8. Terry, Dorothy. "An Analysis by the Use of Rating Scales of Thematic Apperception Test Protocols Obtained under Different Conditions of Test Administration." Unpublished Doctor's dissertation, University of Wisconsin, 1950.
9. ———. "The Use of a Rating Scale of Level of Response in TAT Stories," *Journal of Abnormal and Social Psychology,* 47 (1952), 507–511.

SUGGESTED READINGS

Cronbach, Lee J. *Essentials of Psychological Testing* (2nd ed.). New York: Harper & Brothers, 1960. Chapter 3.

Chapter 3 of this text deals with test administration. The last half of the chapter discusses motivation of the test taker, and several interesting reports of observations of test taking behavior are noted. The reader may be especially interested in the section on anxiety and test performance.

Ross, C. C., and Stanley, Julian C. *Measurement in Today's Schools* (3rd ed.). Englewood Cliffs, N.J.: Prentice-Hall Inc., 1954. Chapter 11.

This chapter deals with topics of learning and performance as represented in test taking behavior. Although many of the studies reported are not recent, they still have much to offer the discerning student.

Super, Donald E., and Crites, John O. *Appraising Vocational Fitness*. New York: Harper and Row, Publishers, 1962. Chapter 4.

The outlines here deal with a variety of conditions surrounding test administration, including conditions of the examinee. Also included is a check list to be used in observing behavior of examinees.